KV-144-460

# Conservatism and American Political Development

*Edited by*

Brian J. Glenn
Steven M. Teles

OXFORD
UNIVERSITY PRESS
2009

# OXFORD
UNIVERSITY PRESS

Oxford University Press, Inc., publishes works that further
Oxford University's objective of excellence
in research, scholarship, and education.

Oxford    New York
Auckland    Cape Town    Dar es Salaam    Hong Kong    Karachi
Kuala Lumpur    Madrid    Melbourne    Mexico City    Nairobi
New Delhi    Shanghai    Taipei    Toronto

With offices in
Argentina    Austria    Brazil    Chile    Czech Republic    France    Greece
Guatemala    Hungary    Italy    Japan    Poland    Portugal    Singapore
South Korea    Switzerland    Thailand    Turkey    Ukraine    Vietnam

Copyright © 2009 by Oxford University Press, Inc.

Published by Oxford University Press, Inc.
198 Madison Avenue, New York, New York 10016
www.oup.com

Oxford is a registered trademark of Oxford University Press

All rights reserved. No part of this publication may be reproduced,
stored in a retrieval system, or transmitted, in any form or by any means,
electronic, mechanical, photocopying, recording, or otherwise,
without the prior permission of Oxford University Press.

Library of Congress Cataloging-in-Publication Data
Conservatism and American political development / edited by
Brian J. Glenn and Steven M. Teles.
    p.   cm.
Includes bibliographical references and index.
ISBN  978-0-19-537392-9; 978-0-19-537393-6 (pbk.)
1. Conservatism—United States—History—20th century.   2. Environmental
policy—United States—History—20th century.   3. Social security—United
States—History—20th century.   4. Education and state—United States—
History—20th century.   I. Glenn, Brian J., 1969–   II. Teles, Steven Michael.
JC573.2.U6C654 2008
320.520973—dc22     2008015919

BLACKBURN COLLEGE
LIBRARY
Acc. No. BB51095
Class No. UCL 320. S 209 GLE
Date 20/08/09

9 8 7 6 5 4 3 2 1
Printed in the United States of America
on acid-free paper

Conservatism a                    elor m  t

# Preface

When the two of us began this project, we knew that we wanted to create a study of conservatives and American political development from the genesis of the modern state to the present. This was an ambitious undertaking, and we realized that the usual "bunch of chapters roughly on a theme" structure of most edited books would not allow us to derive robust conclusions. Still, we wanted to pull from the expertise of a large number of experts. So we drew from the best of both worlds, building on the format employed so successfully by Stephen Skowronek in *Building a New American State,* in which he examined three major policies over two time periods. Given that our study encompasses over seven decades of policy making, we have extended his format to three time periods—and rather than ask one author to cover that much material, we reached out to a dozen authors who were specialists in both the individual policy and the respective time periods to generate our nine chapters.

Although it was a bit of work to produce, this book has been worth the efforts, as we have derived a number of rather surprising conclusions that were uncovered only because we employed the format we did. We hope that this book serves as a useful tool for readers trying to learn more about the relationship between conservatives and the development of American public policy, and we also hope that it will serve as a methodological template for others seeking to answer the kinds of questions we have.

Our authors met together in early spring of 2005 on the campus of the University of Pennsylvania to go over outlines of their prospective chapters. When did each respective chapter begin? When did it end? What were the key issues at stake, who was involved, who was not involved but might have been, and why? After the mini-conference, our authors wrote the first drafts of their chapters, which they then circulated for comments by the other authors. We met together for a second time in February 2006 at the Center for the Study of American Politics at Yale for an all-day conference where authors presented their chapters. Each author or set of authors also presented at least once at either the 2006 Policy History conference at the University of Virginia, the 2006 American Political Science Association conference in Philadelphia, and the 2006 New England Political Science Association conference in Portsmouth, New Hampshire.

An undertaking such as this is only possible with the support of generous funding, which for our project came from the Gentle Foundation of Philadelphia, associated with the University of Pennsylvania, along with Rogers M. Smith, who helped facilitate this work. Among other things, this grant allowed us to gather together at the start of the project. We are also grateful to the Yale Center for the Study of American Politics for funding our conference there the following year. Special thanks go to Alan Gerber, who found room in his budget for the conference, and Pamela Greene, who made sure the trains ran on time. Jon Dach is owed a great debt for his timely and thorough editing of the manuscript, and for his endless patience. Beverly Gage, Marc Landy, David R. Mayhew, R. Shep Melnick, James Morone, Peter H. Schuck, and McGee Young all provided us with useful comments as conference discussants, in many cases drawing attention to serious questions that sent our authors back to the drawing board. Finally, we count ourselves extremely fortunate to have such an impressive collection of authors: Nancy Altman, Edward Berkowitz, Gareth Davies, Martha Derthick, Larry DeWitt, Marc Allen Eisner, Richard M. Harris, Jeffrey Henig,[1] Judith Layzer, Ted Marmor, Patrick McGuinn, and Stephen Skowronek. Each of them willingly accepted round after round of revisions, and actively consulted with the other authors in order to ensure that the book held together as a whole. Without their team spirit, this might have been an interesting collection of essays, but not a *book*.

*Note*

1. To whom we offer our warmest congratulations. Jeff's chapter earned the John C. Donovan for the best faculty paper presented at the 2006 New England Political Science Association Conference.

# Contents

# Contributors

Nancy Altman is a lawyer and the author of *The Battle for Social Security: From FDR's Vision to Bush's Gamble*. She has taught about Social Security at Harvard University's Kennedy School of Government and at the Harvard Law School. In 1982 she was Alan Greenspan's assistant in his position as chairman of the bipartisan commission that developed the 1983 Social Security Amendments.

Edward Berkowitz is professor of history and public policy and public administration at George Washington University. He writes on the history of social welfare policy. His most recent book is *Something Happened: A Political and Cultural History of the Seventies*. Along with Larry DeWitt, his coauthor in this volume, and Daniel Beland he has produced *Social Security: A Documentary History*.

Gareth Davies is university lecturer in American history at St. Anne's College, Oxford. He is the author of *From Opportunity to Entitlement: The Transformation and Decline of Great Society Liberalism* and *See Government Grow: Education Politics from Johnson to Reagan*.

LARRY DEWITT is the public historian at the U.S. Social Security Administration. A recognized authority on Social Security history, he is a member of the National Academy of Social Insurance and the Society for History in the Federal Government.

MARTHA DERTHICK is retired from the Department of Government and Foreign Affairs at the University of Virginia. She is the author of numerous books on American political institutions and public policy, including *Policymaking for Social Security* and *Agency under Stress: The Social Security Administration in American Government.*

MARC ALLEN EISNER is the Henry Merritt Wriston Chair of Public Policy and professor of government at Wesleyan University. His research focuses on problems of institutional and regulatory design and, most recently, the evolution of environmental governance regimes.

BRIAN J. GLENN is an assistant professor of political science at Emerson College. He writes on the politics of mutual assistance in America and has received awards from the Law & Society Association, the New England Political Science Association, and the American Risk and Insurance Association.

RICHARD HARRIS has a joint appointment as professor in political science and public policy and administration at Rutgers University Camden. His research focuses on business-government relations as well as regulatory and environmental policy. He has published numerous articles and four books and is currently working with Daniel Tichenor on a project about the development of organized interest politics in the United States, entitled *Abiding Interests: The Development of Organized Interests in America.*

JEFFREY HENIG is a professor of political science and education at Teachers College and professor of political science at Columbia University. He has written broadly on the politics of privatization and on education policy. Among his books are *Rethinking School Choice: Limits of the Market Metaphor, The Color of School Reform: Race, Politics and the Challenge of Urban Education; Building Civic Capacity: The Politics of Reforming Urban Schools;* and, most recently, *Spin Cycle: How Research Is Used in Policy Debates, The Case of Charter Schools.*

JUDITH A. LAYZER is Linde Career Development Associate Professor of Environmental Policy in the Department of Urban Studies and Planning at MIT. She is a political scientist whose research and teaching focus on the roles of science, values, and storytelling in environmental politics, as well as on the effectiveness of different approaches to environmental planning and management. She is the author of *The Environmental Case: Translating Values Into Policy*, 2nd ed., and *Natural Experiments: Ecosystem Management and the Environment*.

PATRICK MCGUINN is an assistant professor of political science at Drew University. His first book, *No Child Left Behind and the Transformation of Federal Education Policy, 1965–2005*, was published in June 2006 and was honored as a Choice outstanding academic title.

TED MARMOR is professor emeritus of management at Yale University, where he taught from 1979 to 2007. Among his writings are *The Politics of Medicare* (1970, 2000), *America's Misunderstood Welfare State* (with Jerry Mashaw and Philip Harvey), and, most recently, *Fads, Fallacies, and Foolishness in Medical Care Management and Policy* (2007). Marmor is now an adjunct professor of Public Policy at Harvard's John F. Kennedy School of Government.

STEPHEN SKOWRONEK is the Pelatiah Perit Professor of Political and Social Science at Yale University. He is the author of *Building a New American State: The Expansion of National Administrative Capacities, 1877–1920; The Politics Presidents Make: Leadership from John Adams to Bill Clinton; The Search for American Political Development* (with Karen Orren), and *Presidential Leadership in Political Time: Reprise and Reappraisal*. With Karen Orren he started the journal *Studies in American Political Development* and edited it from 1986 to 2007.

STEVEN M. TELES is associate professor of political science at Johns Hopkins University. He is the author of *The Rise of the Conservative Legal Movement: The Battle for Control of the Law*, and *Whose Welfare? AFDC and Elite Politics*. He is currently writing a book on the role of political and historical factors in public policy analysis. He has also written articles and book chapters on Michael Oakeshott, Social Security, the international diffusion of libertarianism, federalism, and U.S.–China policy.

Conservatism and American Political Development

# INTRODUCTION

## Studying the Role of Conservatives in American Political Development

*Brian J. Glenn and Steven M. Teles*

For more than a quarter-century, conservatives have been the source of most of the "action" in American politics. Their initiatives have led to dramatic reductions in taxes on income and capital, a comparatively unprecedented drop in the power of labor, a considerable reorientation of our foreign policy, and a wholesale change in crime policy. As the old liberal establishment lost its dominant position in a wide range of policy debates, conservative perspectives have increasingly taken root, pushing ideas into polite conversation that would have been considered—at best—off the wall just a few decades ago. Until quite recently, the grip of conservative leaders over America's political institutions was tightening, and talk of a long-term realignment to the right had become the conventional wisdom.

The extraordinary rise to power of conservatives in contemporary politics has led historians to produce impressive studies of their leaders, movements, and organizations, largely in effort to explain the sources of this massive shift in American politics.[1] By contrast, in the vast public policy and American political development (APD) literature, conservatives are almost always the bridesmaids and never the brides. In fact, almost every analysis of twentieth-century American public policy follows a set pattern. The author starts with the status quo and then introduces the policy entrepreneurs or political movement that sought to expand the reach of the state. These individuals form the center of the study. Their organization's minutes, correspondence, and newsletters are read intensely, we learn their leaders' personal histories and follow their lobbying efforts and attempts to mobilize the public. Somewhere into the story the entrepreneurs encounter opposition—for the moment let's call them "conservatives"—who rarely receive more than a remote fraction of the attention the entrepreneurs do. The policy's path unfolds in the halls of Congress or in the broader public sphere, and by the time the author concludes with a discussion of how the attempts succeeded or failed, the conservative characters in the story have long since faded from view.

At first glance there are strong methodological reasons for centering one's focus on the proponents of state expansion. After all, without them there would be no story to tell. But this understandable move runs the danger of missing insights that can only be generated through studying those opposed to the growth of the state. Conservatives have always been influential in shaping federal domestic policies, from the New Deal to present, but their effects are easy to miss unless we focus on them as leading characters in the story rather than shunt them into roles as cardboard-cutout villains of the forces of progress.

This volume, then, is a study of conservatives and American political development, with the word "and" carrying a lot of weight. This work is both a study of the influence that conservatives have had on domestic policy from the New Deal to present and an examination of how the growth of the state has shaped the development of conservatism. These two objects of investigation, as we shall soon see, go hand-in-hand in a dynamic, mutually reinforcing process. The components of conservative policy coalitions evolve dramatically over the period under study, largely in response to changes in the scope or character of the American state that helped draw groups in or peeled them off. American conservatism has been a response to the development of the state, developments that previous generations of conservatives had a hand in shaping.

By placing conservatives at the very center of our inquiry, we can see them both holistically and with nuance. The result is a picture of conservatives that can be quite surprising, since conservatives have played a much more complicated role than simply obstructing the development of the American state. Sometimes they were co-opted into facilitating its growth, at other times they inadvertently assisted it, and in still others they accepted the goals of liberalism and worked to design policies to achieve those goals through conservative means. The state has helped to shape American conservatism, and conservatism helped to shape the state.

In this chapter, we introduce the reader to the logic of our inquiry, explaining what our unusual format can offer, and then discuss the definition of the object under study—conservatism—and how we understand its development over time.

## The Format

As our goal is to understand the dynamic relationship between conservatives and American political development in the twentieth century, we adopted a format that permitted comparison across time and policies in order to discover patterns and processes not immediately obvious from either a single-issue or single-period approach. Our policies had to be broad and significant enough that we felt comfortable generalizing from them about the nature of conservative coalitions and strategies. Likewise, we needed to structure the inquiry in a manner that allowed us to uncover the impact that conservatives have had on major domestic policies. Our solution was to study multiple issues across a very long period of time, and to give our authors a set of questions to address that was structured enough to allow for comparisons yet flexible enough for them to tell their stories straight, rather than warping them into a predetermined theoretical framework. We selected three domestic policy areas at the federal level—K-12 education policy, environmental regulation, and Social Security—and divided the study into three loosely defined time periods: the New Deal to the late 1950s, the 1960s to the late 1970s, and the 1980s to present. This approach produced nine separate units of analysis, each of which has been handled by an expert or a pair of experts who answer the exact same set of questions regarding the relevant political actors, their goals, and the ideational and institutional constraints and support they encountered in pursuing their goals.

No choice of cases is perfect, as any three would be overinclusive in focusing the spotlight on certain actors or processes and underinclusive in leaving others in the dark. We selected our cases because they represent as broad a swath of actors and issues as possible in the domestic sphere, covering business regulation (environment), the social safety net (Social Security), and the direct delivery of public goods influential in shaping the social and political attitudes, along with the economic mobility, of rising generations of Americans (education). Viewed from contemporary times, these three policy cases can also be seen as representing the toughest challenges to conservative power, as they arguably represent the components of the modern state that have been least immediately responsive to shifts in electoral power. After all, in the wake of the 1994 Congressional elections, when conservatives seemed to be at the cusp of a wholesale reconstruction of the modern state, it was these three issues that a centrist, unorthodox Democratic president laid down as the nonnegotiable essence of liberalism, the ground on which he would stand and fight. Furthermore, while other components of liberalism, like taxation, public housing, foreign policy, and unionization, have dwindled in popularity, public support for the environment, education, and Social Security have remained strong. Finally, in all three areas, the organizational forces of liberalism continue to be vigorous in their defense of the legacy of liberalism, and capable of expanding it even in conservative times. Thus, education, Social Security, and the environment represent a good test of the fate of conservatism's ability to face off with liberalism's "inner citadel."

Environmental policy represents the area in which business and industry should have been at their strongest. Our study does not assume that business is necessarily conservative, but there are strong reasons to believe that most business interests, most of the time, find the conservative end of the spectrum a comfortable ideological fit. For a variety of reasons manufacturers and extractors especially should have been expected to put up a united front against federal intrusion into their affairs, and to have done so successfully with the help of conservative elected officials. First, industry had impressive financial and human resources across all three time periods. Especially when it comes to environmental regulation, single corporations alone had so much at stake and resources so vast that they would have been expected to spend what was necessary on their own to protect their interests. This concentration of interests was contrasted against the relatively diffuse benefits offered by environmentalists, as, while individuals may value open spaces or clean air, the incentives for political free-riding are considerable. Second, there is the fear of the slippery slope, since concern over "creeping socialism" or incremental intrusion into business affairs should have given ample incentive for long-term repeat players to follow a strategy of fighting every inch of federal intrusion into their affairs. Finally, because industries have ample resources, and for much of the twentieth century possessed expertise typically unmatched by opponents (either in academe or the nonprofit sector), any preexisting issue networks should have been between manufacturers and congressional committees, allowing them to dominate the lawmaking process.

We expected that K-12 education policy would involve a rather different set of actors and that they would be mobilized for different reasons. Education is the primary method by which the government, on both the state and federal levels, involves itself in questions of American identity. Rightly or not, it has long been held that education is a powerful force in shaping the perspectives of the next generation of citizens, who for the most part are a captive audience until the age of sixteen. If environmental politics is the realm of business and property rights, education has been the realm of identity and cultural politics, especially as they centered on the deep and enduring question of race. Education also speaks directly to questions of federalism, as, for the two and half centuries preceding the New Deal, education was almost exclusively a concern of the states and their localities.

Social Security, finally, addresses the questions of poverty and, to a lesser extent, social justice. This issue was selected as a classic pocketbook voting issue, where wealth is redistributed from the working generations to the retired ones, and to a lesser degree from wealthier to poorer workers. To the degree that there is an antitax, antiredistribution, antistatist element to American conservatism, Social Security should have been a prime target across the twentieth century, growing as it did into a policy behemoth that had the potential to impact the American economy and the distribution of wealth in profound and lasting ways.

We made a decision to study the impact of conservatives on policy development at a relatively intensive level, allowing enough room for authors to flesh out the boundaries of who the relevant conservative actors were (and were not), what issues were under contestation, and how ideas and institutions shaped the outcomes. Our approach mirrors that adopted by Stephen Skowronek in his classic study *Building a New American State,* which examined civil administration, the army, and business regulation during the Progressive Era, over two separate time periods.[2] While our conclusions apply directly only to the three issues under examination, our study, like Skowronek's, is built on three broad, salient, politically significant issues that commanded an enormous amount of political space in the periods under study, and consequently should be broad enough to reach beyond the cases.[3]

To facilitate comparisons across time, our chapters have been divided into three somewhat loosely defined time periods: the New Deal until the Great Society, the Great Society to the 1980s, and the 1980s to present. Before our authors produced their analyses, we expected to see distinct policy responses on the part of conservatives in each era. The first period, we thought, would be characterized by conservative strategies designed to stop expansion in its tracks, through either coalitions of senior conservative Democrats and Republicans who controlled committees in Congress, business organizations, or the courts, where we expected to see constitutional arguments that the federal government lacked authority to involve itself in the various policy areas. By the time of the Great Society, we assumed that federal involvement in all three policy areas would have been grudgingly conceded, and that conservative strategies would have evolved to ones of obstruction and containment. Finally, starting with the election of Ronald Reagan to the presidency, the various conservative coalitions would have altered their strategies again, this time toward the dismemberment of the liberal regime.

We have been extremely careful to allow our authors the flexibility of starting and completing their respective narratives where they themselves thought the boundaries should lie. As a result, the first and second periods have some variation between them as to where the first chapter ends and the next picks up, depending on the issue area. Moreover, our authors were not asked to address the larger theoretical questions regarding conservatives and American political development, but rather were asked to focus on their respective areas. Thus, our study has not (we hope) placed artificial boundaries on changes either in policies or conservative coalitions by forcing the stories to end when the chapters do. Indeed, much to their credit, our authors have done an admirable job in ensuring that following chapters pick up where the earlier one left off, and of course, the bigger picture is addressed not by the authors in their respective chapters, but in the conclusion, where we are able to look to the chapters *as a whole* to see the larger picture as it emerges from them.

Given that we have a dozen authors producing the nine policy histories, it was important that they all be on the same page analytically. To that end, our authors have grappled with the role of both ideas and institutions in order to present their causal narratives in a comprehensive and coherent manner. While all political historians claim to respect both ideas and institutions, in practice this more often than not appears to be the exception rather than the rule.[4] Historical institutionalists focus primarily, and in many cases exclusively, on actors attempting to achieve their goals through a given set of institutional constraints, which are occasionally (but rarely) capable of being manipulated. The place of ideas, issue framing, and ideology sits uncomfortably with many practitioners of this school, who see them either as too ephemeral to serve as independent variables, or moving too glacially to serve as engines of change in any but the rarest of events. Conversely, ideational scholars focus intensively on the role of ideas in the interpretation of problems, discourse over them, and how they shape perceptions of outcomes, at times to the detriment of giving institutional influences their rightful place in the analysis.[5] One can see how adopting a methodological perspective at either of these extremes can cause difficulty in studying the kinds of questions we want to explore. As a result, we have asked our authors to speak to both ideas and institutions in a manner that allows the reader to follow the development of both across time and issues.

Each set of authors was asked to answer the same broad set of questions regarding conservative actors and the political environment in which they worked. Those questions were: Given their issue and their time period, how were conservatives organized to pursue their policy goals? What was the nature of conservative coalitions? Who was in them, and who was not but might have been? In short, we wanted to understand just who the relevant conservatives were, allowing us to track changes in conservative coalitions both across time and issues.

Beyond identifying the actors, we wanted to understand the institutional constraints under which they operated. What was the nature of their coalition building efforts? Who funded the actors involved? What role, if any, did federalism play? How much, if at all, did groups coordinate across policy areas? What were the interests of those involved, and were there groups we might have expected to see involved but were not, and if so, why? As mentioned above, in today's political realm every important policy area is amply covered by public intellectuals operating out of well-financed think tanks and other organizations, but this is a relatively recent phenomenon, especially on the right. When did think tanks and other policy organizations become important policy players and what, if anything, filled their space before their development?

The complimentary analytical focus for our authors is on the role of ideas. Each chapter focuses in part on how political culture shaped the nature of the debate. What arguments did conservatives make in pursuing their goals? Which ones were they inhibited from making? What arguments were made but poorly received at a given time? Did ideology inhibit certain coalitions from forming? As with institutions, a vital goal of each chapter is mapping out the terrain on which conservatives were forced to operate in order to understand what options were open to them and how their strategies faired given these ideational and institutional constraints.

## Who Were Conservatives?

Given that this is a book about conservatives, our most daunting challenge was defining the object of study in a way that could be used by our authors in their respective analyses and still reflect the dynamic nature of conservatism across both time and issues in the eighty-year period of our study. Conservatism has never been a single, monolithic perspective that is universally held by all members; instead it is and always has been a coalition of actors who for most of the time agree on a desired policy outcome, although often for dramatically different reasons. Regarding K-12 education policy, for example, both Gareth Davies and Patrick McGuinn refer to coalitions concerned with "race, reds, and religion" that wanted to keep the federal government out of local schools. Race motivated whites (especially but not exclusively in the South) to reject federal assistance for local education out of fear that there would be strings attached mandating desegregation. "Reds"

referred to groups seeking to maintain local control over schools out of
ear of creeping socialism, while religion referred to Catholics who did not
want their taxes going to public schools when their children were attending
parochial ones.

The challenge of finding a definition that captured all the groups of individuals motivated by "race, reds, and religion," along with all the other ideas
driving conservatism, proved to be a daunting one. We knew immediately
that focusing on public intellectuals to discover the contours of conservatism
would not suit our purposes, since we were concerned with conservatism at
the policy-relevant level. New Deal liberalism most certainly was an ideology, and almost immediately a number of brilliant thinkers such as Friedrich
Hayek, Russell Kirk, and Albert Jay Nock, among others, began both critiquing liberalism and forwarding a positive argument for various conservative perspectives. At an intellectual level, the role of Frank Meyer, Richard
Weaver, and William F. Buckley Jr. (the writings in *The National Review*
especially) were vital and central in constructing a "fusionist" understanding
of conservatism that allowed a wide variety of conservative individuals to
see themselves as pursuing a common project. Yet public intellectuals have
for the most part, and especially until the rise of conservative think tanks,
been less focused on specific policies than in constructing an overarching
public philosophy. Journals such as *Public Interest* and *First Things* and magazines such as *The Weekly Standard* and *The National Review* have of course
served as arenas for policy-relevant discussions, but until the late 1970s, when
think tanks allowed individuals to focus intensively on particular policy areas,
public intellectuals were often more concerned with producing a conservative outlook painted in broad terms than in specifically using their venues to
influence specific policies.

A second option would have been to follow the emergence of various
conservative groups and tell the story through their successes and setbacks.
This has been fruitful in specific policy areas,[6] but would not have served
our purposes methodologically. We needed to give our authors the flexibility to tell their stories entirely and holistically without being constrained
artificially, and, as with public intellectuals, predicating our story on the
basis of groups would have created the potential for significant selection
bias to slip in. The concern is not so much with the groups selected, but
rather with excluding groups that might have fallen under the conservative
fold and could have mobilized but did not. Indeed, a huge part of our story
involves studying the dog that didn't bark. Especially in Period Two, there
were potential members of conservative coalitions that did not join the
fight, having been peeled off by accident or clever policy design. Thus, we
not only need to look at groups that were politically active, but those that
might have been but were not.

A third option for finding a common definition was to base it on an *a priori,* philosophical definition of conservatism held across time and issues. Of all the options, this would be the most appealing, since it would have allowed our authors the freedom and flexibility to apply the standard to their respective cases without having to be told in advance whom specifically to include. But what ideology defined conservatism across all our time periods? While conservatives have devoted considerable resources to trying to define the essential idea that holds together all of their various factions, even the movement's semi-official historians have recognized that the task is, essentially, hopeless. No definition that is sufficiently aware of the actual heterogeneity of conservatism is capable of capturing the movement across time and policies.[7]

## Our Choice: Conservatism as an Evolving Identity

As there is no fixed definition of conservatism that works for all periods and policies in American political development, we made the sensible decision not to provide one to our authors. Instead, we encouraged our authors to treat the definition of conservatism as one of the central objects of their inquiry. Avoiding an *a priori* definition of conservatism has the critical advantage of sidestepping potentially crippling problems of selection bias, allowing our authors the freedom to investigate groups of actors who might have been coalition members but who, for one reason or another, were not. Of special importance, viewing conservatism as a plastic and dynamic concept left our study open to seeing conservatism itself as a developmental phenomenon, part of an evolving process by which social groups and ideas—including some that were anathema to previous generations of conservatism—were folded into a changing, internally diverse movement.

Once our authors produced their respective analyses, we then stepped back to see what their work in aggregate revealed. What we discovered is that conservatism is actually a phenomenon that has, over time, developed into something somewhat coherent, even across relatively disparate domestic policies. Even following their own particular logics, the three fields revealed similar patterns, especially since the 1980s, when the increasing density of conservative organization allowed for long-term, systematic generation of ideas across policy lines. Bearing in mind that we are discussing coalitions of actors who do not always agree on the reasons they share similar policy preferences, and that even the policy preferences themselves evolve over time, our focus on conservatives has revealed that American conservatism has evolved across two fairly distinct generations.

## The Evolving Generations of Conservatism

Working upward from policy making on the ground, our analysis reveals two quite distinct generations of conservatism, which, to avoid the baggage associated with previous terms, we will call antistatist (formed by paleoconservatives, libertarians, and fusionists, along with their "Old Right" predecessors), and statist or "modern" conservatism (formed by neoconservatives and more recent "compassionate" and "big government" conservatives, among others). Both forms have been dynamic, evolving over time in response to bottom-up pressures from social movements and electoral change, and top-down from changes in the movement's elected officials and public intellectuals.

Antistatist conservatives existed long before the New Deal, but calling them "conservatives" does not hold much meaning intellectually before the rise of policies that threatened to alter traditional social and economic systems. Antistatist conservatives opposed the expansion of the federal government into new policy areas, in any shape or form, on the basis of either ideology or interest. There were and are individuals who would have been more than happy to dismember the state and retract its reach at any moment, believing the growth of government to be unconstitutional, anti-American, and a threat to their fundamental group interests. Antistatist conservatives dominated our first period. To understand their thinking we can look to the leader of the Sentinels of the Republic, who wagged his finger at members of Congress in a hearing during the markup of the Social Security Act of 1935, informing them that the federal government lacked the constitutional authority to tax and spend in anything like the manner Congress was proposing. Antistatists were held together by an ideology of constitutional fidelity, which attracted Southern segregationists defending federalism, businesses committed to limits on governmental "takings" of private property, and opponents of executive power devoted to a strict understanding of Congress's power to delegate power to administrative agencies. In Gareth Davies's telling of federal education policy, this constitutional prism focused on the issue of federalism, colored opposition to the growth of federal education spending, and, as Mark Eisner argues, was the key concern of conservatives interested in limiting federal claims over natural resources. This was a powerful—and at times effective—claim before government entrenched itself in various policy areas, but grew quite weak once it had. This older conservatism, which has variously been called "paleoconservatism" or the "Old Right," was also limited politically by its narrow, WASP, big business and small town constituencies at a time when the New Deal Democratic Party was incorporating new groups and becoming a powerful electoral machine because of it. While they could at times shape or obstruct legislation, this older generation of conservatives lacked the political reach and ideological depth to control the political agenda. They had become, in the literal sense of the term, reactionaries.

In the face of the success of liberalism's expansion of the state under the New Deal and with the coming of the Cold War, a new strain of antistatism began to emerge. The "fusionist" conservatism created by Frank Meyer and William F. Buckley at *The National Review,* and injected into the political arena by Barry Goldwater and Ronald Reagan, built on the commitments of their paleoconservative and Old Right predecessors while also creating a political philosophy with the potential to reach well beyond their limited political constituency to a wider swath of Americans. Fusionism added a deeper philosophical basis to paleoconservatism's belief in tradition and a religiously based morality and combined it with a broader, public-spirited justification for the market economy and limited government linked to a vigorous anticommunism. Previous generations of conservatism were more associated with Northeastern big business, but fusionism threw in its lot with the rising class of Sun Belt entrepreneurs thrown up by the post–World War II economy. The Old Right was almost exclusively mainline Protestant in its devotional life; the fusionism of Buckley and Meyer brought into the fold Catholics and Southern evangelicals. Finally, while earlier generations of conservatives defended institutions like the Ivy League universities and the religious establishment, fusionism pointed conservatism in the direction of populism, fired by the belief that much of the establishment had sold out to and become instruments of New Deal liberalism.[8] This newer form of antistatist conservatism helped to detach the movement from its formerly cramped coalitional limits and provided a powerful basis for attracting new converts. Out of this ideological ferment came many of the organizational building blocks of a revived conservatism, which in addition to the *The National Review* included the Intercollegiate Studies Institute, and Young Americans for Freedom, as well as the Goldwater campaign.

This revived antistatist conservatism continued to be hobbled by the constraints of its (still active but much-weakened) conservative predecessors. Operating at a high level of abstraction, and without the dense, policy-specific organization of its liberal adversaries, fusionism was an increasingly powerful electoral and philosophical force, but it lacked the weapons for policy combat. As our middle chapters show in great detail, the combination of intellectuals and grassroots social movements that characterized conservatism in this period was distinctly ineffective at constraining the growth of the state, as conservative interests were co-opted through clever policy design, out-competed strategically, and defeated at the brass-tacks level of policy ideas. Mining and other environmental interests were divided, tempted in many cases to serve their short-term corporate goals rather than their larger ideological ambitions. Opponents of Social Security became entangled in a series of strategic errors that allowed the policy (along with Medicare) to expand dramatically. Catholics were bought off with funding mechanisms that followed children even to religious schools, and race was (temporarily) defanged by a flood of federal dollars to Southern schools. In all these cases, conservatives found that, even as their broader ideas were attracting new adherents, their ability to connect this to political outcomes was limited by their inability to develop viable alternatives to liberal programs. Antistatists of all stripes were for the most part reactionaries in a period in which control of the political agenda was at a premium, and so the state continued to grow, even as support for liberalism withered.

Beginning in the late-1970s, conservatism as a force in public policy—as contrasted to an electoral and philosophical movement—developed a new and distinct second strain that we call modern conservatism. While the antistatist elements of conservatism certainly did not disappear, in day-to-day policy combat since the late 1980s they began to wane until nearly collapsing by the time of the George W. Bush administration. Modern conservatism rose as the result of two key forces. First, the election of the antistatist Ronald Reagan kicked off twelve years of Republican control of the executive branch, followed by a dozen more years of Republican control of Congress starting in 1994. This gave conservatives an opportunity to govern, rather than simply criticize from the outside, and many came to see the state as a vehicle for pursuing conservative social and economic ends. Just as important, the experience of governing (which can be seen in the early years of Period Three, in all our cases) made clear to conservatives just how powerful were the constraints on wholesale destruction of the liberal state, and that further conservative advances would depend upon adapting to the liberal inheritance, rather than directly reversing it.

Second, conservatism brought into its fold a group of former liberals and leftists who came to be known as *neoconservatives,* and who brought two key assets to the conservative movement. First, neoconservatives had experience with the modern tools of social science and were comfortable arguing with liberals on the level of specific policy proposals. Second, neoconservatives also brought with them a new understanding of conservatism, one that accepted (sometimes grudgingly, sometimes enthusiastically) liberal goals, such as educating poor and minority children, supporting civil rights, defending the elderly from old age poverty, and protecting the environment, which they knew were supported by overwhelming majorities of Americans. Unlike their antistatist predecessors, modern conservatives largely abandoned the hope of rolling back the state and instead sought ways that government could be turned to conservative ends. In the wake of conservatism's failure to roll back the state in the early Reagan years (described in detail in the chapters by Henig, Teles and Derthick, and Layzer), the movement as a whole became increasingly open to the neoconservatives' message, culminating in the "compassionate conservatism" of the 2000 Bush campaign. If federal funding for public education must remain, then the question becomes whether the nation's public schools are educating all of its children adequately. If not, perhaps there are other options that serve children in challenged areas better, such as vouchers to allow them to attend private, parochial, or charter schools. If protecting the elderly in old age is the goal, perhaps allowing them to invest their Social Security premiums in a carefully regulated range of mutual funds could result in higher benefits during retirement, or lower taxes for the rest of us. Likewise, if the federal government must regulate environmental pollution, perhaps a market-based system of incentives rather than "command and control" will serve the process best.

Modern conservatives did not simply accept the growth of the state, however, as they hoped that these new mechanisms of public provision would detach citizens from the commitments to the state that previous generations of liberals had carefully constructed. In this way, they built a bridge to the earlier, antistatist, parts of the conservative coalition, including libertarians. Private, nonunion contractors would welcome visitors to public parks, mow the lawns, and sell the food. Students would learn from nonunion teachers at charter schools, private schools, and even parochial schools on vouchers offered by states or localities. Senior citizens would interact with large mutual funds and not the Treasury Department for their Social Security benefits, and in time, perhaps, citizens will come to see these services as provided less and less by the government, and even come to see their goals as less and less an obligation of the government to provide. Only time will tell whether these statist conservative strategies will in fact serve the older conservative goals of limiting the growth of the state, or merely entrench it even further, as libertarian skeptics contend.[9]

In any event, one potentially important long-term contribution of modern conservatives has been to help build an organizational infrastructure for the movement capable of allowing it to compete head-to-head with liberalism at the level of concrete public policy. Think tanks like the Heritage Foundation, the American Enterprise Institute, and others in Washington and in state capitals, conservative public interest law firms, and university-based institutes were all designed to give conservatives the tools to allow the movement to control the political agenda, rather than simply react to it.[10] Conservatives can now design their own policies, with the goal of splitting liberal constituencies, preempting pressure for policy action that would have culminated in liberal victories in previous eras, transforming the political terrain of future battles and preventing the co-optation of allied interests. Whereas the chapters examining the 1960s and 1970s document numerous cases in which conservatives lost simply because they were nowhere to be found, this new organizational infrastructure would ensure that conservatives would be present where the action was, in a timely manner and often with their own proposals in hand. Conservatives could develop their own long-term strategy, leaving behind the reactionary tactics of the past.

By the time that George W. Bush took office in 2001, modern conservatism had reached its high point. The president's commitment to "compassionate conservatism" reflected all of its key principles, and Bush embraced its most important policy manifestations: Social Security privatization, free market environmentalism, education choice and national standards. Despite conservatism's recently rocky political fortunes, and the ire that many antistate conservatives have for what they see as Bush's (and modern conservatism's) abandonment of Reaganite antistatism, there seems to be little prospect of conservatism shaking off its uneasy rapprochement with the state.

The implications of this shift for the character of the movement, and for the future of American policy development, are certain to be profound. The chapters before you will show how this shift happened and why, and in the process it will tell an unusual, but we hope illuminating, story of the growth of the modern activist state.

## Notes

1. A small sampling of this literature includes: Rick Perlstein, *Nixonland* (New York: Scribners, 2008); Kevin Kruse, *White Flight: Atlanta and the Making of Modern Conservatism* (Princeton, NJ: Princeton University Press, 2005); Lisa McGirr, *Suburban Warriors* (Princeton, NJ: Princeton University Press, 2001); Rick Perlstein, *Before the Storm: Barry Goldwater and the Unmaking of the American Consensus* (New York: Hill and Wang, 2001); Sam Tannenhaus, *Whittaker Chambers: A Biography* (New York: Random House, 1997); John Andrews, *The Other Side of the 60s: Young Americans for Freedom and the Rise of Conservative Politics* (New Brunswick, NJ: Rutgers, 1997); Dan T. Carter, *The Politics of Rage: George Wallace, the Origins of the New Conservatism, and the Transformation of American Politics* (Baton Rouge: LSU, 1995); John B. Judis, *William F. Buckley: Patron Saint of the Conservatives* (New York: Simon and Schuster, 1988); George H. Nash, *The Conservative Intellectual Movement in America* (New York: Basic Books, 1976).

2. Stephen Skowronek, *Building a New American State: The Expansion of National Administrative Capacities 1877–1920* (Cambridge: Cambridge University Press, 1982). In fact, Skowronek's study has elements of a three-period analysis, since he also examines the status quo ante "state of courts and parties." But this chapter does not study his three policies in detail, so it seems more accurate to call it a two-period analysis.

3. We should also note that one important recent study of federal tax policy closely parallels the findings in this book. Michael J. Graetz and Ian Shapiro have studied the causes of public support for the demise of the federal

inheritance tax and discovered stunning similar institutional developments in that field, as we do in ours in the final time period. See Michael J. Graetz and Ian Shapiro, *Death by a Thousand Cuts: The Fight over Taxing Inherited Wealth* (Princeton, NJ: Princeton University Press, 2005).

4. For discussion, see Brian J. Glenn, "The Two Schools of American Political Development," *Political Studies Review* 2, 2 (2004): 153–65.

5. Exemplary recent studies in the ideational tradition include Sheri Berman, *The Primacy of Politics: Social Democracy and the Making of Europe's Twentieth Century* (Cambridge: Cambridge University Press, 2006); Erik Bleich, *Race Politics in Britain and France: Ideas and Policymaking since the 1960s* (Cambridge: Cambridge University Press, 2003); Mark Blyth, *Great Transformations: Economic Ideas and Institutional Change in the Twentieth Century* (Cambridge: Cambridge University Press, 2002); and Katherine McNamara, *The Currency of Ideas* (Ithaca: Cornell University Press, 1998).

6. Sarah Diamond, *Roads to Dominion: Right-Wing Movements and Political Power in the United States* (New York: Guilford Press, 1995).

7. Nash, *The Conservative Intellectual Movement in America,* xi–xiv.

8. Buckley first came to public consciousness, of course, with his assault on the Ivy League in *God and Man at Yale* (Chicago: Regnery, 1951), followed quickly by his defense of Joe McCarthy, in particular his accusation that America's establishment could not be trusted to defend the country against communism—and had in fact become infested with actual supporters of the Soviet Union. Later, the *National Review* would even challenge the hierarchy of Buckley's own Catholic Church, for example when it entitled its cover story (which criticized John XXIII's encyclical "Mater et Magistra") "Mater Si, Magistra No." John Judis, *William F. Buckley: Patron Saint of the Conservatives* (New York: Simon and Schuster, 1988), 186.

9. For an example of libertarians who have concluded that the antistatist promises of modern conservatism were a fraud, see Brink Lindsey, "Liberaltarians: A Progressive Manifesto," *The New Republic,* December 11, 2006, v. 235, Issue 24, 14–17.

10. Steven Teles, *The Rise of the Conservative Legal Movement* (Princeton: Princeton University Press, 2008).

PART I

The New Deal to the Great Society

# CHAPTER I

Environmental Policy from the New Deal
to the Great Society: The Lagged Emergence
of an Ideological Dividing Line

*Marc Allen Eisner*

E nvironmental protection constitutes one of the more significant expansions of state authority during the last decades of
the twentieth century. The Environmental Protection Agency was created in
1970 and was granted the authority to regulate corporate practices on an
economy-wide basis. It quickly developed the capacity to translate complex
scientific research into detailed regulations and manage pollutants measurable in parts-per-million or parts-per-billion. For environmental advocates,
the flurry of new regulations, the imposition of expensive mandates on the
states, and the unprecedented compliance costs were justifiable expressions of
governmental authority. For conservative opponents, the new social regulation was little more than elite social engineering committed to expanding the
administrative state and running roughshod over private property, markets,
and states' rights. Although environmental and public interest groups realized
some considerable victories in the early 1970s, the new regulations stimulated

a conservative countermobilization. Corporations and conservative foundations made heavy investments in policy think tanks and Republican candidates committed to restraining the expansion of regulatory authority.[1]
Although the reaction to the new environmental regulations does not provide
a complete explanation of conservative ascendancy, it was most certainly an
important part of the story, with ramifications that extended well beyond the
policy subsystem.

The role of conservatives in shaping contemporary regulatory politics during this critical period is the subject of subsequent chapters. This chapter is
concerned primarily with the decades immediately following World War II.
Making sense of conservatives and the environment is this period is an
intriguing task for three reasons. First, the conservative movement was in
its formative stage. In Sara Diamond's words: "the Right was more of an
intellectual ideological current than a proper social movement."[2] Traditionalists and libertarians, in particular, were battling over the core definition
of conservatism; nothing rising to the level of a coherent conservative position had yet emerged. Second, conservatism had yet to gain much influence
over the Republican Party. President Eisenhower, in particular, was intent on
building a "modern" Republican Party that accepted much of the New Deal
order; marginalizing elements of the Old Right were viewed as being an electoral liability. Third, the "environment" as it would be understood during the
modern environmental era (e.g., as contrasted to conservation or preservation) had yet to emerge as an issue.

Nonetheless, key policy debates of the period involved a host of conflicts
that would be central to subsequent environmental debates. First and most
obvious, there were sharp divisions over the correct balance between preservation or conservation, on the one hand, and commercial development, on
the other. Although these divisions had a strong sectional component, they
were frequently framed as involving the security of property rights. The promotion of conservation—as well as claims that natural resources constituted
a national trust to be administered by the national government—was portrayed by opponents as national resource planning that was tantamount to
socialism. Second, and more important, policy issues were inseparable from
debates over institutions. Consider the role of federalism. Claims of the federal government over natural resources inevitably involved a diminution of
states' rights. Hence, conservatives contrasted centralized resource planning
with the preservation of local control over questions of economic development and the revenue streams that would be generated from the sale or leasing of resources. If the determination was made that the national government
had authority over resources, attention focused on whether such authority
would be vested in the president and executive branch agencies, or would
remain with Congress. Congressional conservatives, responding to the broad

delegations of authority that had characterized the New Deal, had a strong preference for the latter.

This chapter proceeds in several stages. It begins with a brief discussion of the status quo ante at the beginning of the period in question. Next, it turns to an examination of the position of the environment in postwar conservative thought. With these foundations in place, the paper examines two major controversies—the tidelands debates and wilderness preservation—which, when combined, extend across the period in question. These two cases reveal the ways in which environmental disputes were framed relative to larger ideological conflicts and issues of institutional design. Moreover, while they illustrate the extent to which the fluctuating fortunes of conservatives shaped the outcomes, they also reveal the overwhelming power of business and development interests in forcing legislative compromises, regardless of the partisan control of the national government.

## The State and the Environment

Since the 1970s, conservative critics have portrayed environmental regulation as an instance of statist social engineering, drawing implicit comparisons with some golden age of free markets and local control. Yet, such comparisons neglect an inconvenient fact: in the United States, there has always been a strong statist element in the treatment of land and natural resources more generally. The focus of policy has changed over time, largely reflecting changes in broader policy regimes. These changes have not brought about the wholesale elimination of preexisting policies and institutions. Rather, new policies have been layered upon past policies contributing to a seemingly incoherent whole. Indeed, policies involving the environment, broadly construed, constitute a striking example of a "path-dependent layering process." Preexisting policies representing disparate interests have given rise to a host of tensions and conflicts that compromise the extent, direction, and rapidity of institutional change.[3] Thus, since its creation in 1970, the Environmental Protection Agency has been forced not only to implement its own complicated statutory mandates, but to compensate for the negative externalities of policies implemented by other agencies (e.g., the Department of Agriculture, the Department of Interior), each with its own distinctive history, organized constituents, and congressional patrons.

During the nineteenth century, American land policy was defined by multiple goals, including the rewarding of war veterans, the generation of public revenues through land sales, the funding of education and internal improvements and, most importantly, the promotion of development.[4] The General Land Office promoted the rapid transfer of public lands to the private sector.

"While preference was nominally given to family farms, actual administrative practice also relinquished every type of resource—land, forests, mineral, and later, water power—to corporate interests as well" creating a "momentum of feverish exploitation."[5] The disposition of public lands had important sectional impacts. Although the thirteen original states and Vermont, Kentucky, Tennessee, Maine, and Texas retained ownership of public lands, in new states the federal government claimed ownership of vast tracks of public lands and determined the conditions under which land (and rights to the resources they contained) would pass to the private sector. Obviously, states had a financial stake in the ongoing exploitation of public lands. Congressional committees were routinely dominated by Western legislators who promoted "a wide-open land policy to hasten the transfer to private ownership" and rapid resource extraction.[6]

Although conservation efforts emerged at the state level in the 1870s, the presidency of Theodore Roosevelt is commonly viewed as a watershed. Roosevelt, along with his Chief Forester Gifford Pinchot, used federal powers to aggressively promote resource planning and management. Under Roosevelt, the size of the national forests was tripled and control was transferred to the Department of Agriculture (USDA). The executive branch assumed greater control over the disposition of mineral resources, waterpower sites, forests, and grazing land; revenues were increasingly devoted to management. Under the Newlands Act of 1902, for example, 95 percent of land sales revenues in sixteen Western states was placed in a revolving fund to finance dam construction and irrigation. Similarly, under the Mineral Leasing Act of 1920, 52.5 percent of the revenues from leases on coal, oil, gas, potash, and phosphate resources was placed in a reclamation fund and 37.5 percent was paid to the states of origin.[7] This system of funding internal improvements did little to moderate sectional conflicts. As Paul W. Gates explains, Western states "came to think of the extensive federal lands within their borders, reserved or withdrawn from entry, as retarding their development, slowing down their progress, and keeping them in thralldom to a remote government not capable of understanding their needs."[8]

Although Progressive Era conservation efforts marked a significant departure from the past, there remained persistent tensions. Under the influence of Pinchot, the USDA was often the strongest advocate for conservation, whereas the Department of Interior remained wedded to a developmental agenda. Thus, while San Francisco's efforts to acquire a permit to build a dam and flood Yosemite National Park's Hetch Hectchy Valley were initially thwarted, Roosevelt's secretary of the Interior acquiesced in 1908 in the wake of the 1906 earthquake and fires.[9] Two years later, during the Taft administration, the conflicts between conservation and development came to a head when Pinchot alleged that Interior Secretary Richard Ballinger had succumbed to corruption in the opening of Alaskan coal reserves to private mining interests. The Ballinger-Pinchot controversy resulted in highly publicized congressional hearings and, ultimately, Pinchot's 1910 dismissal for insubordination. The firing of the strongest advocate of the Progressive vision exacerbated the conflicts between Taft and Roosevelt and marked the end of Progressive conservation.[10] Although John Muir and the Sierra Club had achieved some success in delaying the flooding of Hetch Hetchy, in 1913 the newly inaugurated Woodrow Wilson appointed former San Francisco attorney Franklin Lane as Interior secretary. Congress moved quickly to authorize the flooding of the valley, and construction of the O'Shaughnessy Dam began the next year.

Even if conservation continued to attract attention in subsequent decades, it was with a few exceptions,[11] subordinated to the more pressing concerns associated with war mobilization and economic recovery.[12] While the New Deal was rife with new conservation and resource management programs, they were "born of the necessity to deal productively with the problems of vast unemployment during the depression of the 1930s: reforest the land, build a dam or bridge or other public work, and maintain the dignity of labor."[13] Thus, while the Public Works Administration, the Works Progress Administration, and the Civilian Conservation Corps deployed peacetime armies on conservation projects, they were primarily public works programs. Similarly, while the Soil Conservation and Domestic Allotment Act authorized the USDA to distribute $500 million annually in "conservation payments" to farmers, it was primarily a means of continuing income support in the wake of *U.S. v Butler* (1936).

New Deal conservation programs provided a context for experiments in planning. As Whitney R. Cross observed: "Every New Deal policy inevitably involved planning (some of it most casual, to be sure), but conservation policies did so to a peculiar, perhaps a unique, extent."[14] The Taylor Grazing Act of 1934, for example, created a general land classification system. Some 80 million acres of public domain land not suited for agriculture were placed within a grazing system and managed to reduce overgrazing and erosion.[15] Even more impressive, the Tennessee Valley Authority was created in 1933 to control the Tennessee River for the generation of hydroelectric power, navigation, and flood control. Although one might view the TVA primarily as a conservation project, the decision to place the government in competition with the private sector over the sale of electricity reinforced the perception that it was simultaneously "an experiment, a political laboratory for democratic social and economic planning on a less-than-national scale,"[16] one that would have devastating environmental consequences. Similarly, although the National Resources Planning Board was responsible for developing regional plans and conducting research on trends in national resources and land use, its broad mandate extended to a far wider range of issues, including industrial organization, public housing, and welfare policy. In the end, the lack of staffing and administrative power forced the board to serve little more than an advisory function.[17]

The combination of promotion, scientific resource management, and planning inherent in the conservation policies introduced in the first half of the twentieth century were often difficult to reconcile. For Western states, they often raised the fear that Eastern interests were hampering economic development. For constitutional formalists, the concentration of power in the executive branch raised concerns over the robustness of federalism and the delegation of authority to administrative agencies. For advocates of market governance, they raised the fears of central state planning running roughshod over property rights, a critique that would merge in the postwar period with Cold War concerns over the specter of communism. When combined, one should not be surprised that environment would become embroiled in ongoing struggles over the role of the state.

## Conservatism and the Environment in the Wake of the New Deal

Given the cluster of issues inherent in the state's relationship to the environment, one would expect, in the wake of the New Deal, great conservative interest in the subject. The key divisions in the immediate postwar period were between traditionalists and libertarians or classic liberals. Traditionalists[18] adopted a Burkean vision of society as "a partnership not only between those who are living, but between those who are living, those who are dead, and those who are to be born."[19] They sought to preserve traditional society and morality in the face of an emergent mass society. Libertarians embraced the spontaneous order of the market and were far less inclined to join the traditionalist assault on modernity. Despite the ongoing efforts to find common ground (most clearly expressed in the fusionist project of Frank S. Meyer) these strands represented more or less separate intellectual camps.[20] The internecine struggles to define conservatism impeded the emergence of a clear and coherent conservative position on the role of the state in the environment. Let us examine the competing positions in greater detail.

From the perspective of the 1940s and 1950s, the past several decades had brought a remarkable transformation in the political economy. A new organizationally dense economy had displaced the decentralized system that carried so much appeal for traditionalists. In his 1948 book *Ideas Have Consequences*, Richard M. Weaver made sense of the revolutionary changes that had occurred in the West by tracing them back to the rise of nominalism and the denial of a transcendent order.[21] At the individual level, Weaver observed that self-discipline, order, and prudence had been replaced by an egotistical materialism and a "spoiled-child psychology." These changes had significant ramifications for our relationship with the environment: "The modern position seems only another manifestation of egotism, which develops when man has reached a point at which he will no longer admit the right to existence of things not of his own contriving."[22] Weaver continued: "It is a matter of elementary observation that nature reflects some kind of order which was here before our time and which, even after atomic fission, defies our efforts at total comprehension."[23] He decried the "continual warring upon nature" and concluded that "an essential step in retaining our hold upon the real reality" is the recognition that nature has "a place in the order of things which is entitled to respect."[24] Indeed, Weaver believed that nature constituted part of a divinely ordained order; piety, rather than the search for profit, should govern our attitudes toward nature.[25]

In what would become the key statement of traditionalism, Russell Kirk's 1953 *The Conservative Mind* cited the "affection for the proliferating variety and mystery of traditional life"[26] as a core canon of conservatism. In his 1954 book, *A Program for Conservatives,* he developed the policy implications of this position. When he looked to the changes occurring in postwar America, he saw the "cosmopolis of modern mass society" assimilate "every community that retains something of its peculiar character."[27] This is "the pure Utilitarian mind at work: Production is the only important task of life, and Profit the only important end. The conservative thinks otherwise."[28] How does one revive "a sense of traditions among a crowd who have forgotten the whole concept of tradition?" Part of the answer involved reversing the trends toward urbanization and industrialization: "The conservative will do everything in his power to prevent the further diminution of our rural population; he will recommend decentralization of industry and deconcentration of population; he will seek to keep as many men and women as possible close to the natural and customary world in which tradition flourishes."[29]

Two comments are necessary at this juncture. First, although it is convenient to view conservatives as the shills of corporate America, traditionalists expressed contempt for the corporate behemoths that had come to dominate the American economy and the mass-production/mass-consumption culture they fostered. Indeed, when Weaver spoke of property rights—"the last metaphysical right"—he was clear to distinguish individual property holdings (e.g., the farm, a small commercial concern) from the "kind of property brought into being by finance capitalism" which was "a violation of the very notion of *proprietas*."[30] Whereas the former was a metaphysical extension of the individual to be nurtured with stewardship and preserved for future generations, the modern form of property was a product of imprudence and a rejection of the divinely ordained order.

Second, although one might see the likes of Kirk and Weaver as having much in common with an earlier generation of Republican Progressives who recognized the symbolic importance of the frontier and mourned its closing, there were, once again, fundamental differences. Both shared a romantic attachment to nature. Progressive Republicans, armed with a faith in scientific management and bureaucratic neutrality, promoted new state agencies with expansive mandates. Postwar traditionalists, in contrast, were wary of "sophisters and calculators," to use Kirk's gloss on Burke. They experienced the proliferation of New Deal agencies and their impact on traditional doctrines of property rights and freedom of association; they witnessed the dark side of social engineering in war collectivism. They sought the preservation of nature and the traditional life and folkways it supported, not a full-blown revivification of planning.

The antiplanning animus and fealty to property rights were strongest among classic liberals or libertarians. For libertarians, individual autonomy and freedom of association were elevated above all other values. Competitive capitalism, grounded in well-defined property rights and market exchange, "promotes political freedom because it separates economic power from political power."[31] All parties to economic transactions benefit from exchanges insofar as they enter into the relationships voluntarily. Any form of planning substitutes the will of some external power for the voluntary decisions of free individuals and violates the right to freedom of association. The state's legitimate role was limited to national defense, the preservation of domestic order, and the definition, maintenance, and defense of property rights. With respect to the moral content of individual action, libertarians promoted maximum freedom but, in sharp contrast with traditionalists, had "nothing to say about what an individual does with his freedom."[32]

The differences between libertarians and traditionalists were best presented in Friedrich A. Hayek's postscript to *The Constitution of Liberty* (1960). According to Hayek, traditionalists were characterized by "fear of change" and an inclination "to use the powers of government to prevent change or to limit its rate to whatever appeals to the more timid mind." In contrast, the libertarian position was based on "a preparedness to let change run its course even if we cannot predict where it will lead." Libertarian "faith in the spontaneous forces of adjustment" created a willingness to "accept changes without apprehension" even if one did not "know how the necessary adaptations will be brought about."[33] Where the libertarian was suspicious of the state relative to the market, traditionalist "opposition to too much government control" was "not a matter of principle."[34] What some traditionalists might accept as legitimate public conservation efforts, libertarians would reject as forays into economic planning. Anticipating the free market environmentalism of the 1990s, libertarians claimed that most pollution and resource depletion problems arose from a failure to assign private property rights that would create incentives for conservation.[35] Traditionalists, in contrast, portrayed pollution as an impious assault on nature justified through modern notions of corporate property. The positions were difficult to reconcile, as were the ramifications for policy.

Yet, even if we stipulate that there were sharp divisions within conservatism, one can identify common ground. Centralizing control in the federal government was abhorrent for traditionalists and libertarians alike. Even if they would disagree over when (or if) government intervention was justified, they would share a strong predisposition for vesting control in the states rather than the federal government. If federal control were inescapable, power should rest in Congress rather than in the president and the bureaucracy. Regardless of where power was exercised, there should be strict limitations on the extent to which intervention could undermine existing property rights. Traditionalists, concerned with the rise of a mass-based consumer society, might be willing to entertain restrictions on environmental exploitation. Libertarians, in contrast, would disallow any efforts to foreclose commercial activities.

Even if one acknowledges the diversity of corporate interests, one can discern a "business" position during this period that is not strictly conservative. Certainly, both conservatives and business affirmed the sanctity of existing property rights. Many businesses supported a decentralization of authority, albeit for instrumental reasons: they could have far greater influence at the state level than at the federal level. The key differences came in the pace or magnitude of exploitation and the role of the state. Businesses preferred unfettered access to resources—a posture that was difficult to reconcile with traditionalist positions. More important, however, businesses rarely mounted principled opposition to market interventions as long as they came in the form of public support (e.g., subsidized access to public lands and resources) whereas conservatives eschewed any government subvention of corporate activity, fearing it would lead inexorably to the politicization of the market. Of course, these differences never prevented moderate Republicans from appropriating conservative rhetoric to justify their support for business. But the effort to equate conservatism with blind support for business was, in the words of Clinton Rossiter, "the Great Train Robbery of American intellectual history" executed by "men who would have found Burke and Adams a pair of 'cranky old bores.'"[36]

## Resurgent Republicans and the Modern Republican Party

In the decades following the late 1970s, the political landscape was dominated by a dense network of conservative advocacy groups and think tanks, integrated into the Republican Party and framing key policy debates on the environment. In the immediate postwar period, in contrast, the conservative movement was in its formative period. The Republican Party, pursing an explicit strategy of recasting itself as a moderate force, had little patience for conservatives. Repulsed and rejected by the "modern" Republican Party, conservatives remained somewhat alienated from popular politics, choosing to follow the path of Albert Jay Nock and speak to the "Remnant" rather than "aim[ing] consciously at the lowest common denominator of intellect, taste and character" among the masses.[37] Their battles were being fought out in the pages of *National Review, Modern Age,* and *Human Events,* not the chambers of Congress.

After enduring two decades as the minority party, the electoral fortunes of the Republican Party improved significantly in the 1950s. In the midterm elections of 1950, Republican gained seats in the House (from 171 to 199 seats) and Senate (from 42 to 47 seats). Although the Democrats retained nominal control, a bipartisan coalition of Republicans and Southern Democrats increasingly cooperated in opposition to Truman and the Fair Deal.[38] In 1952, Eisenhower's victory was decisive; with 55.1 percent of the popular vote, he had carried 39 states (including Texas, Florida, and Virginia) and 442 electoral votes. The Republicans also assumed control of the Congress, albeit by a narrow margin (221 to 214 in the House and 49 to 47 in the Senate).

There was little evidence that unified Republican control of the presidency and Congress constituted a renunciation of the New Deal. Senator Henry Cabot Lodge, Jr, (R-MA) had convinced Eisenhower to enter the Republican primary to defeat the Old Guard, which appeared "unaware of the realities of the modern world." After being "cast in an opposition role for twenty long years," he argued, they "gave the country a negative impression...that Americans faced the choice of doing the wrong thing under the Democrats or doing nothing at all under the Republicans."[39] This Old Guard, which included Ohio's Robert A. Taft, Wisconsin's Joseph McCarthy, Iowa's Bourne Hickenlooper, Ohio's John Bricker, and New Hampshire's Styles Bridges rejected the New Deal and represented an amalgam of populism, virulent anticommunism and isolationism.[40] The Old Guard gravitated around Taft, until his untimely death in 1953.[41]

Although Eisenhower initially made concession to the Old Guard (e.g., support for Chinese nationalists, opposition to some price supports),[42] following the reversals of the 1954 midterm elections, which he blamed squarely on the Old Guard, he devoted his efforts to transforming the GOP into a "modern" party that recognized a more activist state role in domestic politics and embraced internationalism. Eisenhower understood a practical fact: "Should any political party attempt to abolish social security, unemployment insurance, and eliminate labor laws and farm programs, you would not hear of that party again in our political history."[43] The New Deal had successfully mobilized economic interests and given them a stake in the preservation of core public policies. As George H. Mayer notes: "By 1953 the pressure groups had multiplied to the point where Eisenhower could reduce neither expenditures nor services without risking organized retaliation."[44]

Old Guard Republicans and conservative intellectuals cast Eisenhower's republicanism as unprincipled "me-tooism." As William Henry Chamberlin explained, Eisenhower's "idea was to 'modernize' the party outlook and offer a good deal of liberal bait in the platform. Conservatives could be taken for granted; they would vote Republican anyway. Hence the winning strategy would be to accept, in the main, the political, economic, and social legislative changes of the last generation, promising better performance and implementation."[45] Where the president sought accommodation with the New Deal order, conservatives sought "retrenchment—in the size of government, its budget, its debt, its impact on private enterprise, and its tax rate."[46]

## Public Resources and Wilderness Preservation

During the late-1960s and early 1970s, the "environment" emerged as a salient issue, and Congress responded by introducing a series of statutes that redefined the role of the state in the economy and imposed unprecedented costs on businesses. Nonetheless, prior to the "environment decade," important legislative debates directly addressed the role of the state in resource management and wilderness preservation. This section explores two of the most important issues of the period, the control over resources in the tidelands and the creation of the national wilderness system. In each case, conflicts engaged the priority to be placed on economic development relative to conservation and preservation. Equally important, both controversies engaged larger institutional questions. In the case of the tidelands, the key question was whether the federal government was to exercise dominion over resources or whether control would be vested with the states. In the creation of the wilderness system, in contrast, attention focused on the balance of power between the executive branch and Congress. Conservatives, predictably, were unified in their recognition of states' rights and concerns over the delegation of authority to the president and the executive bureaucracy.

These cases are enlightening for another reason: they were concluded under very different political circumstances. The first controversy, resolved with the passage of the Submerged Land Act of 1953, occurred when the Republican Party had unified control of Congress and the presidency. Robert Taft, the central solon of the Old Guard, led the Senate. Although the GOP was rife with divisions, this issue unified the Old Guard, many modern Republicans, and Southern Democrats. The second controversy—wilderness preservation—began three years after the passage of the Submerged Land Act and culminated with the passage of the Wilderness Act of 1964. The creation of the wilderness system involved a similar set of disputes over federal authority and the proper balance between administration of public resources and economic development. But the political context could not have been more dissimilar. By the time the Wilderness Act was passed, the Democrats had assumed unified control of the Congress and the Presidency. Yet, even with the Right in retreat, it would be nonetheless impossible to secure preservation without accommodating business interests.

## Contesting the New Deal in the Tidelands

Prior to the 1940s, the federal government's control over submerged lands was largely defined by a series of nineteenth-century cases[47] that embodied a common set of propositions. At the time of independence, the original states had gained title to resources in submerged lands within navigable waters— that is, inland waters and the maritime belt within three miles of the low water mark. States that joined the Republic subsequently did so on "equal footing." States had the authority to sell or lease property rights; the federal government could acquire access to coastal resources if it paid for the rights. Although Interior Secretary Ickes had acknowledged state control during the early phases of the New Deal, his growing interest in petroleum reserves led him to reverse his position in the late 1930s. When his efforts to acquire legislation to declare lands under the marginal seas part of the public domain failed, he appealed to Roosevelt, who, shortly before his death, authorized Attorney General Francis Biddle to file suit in hopes of getting the courts to recognize federal claims over these resources.[48]

Biddle filed suit against Pacific Western Oil Company in the District Court for the Southern District of California. Ickes argued that a suit should have been filed against the state of California, thereby invoking the Supreme Court's original jurisdiction. With Truman's assumption of the presidency and Biddle's resignation, Attorney General Tom Clark was ordered to abandon the Pacific Western case and file suit against California.[49] Thus, in the fall of 1945, Clark filed an action claiming that the United States "is the owner in fee simple of, or possessed of paramount rights in and powers over, the lands, mineral and other things of value…lying seaward of the ordinary low water mark on the coast of California and outside of the inland waters of the State."[50]

The majority decision in *United States v. California* (1947), delivered by Justice Hugo Black, affirmed the administration's position, concluding that "California is not the owner of the three-mile marginal belt along its coast, and that the Federal Government rather than the state has paramount rights in and power over that belt, an incident to which is full dominion over the resources of the soil under that water area, including oil."[51] In part, the decision rested on the belief that the federal government had "the right and responsibility to exercise whatever power and dominion are necessary to protect this country against dangers to the security and tranquility if its people."[52] The majority was not influenced by the Interior Department's prior denials of lease applications in the coastal belt "on the grounds that California owned the lands." Indeed, "short of a congressional surrender of title or interest," such actions were deemed irrelevant.[53] Similarly, investments that had been made on the assumption of state property rights were of little concern: this "great national question is not dependent upon what expenses may have been incurred upon mistaken assumptions."[54]

In his dissent, Justice Frankfurter objected that the Court referenced "the 'national dominion' of the United States over this area." "Dominion," drawn from the Roman concept of *dominium*, assumed ownership and property rights; *imperium*, in contrast, addressed sovereign authority. "Ownership implies acquisition in the various ways in which land is acquired—by conquest, by discovery and claim, by cession, by prescription, by purchase, by condemnation." The majority had not established that such property rights existed. Rather, it simply assumed that "the power to regulate" was sufficient to "change the imperium of the United States into dominion." His brief dissent ended with an invitation for Congress to address this issue, noting that the determination of these property rights "is a political decision not for this Court."[55]

Congress did not wait for the resolution of *U.S. v. California*. Following the 1945 filing (and the parallel filings against Louisiana and Texas),[56] Congress twice passed quitclaim legislation assigning rights to the states, only to encounter Truman's veto. Truman rejected the legislation as a product of "the private oil interests, seeking to exploit these oil-rich areas without federal control and supervision." He continued: "No state in the Union is a free and independent entity. Each one is part of the United States, and the national government embodies the interests of all the states."[57] The Republican Party quickly embraced the tidelands as a campaign issue, assigning it planks in the 1948 and 1952 platforms. The 1952 platform, for example, advocated "a full and orderly program for the development and conservation of our natural resources" and proclaimed: "We favor restoration to the States of their rights to all lands and resources beneath navigable inlands and offshore waters within their historic boundaries."[58]

On the campaign trail, Eisenhower charged that the "attack on the tidelands is only a part of the effort of the administration to amass more power and money." He questioned where this expansion of federal authority would lead:

> The policy of the Washington powermongers is a policy of Grab.
> I wonder how far a consistent pursuit of this policy would take us.
> If they take the Louisiana, Texas and California Tidelands, then
> what about the Great Lakes? They have been held to be open sea.
> A good part of Chicago has been built on lands once submerged by
> Lake Michigan. What of the Inland Lakes? Rivers and streams in
> Oklahoma, Iowa, Illinois and Kansas? What about the iron ore under
> the navigable waters of Minnesota and the coal under the waters
> of Pennsylvania, West Virginia, and other States?"[59]

In what Eisenhower referred to as the "Shoddy Deal," the federal government would claim control over natural resources and "dole out to the tin cups of the states whatever part of the revenues Washington decided might be good for them."[60] He pledged "to shore up the rights of the states against the implacable expansionism of the federal government,"[61] and in so doing, embraced an issue that could unify the disparate factions in the GOP and Southern Democrats.

Following the 1952 electoral victories[62] and bolstered by promises of presidential support, Republicans made tidelands legislation a major order of business during the first session of the 83rd Congress. On March 27, 1953, the Committee on Interior and Insular Affairs reported Senate Joint Resolution 13, "to confirm and establish the titles of the States to lands beneath navigable waters within State boundaries and to the natural resources within such lands and waters, and to provide for the use and control of said lands and resources." The bill appeared to be unstoppable, with 40 cosponsors (including 15 Southern Democrats)[63] and the endorsement of the Council of State Governments, the Governors Conference, National Conference of Mayors, the American Association of Port Authorities, the American Bar Association, the U.S. Chamber of Commerce, and a long list of trade associations. The bill passed with relative ease in the House (258–108) on April 1, 1953. The Senate debates, in contrast, were raucous and spanned over a month. The majority of Republicans (with the critical support of Southern and Western Democrats) viewed the actions of Ickes, Truman, and the Court as promoting a dramatic expansion of federal authority, a usurpation of state rights, a violation of property rights, and a disdain for market mechanisms. Northern and Eastern Democrats objected that natural resources were a national trust that should be administered in the public interest.

Advocates of the Submerged Land Act focused much of their attention on the statist implications of *United States v. California*. Spessard Holland (D-FL) noted that the controversy pitted the "active proponents...who seem to think that an all-powerful Federal Government is a panacea for all the ills of the people of this country" against those who are "strongly opposed to the nationalization of resources" and "feel that the ownership and control of these resources should remain in the States and be subjected to State and local control where it will be very close to the people who are greatly affected."[64] The paramount powers central to the Court's decision were particularly troubling. As Senator Price Daniel (D-TX) explained:

> The Supreme Court of the United States has held that the paramount governmental powers which the Federal Government has over every farm, home, mine, and factory in the United Sates, as well as over the submerged lands, give the Federal Government the right to take property without paying compensation. It is closely akin to the "inherent powers" doctrine which was announced by President Truman toward the end of his administration. I say it is a dangerous doctrine. I do not believe that the present Supreme Court ever intended that its doctrine should be extended to cover private property.[65]

In response to a subsequent challenge by Senator Paul Douglas (D-IL), Daniel went on to argue that the theory of paramount rights "carried to its logical conclusion" would lead, invariably, to socialism. While these appeals may have been transparent efforts to capitalize on anticommunist sentiments, supporters of the legislation could draw on the judgment of the American Bar Association: "The new concept that the Federal Government has the paramount right to take property without compensation...can have no logical end except that the Federal Government may take over all property, public and private, and under this theory the Federal Government could nationalize all of the natural resources of the country without paying the owners therefore, wholly in disregard of the fifth amendment." The National Association of Attorneys General similarly warned: "The principles of the tidelands decisions...could lead to nationalization of private lands as well as State lands without compensation."[66]

Concerns over the expansion of the federal government were impossible to untangle with the related issues of states' rights and property rights. States' rights loomed large among those who objected to the intrusions (real or perceived) of the Fair Deal. During the Interior and Insular Affairs Committee hearings, several state attorneys general testified in support of the Submerged Land Act. Michigan Attorney General Frank G. Millard provided the clearest expression of state concerns, when he argued: "Only if the States can maintain their sovereignty will they be able to check the untrammeled exercise of Federal power with its resultant centralization of government...we are stemming a tide which has been running during the past 20 years toward the concentration of extensive powers in the Federal Government resulting in the disintegration of the sovereignty of the States."[67] State-level opposition to the federal government's position was expressed is a wave of resolutions in thirteen states demanding that the federal government quitclaim to the submerged lands.[68]

Until the Supreme Court decision, there had been a strong consensus that states held title to the submerged lands; they had awarded private parties property rights over the resources. As Senator Guy Cordon (D-OR) noted, "the people of the United States, supported as they thought, by court decisions, supported as they knew, by words coming from the highest officers up to the department level of the United States...bought, sold, and improved [lands] throughout more than a century of our history....Title insurance companies have guaranteed the titles, and men have spent millions of dollars upon such lands."[69] Thomas H. Kuchel (R-CA) argued that uncertainty over property rights in the states were the inevitable byproduct of this "novel 'paramount rights' doctrine." It had created "a new concept of Federal rights to property within State boundaries" and a legitimate fear that "this paramount rights doctrine may someday be applied to other lands presently believed to be under State jurisdiction."[70]

Opponents of the Submerged Land Act called on the majority to reaffirm the GOP's legacy of conservation and eschew the demands of special interests. The minority report, filed by Senators Clinton Anderson (D-NM), Henry Jackson (D-WA), and James Murray (D-MT) warned of a return to the past when "we allowed our natural riches to waste with startling rapidity" and "erosion and rape of mineral resources were the rule." The minority presented the tidelands legislation as the first step in reversing "the few good chapters of our conservation history" and opening the door "for the attack on our whole public domain." Cattle interests "complain that under Federal regulation designed to save the ranges, the largest cattle owners cannot graze their cattle when they please" and "private forestry interests are making wild attacks on Government policies." They decried the framing of the Court decision as national planning as a crude exploitation of anticommunist sentiments: "From many sides the special interests cry 'socialism.' This is nonsense. The policies were initiated by staid Republican Presidents and governors."[71]

Critics also clearly understood that the Submerged Land Act would transfer decisionmaking authority to a venue that was far more amenable to corporate interests. In the words of O. A. Knight, president of the Oil Workers International, and vice president of the Congress on Industrial Organization, "the special interest[s]...always fight to give their custody to the States, because they know that they can get a better deal that way. They sound off at great and impressive length about the States' rights but they debase this perfectly sound principle into a cloak for their boundless greed."[72] Similarly, J. T. Sanders, legislative counsel of the National Grange, predicted that "these resources in the hands of the various states will not be judiciously conserved and used, but will be soon and recklessly squandered."[73] As Senator Herbert H. Lehman (D-NY) explained, the Act proposes that "we vacate the National Government's sovereign regulatory powers...if this is anything, it is a usurpation of States rights—a usurpation of the rights of 45 States, and of all the people of the nation."[74] Similarly, Hill observed that "senators from coastal States" who support the legislation were "reaching eagerly for a shadow, while letting the substance slip from their grasp." Rights would be granted to all coastal states, but the benefits would accrue to three states with vast oil resources.

Indeed, the asymmetry of benefits was rather striking. The 1954 Economic Census revealed that the oil and gas industries (including operations in manufacturing) for California, Texas, and Louisiana employed 193,400 workers and generated $5.5 billion in value added. Other coastal states paled in comparison. Florida had no oil and gas industry to speak of, whereas the industries in Alabama and Mississippi, when combined, employed 3,300 workers and generated value added of $89.6 million.[75] One might conclude from these figures that most of the advocates of the Submerged Land Act failed to perceive their own economic self-interest and were, in fact, "reaching eagerly for a shadow." Alternatively, one might conclude that economic self-interest was not the primary force outside of the three major beneficiaries. Certainly, the majority of states that passed quitclaim resolutions in the previous decade lacked offshore reserves. Rather, they viewed the expansive claims of federal authority over the tidelands as emblematic of an activist federal government intent on expanding its control over what had traditionally fallen within the jurisdiction of individual states.

Democrats proposed two inventive substitutes for the key provisions of the Submerged Land Act, hoping to give the states a greater stake in federal control. Senators Anderson, Jackson, and Murray recommended alternative S. 107, which would place the offshore deposits under the control of the secretary of the Interior, with 37.5 percent of the royalties proportionately allotted to the 48 states.[76] Even more inventive, an "oil-for-education" amendment would earmark 62.5 percent of revenues within 3 miles of the shoreline and

100 percent thereafter for the building of schools, and hiring of teachers via grants-in-aid.[77] Efforts were made to link the investment in education to the Cold War, albeit unsuccessfully. In the end, these proposals to impose federal regulation failed to carry the day. When a record-setting 22-hour filibuster by Senator Wayne Morse (I-OR) failed, the resolution passed the Senate, and President Eisenhower signed the Submerged Lands Act on May 22, 1953, noting: "I deplore and I will always resist federal encroachment upon rights and affairs of the States. Recognizing the State's claim to these lands is in keeping with basic principles of honesty and fair play."[78]

## Preserving Wilderness and Congressional Authority

The Submerged Land Act and the Wilderness Act evolved in vastly different political environments. Senator Taft died weeks after the passage of the Act, and conservatives continued to lose influence in a party that had developed along the lines envisioned by Eisenhower. In the 1954 midterm elections, the GOP lost 18 seats in the House and one seat in the Senate, turning control over to the Democratic Party. Two years later, the GOP lost an additional seat in each chamber, despite a landslide victory for Eisenhower. In 1958, the GOP hemorrhaged, losing 58 seats in the House and 12 seats in the Senate.[79] With the Old Guard largely eradicated from elective office, Congress largely consisted of Democrats (increasingly divided between their Southern and Northern factions) and modern Republicans who claimed the support of a large business coalition and were disposed to use the public policy to retain its support.

In 1956, Senator Hubert Humphrey (D-MN) and Representative John Saylor (R-PA) introduced legislation, written largely by Wilderness Society executive director Howard Zahniser, to create a federal wilderness system. After eight years, Congress passed "the most far-reaching land preservation statute ever enacted."[80] John Saylor, the sponsor of the legislation in the House, a traditionalist conservative, promoted wilderness preservation in terms that would appear quite defensible to the likes of Russell Kirk and Richard Weaver.[81] In his 1956 speech introducing the Wilderness Act, he noted: "In the wilderness, we can get our bearings. We can keep from getting blinded in our great human success to the fact that we are part of the life of this planet, and we would do well to keep our perspectives and keep in touch with some of the basic facts of life."[82] Wilderness preservation was a corrective to modernity. The "encouragement of the hardy recreation that puts a man or a woman or a red-blooded child on his own in the face of primitive hardships" would create "a nation of strong, healthy citizens," something that Saylor contrasted with the "softness" that had been produced by modern conveniences ranging from regulated heat to inner-spring mattresses.[83] Saylor framed environmental stewardship in Burkean terms as an intergenerational contract: "We want to know that there will always be these areas of wilderness remaining unspoiled, not only for ourselves but for our children, and their children, on and on into the future."[84] While he would continue to represent a traditionalist position on preservation for the remainder of his congressional career, there were few in the Republican ranks who shared his vision. Saylor's original bill permitted for no new mining or prospecting; fellow Republicans and a sizable contingent of Democrats were loath to foreclose future opportunities for resources exploitation.

The original legislative proposal defined wilderness in lofty terms as "an area where the earth and its community of life are untrammeled by man, where man himself is a member of the natural community who visits but does not remain and whose travels leave only trails."[85] Although there was some nominal recognition of "multiple use," the ramifications for development were unambiguous. As stated in Section 3(b):

> Except as otherwise provide in this section, and subject to existing private rights (if any) no portion of any area constituting a unit of the National Wilderness Preservation System shall be devoted to commodity production, to lumbering, prospecting, mining, or the removal of mineral deposits (including oil and gas), grazing by domestic livestock (other than by pack animals in connection with the administration or recreational, educational, or scientific use of the wilderness), water impoundment or reservoir storage, or to any form of commercial enterprise except as contemplated by the purposes of this act.[86]

Opposition to preservation emerged immediately from representatives of the mining industry who clearly understood that the bill, if passed, would foreclose large tracts of land from prospecting and mining.[87] Western and mountain state legislators clearly understood the stakes: in 1958, mining (excluding gas and oil) employed some 95 thousand workers and generated $1.3 billion in value added.[88]

Between 1957 and 1961, House and Senate committees considered the creation of a wilderness system but legislation never broken free of the committee system. Finally, in 1961, the Senate Committee on Interior and Insular Affairs reported the Wilderness Bill (S. 174) to the Senate with the support of the administration. President Kennedy's Natural Resources Message of February 23, 1961 called on the nation to "chart a proper course of conservation and development" noting that all citizens "have a stake in a sound resources program under the progressive principles of national leadership first forged by Pinchot and Theodore Roosevelt, and backed by the essential cooperation of State and local governments." He urged Congress to enact "a wilderness protection bill along the general lines of S. 174."[89] The Wilderness bill designated 6.8 million acres to be included in a newly created Wilderness System and mandated the review of an additional 44 million acres for potential inclusion at the president's discretion, subject to a two-house legislative veto exercised during the first full session after the changes were made. Once designated as parts of the Wilderness System, lands could not be removed or modified in use except through an act of the president subject to a legislative veto.[90]

During the Senate hearings of February 27 and 28, 1961, representatives of the grazing, mining, petroleum, and timber industries testified that their existing property rights in public lands would be abrogated under S. 174, albeit to no avail. During the debates, floor manager Senator Frank Church (D-ID) sought to mollify commercial interests by emphasizing continued recognition of the principle of "multiple use" (where it was currently being observed) and provisions granting the president discretion to make exceptions where deemed in the national interest. However, the Senate floor debates were marked by disquiet over the broad grants of authority to the president and growing sectional divisions between Eastern Republicans and their counterparts from the Rocky Mountain West and Southwest. Thus, the minority report filed by Senators Henry Dworshak (R-ID), Barry Goldwater (R-AZ), Gordon Allott (R-CO), and J. J. Hickey (D-WY), had suggested that "the 'sense of urgency' that lies behind the drive for enactment of this legislation" was "artificial and fictitious" given the vast lands that were currently designated as "wilderness."[91]

The greatest concern during the floor debates involved the massive grant of authority to the president inherent in the legislation and its inconsistency with constitutional principles. Republican Senator Gordon Allott offered sustained opposition to the broad grant of authority to the executive. Citing Article IV, Section 3 of the Constitution, he noted:

> The theory and practice of American constitutional government has been for Congress to initiate proposals and for the Executive to retain the veto power.... What the committee has done in respect to the bill before us is to reverse that process.... For Congress to delegate to the Executive the power to initiate legislation, and retain to itself only a limited veto power, in my opinion would be a clear abdication of congressional responsibility.[92]

Rather than ceding control to "some bureaucrat over whom Congress has no direct control, and who is part of the executive branch of the Government,"

Allott proposed that Congress hold hearings and pass separate bills for each tract of land that would be added to the Wilderness system. Senator Karl Mundt (R-SD) agreed with Allott's proposal, decrying "the strange idolatry of the Chief Executive" inherent in the bill and noting "the zest for increased Executive power which seems to pervade bill after bill which has been brought forward by the administration at this session."[93]

The amendment was defeated for two reasons. First, by mandating the passage of 100 to 150 bills, it would simply overwhelm the Committee on Interior and Insular Affairs and create "a constant logrolling debate in the Senate" over every parcel of public land.[94] Second, there was a strong argument to be made that the system prescribed by the bill actually *increased* congressional power. Executive departments had been designating land use (e.g., declaring lands as "wilderness" or "primitive") since Congress had granted such authority in 1924.[95] Under the proposed Wilderness Act, Congress would finally claim the power to review these determinations with a legislative veto. Although opponents might concede this point, they would go on to argue that this was not nearly sufficient, given that the act would essentially foreclose future development without explicitly considering alternative uses for the lands in question. When this amendment was defeated, Allott retreated from constitutional formalism to offer a second amendment to authorize the secretaries of Interior and Agriculture rather than the president to make exceptions for commercial development within the system. One might argue that the secretaries would be more responsive to Congress; others predicted that such a provision would lead inexorably to agency capture. With the defeat of this second amendment, the Wilderness bill passed the Senate by a 78 to 8 margin.[96]

Commercial interests that had encountered stiff resistance in the Senate found a more receptive audience when the Public Lands Subcommittee of the House Interior and Insular Affairs Committee held hearings in May 1962. The configuration of interests was much as one might expect. Representatives of the Kennedy administration, Interior Secretary Udall and Agriculture Secretary Freeman, supported S. 174, dismissing concerns over commercial use and opposing efforts to dilute presidential control. Representatives of conservation and environmental groups, including the Wilderness Society, the Izaak Walton League, the National Audubon Society, the Citizen's Committee on Natural Resources, and the National Speleological Society, joined with the administration in strongly supporting the bill. Representatives of commercial interests exploited the divisions evident in the Senate debates by focusing on the broad grant of executive authority. Floyd Beach of Western Colorado Cattlemen's Committee called for amendments "so that Congress does not follow and accelerate the alarming trend of abdicating its responsibilities and delegating its authority to the Executive Branch."[97] John I. Taylor of the American Farm Bureau Federation argued that primitive areas should not be incorporated by presidential fiat but only by explicit congressional authorization after careful consideration had been given to the use of lands for forestry, mining, hunting, and grazing. Gordon A. Goodwin, representing the American Petroleum Institute, the Rocky Mountain Oil and Gas Association, and the Western Oil and Gas Association, argued that amendments should require positive act of Congress and provide for multiple use of all lands, a position echoed by representatives of the National Association of Manufacturers, the US Chamber of Commerce, and the National Lumber Manufacturers Association.

In September 1962, the House Interior and Insular Affairs Committee voted to report a wilderness bill (H.R. 776) that departed significantly from its Senate counterpart. Although both the Senate and House agreed on the lands to be placed in the Wilderness System, the House version denied the grant of authority to the president, requiring an affirmative act of the Congress, and prohibited the president from making future changes in classification without congressional authorization. Moreover, the House bill allowed for a continuation of mining and prospecting for 25 years and required that each area included in the Wilderness area be reviewed at least once every 25 years.[98] When the Interior Committee voted to report the bill to the floor under a closed rule, conservationists mobilized in opposition to H.R. 776, arguing that it was worse than no legislation at all.[99] In the end, Interior Committee Chairman Wayne Aspinall (D-CO) gave conservationists their wish. Following the committee approval of H.R. 776, he noted that "propagandists for the wilderness preservationists and their newspaper allies" mobilized and "demonstrated that they have no desire to compromise and, in their reckless and ruthless demand, to rule or ruin." He took no further action to bring H.R.776 to the floor and the measure died with the adjournment of the 87th Congress.

By April 1963, the Senate had passed (73–12) an amended bill (S. 4) establishing a National Wilderness Preservation System, largely along the lines of the earlier legislation. After a year of House inaction, attention returned in April 1964 to the Public Lands Subcommittee of the House Committee on Interior and Insular Affairs. The subcommittee considered two proposals in addition to S. 4. Representative John Dingell (D-MI) sponsored H.R. 9162, which was much the same bill as had passed the committee in the last round. It directed the departments of Agriculture and Interior to review additional lands for inclusion into the system but required that Congress retain control by passing legislation rather than simply exercising a legislative veto. The Dingell bill differed from its predecessor in permitting a continuation of mining for 10 years instead of 25. Republican John Saylor sponsored H.R. 9070, which similarly required affirmative action on the part of Congress. However,

H.R. 9070 prohibited any new mining in wilderness areas. Prospecting for mineral resources was permitted where compatible with wilderness preservation and mining could continue in "primitive" areas pending action by Congress.[100]

The hearings proved to be something of a surprise. The administration supported S. 4 but found merit in the Dingell bill and endorsed inclusion of new lands through affirmative congressional action, a significant reversal of Udall's position in 1962.[101] Representatives of environmental groups followed the administration's lead and conceded the legitimacy of provisions requiring the affirmative action of Congress. Although they remained more supportive of S. 4 and H.R. 9070, they signaled willingness to compromise on mineral leasing. The corporate response remained what one might expect. Although the National Association of Manufacturers promoted the 10-year extension of mining rights under H.R. 9162, the American Mining Congress stood fast in its advocacy of the original 1962 bill that extended mining for 25 years.[102]

Ultimately, the Committee reported an amended version of the Saylor bill and in August 1964, the House passed the bill 373–1. The compromises struck by conservationists and the administration were deemed critical in the outcome. Yet, the concessions were more than trivial. The House required an affirmative act of Congress rather than the Senate's preferred legislative veto. Moreover, the House prohibited the USDA Secretary from declassifying lands that were already classified as primitive, thereby retaining congressional control in this area as well. Most troubling for conservationists, the final House bill preserved existing mining rights and decided to permit new mining patents for 25 years with no new mining operations after December 31, 1989.[103] After eight long years and 66 drafts, the House and Senate approved the conference report on the Wilderness Act on August 20, 1964. The final Act placed 9.1 million acres of federal land permanently into the wilderness system and created a mechanism for expansion by directing the USDA to review "primitive" national forests (5.4 million acres), the Department of Interior to review roadless national park areas (22.1 million acres) and wildlife refuges and game ranges (24.4 million acres) for possible inclusion. Opponents of executive expansion had been successful in their efforts to limit the president's discretionary authority. Ultimately, the Wilderness Act allowed for ongoing economic development. With respect to mining, "valid existing rights" were recognized, but no new mining rights would be issued and no new mining activities would begin after December 31, 1986—one of the few concessions that the Senate won in conference. Similarly, livestock grazing was allowed to continue under the supervision of the USDA. In addition, the Act permitted water prospecting and the establishment of reservoirs, power projects, and transmission lines.[104]

## Conclusion

The legislative histories provide some insights into conservatism and environmental politics prior to the environmental decade. With unified Republican control of the presidency and the Congress during the tidelands debates, one should not be surprised that the final product was a law that rejected claims of federal authority over natural resources. Property rights were vested in the states and, in many cases, transferred to the commercial interests that effectively mobilized in support of the Submerged Land Act. On this issue, a powerful coalition of Old Guard and moderate Republicans and Southern Democrats prevailed with the support of states and business associations. In stark contrast, the Wilderness Act was passed under unified Democratic control of the presidency and the Congress. Conservation groups—largely absent in the tidelands debate—mobilized in support of policy but proved incapable of overcoming the stiff opposition of business associations and development interests, particularly in the House. Despite the efforts of the Western Republicans, the Wilderness Act succeeded in setting aside an unprecedented amount of public lands. Whereas the Submerged Land Act had rejected federal management for economic development, the Wilderness Act secured preservation. Yet, preservation was possible only after the Senate conceded to the House, which proved far more interested in facilitating development and protecting its institutional authority. Mining rights would receive a quarter-century lease on life. Authority over the expansion of the Wilderness System would rest firmly with Congress, thereby securing access points for development interests wary of further restrictions.

These debates were intertwined with larger contests over institutional design and the role of the state in society. Concerns over the relationship between the federal government and the states were central to the tidelands controversy. To what extent could the federal government use claims of "paramount rights" to extend control over natural resources? Although many of the states that supported quitclaim legislation lacked petroleum reserves and would have benefited from Democratic proposals to nationalize control, the claims of federal authority was emblematic of a much larger transfer of authority that had occurred during the Roosevelt and Truman administrations. During the wilderness debates, attention turned instead to executive-legislative relations. To what extent did the constitution place formal constraints on the delegation of discretionary authority to executive agencies? Legislative advocates, ready to crown the president with broad grants of discretionary authority, were thwarted and the Wilderness Act established a precedent by taking the decisions on wilderness designation away from the bureaucracy and vesting them in Congress.[105] Following this precedent, in the core regulatory statutes of the 1970s, Congress would delegate minimal discretionary authority to regulators, essentially replacing the broad grants of authority that had been common in the past with exhaustive statutes that would severely constrain bureaucratic action.

And what of the role of the state in the economy? Republicans (at times supported by Southern Democrats) argued that the state should not subjugate private property rights to the national interest, however conceived. Yet, one might view these objections as rhetorical tools rather than as principled traditionalist commitments to inalienable rights or libertarian celebrations of spontaneous order. Much in keeping with the historical legacy of the state in its developmental capacity, opponents of national control (in the tidelands controversy) and preservation (in the wilderness debates) envisioned a state that would provide commercial interests with access to resources, often at fire sale prices. The demands of business found a ready constituency regardless of the partisan composition of Congress or the fluctuating fortunes of conservatives. This great constant of business influence should be of little surprise for observers of American politics, whether they employ neopluralist, elite-managerial, or class frameworks for explaining policy outcomes.[106]

The ways in which the debates were framed would prove to have remarkable longevity. Appeals to constitutional formalism would find ongoing expressions in regulatory politics, both in the perennial congressional quest to reign in bureaucratic discretion through exhaustive statutes and in the efforts to impede environmental restrictions on private property (e.g., the "regulatory takings" debates).[107] Continued appeals to the sanctity of market processes and property rights would find continuing expressions in libertarian critiques of regulation and "free market environmentalism."[108] As in the earlier debates, references to the marvels of the market would be deployed for their instrumental value. The arguments regarding the "multiple use" of public lands presaged the "wise use" arguments of the future in which development interests would argue that resource exploitation was compatible with environmental protection. The tensions between preservation and commercial development would remain central to national management of public lands, as exhibited by the continued subsidization of grazing and mining rights on public lands and ongoing efforts to extend oil exploration to the Alaskan National Wildlife Refuge.

The strands of continuity should not obscure the larger change that would occur in the decade following the passage of the Wilderness Act. Richard Nixon provides a convenient study in contrasts. In his speech accepting the 1960 Republican nomination, Nixon embraced a developmental agenda, stating that to achieve greater prosperity, "we will develop to the full the untapped natural resources, our water, our minerals, our power, with which we are so fortunate to be blessed in this rich land of ours."[109] A decade later, Nixon signed the National Environmental Policy Act with great fanfare on

New Year's Day. Later that month, in his 1970 State of the Union address, he argued that clean air and water were a birthright of all Americans and proclaimed: "Clean air is not free, and neither is clean water. The price tag on pollution control is high. Through our years of past carelessness we incurred a debt to nature, and now that debt is being called."[110] By year's end, Nixon created the Environmental Protection Agency and Congress passed the Clean Air Act Amendments. The modern environmental era was underway.

What of conservatives? Although they would realize some fleeting success in Barry Goldwater's disastrous bid for the presidency, the humiliating 1964 defeat seemed, at the time, to mark the end of conservatism as a political force. Yet, with the emergence of the "environment" as an issue and the regulatory revolution of the early 1970s, many conservatives would discover a new *cause célèbre*. Environmental protection—an issue that could be framed as part of a policy agenda embraced by elite social engineers and countercultural fringe groups hostile to free-market capitalism—joined affirmative action, women's rights, and social welfare to unify disparate conservative factions. Corporate foundations provided massive infusions of financial support as they began to invest heavily in policy advocacy. Henceforth, the American Enterprise Institute, the Heritage Foundation, and the Cato Institute would prove far more influential than *Modern Age* or the *National Review* in framing future regulatory contests. Although the divisions between traditionalists and libertarians would never be fully resolved, they would join forces frequently to contest the policies of the Environmental Protection Agency and other social regulatory agencies, even if they would frequently part ways when offering alternatives. The Republican Party would continue to evolve along the path of modern Republicanism forged by Eisenhower, deploying conservative arguments where instrumentally valuable, but rarely embracing their implications when they ran afoul of public opinion. Given the salience of environmental protection in the decades following Earth Day 1970, a frontal assault on the EPA or efforts to revoke key statutes would have carried significant political costs that the GOP was unwilling to endure.

## Notes

1. See David Vogel, *Fluctuating Fortunes: The Political Power of Business in America* (New York: Basic Books, 1989).
2. Sara Diamond, *Roads to Dominion: Right-Wing Movements and Political Power in the United States* (New York: The Guilford Press, 1995), 35.
3. Eric Schickler, *Disjointed Pluralism: Institutional Innovation and the Development of the U.S. Congress* (Princeton: Princeton University Press, 2001), 16. See also Karen Orren and Stephen Skowronek, "Beyond the Iconography of Order: Notes for a 'New' Institutionalism," in *The Dynamics of American*

*Politics: Approaches and Interpretations,* ed. Larry Dodd and Calvin Jillson (Boulder: Westview, 1994), 331–365.

4. Paul W. Gates, "Public Land Issues in the United States," *The Western Historical Quarterly* 2, 4 (1971): 365.

5. Merle Fainsod, Lincoln Gordon, and Joseph C. Palamountain, Jr., *Government and the American Economy,* 3rd ed. (New York: W. W. Norton, 1959), 707.

6. Gates, "Public Land Issues," 374.

7. Paul W. Gates and Lillian F. Gates, "Canadian and American Land Policy Decisions, 1930," *The Western Historical Quarterly* 15, 4 (1984): 389–91.

8. Gates, "Public Land Issues," 375.

9. See Elmo Richardson, "The Struggle for the Valley: California's Hetch Hetchy Controversy, 1905–1913," *California Historical Society Quarterly* 38 (1959): 249–58.

10. Rickey L. Hendricks, "The Conservation Movement: A Critique of Historical Sources," *The History Teacher* 16, 1 (1982): 85.

11. See Kendrick A. Clements, "Herbert Hoover and Conservation, 1921–33," *The American Historical Review* 89, 1 (1984): 67–88.

12. Stephen Raushenbush, "Conservation in 1952," *Annals of the American Academy of Political and Social Science* 281 (1952): 1.

13. Jack C. Oppenheimer and Leonard A. Miller, "Environmental Problems and Legislative Responses," *Annals of the American Academy of Political and Social Sciences* 389 (1970): 79.

14. Whitney R. Cross, "Ideas in Politics: The Conservation Policies of the Two Roosevelts," *Journal of the History of Ideas* 14, 3 (1953): 436.

15. Luther Tweeten, *Foundations of Farm Policy* (Lincoln: University of Nebraska Press, 1970), 96–7.

16. Norm Wengert, "TVA—Symbol and Reality," *The Journal of Politics* 13, 3 (1951): 378; Fainsod, Gordon, and Palamountain, *Government and the American Economy,* 759.

17. See Marion Clawson, *New Deal Planning: The National Resources Planning Board* (Baltimore, MD: Johns Hopkins University Press, 1981).

18. For a good overview of conservatism from a traditionalist perspective, see William Henry Chamberlin, "The Conservative Message for Our Time," *Modern Age* 3, 3 (Summer 1959): 300–6.

19. Edmund Burke, *Reflections on the Revolution in France* (Indianapolis: Library of Liberal Arts 1790/1955), 110.

20. See Frank S. Meyer, *In Defense of Freedom: And Related Essays* (Indianapolis: Liberty Fund, 1996).

21. See George H. Nash, *The Conservative Intellectual Movement in America since 1945* (Wilmington, DE: Intercollegiate Studies Institute, 1996), chap. 3.

22. Richard M. Weaver, *Ideas Have Consequences* (Chicago: University of Chicago Press, 1948), 171.

23. Ibid., 172. See the discussion of Weaver in Nash, *Conservative Intellectual Movement*, 32–5.

24. Weaver, *Ideas Have Consequences*, 173, 175.

25. For a fascinating overview of the traditionalist position and its environmental implications, see John R. E. Bliese, "Richard M. Weaver, Russell Kirk, and the Environment," *Modern Age* 38 (Winter 1996): 148–58.

26. Russell Kirk, *The Conservative Mind: From Burke to Eliot*, 7th ed. (Washington, DC: Regnery Publishing, 1985), introduction. For another influential statement of core principles, see Peter Viereck, *Conservatism Revisited: The Revolt against Revolt, 1815–1949* (New York: Charles Scribner's Sons, 1949).

27. Russell Kirk, *A Program for Conservatives* (Chicago: Henry Regnery), 294.

28. Ibid., 291.

29. Ibid., 308.

30. Weaver, *Ideas Have Consequences*, 130. See George H. Nash, "The Influence of Ideas Have Consequences in the Conservative Intellectual Movement in America," in *Steps Towards Restoration: The Consequences of Richard Weaver's Ideas*, ed. Ted J. Smith (Wilmington, DE: Intercollegiate Studies Institute, 1998), 81–124.

31. Milton Friedman, *Capitalism and Freedom* (Chicago: University of Chicago Press, 1962), 9.

32. Ibid., 12.

33. Friedrich A. Hayek, *The Constitution of Liberty* (Chicago: University of Chicago Press, 1960), 400. Hayek uses the term "liberalism" to connote classic liberalism, finding the term "libertarianism" to be "singularly unattractive," having "too much the flavor of a manufactured term and of a substitute" (408). The term "libertarian" will be used here to avoid confusion and comport with contemporary usage.

34. Ibid., 403. See Diamond's discussion of the fragile relationship between traditionalists and libertarians in *Roads to Dominion*, chap. 1.

35. See Hayek's discussion of conservation in *The Constitution of Liberty*, 366–75.

36. Clinton Rossiter, *Conservatism in America* (New York: Alfred A. Knopf, 1955), 221. Rossiter notes that genuine conservatives (characterized by their "obstinate refusal to delight in the 'progress' of industrialism or the make peace with the 'shallow optimism,' 'selfish individualism,' and 'hedonistic materialism' of the scheme of values that this progress has sustained") were, at best, "a goad to the conscience of the Right . . . and a reminder that some conservative Americans are as troubled by the harsh dogmas of individualism as by the false promises of collectivism" (212).

37. Albert Jay Nock, "Isaiah's Job," in Albert Jay Nock, *The State of the Union: Essays in Social Criticism*, ed. Charles H. Hamilton (Indianapolis: Liberty Fund, 1991), 130.

38. George H. Mayer, *The Republican Party, 1854–1966*, 2nd ed. (New York: Oxford University Press, 1967), 480–1.

39. Dwight D. Eisenhower, *Mandate for Change, 1953–1956* (Garden City, NY: Doubleday, 1963), 17–18.

40. See David A. Horowitz, *Beyond Left and Right: Insurgency and the Establishment* (Urbana: University of Illinois Press, 1997), chap. 10.

41. John W. Sloan, *Eisenhower and the Management of Prosperity* (Lawrence: University Press of Kansas, 1991), 61; Stephen E. Ambrose, *Eisenhower,* vol. 2, *The President* (New York: Simon and Schuster, 1984), 76.

42. Ambrose, *Eisenhower,* 47.

43. Quoted in Sloan, *Eisenhower and the Management of Prosperity,* 62.

44. Mayer, *The Republican Party,* 498.

45. William Henry Chamberlin, "Rallying Cry for American Conservatives," *Modern Age* 8, 4 (Fall 1964): 344. See William F. Buckley, "The Tranquil World of Dwight D. Eisenhower," *National Review* 5 (January 18, 1958): 59, and Clinton Rossiter, *The American Presidency* (New York: Harcourt, Brace, 1956), 134.

46. James L. Sundquist, *Politics and Policy: The Eisenhower, Kennedy, and Johnson Years* (Washington, DC: Brookings Institution, 1968), 416.

47. 41 U.S. (16 Pet.) 367 (1842).

48. Ernest R. Bartley, *The Tidelands Oil Controversy: A Legal and Historical Analysis* (Austin: University of Texas Press, 1953), 101–11.

49. Ibid., 137–41.

50. Quoted in *United States v. State of California,* 332 U.S 19 (1947), 22.

51. 332 U.S. 19, 38–9.

52. 332 U.S. 19, 29.

53. 332 U.S. 19, 39.

54. 332 U.S. 19, 41.

55. 332 U.S. 18, 45.

56. See the discussion of relevant court decisions in Aaron L. Shalowitz, *Shore and Sea Boundaries* (Washington, DC: Government Printing Office, 1962), vol. 1, chap. 1.

57. Harry S. Truman, *Memoirs,* vol. 2, *Years of Trial and Hope* (Garden City, NY: Doubleday, 1956), 481–2, 483.

58. Republican Party Platform of 1952, in *National Party Platforms, 1840–1960,* 502. Kirk H. Porter and Donald Bruce Johnson, eds. (Urbana: University of Illinois Press, 1961).

59. "Speech by General Eisenhower on Tidelands Oil, New Orleans, October 13, 1952," in *The Eisenhower Administration, 1953–1961: A Documentary History,* ed. Robert L. Branyan and Lawrence H. Larsen (New York: Random House, 1971), vol. 1, 123–4.

60. Ibid.

61. Eisenhower, *Mandate for Change,* 203.

62. Robert Allen Rutland, *The Republicans: From Lincoln to Bush* (Columbia: University of Missouri Press, 1996), 209.

63. Cosponsors of S.J. Res. 13 included Spessard Holland (D-FL), Hugh Butler (R-NE), George Smathers (D-FLA), Harry Byrd (D-VA), Absalom

Robertson (D-VA), Wallace Bennett (R-UT), Arthur Watkins (R-UT), John Bricker (R-OH), Robert Taft, (R-OH), John Butler (R-MD), James Beall (R-MD), Guy Cordon (R-OR), Frank Carlson (R-KS), Andrew Schoeppel (R-KS), Price Daniel (D-TX), Lyndon Johnson (D-TX), James Duff (R-PA), Edward Martin (R-PA), Allen Ellender (D-LA), Russell Long (D-LA), James Eastland (D-MS), John Stennis (D-MS), Joseph Frear (D-DE), Ralph Flanders (R-VT), Barry Goldwater (R-AZ), Robert Hendrickson (R-NJ), Howard Smith (R-NJ), Bourke Hickenlooper (R-IA), William Jenner (R-IN), William Knowland (R-CA), Thomas Kuchel (R-CA), John McClellan (D-AK), Burnet Maybank (D-SC), Karl Mundt (R-SD), Charles Potter (R-MI), Leverett Saltonstall (R-MA), Willis Smith (D-NC), Edward Thye (R-MN), Herman Welker (R-ID), and Patrick McCarran (D-NV).

64. *Congressional Record,* 83rd Cong., 1st sess., vol. 99, part 2 (April 7, 1953), 2774–5.
65. *Congressional Record,* 83rd Cong., 1st sess., vol. 99, part 2 (April 8, 1953), 2818, 2819.
66. *Submerged Lands,* Hearings before the Committee on Interior and Insular Affairs, United States Senate, Eighty-Third Congress, First Session. (Washington, DC: Government Printing Office, 1953), 58.
67. Ibid., 80.
68. Ibid., 52. State resolutions were passed by Alabama in 1939 and 1951, California in 1948, 1949, and 1951, Florida in 1945 and 1949, Louisiana in 1946, Maine in 1949, Maryland in 1948 and 1949, Michigan in 1948, Mississippi in 1948, New Jersey in 1939, New York in 1946 and 1950, North Carolina in 1949, Oregon in 1949, and Virginia in 1950.
69. *Congressional Record,* 83rd Cong., 1st sess., vol. 99, part 2 (April 1, 1953), 2615.
70. *Congressional Record,* 83rd Cong., 1st sess., vol. 99, part 3 (April 13, 1953), 2984.
71. *Congressional Record,* 83rd Cong., 1st sess., vol. 99, part 2 (April 8, 1953), 2844–45.
72. *Submerged Lands,* 469–70.
73. Ibid., 485.
74. *Congressional Record,* 83rd Cong., 1st sess., vol. 99, part 3 (April 13, 1953), 2974.
75. Figures for the 1954 Economic Census reported in U.S. Department of Commerce, Bureau of the Census, *Census of the Mineral Industries, 1972* (Washington, DC: US Government Printing Office, 1976), 5-13, 6-7, 6-8, 7-7, 7-8, and 8-9.
76. *Congressional Record,* 83rd Cong., 1st sess., vol. 99, part 2 (April 8, 1953), 2839–41.
77. The "oil-for-education" amendment was sponsored by Paul Douglas (D-IL), Matthew Neely (D-WV), Charles Tobey (R-NH), William Langer (R-ND), Morse (I-OR), John Sparkman (D-AL), Estes Kefauver (D-TN),

Dennis Chavez (D-NM), Hubert Humphrey (D-MN), Thomas Hennings (D-MO), Herbert Lehman (D-NY), James Murray (D-MT), Guy Gillette (D-IA), James Fulbright (D-AK), Francis Case (R-SD), Harley Kilgore (D-WV), Theodore Green (D-RI) Warren Magnuson (D-WA), Henry ackson (D-WA), Michael Mansfield (D-MT), John Pastore (D-RI), and Lister Hill (D-AL).

78. "Statement by President Eisenhower upon Signing the Tidelands Oil Bill, May 22, 1953," in Branyan and Larsen, eds., *The Eisenhower Administration, 1953–1961,* 134.

79. See Louis L. Gould, *Grand Old Party: A History of the Republicans* (New York: Random House, 2003), 336–51.

80. Robert L. Glicksman and George Cameron Coggins, "Wilderness in Context," *Denver University Law Review* 76 (1999): 387.

81. Keith Easthouse, "The Party That Was Green." *Forest Magazine,* July/August 2001 (www.fseee.org/index.html?page=http%3A//www.fseee.org/forestmag/0104east.shtml).

82. *Congressional Record,* 84th Cong., 2nd sess., vol. 102, part 9 (July 12, 1956), 12584.

83. Ibid., 12583.

84. Ibid., 12583.

85. H.R. 11703, Sec. 1 (c). *Congressional Record,* 84th Cong., 2nd sess., vol. 102, part 9 (July 12, 1956), 12590.

86. H.R. 11703, Sec. 3(b) at *Congressional Record,* 84th Cong., 2nd sess., vol. 102, part 9 (July 12, 1956), 12591.

87. See Kenneth D. Hubbard, Marilyn Nixon, Jeffrey A. Smith, "The Wilderness Act's Impact on Mining Activities: Policy versus Practice," *Denver University Law Review* 76 (1999): 591–609.

88. U.S. Department of Commerce, *Census of the Mineral Industries, 1972,* 7-7, 8-7, and 9-8.

89. President John F. Kennedy, Natural Resources Message of February 23, 1961 (www.jfklink.com/speeches/jfk/publicpapers/1961/jfk49_61.html).

90. "National Wilderness System," *Congressional Quarterly Weekly Report* 19, 31 (August 4, 1961): 1360.

91. Quoted in *Congressional Record,* 88th Cong., 1st sess., vol. 109, part 5 (April 8, 1963), 5885.

92. *Congressional Record,* 87th Cong., 1st sess., vol. 107, part 14 (Sept 6, 1961), 18358.

93. Ibid., 18362.

94. Ibid., 18369–70.

95. The U.S. Forest Service established the first protected wilderness area under its own discretion in 1924. See Ross W. Gorte, *Wilderness: Overview and Statistics,* Congressional Research Service Report for Congress No. 94–976 ENR, 2 December 1994.

96. "Senate Passes Wilderness Bill, 78–8," *Congressional Quarterly Weekly Report* 20, 36 (September 8, 1961): 1543–4.

97. Quoted in "Committee Roundup," *Congressional Quarterly Weekly Review* 20, 20 (May 18, 1962): 854.

98. "House Committee Approves Modified Wilderness Bill," *Congressional Quarterly Weekly Report* 20, 36 (September 7, 1962): 1488–9.

99. "Aspinall Strategy Blocks Wilderness in Session-End Jam," *Congressional Quarterly Weekly Report* 20, 47 (November 23, 1962): 2197–8.

100. See comparison of bills in "Outlook Improves for Compromise Wilderness System Bill," *Congressional Quarterly Weekly Report* 22, 21 (May 22, 1964): 1008–10.

101. "Wilderness System," *Congressional Quarterly Weekly Report* 22, 18 (May 1, 1964): 873.

102. "Wilderness System," *Congressional Quarterly Weekly Report* 22, 19 (May 8, 1964): 5–6.

103. "House Votes to Establish Wilderness System, 373–1," *Congressional Quarterly Weekly Report* 22, 32 (August 7, 1964): 1678–9.

104. "Congress Clears Bill Establishing Wilderness System," *Congressional Quarterly Weekly Report* 22, 35 (August 28, 1964): 1969–70.

105. Samuel P. Hays, *Explorations in Environmental History: Essays by Samuel P. Hays* (Pittsburgh: University of Pittsburgh Press, 1998), 133.

106. See, for example, Robert R. Alford and Roger Friedland, *Powers of Theory: Capitalism, the State, and Democracy* (Cambridge: Cambridge University Press, 1985).

107. See Richard Epstein, *Takings: Private Property and the Power of Eminent Domain* (Cambridge: Harvard University Press, 1985).

108. See Terry L. Anderson and Donald R. Leal, *Free Market Environmentalism,* rev. ed. (New York: Palgrave, 2001).

109. Richard M. Nixon, Acceptance Speech, July 28, 1960, Chicago, (www.presidency.ucsb.edu/shownomination.php?convid=23).

110. President Nixon, 1970 State of the Union Address. (www.janda.org/politxts/State%200f%20Union%20Addresses/1970–1974%20Nixon%20T/RMN70.html).

# CHAPTER 2

## Social Security from the New Deal to the Great Society: Expanding the Public Domain

*Edward Berkowitz and Larry DeWitt*

At the beginning of the 1935 congressional session that resulted in the passage of the Social Security Act and the creation of the old-age insurance program that we now call Social Security, the *New York Times* reported, "there is every indication that Mr. Roosevelt will have his way from beginning to end."[1] The article implied a sense of inevitability about the legislative passage of the items on the president's agenda. In this view of contemporary events, the impressive victory of the Democrats in the 1934 election paved the way for the second New Deal, including the Social Security Act that the president signed into law on August 14, 1935. In fact, however, little about the creation of Social Security was inevitable. The narrative that has the liberal Franklin D. Roosevelt dictating the terms of the legislation leaves out the vital role of conservative ideas and conservative politicians in the process. Conservative forces delayed the passage of the legislation and nearly caused it to be carried over to the next congressional session. Even after the passage of the law, conservative ideas and institutions continued to influence the development of the program.

The program required two additional "starts" after 1935 in order to acquire the political momentum that made it the cornerstone of America's welfare state. Conservative critiques of the financing aspects of the program framed the political discussion that led to the 1939 amendments, and conservative predilections for locally run programs influenced Social Security politics in the 1940s. Only after 1950 did the program acquire the expansionary characteristics that academic observers have come to associate with Social Security, and even then conservative notions of economic behavior slowed the extension of the program into new areas, such as disability. Hence, the period between 1935 and 1956 differs from the two other periods discussed in this volume. In this period, questions about the state's role in provisions for the elderly remained open, and hence conservatives had a greater opportunity to shape the program.

Roosevelt himself made conservative choices in the Social Security proposals that he sent to Congress in 1935. In particular, he did not call for federally funded payments to all of America's elderly citizens. Instead, he relied on the concept of social insurance to link the eventual receipt of Social Security benefits to the previous state of working in an industrial or commercial job. Furthermore, he depended on the states, rather than the federal government, to administer many of the programs that he included in the omnibus Social Security Act. If Roosevelt made Social Security "the cornerstone" of American social provision and considered it the proudest achievement of his presidency, he built his grand edifice on materials that were quite conservative in origin and conception. Between 1935 and 1950, furthermore, the grand edifice was neither grand nor close to being completed. Those developments would come in the period described by Marmor and Altman in this volume, although even then the creation of Medicare in 1965 occasioned a lively partisan political debate between liberals and conservatives. An indifference to Social Security on the part of liberals and a surprising convergence of liberals and conservatives on developing alternatives to old-age insurance characterized the initial period.

The conservative in the era of Newt Gingrich faced a world far different from that of the conservative in the age of FDR. For that reason, conservatives as a political force and conservatism as a political ideology changed their characteristics and arguments over time. In the New Deal, essential boundary questions concerning public and private responsibility for the maintenance of the elderly were debated. Conservatives in Congress, who were largely Republicans but might also be southern Democrats or even western progressives, favored granting discretion to the states and localities over broadening the power of the federal government. They questioned the wisdom of saddling employers with high payroll taxes and having the government hold large amounts of money in reserve for the program, and they sought to protect what they regarded as constitutionally sanctioned rights such as freedom of contract. These feelings united a very loose coalition of New Deal opponents from Republican members of Congress, to federal judges appointed before the New Deal, to leaders of the business community and the organizations that expressed these individuals' points of view, such as the Chamber of Commerce or the Republican Party. Over time, this coalition would change. In the 1950s, for example, a majority of Republicans favored the expansion of Social Security to pay higher benefits. After 1937 the opposition of the courts to Social Security lessened. Later generations of conservatives faced a situation in which the wall between public and private provision for the elderly had been significantly breached and Social Security policy was inevitably a matter of federal policy. The questions shifted from boundary questions (Should there be Social Security?) to maintenance questions (How could Social Security benefits be preserved? How much should they be expanded?). During the initial boundary phase, every bit as much as during the modern privatization debates, policy makers needed to be attentive to conservative ideas and policy proposals.

## The Condition of the Elderly and the Movement for State Pensions

In the immediate sense, the process that led to the passage of the Social Security Act began with a 1934 decision by President Roosevelt to prepare a comprehensive economic security bill that he could present to Congress at the beginning of 1935. To produce a bill according to his specifications, the president created a cabinet-level committee that supervised a staff of experts on topics related to social welfare. This apparatus produced a bill that was eventually sent to the tax committees of Congress early in 1935. With the exception of businessmen from large national corporations such as Standard Oil and General Electric and actuaries from the insurance industry, the administration made little effort to reach out to what might be described as the conservative political community. Instead, it relied on social insurance experts, with a predilection toward state-sponsored solutions to the problems of unemployment and old age. To be sure, businessmen and insurance company executives—the voices of experience—could not be ignored without a serious loss of credibility. These businessmen, after all, had attempted to offer old age pensions on a national basis and had better access to at least some of the relevant data than did government bureaus such as the Bureau of Labor Statistics. Nor were these businessmen particularly conservative members of their communities. Instead, they might be considered corporate liberals.[2] Although actuaries were bound by what might be described as numerical precedent that tended to cast their projections in conservative terms, they worked in an industry with a strong sense of social purpose in matters such as industrial safety and the maintenance of good health.[3]

The problem of old age came to the agenda of this working group in part because it had been on the reform agenda at least since the Progressive Era.[4] Advocates for old-age pensions portrayed old age as a harrowing time in which workers lost their ability to keep up the pace of production in an industrial economy. In this spirit, Abraham Epstein referred to "the tragedy of old age" and argued that what he called "superannuation" was unknown before the development of the factory system. He cited statistics that showed employment rates for older workers were lower than the rates for younger workers and pointed to such practices as age limits on the employees that companies would hire. The unemployment rate, he noted, went up steeply after age 45. Over 90 percent of workers aged 16 to 64 found gainful employment in 1930, compared with 58.3 percent of those over 65. The depression made a bad problem that much worse.[5]

Modern researchers think that Epstein and others might have over-dramatized the problem. Haber and Grattan note, for example, that between the 1850s and 1930, older people became more likely to own their homes. In general, the savings and income of the elderly increased, rather than decreased, during the industrial era, softening Epstein's tragedy of old age.[6] At the beginning of the depression, furthermore, older male employees were less likely to be laid off than their younger counterparts. As the depression deepened in the period that coincided with Roosevelt's creation of the Committee on Economic Security, however, conditions grew worse for the elderly, who suffered disproportionately from unemployment.[7] Adding to the problem, the depression eroded their assets more than the assets of younger Americans, simply because the elderly had accumulated those assets over a greater period of time. The homes on which the elderly prided themselves could be lost to the bank or the sheriff. Banks in which the elderly invested and protected their savings closed. Public and private pension schemes, which at best covered 15 percent of the elderly, went bankrupt. These developments "proved the incapacity of the private market to guarantee autonomy in middle age" and helped to strengthen movements for state-sponsored old-age pensions that had existed at least since 1912.[8]

The image of the almshouse exercised a great deal of symbolic power over the debate. Here, too, appearances were deceiving. In the nineteenth century the majority of almshouse residents were relatively young members of indigent families or people with disabilities. As specialized institutions, such as mental hospitals and orphanages, claimed an increasing percentage of these young people, the elderly became the primary group domiciled in community poorhouses. By 1904 more than half of the people in almshouses were elderly, and the percentage continued to rise in the period before the enactment of Social Security. Still, a very small percentage of the elderly—no more than 2 percent—resided in an almshouse at any time. Despite this fact, the movement for old-age pensions gained strength as a dignified alternative to the poorhouse for people whose only offense to the community was to be old.[9]

To say that there was a growing movement for state-sponsored pensions for the elderly begged the question of what form the pensions would take. As the Committee on Economic Security conducted its business in the summer of 1934, its members knew that in the past advocates had focused on securing state, rather than federal, pensions, with the result that over half of the states would have old age pensions by 1935.[10] Federal authorities could offer financial inducements to extend the pensions to all of the states and improve the financial circumstances of the state programs that were strapped for cash. In the summer of 1934 that appeared to be a far more conservative response to the problem than, for example, granting pensions to all of the elderly. Frances Townsend, a retired doctor living in Long Beach, California, led a movement that came to the attention of every member of Congress and called for every person over 60 to receive a monthly payment of $200 a month, provided they agreed to spend the money that month.[11]

## Reflexive Conservatism

Whatever the Roosevelt administration proposed, it knew that a group of conservative opponents of the New Deal, such as former president Herbert Hoover, would oppose any extension of federal power, even if only to fund state programs. Although Hoover thought of himself as, among other things, a progressive, a Wilsonian, and a humanitarian, the former president had become a reflexive critic of the New Deal. As Congress debated the Social Security Act, Hoover told a group of California Republicans that, "The American people have directly before them the issue of maintaining and perfecting our system of orderly individual liberty under constitutionally conducted government, or of rejecting it in favor of the newly created system of regimentation and bureaucratic domination in which men and women are not masters of government but are the pawns and dependents of a centralized and potentially self-perpetuating government."[12] The New Deal, in other words, marked an unconstitutional extension of federal power that threatened the fundamental freedoms of the American people. The Social Security Act would be another engine of a centralized, self-perpetuating government.

The Liberty League, founded in 1934 just as the Social Security Act was being created, became the most publicized of anti–New Deal organizations. The group included business executives with a conservative bent, such as executives from the Dupont and General Motors corporations, corporate lawyers, and politicians whom Roosevelt had alienated. Foremost among these disaffected politicians was former New York governor Alfred E. Smith, at one time identified as a leading urban progressive but transforming into a conservative in his years out of power. Members of the conservative wing of the Democratic Party, many with ties to big business, who could trace their lineage back to Grover Cleveland, also belonged to the League. Democrats of this type included the party's candidates for president in 1924 (John W. Davis) and 1928 (Smith). In various speeches and pamphlets, many drafted by corporate lawyers, the League offered a coherent critique of New Deal programs such as Social Security. The critique highlighted how payroll taxes and other compulsory forms of government activity retarded economic growth, contributed to unemployment and other forms of economic inefficiency, and, at the same time, deprived citizens and corporations of their fundamental liberties. Despite the coherence of the critique and the appeal to fundamental American values, the League, by most accounts, failed to gain much political traction in 1935.[13]

The Liberty League, like many of the opponents of the Social Security Act, was a disparate coalition that brought together advocates of prohibition and the leaders of the highest tech industries in America. In general, those who might be classified as conservative lacked the coherence of the administration forces pushing for passage of Social Security. Business, a natural enemy of increased government taxation, nonetheless included some companies, led by so-called corporate liberals, who believed that a federal old age pension law could do little to harm them and might force added costs on their smaller competitors. In this spirit, Gerard Swope of General Electric wrote "the plea of certain business interests that the time is not ripe [for Social Security] is a mistaken one; so long as the legislation is applied on a nationwide basis, it makes no difference to industry that unemployment insurance [and pensions] may slightly increase costs." Of course, slightly increased costs were relative matters. For some employers, closer to the margins of profit and loss, increased costs could make all the difference.[14] Hence, some organizations, such as the Chamber of Commerce and the National Association of Manufacturers, were somewhat conflicted on the question of Social Security, which lessened their ability to intervene in the complicated political debate about many different programs in an effective way.

As for reflexive conservatism, the Senate hearings on the Social Security Act featured the testimony of Frank I. Peckham, a self-appointed guardian of Republican virtue, who appeared on behalf of the Sentinels of the Republic.

He described the group, created in 1922, as one "in opposition to all measures that tend further and further to centralize power and responsibility in the Federal Government of Washington over various sorts of matters that primarily should not only be under the control of the States and local governments but for which those local governments are primarily responsible as well."[15] Before disbanding in 1944, the group gained notoriety for having anti-Semitic and fascist tendencies, although its leader insisted that it opposed all forms of autocratic government, whether on the Left or Right.[16] In his Senate testimony, Peckham argued that Congress had no power to legislate on such matters as old-age pensions. The constitution mandated that these pensions were not federal concerns.

## Federalism

Neither Hoover or Peckham, nor the ideological critics of the Liberty League, exercised any influence over Social Security, yet conservative ideas in the form of federalism did play a major role in the legislation. Raymond Bill, a self-described businessman, in a statement that appeared in the Senate hearings, described federal social welfare legislation as "impractical and unintelligent" because of the diverse conditions that prevailed across the United States. The heterogeneity of the American labor market led him to advocate that "such measures should be handled strictly by the States or subdivisions thereof."[17] As Henry I. Harriman of the United States Chamber of Commerce—a representative of business who the administration often considered to be an ally—noted, states should be given wide latitude "because living conditions and costs of living vary greatly in the United States."[18] Harriman did not oppose federal aid for things like unemployment compensation or old-age pensions, but he insisted on the primacy of state administration.

President Roosevelt, himself a former state governor, and Secretary of Labor Frances Perkins, herself a former state official, tended to agree with these sentiments. Even though they were Democrats who would be responsible for creating key components of an activist state, they shared a Progressive Era suspicion that the federal government lacked the administrative competence to undertake complex tasks (in this sense they shared similar political roots with the Democrats in the Liberty League). In January 1935, President Roosevelt said that his program of old age pensions, unemployment compensation, public assistance, and public health measures was one that appealed to "the sound sense of the American people."[19] As such it left the actual management of most parts of the program to the States and in this way respected the "rights and responsibilities of the states."[20] Congress, for its part, consistently favored state over federal administration of social security programs and did its part to weaken federal standards as conditions for state receipt of federal money. Hence, welfare, unemployment compensation, and nearly everything else became a state, rather than a federal, responsibility. The only exception was old-age insurance or, as we call it today, Social Security, and this exception did not pass Congress without some critical examination.

## Contextual Conservatism: The Reserve Question

Other conservative arguments about Social Security were less overtly ideological and more contextual. They centered on key details, rather than on the overall legitimacy of the legislation. One idea, advanced by many businessmen and later shared by advocates of Keynesian economics, was that passage of the Social Security Act and its incorporated payroll taxes would retard the process of economic recovery from the ravages of the great depression. L. C. Morrow, an executive with the McGraw-Hill Publishing Company, told the Senate Finance Committee that business favored some sort of Social Security plan. He worried, however, that the bill with its payroll taxes of up to 5 percent to fund unemployment compensation and old-age insurance would retard the recovery that was under way.[21] Hence, Morrow complimented the New Deal's macroeconomic policy in order to criticize one of its key social policies. H. O. Andrew, who edited a trade journal for the petroleum industry, described himself as a "rugged individualist" but knew that such a style was out of favor. He, like many of his colleagues, regarded the passage of some sort of Social Security bill as inevitable. He based his argument on the need for the legislation to be workable and noted, "If the cost of sound legislation is to be added to present burdens it means still further delay of recovery regardless of how desirable these plans may be."[22]

Related to conservative opposition to payroll taxes was the argument that the design of old-age insurance was inherently impractical and invited corruption and unsustainable expansion of government benefits. The reasons went to the heart of the president's efforts to create a program that was not too extravagant and that was self-financing in the sense of never having to take money from general revenues. In other words, his efforts to respect conservative principles of governance and finance led him to propose a program that conservatives argued was impractical and extravagant. Furthermore, the conservatives, rather than the administration, ultimately prevailed on this question. The large reserves that the president envisioned in 1935 never developed, and something closer to a pay-as-you-go system characterized Social Security for much of its history.

Actuaries from the private insurance industry, such as W. R. Williamson of the Travelers Insurance Company, spoke with the most authority on financing questions. The key to the argument was to point out differences between private and public insurance programs. The government sought to start a public insurance program that would collect premiums from workers and their employers in the form of payroll taxes and pay them benefits in the form of old-age pensions. The very concept was a tribute to the notion that business should be a model for government, even in a period when the business community was as discredited as it ever would be and when the government enjoyed an uncommon mandate to expand its activities. According to Williamson, the analogy between private and public companies was misleading. Private insurance companies needed to maintain reserves so as to meet their contractual obligations, even if they were to go out of business. Government, by way of contrast, could always rely on the taxing power—assuring it of available funds—and, presumably, would never go out of business. Hence, the federal government, unlike the Travelers Insurance Company, did not need to maintain large reserves to sustain an insurance program.[23]

Despite this advice from Williamson, who would go on to have a career as a Social Security actuary, the president wanted his Social Security program to be funded solely by payroll taxes, rather than through current general revenues. This constraint introduced all sorts of complications. It meant that, if future tax rates were not to be prohibitive, the program needed to collect too much in the beginning in order to meet its future obligations. In the future, after all, a greater percentage of the retired population would have paid into the Social Security fund and hence costs would be higher. The government plan, as modified by the president, thus entailed the building up of large reserves. Reserves, warned Williamson, were inherently unstable. They could lead, for example, to interest payments of $3 billion a year by 1980. An eventual reserve of $100 billion was, as Williamson put it, "too large to contemplate."[24]

Williamson and others who shared his conservative viewpoint believed that government reserves achieved through payroll taxes would be similar to any other government tax payments. As money came into the federal treasury, it would be spent, particularly since the government was running a deficit. Hence, when it came time to draw upon the reserve, it would not be there. Congressman Fred Vinson, a Democrat who was sympathetic to the administration, asked Williamson if the interest on the reserve (that would be used to help pay benefits in the future) came "out of the taxpayer." "I don't know any other place where it comes from," Williamson replied.[25] Nor did the mischief end there. On paper the Social Security fund would show a large surplus and initial benefits under Social Security would be relatively modest. The result would be a demand that the federal government spend some of the reserve on larger benefits. Williamson lamented that, "no actuary could convince Congress it was necessary to hold down to these small amounts or it would go out of balance." It would, therefore, seem "unreasonable to hold back from a liberalization of the plan," or, as conservative Republican congressman Daniel Reed noted, "there would be a constant demand on Congress" to make Social Security benefits higher.[26]

Marion Folsom, an executive with Eastman Kodak who played an influential role among businessmen on the Social Security question and who would later become secretary of Health, Education, and Welfare in the Eisenhower administration, also argued against the building up of large reserves. Such a large reserve would adversely affect investment markets and business more generally. More to the point, "within a short time the income will be much greater than the outgo" and with a large fund built up, "there will be a tendency to increase benefits, with a big deficit resulting later."[27] John Harrington of the Illinois Manufacturers Association agreed that such a plan was unwise. He doubted the wisdom of collecting payroll taxes to "pay annuities of doubtful value to the aged after 1942."[28] In other words, why should the nation hurry into a plan that only promised to pay regular benefits beginning in 1942 and that contemplated the building up of large and possibly dangerous reserves when such a plan would retard recovery and not help anyone already old or unemployed?

Arguments specific to the financing plan for old-age insurance fed into a more general conservative critique of government spending. Businessmen repeatedly spoke of the need to separate the administration of unemployment and pension plans from "political influence." This argument reflected a reasonable reading of American history. Previous federal pension plans, and in particular the Civil War pensions, had grown into immense social giveaways that were explicitly used by the Republican Party to gain partisan advantage over the Democratic Party in the highly contested political era in the last quarter of the nineteenth century.[29] The New Deal might be trying the same thing in reverse. In a typical statement, Warren Platt of the *National Petroleum News* said that he feared "for the incompetence and dishonesty of management" in any government-run plan.[30]

## Congressional Opposition and Indifference to the Social Security Act

Contrary to the expectations of the administration, passage of the Social Security Act was neither speedy nor free of controversy. At key points the bill threatened to become unraveled and postponed to a future session of Congress, which might have doomed the bill. Early in 1935, the president hoped to make it one of the first measures passed in the legislative session. Trouble developed almost immediately. Most members reacted with indifference to the bill, except for the section that allowed states to begin old-age pension programs immediately with federal assistance (a program that we would today call welfare because it was discretionary on the part of the states and involved not a universal right to benefits or an entitlement but rather a means test in which applicants had to demonstrate their poverty in order to receive benefits). The other parts of what was then called the Economic Security Act, with their payroll taxes and their promises of future, rather than immediate, benefits, offered little of immediate political value. Coverage restrictions, such as limiting old-age insurance to industrial and commercial workers, made Social Security appear irrelevant to the many members who came from agricultural districts. At precisely this time, furthermore, the Congressmen faced pressures from the supporters of the Townsend Movement who, in the spirit of veterans pensions, wanted immediate payment of very generous pensions, without any need for a person to have contributed to these pensions.

By March 20, 1935, the *New York Times* ran a story by reporter Louis Stark, who had already filed a series of unsympathetic reports on the legislation, under the headline "Hopes Are Fading for the Social Security Bill." Stark wrote that, "The confusion that has arisen since hearings of the Ways and Means Committee on the omnibus bill, the apathy of members of Congress on the measure, and the split between the bill's adherents, serve to support the opinion of those who are convinced that President Roosevelt's elaborate plans for social security will probably result in the enactment of but one major measure—old age assistance for indigent persons over 65 years of age." Representative Isabella Greenway, described as a "close friend of President and Mrs. Roosevelt," wanted to split up the various portions of the bill and preserve the grants to the states for old-age pensions in an effort "to save something from the wreck."[31] The next day the *Times* editorialized that the president's Social Security program was simply "too large" and that it should be broken up with only the state old-age pensions passed and the rest carried over into the next year.[32] Arthur Krock, already a veteran hand in the *Times*' Washington bureau and already trending conservative in his personal opinions, argued that members of Congress just did not understand the complicated legislation and "in the new mood of Congress it is not willing to ratify that which even its leaders do not understand."[33]

These views echoed those of prominent Baltimore retailer Albert D. Hutzler, who in testimony on behalf of the National Retail Dry Goods Industry told the House Committee on Ways and Means that "we might as well divorce...old-age insurance from the bill." That would make it possible to speed up the other sections of the bill and "get a real start for our social security program."[34] The Chamber of Commerce also urged postponement so that Congress could undertake further study of the measure.[35] Here again the conservative strategy was one not of opposition but of delay.

The tactic of urging delay to prevent passage ultimately failed. During the crucial month of April 1935, the Ways and Means Committee passed what the *Times* described as a "drastically altered" bill, but one that retained old-age insurance. Committee members worried, though, about what would happen to the bill on the floor. They feared that the measure would be "Townsendized," split into separate measures, or changed to reduce the reserve financing features of the bill. The members played up the conservative features of the measure, such as the wide latitude it gave to the states.[36] Such latitude, it was hoped, would "placate much of the opposition that might otherwise have confronted the measure on the floor from members set against further invasion of the Federal Government of the field of private enterprise."[37] In other words, it was fear of the Right, and not just fear of the Left, that motivated the Ways and Means Committee's handling of the bill. Even so, Turner Catledge reported on the continuing scuttlebutt that the bill would be put off until the next Congress in order to protect it from "emasculation."[38] Roosevelt, realizing he could lose a key piece of legislation, called the House leaders to the White House and urged them to pass the Social Security Act as a matter of personal loyalty to him. The members swallowed their doubts and demonstrated their loyalty by passing the bill in the House by a substantial 372 to 33 margin.[39]

## The Clark Amendment as Legislative Barrier

Even so, opposition to old-age insurance refused to die. The Senate, where conservative Republicans once again tried and failed to take the old-age insurance provisions out of the bill in committee, provided another opportunity for opponents of Social Security to derail the bill. The chosen vehicle came to be known as the Clark Amendment, after its sponsor Senator Bennett Champ Clark. It originated in a suggestion by Walter Forster, who worked for a pension-consulting firm, that the more than 600 corporations that already maintained pension plans be allowed to keep them. He asked that the new law not require the employers to abandon their plans or to be forced to adopt the federal plan. Forster noted that federal employees were already exempt from the proposed old-age insurance. Why not, then, extend that same privilege to employers who had or would subsequently have plans that were "more liberal" than the proposed old-age insurance plan? Such a measure would ease federal deficits and leave many people with better protection than that promised under Social Security. Democrats, particularly those in the districts with people joining the newly forming industrial unions, were wary. They worried that workers who went out on strike might lose their benefits or that employees who switched jobs would somehow be disadvantaged by Forster's plan.[40]

Nonetheless, the Clark Plan passed the Senate and became a real issue in the conference committee, which dragged deep into the summer of 1935. A compromise needed to be jerry-rigged in which the Senate agreed to the legislation with the proviso that there would be further study of the Clark Amendment. The real worry occasioned by the Clark Amendment could be seen in the private correspondence of Social Security proponents, such as Edwin Witte, the Wisconsin professor who had directed the staff of the Committee on Economic Security (CES). "I feared," Witte wrote upon learning of the bill's final passage, "that it would be necessary to take the Clark Amendment in some form; but it is certainly much better that it has been eliminated, even if (as I am told here) there is some sort of understanding that the Clark Amendment is to be introduced as a separate bill."[41]

## The Court as a Conservative Restraint on Social Security

Often, the passage of a law foreclosed further debate as interest groups adjusted to its presence and headed off on the historical path set by the legislation.[42] Including a contributory old-age insurance program in the Social Security Act gave such a program more legitimacy than it would otherwise have had, but the fiscal structure of old-age insurance made it a highly tentative program even after passage. In order to observe the principles of social insurance, the Social Security program would not begin to collect payroll taxes until 1937 or pay permanent benefits until 1942. That gave its opponents additional time to derail it, since it would take at least until 1942 for voters to develop any sort of attachment to the program. In the five years in which the program would function as a tax, rather than a benefit, it would be particularly vulnerable to political attack on financial, ideological, or constitutional grounds.

The constitutional issue became a very real one after the Supreme Court issued its decision in the *Schechter* case in May, 1935, which invalidated key parts of the National Industrial Recovery Act (NIRA). The Court promulgated the decision just after the Senate Finance Committee approved its version of the Social Security bill but before final passage. *Schecter,* widely interpreted as a defeat for the New Deal, called into question the constitutionality of the legislation under consideration in 1935. "Wall Street Hails New Deal Defeats," the *Times* headlined at the end of May.[43] Roosevelt hastened to assure Congress that Social Security, unlike the Railroad Retirement Act and the NIRA, would be upheld by the Court.[44]

The Supreme Court, with its lifetime tenure for judges and its reliance on legal precedent, operated on a different political time line than did the

Congress. Even in the face of Progressive Era and New Deal reforms, the Supreme Court had been following a traditional jurisprudence on issues related to the government's ability to amend employment contracts in the public interest. The 1905 *Lochner* case, which overturned the state regulation of hours and working conditions in the baking industry, was typical. No stronger evidence existed of the effectiveness and persistence of a conservative tradition in America—a force that might be described as judicial conservatism reinforced through legal precedent and amplified by judicial review.

Frances Perkins and key CES staff struggled with the constitutionality questions inherent in Social Security throughout the summer and fall of 1934.[45] Invited to an afternoon tea at the home of Supreme Court Justice Harlan Stone, Perkins found herself in private conversation with Stone and, surprisingly, started to discuss the constitutionality of the new CES program. Justice Stone offered a whispered tip to Perkins on how the administration might design a constitutionally sound Social Security scheme, hinting that the government's broad taxing power would likely pass the Court's muster. "I went back to my committee," Perkins recalled, "and I never told them how I got my great information. As far as they knew, I went out into the wilderness and had a vision. But, at any rate, I came back and said I was firmly for the taxing power. We weren't going to rig up any curious constitutional relationships. 'The taxing power of the United States—you can do anything under it,' said I."[46]

The tea party incident illustrated the uncertainty of the legal ground on which the Social Security program was poised. Even with Stone's hint, the CES continued to worry about the constitutionality question; so much so that it devised a transparent legislative maneuver that it hoped would serve as a kind of hedge against an adverse legal ruling. It separated the program-benefits title of the Social Security Act (which appeared in Title II of the law) from the revenue or tax collection title of the Act (which appeared in Title VIII) so as to maintain the fiction that the two titles had nothing to do with each other. It was as if the federal government was imposing a new form of taxation just for the sheer caprice of it, and then, discovering a large pot of new money, quite independently decided to disperse it in the form of Social Security benefits.

Four Social Security cases testing the Social Security Act came before the Court during its October 1936 term, including *Helvering v. Davis,* which challenged the old-age insurance scheme. In three of the cases, businesses sought to avoid the imposition of the new taxes on payrolls, and in the fourth a shareholder complained that the imposition of these taxes diminished the value of his equities. The Supreme Court handed down its decisions in all four cases on the same day in May 1937. Justice Benjamin Cardozo wrote the majority opinion in *Davis.*

Mirroring the situation in Congress when the legislation was considered, the old-age insurance program passed the Court by a wide margin but not without considerable doubt and anxiety. The Court ruled 7 to 2 in *Davis* in support of the old-age insurance program, and even though two justices disagreed with the decision, no separate dissents appeared.

The plaintiff's brief in *Davis* dealt exclusively with the relevant precedents, theories of constitutional construction, and the interpretation of various terms of legal art; the government, by way of contrast, argued that the Social Security program contributed to the general welfare and presented a detailed socioeconomic study of the plight of the poor and the elderly in the depression economy. The newly formed Social Security Board researched this aspect of the case—one of the first examples of the bureaucracy as an agent of its own preservation and expansion that would become commonplace in Social Security. The government had much more at stake than did any individual company and at least as much manpower to research the case.[47] Marjorie Shearon, of the Board's Bureau of Research and Statistics, who would later become an outspoken conservative critic of Social Security, produced a 221-page study of "Economic Insecurity in Old Age: Social and Economic Factors Contributing to Old-Age Dependency." This study made up two-thirds of the government's brief in *Davis*. The plaintiff's 61-page brief ignored any empirical data about the condition of the nation in favor of reciting the text of the Act, the relevant provisions in the Constitution, and the legal precedents. The argument, then, pitted current conditions against legal precedent, a gamble in legal strategy that the government took and won.

Typical of Cardozo's ruling was this evocative language, "The purge of nation-wide calamity that began in 1929 has taught us many lessons.... The hope behind this statute is to save men and women from the rigors of the poor house as well as from the haunting fear that such a lot awaits them when journey's end is near."[48] Hence, the fear of the almshouse served to reaffirm the goals of Social Security's proponents. The fact remained, however, that the interval between *Schechter* and *Davis* marked a time of uncertainty in the development of the Social Security program and an effective check upon the early expansion of the program.

## Solving the Clark Amendment, Continuing the Reserve Controversy

The Supreme Court's approval of the Social Security Act occasioned considerable relief among the Act's supporters. So did the resolution of the problems posed by the Clark Amendment. In 1936, the year after the passage of the Social Security Act and the year before the system started to collect payroll taxes, supporters from the private pension industry tried once again to pass a version of the amendment. This time they met with little success. Eastman Kodak's Marion Folsom began as a supporter of the amendment in 1935 but decided in 1936 that the existence of Social Security hardly posed a threat to firms such as Kodak. "In the future," Folsom said, "the employee will accumulate part of his annuity with the insurance company and part with the government."[49] Folsom's prediction proved to be right. The existence of Social Security seemed to stimulate interest in private products aimed at easing the problems of financial insecurity in old-age. Life insurance salesmen used the limited scope of Social Security as a selling point for the sale of life insurance.[50] Business, at least that segment of the business community that represented large corporations operating in a national market, had already pulled out of the coalition opposed to Social Security, if indeed it was ever a member.

Despite this apparent conjunction of private and public interests, private businessmen in the insurance industry and conservatives more generally maintained an interest in limiting the size and scope of Social Security. Hence, the issue of large reserves had legs that ran beyond the settlement of the Clark Amendment question in 1936 and the Supreme Court decision of 1937. As a result, the Republicans decided to make Social Security an issue in the 1936 election, a decision that would be unthinkable in the period between 1953 and 1973. In the period from 1936 through 1950, however, Social Security was far from a winning issue for the Democrats and a losing issue for the Republicans.[51]

The late start for Social Security, coupled with the five-year period of tax collection without regular benefits, added to the program's political vulnerabilities. These, in turn, fueled conservative critiques of the program. As an example, when the first payroll deductions began to show up in workers' checks at the beginning of 1937, conservatives could argue that these taxes were a form of theft. Furthermore, the program engulfed workers and their employees in a sea of paperwork that highlighted the program's bureaucratic, rather than beneficial, aspects. Employers complained about having to give workers receipts for their Social Security contributions and having to report on payroll taxes to the Social Security Board. The government had difficulty matching the tax receipts with a person's Social Security account. These arguments had salience because the program had not yet gone into permanent effect and might still be repealed before it began to pay regular benefits.

The reserve-financing issue lurked behind these complaints. Employers and employees paid Social Security taxes. Employers sent the money to the U.S. Treasury Department, which used it just as it used any other form of revenue. Until 1939, the money raised was not legally dedicated to Social Security. Instead, Congress needed to appropriate the money to the Social

Security account. Once in this account, the money was used to pay benefits, and the money left over, which was a considerable amount, was invested in government securities. In 1937, for example, Congress appropriated $511 million into the Social Security account but only $6 million was needed for current expenses. In 1937, therefore, most of the Social Security money went into the reserve account. At the far end of the actuaries' calculations, in 1980, appropriations would reach more than $2 billion and benefits more than $3.5 billion. By 1980, however, the balance on the reserve would have reached more than $46 billion, and the interest would, at least in theory, be enough to make up the difference between income and expenditures.

The problem with this scheme was that the sheer size of the projected reserve attracted people's attention. The figure represented eight times the amount of money then in circulation in the United States. A large reserve, even one that existed largely only on paper, represented an unstable political construct in the late 1930s. From the Left, people could argue that it made no sense not to spend all of the available money on the nation's poor as they faced an apparently never-ending depression. From the Right, people could argue that the reserve would never achieve its objective because the government would not allow it to accumulate. A few—Edwin Witte, the Wisconsin economics professor who had headed the staff of the Committee on Economic Security, being the prime example—argued that a large projected reserve was an explicit way to acknowledge long-range financial commitments, and hence was a tool for responsible financial management. But by far the predominant concern was that the existence of a large reserve, even as a fictitious entity, could provide an open invitation for the government to expand its social programs without any sense of discipline or any sense of the obligations it was creating for the future. Hence, in general, people on the Left worried that the money would not be spent on social welfare and people on the Right worried that it would be. Neither side liked the arrangement.

The Republicans sensed a winning issue. In their 1936 platform, the Republicans charged that the 1935 act was unworkable. "The so-called reserve fund," the platform stated, "is no reserve at all because the fund will contain nothing but the government's promise to pay, while the taxes collected in the guise of premiums will be wasted in reckless and extravagant schemes." On September 26, 1936, Republican nominee and Kansas governor Alfred Landon elaborated on this theme. In a Milwaukee speech, he blasted Social Security as "unjust, unworkable, stupidly drafted and wastefully financed." Landon reserved the brunt of his attack for the reserve financing plan. "We have some good spenders in Washington," he said. "With this Social Security money alone running into billions of dollars, all constraints on Congress will be off."[52]

Other organizations, such as the Brookings Institution (not yet a center of liberal, Keynesian wisdom but rather a relatively conservative advocate of good government), the Chamber of Commerce (which would continue to take an active role in the Social Security financing debate through the 1950s) and the *New York Times* (which had never given the Social Security Act its blessing) agreed that the reserve financing plan was a bad idea. Hence, even though the Republicans lost the 1936 election in a landslide, they refused to let go of the Social Security issue. Indeed, criticism of Social Security increased, rather than abated, after the 1936 election and the beginning of payroll tax collections.

Arthur Vandenberg, a prominent Republican senator from Michigan who, despite his internationalist tilt in the World War II era, would have described himself as a conservative, offered a resolution in January 1937 to his Senate colleagues in which he called the reserve method of financing "a perpetual invitation to the maintenance of an extravagant public debt."[53] That led to a Senate Finance Committee hearing at which Vandenberg suggested, and the Roosevelt administration agreed, that a congressional commission should be created to inquire into the matter.

This commission marked the start of a Social Security tradition of creating officially sanctioned but nonbinding bodies to deliberate over sensitive Social Security issues. Then, as now, Congress eagerly accepted a means of handling a problem that committed the politicians to nothing and helped to legitimate what might otherwise have been an unpopular alternative. The format called for a third of the members to be drawn from the ranks of business. The businessmen chosen tended to be from the ranks of the corporate liberals who were generally favorable to Social Security and the administration, although such businessmen were increasingly hard to find by the end of the 1930s. Still, the insurance industry claimed a place on the commission, which resulted in the appointment of M. Albert Linton, the head of the Provident Mutual Company. Linton, a trained actuary with a reputation for personal integrity, was knowledgeable, invested in the discussion, and articulate. He made the conservative case against large reserves within the Advisory Council.

Linton's main protagonist on the Council was Edwin Witte. Witte, a student of John R. Commons in the Wisconsin tradition, believed deeply in the principles of social insurance and took pride in the Social Security Act that he had helped to create. Witte was wary of using general revenues as an alternative to the reserves in funding the Social Security system. He feared that in the future Congress might not appropriate money for the program, and he believed that the commitment to reserve financing was the surest way to guarantee that a future Congress would not shortchange the system. Linton had the opposite worry. He objected to any system that required the government to hold large reserves, asserting that $46 or $47 billion represented too much of a temptation for Congress. Instead of letting the reserves accumulate, Congress would make benefits more liberal and leave a crushing burden for the future. "I think we are going to come to 1980 without the help of the reserve fund and we are going to be faced with the benefits of 9½ percent of payroll and none of these helps to bear the load," he said.[54] Witte, the liberal, thought in pessimistic terms that Congress would not support Social Security. Linton, the conservative, thought in pessimistic terms that Congress would support Social Security in too lavish a manner. Witte wanted a guaranteed source of funds; Linton wanted to starve the program of revenue to contain its size.

More people on the Council agreed with Linton than with Witte. The Council issued a report that traded an expansion of the program's scope for a tacit retreat from the large reserves. The report formed the basis for what became the 1939 Social Security Amendments. As a result of this legislation, regular benefits became payable in 1940, rather than in 1942, as originally intended. The legislation transformed old-age insurance into old-age and survivors insurance, with higher benefits for married couples than for single individuals and benefits for widows (not yet widowers) and the dependent children of deceased workers. As a form of life insurance, Social Security could be of more immediate help to younger workers, who would not reach retirement age for many years but who were at risk to die and leave behind a struggling family.

In 1939 the Roosevelt administration, by now distracted by foreign affairs, backed away from its earlier commitment to the reserve financing plan. On this point, the conservatives had clearly won. Treasury Secretary Henry Morgenthau told Congress that the 1939 amendments would make benefits more widely diffused. Therefore, a general revenue contribution could be considered as a financing mechanism and "the argument for a large reserve does not have the validity which 4 years ago it seemed to possess."[55] Morgenthau chose to ignore the fact that old-age insurance still only covered industrial and commercial workers. So, even with the new survivors benefits, Social Security only had the potential to reach about half of the people in the country. Furthermore, Congress left vague the details of exactly when and how the federal contribution would kick into the Social Security funds. Instead, it approved what people called a "reasonable contingency reserve"—enough to meet the program's payments and to tide it over in emergencies such as a sudden rise in the unemployment rate.

The reserve controversy receded in part because of the 1939 amendments and in part because the nation became desensitized to large financial obligations during World War II, as federal expenditures rose at an exponential rate. Perhaps more to the point, periodic tax raises remained in the law. During the 1940s, as the dates for each of the tax increases approached, Congress repealed them, maintaining the notion of a reasonable contingency reserve (although a favorable economy continued to bring more into the Social Security system than anticipated).

## The Perils of the 1940s: Coverage

Despite the 1939 amendments, however, Social Security did not vault into a new position of popularity. Instead, it remained a relatively neglected program. Programs more directly related to national service and hence more favored by conservatives predominated over Social Security. In 1940, for example, even before the nation's entrance into World War II, the United States spent more on veterans' payments and workers' compensation than it did on old-age and survivors insurance. Even in the area of old-age security, social insurance—a national program—played a distinctly secondary role to welfare—a state and local program. Hence, on the question of federalism, the nation's social welfare system continued to reflect the predilections of conservatives rather than liberals. By the end of the 1940s, just over one-fifth of the elderly received old-age assistance (welfare) benefits, and in a few states over half received such payments. The average monthly welfare benefit was $42 in 1949 (although with considerable variance from state to state), compared with an average Social Security benefit of $25.[56] As late as 1950, more than twice as many people were on state welfare rolls receiving old-age assistance as were receiving retirement benefits from the federal government under Social Security. In the more rural and agricultural states, the disparity was extreme. Conservatives had not defeated Social Security, but they had apparently limited its growth. State welfare programs mattered more than the federal old-age insurance program.

The coverage issue proved particularly vexing for the Social Security program in the 1940s. Only about half the jobs in the economy were covered by the social insurance program as enacted in 1935. While the Roosevelt administration's 1935 legislative proposal did not advocate universal coverage, it limited its list of excluded occupational groups to three: government employees; railroad workers; and white collar workers earning more than $50 a month (the self-employed and some professionals were implicitly excluded by virtue of not being wage-earners). During the hearings on the administration's bill, the secretary of the Treasury—without the consent of the CES—suggested to the Ways and Means Committee that the exclusions be extended to agricultural workers, domestic workers, and casual laborers—on grounds of administrative difficulties in tax collection—and the Committee added these exclusions to the bill without debate. The Ways and Means Committee also added an exclusion for the merchant marine, again without apparent dissension. Representatives of religious and charitable organizations lobbied both the Ways and Means and the Senate Finance Committees to be excluded from the old-age insurance plan; both committees acceded to the request. None of these exclusions came in for any serious opposition in the House or Senate.

So, during initial consideration of the Social Security Act of 1935, liberals were every bit as likely as conservatives to support excluding various constituent groups from the new program. Put another way, conservatives enjoyed just as much success on questions related to coverage as did liberals between 1935 and 1939.

The bureaucrats of the Social Security Administration remained committed to expanding Social Security coverage, even if Congress remained indifferent throughout the 1940s. On the day after the Supreme Court approved the Social Security program, Board Chairman Arthur Altmeyer gave a major speech in which he advocated moving toward universal coverage.[57] Beginning in 1937, the Social Security Board's Annual Report advocated the extension of coverage. In April 1938, as part of the buildup to the 1939 amendments, Altmeyer arranged to have President Roosevelt send the Board a letter asking it to give consideration to the "feasibility of extending [the program's] coverage."[58]

The Advisory Council agreed to the Board's recommendations to extend coverage to farm and domestic workers and employees of nonprofit organizations. Later, the Board convinced the president to add federal, state, and local government employees to the list. President Roosevelt's January 16, 1939, legislative message explicitly endorsed these recommendations. But Congress, which had become far more hostile to New Deal measures since 1935, declined the president's recommendations. "Doctor, when the first farmer with manure on his shoes comes to me and asks to be covered, I will be willing to consider it," crusty Ways and Means Chairman Robert Doughton told Arthur Altmeyer.[59]

Dropping the administration's list of potential entrants to the Social Security system, the Ways and Means Committee replaced it with an odd mix that included the merchant marine and certain government employees in the banking industry. The Republican minority on the Ways and Means Committee raised no issues about the coverage changes. The Senate Finance Committee adopted the House list of expansions and added two small definitional exclusions, without dissent. The administration concurred in these changes, because survivors' benefits mattered more to it in 1939 than did expanding coverage.[60]

At the end of a House debate that ignored the coverage issue, the chairman and ranking member of the Ways and Means Committee praised one another and emphasized the bipartisan nature of a bill that passed with only two "nay" votes.[61] In the Senate, the only "disagreement" on coverage involved a deal in which Senator Pat Harrison's (D-MS) amendment to exclude the fishing industry from coverage was modified by Senator Schellenbach (D-WA), who wanted the salmon fishermen in his state to be covered.[62] When all was said and done, the 1939 amendments made no net changes in the number of workers covered by the program.

Despite the apparent Congressional disinterest in extending coverage, President Roosevelt signaled his long-term interest in the coverage issue by declaring, in his signing statement for the 1939 amendments, "In my opinion, it is imperative that these insurance benefits be extended to workers in all occupations."[63] The Social Security Board continued its steady advocacy of expanded coverage after 1939, but, with no legislative vehicle to ride, its proposals went nowhere. The Congress, for its part, showed no interest in viewing coverage as a major ideological or policy issue, preferring to tinker at the margins with small bits of legislation affecting tiny cohorts of the workforce. In this regard Congress maintained what might be considered to be a conservative position on Social Security, not eliminating it but not expanding it and hence making it increasingly irrelevant to the nation's social provisions.

The next opportunity to engage this issue came in 1948 during the Truman administration. In 1946 and 1947, the Supreme Court extended the meaning of the employer-employee relationship for Social Security purposes, and the Social Security Administration and the Treasury Department issued draft regulations implementing this expanded understanding of the relationship. The Court rulings and administrative regulations had the potential to modestly expand the scope of the program by defining more occupations as exhibiting an employer/employee relationship and hence obliged to participate in Social Security coverage. In March 1948, Congress enacted a seemingly trivial piece of legislation that exempted about half-a-million newspaper and magazine vendors from Social Security coverage.[64] Vetoing the bill, Truman told Congress that "This legislation...raises the fundamental question of whether or not we shall maintain the integrity of our social security system....The security and welfare of our Nation demand an expansion of social security to cover the groups which are now excluded from the program. Any step in the opposite direction can only serve to undermine the program and destroy the confidence of our people in the permanence of its protection...."[65] The Republican Congress easily overrode the veto, with only 35 votes supporting the President (33 Democrats and two Republicans).

Quick on the heels of this effort, Congress enacted a second law exempting another half-million workers by restoring the prior common-law test of the employer/employee relationship—restoring the *status quo ante* before the earlier court decisions. This time the Congressional Democrats and the administration mounted a full-court press against the change, turning the coverage question into a partisan issue in the 1948 election. The Treasury Department, the Federal Security Administrator, and the Social Security Administration all sent stern warning letters to the Congress. The president vetoed the bill in June, just as he had done in the case of the newspaper vendors two months earlier, using much the same language."[66] This time the Democrats exercised more party discipline. But even with the political stakes raised, the president was again overridden by the Republican Congress. The decade ended as it had begun, with little congressional interest in widespread coverage extension.

## The Perils of the 1940s: Financing

If Congress tended to treat coverage extension in a rather cavalier manner during the 1940s, it paid far more attention to the financing issue. By the terms of the 1939 amendments, the tax rate increase scheduled to take place in 1940 was canceled, at the insistence of the conservatives. Instead, the program was poised for an earlier start of more generous benefits and for regularly scheduled periodic rounds of tax rate increases. The tax rate was scheduled to triple by 1950, from its frozen 1939 rate of 2 percent to an eventual 6 percent of payroll. However, when the next rate increase (scheduled for 1943) loomed, Vandenberg and his fellow conservatives successfully introduced legislation to freeze the rate a second time. Congress repeated this pattern six more times during the decade. The Social Security Board and the Roosevelt administration vehemently resisted the subsequent freezes. Despite these protests, the Social Security tax rate, which had been scheduled to rise four times by 1949, stayed at its 1937 rate until 1950 (see Table 2.1).

Favorable economic conditions aided the conservative cause by easing financing problems. Wartime mobilization kept the unemployment rate low—assuring high flows of revenue to the Social Security system—and encouraged people to postpone retirement—reducing benefit demands on the system. The result was a Social Security system unexpectedly flush with cash. Indeed, the actuarial projections used in the 1939 law anticipated a reserve of $2.6 billion by 1943; the actual reserve was over $4.8 billion by that time. In such an environment, the short-range view that taxes were higher than they needed to be proved irresistible to members of Congress of both parties. The administration tried unsuccessfully to urge the long-range view, arguing that the reserve needed to be maintained as a store of assets to meet future demands. But Ways and Means Committee member Thomas Jenkins (R-OH) probably spoke for many when he complained that Social Security financing was too long-range. "Everything will be all right for 20 years," he told his colleagues. "Why should we worry about it? Sufficient to the day is the evil thereof."[67]

In the atmosphere of inactivity that prevailed in the 1940s, the program gained few accolades from liberals, who worried about the program's effect on

Table 2.1. Projected vs. Actual Social Security Tax Rates (Employee and Employer Rates Combined)

| Year | 1935 Law | 1939 Law | Actual Rates |
|------|----------|----------|--------------|
| 1937 | 2.0 | 2.0 | 2.0 |
| 1938 | 2.0 | 2.0 | 2.0 |
| 1939 | 2.0 | 2.0 | 2.0 |
| 1940 | 3.0 | 2.0 | 2.0 |
| 1941 | 3.0 | 2.0 | 2.0 |
| 1942 | 3.0 | 2.0 | 2.0 |
| 1943 | 4.0 | 4.0 | 2.0 |
| 1944 | 4.0 | 4.0 | 2.0 |
| 1945 | 4.0 | 4.0 | 2.0 |
| 1946 | 5.0 | 5.0 | 2.0 |
| 1947 | 5.0 | 5.0 | 2.0 |
| 1948 | 5.0 | 5.0 | 2.0 |
| 1949 | 6.0 | 6.0 | 2.0 |
| 1950 | 6.0 | 6.0 | 3.0 |

the macroeconomic management of the economy, or from conservatives, who condemned the seemingly arbitrary features of the program. The Brookings Institution, in particular, became a center of program criticism. Social Security was a subject that brought together Brookings's interest in tax policy—for which it would later gain great fame through the work of Joseph Pechman (a noted Social Security critic of the 1960s)—and its interest in public administration. In 1946, for example, Brookings published a 912-page book on *Relief and Social Security* by political scientist Lewis Meriam. The author went out of his way to point out the peculiarities of the Social Security program, such as husbands being treated less fairly than wives or the existence of people who had paid into the program but who were not eligible for benefits. In other words, in a line of thought that went back as far as the Liberty League, he argued that the program was dangerously arbitrary.[68] In 1950 Meriam contributed to another Brookings study critical of Social Security. Carl Schlotterbeck, one of the coauthors of this study, became the staff director of a congressional subcommittee, headed by Representative Carl Curtis, which in 1953 sought to discredit the program by demonstrating that it was not really a form of insurance.[69]

## Changes in the 1950s and Disability Insurance

The situation that allowed conservatives to contain the growth of Social Security did not last. After 1950, Social Security enjoyed a new life and rapidly became America's most important social program. Key to the shift was congressional action in 1950 to raise Social Security benefit levels and expand coverage to reach the self-employed. By this time, the rhetoric of Social Security and welfare had shifted. Once portrayed as a temporary alternative to Social Security that would disappear as the Social Security program matured, welfare now became synonymous with the widely condemned "relief" or "the dole." If welfare remained the predominant form of social provision, argued Princeton professor and Social Security advocate Douglas Brown, it would lead the United States "down the primrose path of state paternalism." In other words, welfare, in Brown's opinion, had a greater potential to spiral out of control than did Social Security. The general revenues that fed welfare were abundant, and politicians would not hesitate to use them. Social Security, by way of contrast, was constrained by the fact that its benefits needed to come from employee contributions. In other words, Brown tried to switch positions with Linton and argue that Social Security was the fiscally responsible alternative to welfare.

The 1950 amendments passed in part because of their position in the cycle of congressional and presidential politics, in part because of the prosperity that nourished the Social Security trust funds, and in part because of the peculiarities of labor-management politics. As with the 1939 amendments, an advisory council that met in 1948 paved the way for the new legislation. Robert Ball, the *wunderkind* Social Security bureaucrat about to become the program's chief operating officer, served as the staff director for this Council and did a masterful job forging agreement between its liberal and conservative factions. Even Ball, however, could not get Linton and Marion Folsom to agree on the desirability of disability insurance. He recognized, though, that higher benefits and extended benefits were the program's primary needs, and he persuaded the Council to go along with recommendations along those lines. His report became the blueprint for the 1950 amendments. Although the Advisory Council met under the auspices of the Republican 80th Congress, the Congress that received the report in 1949 had reverted back to its Democratic majority. In addition, Harry Truman had unexpectedly held the White House for the Democrats. Hence, the members of the 81st Congress were able to exploit the Advisory Council report to the full. They gained an important edge because of changes in collective bargaining agreements that promised pensions to workers inclusive of Social Security. That gave General Motors and the other large automakers little reason to oppose an expansion of Social Security benefits, and the coverage extensions to the self-employed were irrelevant to these companies. With labor and management united during a Democratic administration on a measure that the Democrats tended to favor, the opponents of Social Security expansion had little room to maneuver.[70]

The 1950 amendments alone brought 10 million new covered workers into the system (most self-employed, farm workers, and some government employees). The amendments of 1954, signed into law by Eisenhower, who was happy to claim credit for the Republicans, brought another 10 million workers into the program (farmers, most professional people, and most state and local government employees). The 1956 legislation, in addition to providing cash disability benefits, extended coverage yet again, to members of the uniformed military services and to many of the self-employed professional and agricultural groups not encompassed in 1954. By the end of the Eisenhower administration, the Social Security program was securely on a glide-path to universal coverage—thus fulfilling Arthur Altmeyer's liberal ambitions for the program.

The expansion of Social Security after 1950 fed on itself. As more groups were covered by the program, more Congressmen supported it. Prosperity meant that even with a pay-as-you-go system with only a reasonable contingency reserve, expansion was still possible. As more people went to work and wages rose, Social Security tax receipts also rose, making it plausible for the bureaucracy to design and Congress to vote for benefit increases. Such increases appeared in 1952, 1954, 1956, and 1958.

Actuaries like Albert Linton did try to come up with conservative alternatives. In the period of President Eisenhower's election they worked on these alternatives with particular fervor. Beginning on November 15, 1952, the Chamber of Commerce, still interested in containing the growth of Social Security, polled its members on a proposal called "Social Security for the Aged" that Linton had prepared. This proposal made Social Security coverage universal and called for the abolition of welfare. Every elderly person would receive a payment of at least $25 per month. Hence, Linton played into the tendency to criticize welfare as "the dole" and substituted a form of social insurance for it. His plan would be funded by payroll taxes and run on a strictly pay-as-you-go basis. In theory, then, it would be difficult to expand benefits without also having a tax increase, a form of fiscal discipline on which Linton counted to hold down the size of the program. He hoped, as the Chamber put it, to institute "more checks and balances" into the program. Under the existing program, as new groups came into the system they tended to pay in far more than they received, creating a surplus that was used to expand benefits. Covering everyone would help to end this sort of expansion. Beyond a tax increase, only an increase in employment or wages would lead to benefit raises and presumably a recession would lead to a benefit reduction. Chamber of Commerce members, who probably understood few of the details, endorsed the proposal by a margin of sixteen to one. When Eisenhower began his term, therefore, the Chamber of Commerce proposal was something he needed to consider.[71]

As things turned out, Eisenhower rejected the Chamber proposal and accepted the traditional Social Security program, even sponsoring a major expansion in coverage in 1954. Historical contingency played a large part. As Eisenhower told one of his supporters, "It would appear logical to build upon the system that has been in effect for almost twenty years rather than embark upon the radical course of turning it completely upside down and running the very real danger that we would end up with no system at all."[72] If Eisenhower had somehow managed to run for president in 1948 and beaten Truman, then he might have had more flexibility to respond to conservative Social Security proposals.

Social Security became synonymous with the growth of the state in the 1950s. Even then, however, the ideas of conservatives were not without influence, as the fight over disability insurance revealed. Liberals saw disability insurance as a straightforward extension of old-age insurance to cover people who needed to drop out of the labor force before 65 because of a physical or mental impairment. Conservatives argued that disability was a subjective concept and that the state of disability and hence the size of the disability rolls were heavily influenced by available sources of alternative income. During times of unemployment, the disability rolls would swell as people with impairments sought refuge from the inhospitable labor force. Once on the rolls, a person would tend to stay there, creating a sense of dependency on the government. Historical contingency allowed conservatives to adopt a constructive alternative to disability insurance after World War II. People with disabilities, they argued, should receive personal attention from rehabilitation counselors who would give them the necessary advice and training to reenter the labor force. The emphasis should be on local programs with administrators who understood local conditions and who favored employment over retirement. The great wave of publicity for rehabilitation efforts after the second world war lent at least an air of plausibility to this argument. The argument had such political resonance that the advocates of Social Security expansion sought ways to accommodate it, even after the rise in Social Security's popularity after 1950. Hence, Congress agreed to a new welfare category for disability (in the 1950 law), but not a social insurance program, and in 1950 and in 1954 took the first steps toward disability insurance only as an adjunct to a major expansion of the vocational rehabilitation program. Finally, in 1956, Congress passed a disability insurance program by the barest of margins, limited it to people over 50 who were considered beyond salvage or rehabilitation, and even then required that every applicant for disability insurance be put in touch with a rehabilitation counselor and that the determinations of disability be made at the state, rather than the federal, level. Conservative notions of federalism and labor market economics clearly influenced the development of disability insurance, even in the heyday of Social Security expansion.[73]

## Conclusion

During this formative period, conservatives could not prevent the creation of Social Security, but they could constrain its growth by limiting tax increases and coverage extensions. Conservative congressmen initially triumphed over liberal Social Security administrators on these issues of taxes and coverage, yet much of the content of Social Security policy making involved a bipartisan consensus between 1937 and 1950. Conservatives and liberals jointly shaped policies for at least two reasons.

First, the Social Security program owed its survival in this period to what might be called benign neglect. Few people were initially enthusiastic about the old-age insurance program; most of the political debate focused on state old-age benefits and unemployment compensation. Since welfare benefits were higher than old-age insurance benefits, few people clamored to be covered by Social Security, and politicians responded to specific constituent demands rather than to comprehensive ideological choices.

Second, political actors in both parties shared some conservative political values, such as a commitment to federalism. Moreover, much of the financing debate involved competing alternatives meant to control future behavior. Because the choices were so deeply imbedded in the design of the Social Security program, it was difficult to identify conservative or liberal positions in the debate. In the matter of the Trust Fund, for example, the question of whether the Fund should be large or small asked legislators to choose between making provision for future commitments through a larger reserve or restraining the expansion of current benefits by having a smaller reserve. It was difficult to discern which of these alternatives was the more conservative.

Hence, after the presidential election of 1936, partisan disputes in Social Security were relatively muted, particularly compared to the period described by Derthick and Teles. After 1950, this initial period of policy partnership ended, and conservative influence over the program lessened.

Although in this essay we have deliberately oversampled conservative opinion and undersampled liberal opinion, perhaps this approach corrects an existing imbalance. It reverses the usual approach, one that emphasizes the expansion of Social Security as an outgrowth of New Deal politics and mistakenly assumes that the program's growth was continuous after 1935. Attention to conservative influence helps to explain some apparent paradoxes of Social Security, such as the reasons for the program's lack of popularity in the New Deal era and its increasing popularity in the 1950s. It also underscores the fact that conservative predilections have shaped key elements of Social Security financing and of the federal-state design of the American social welfare system. Hence, an emphasis on conservatives adds an important clarifying dimension to the study of American political development, even in the case of what Ronald Reagan's Budget Director David Stockman would call "the inner fortress of the welfare state."[74]

## Notes

1. "Congress Faces a Heavy Program," *New York Times,* January 2, 1935, 10.
2. For a fuller exposition of corporate liberalism and the place of businessmen in reform see Edward Berkowitz and Kim McQuaid, *Creating the Welfare State: The Political Economy of Twentieth Century Reform* (Lawrence: University Press of Kansas, 1992).
3. The web site for the Metropolitan Life Insurance Company notes, for example, "In 1909, MetLife Vice President Haley Fiske announced that 'insurance, not merely as a business proposition, but as a social program,' would be the future policy of the company. As a first step, Fiske hired the pioneering industrial social worker Lee Frankel to work at MetLife. Frankel envisioned insurance as a powerful means toward improving the lot of the underprivileged. To this end, he established MetLife's Welfare Division." See http://www.metlife.com/Applications/Corporate/WPS/CDA/PageGenerator/0,1674,P279,00.html, accessed on April 13, 2006.
4. See, for example, Roy Lubove, *The Struggle for Social Security: 1900–1935* (Cambridge: Harvard University Press, 1968).
5. Abraham Epstein, *Insecurity: A Challenge to America* (New York: Agathon Press, 1968), reprint of edition originally published in 1938, 421–2, 493–5.
6. Carole Haber and Brian Gratton, *Old Age and the Search for Security: An American Social History* (Bloomington: Indiana University Press, 1994), 79–80.
7. Ibid., 110.
8. Ibid., 180.
9. Ibid., 116, 122–23; see also Michael B. Katz, *In the Shadow of the Poorhouse: A Social History of Welfare in America* (New York: Basic Books, 1986).
10. Edward Berkowitz, *America's Welfare State* (Baltimore, MD: Johns Hopkins University Press, 1991), 116.
11. Sociologist Edwin Amenta's book *When Movements Matter: The Townsend Plan and the Rise of Social Security* (Princeton, NJ: Princeton University Press, 2006) demonstrates the continued resilience and relevance of the Townsend Movement throughout the formative period of Social Security.
12. "Ex-President Hoover's Call to Republicans," *New York Times,* March 24, 1935, 32.
13. Edwin Amenta, *Bold Relief: Institutional Politics and the Origins of Modern American Social Policy* (Princeton, NJ: Princeton University Press, 1998), 117–9; Sheryl R. Tynes, *Turning Points in Social Security: From 'Cruel Hoax' to 'Sacred Entitlement'* (Palo Alto, CA: Stanford University Press), 56–9.
14. Colin Gordon, *New Deals: Business, Labor and Politics in America, 1920–1935* (Cambridge: Harvard University Press, 1994), 272.

15. Statement of Frank I. Peckham, Washington, DC, Vice President Sentinels of the Republic, Senate Finance Committee Hearings on Social Security, 1935, 677.

16. George Wolfskill, *The Revolt of the Conservatives: A History of the American Liberty League, 1934–1940* (Boston: Houghton Mifflin, 1962), 233; Leo Ribuffo, *The Old Christian Right* (Philadelphia: Temple University Press, 1983).

17. Statement by Raymond Bill included in testimony of L. C. Murrow, McGraw-Hill Publishing Company, Senate Finance Committee Hearings on Social Security, 1935, 787–8.

18. Statement of Henry I. Harriman, President, United Chamber of Commerce, Senate Finance Committee Hearings on Social Security, 1935, 916.

19. "Message to the Congress, Transmitting the Report of the Committee on Economic Security," January 17, 1935. Available online at http://www.ssa.gov/history/reports/ces/ces3.html.

20. "President Urges Speed," *New York Times,* January 18, 1935, 1.

21. Testimony of L. C. Morrow, Senate Finance Committee Hearings on Social Security, 1935, 787–8.

22. Statement by H.O. Andrew, ed., *Gas Age Record,* included in testimony of L. C. Morrow, Senate Finance Committee Hearings on Social Security, 1935, 799.

23. Statement of W. R. Williamson, Assistant Actuary, Travelers Insurance Company, Hartford, Connecticut, in House Hearings on Social Security, 1935, 1011.

24. Williamson statement, 1014.

25. Williamson statement, 1013.

26. Williamson testimony, 1018.

27. Testimony of Marion Folsom in House Hearings on Social Security, 1935, 993.

28. Statement of John Harrington, general counsel for the Illinois Manufacturers Association, Senate Finance Committee Hearings on Social Security, 1935, 686.

29. See, among many other books, Jill Quadagno, *The Transformation of Old Age Security,* (Chicago: The University of Chicago Press, 1988) and Theda Skocpol's *Protecting Soldiers and Mothers* (Boston: Belknap Press, 1992).

30. Statement of Warren C. Platt, *National Petroleum News,* in Senate testimony of L. C. Morrow, 796.

31. Louis Stark, "Hopes are Fading for Social Security Bill," *New York Times,* March 20, 1935, 1.

32. "Too Large a Program," *New York Times,* March 21, 1935, 22.

33. Arthur Krock, "Roosevelt Wrestles Shifting Opposition," *New York Times,* March 24, 1935, E3.

34. Statement of Albert Hutzler, Representing the National Retail Dry Goods Industry, House Hearings on Social Security, 1935, 773.

35. "Chamber Denounces Plan of New Deal but Advisers of President Uphold Him," *New York Times,* May 3, 1935, 1.

36. "Recast Social Security Bill Ready for House; 'Gag' Rule Sought," *New York Times,* April 3, 1935, 1.

37. "House Gets Bill on Social Security," *New York Times,* April 5, 1935, 18.

38. Turner Catledge, "Congress Leaders Seek Delay to 1936 in Roosevelt Bills," *New York Times,* April 8, 1935, 1.

39. "Parley at White House Decides on a Program to Speed Up Congress," *New York Times,* April 10, 1935, 1; Turner Catledge, "Filibuster Threat on Lynching Bill Hangs Over Senate," *New York Times,* April 22, 1935, 1.

40. Statement of H. Walter Forster, Vice President of the Pension Consulting Division of Towners, Perrin, Forster, and Crosby Inc., Philadelphia, Pennsylvania, House Hearings on Social Security 1935, 663–4.

41. Edwin Witte to Murray Latimer, August 11, 1935, Murray Latimer Papers, Gelman Library, George Washington University; "Companies Known to Favor Clark Amendment to Social Security Act," in Dr. Rainhard B. Robbins, "Confidential Material Collected on Social Security Act and Clark Amendment," July 11, 1935, Latimer Papers. A good general account of the Social Security's passage is Edwin Witte, *Development of the Social Security Act* (Madison: University of Wisconsin Press, 1963), which could be supplemented with Carolyn L. Weaver, *The Crisis in Social Security* (Durham: Duke University Press, 1982).

42. On the question of path dependency, which is a central construct in the application of history to political science, see Paul Pierson, "Not Just What, but When: Timing and Sequence in Political Processes," *Studies in American Political Development,* Vol. 14, Issue 01 (Spring 2000): 72–92; and "Increasing Returns, Path Dependence, and the Study of Politics," *American Political Science Review* 94, 2 (2000): 251–67; Kathleen Thelen, Timing and Temporality in the Analysis of Institutional Evolution and Change," *Studies in American Political Development* 14, 2 (2000): 101–8.

43. "Wall Street Hails New Deal Defeats," *New York Times,* May 28, 1935, 1.

44. "Holds Social Bill Not Hit by NRA End," *New York Times,* May 7, 1935, 18.

45. The CES staff produced four internal studies of the constitutionality of their various proposals for unemployment and old-age insurance, and the House Ways and Means Committee solicited a formal memorandum from the Attorney General's office on the question before proceeding to any serious consideration of the Administration's legislative proposals. The text of these five studies can be found online via the U.S. Social Security Administration's Web site at http://www.ssa.gov/history/reports/ces/cesvolsix.html.

46. Frances Perkins, "The Roots of Social Security," speech given to Social Security Administration staff on October 23, 1962, at SSA headquarters in Baltimore, MD, available online at http://www.ssa.gov/history/perkins5.html.

47. Martha Derthick, *Policymaking for Social Security* (Washington, DC: The Brookings Institution, 1979).

48. Supreme Court of the United States, no. 910, October Term, 1936, *Helvering v. Davis,* May 24, 1937: 6–7.

49. Marion Folsom to Rainhard B. Robbins, December 18, 1935, Latimer Papers.

50. See Jennifer Klein, *To Secure These Rights* (Princeton: Princeton University Press, 2006).

51. Much of this discussion of the reserve controversy comes from Edward D. Berkowitz, "The Transformation of Social Security," in *Social Security Reform: Links to Saving, Investment and Growth*, eds. Steven A. Sass and Robert K. Triest, Conference Series no. 41 (Boston: Federal Reserve Bank of Boston, 1997), 19–28 and from Edward D. Berkowitz, "The First Advisory Council and the 1939 Amendments," in *Social Security after Fifty: Successes and Failures* (Westport: Greenwood Press, 1987), 55–78.

52. James A. Hagerty, "Landon Condemns the Security Law; Would Amend It," *New York Times,* September 27, 1936, 1. Full text of Landon's speech on p. 31.

53. "Ask Major Changes in Social Security: Republicans in Congress Call for Repeal of Reserves Plan and 'Pay-as-You-Go' Basis," *New York Times,* January 30, 1937, 5.

54. This quotation, like the other material related to the Advisory Council, comes from the transcript of its meetings that is available in Record Group 47 in the National Archives. We have taken these quotations from Berkowitz, "The First Advisory Council."

55. "Statement of Secretary of Treasury Morgenthau before Ways and Means," Friday March 24, 1939, File 705, Record Group 47, National Archives.

56. Berkowitz, *America's Welfare State,* 56.

57. Arthur J. Altmeyer, "Progress and Prospects under the Social Security Act," address to the National Conference on Social Work, Indianapolis, Indiana, May 25, 1937. Available online via the Social Security Administration Web site at http://www.ssa.gov/history/altm5.html.

58. *Third Annual Report of the Social Security Board, 1938,* (Washington, U.S. Government Printing Office, 1938): 17. On Altmeyer's role in drafting the letter see, Arthur J. Altmeyer, *The Formative Years of Social Security* (Madison: University of Wisconsin Press, 1966), 90–91.

59. Altmeyer, *Formative Years,* 103.

60. Altmeyer made a very diplomatic concession to the Ways and Means Committee during its consideration of the bill, telling the Committee that the Administration recognized their authority in these matters of public policy. Cf. *Hearings Relative to the Social Security Act Amendments of 1939, Committee on Ways and Means, House of Representatives, vol. 3* (Washington, U.S. Government Printing Office, 1939), 2328–9.

61. Cf. *Congressional Record,* House, 76th Congress, 1st Session, vol. 84 (June 10, 1939): 6968–9.

62. Schellenbach's view prevailed in Conference.

63. "Presidential Statement on Signing Some Amendments to the Social Security Act," August 11, 1939, http://www.ssa.gov/history/fdrstmts.html#1939b.

64. The bill passed both chambers without any recorded votes, which is an indirect indicator of no serious opposition.

65. *Congressional Record,* 80th Congress, 2nd Session, vol. 94 (April 6, 1948), 4134.

66. *Congressional Record,* (June 14, 1948), 8188.

67. "House Committee Favors Dole over Social Security," newspaper article, 11/28/1944 (paper unknown). Clipping in National Archives II, R.G. 47, Correspondence of the Executive Director and the Chairman of the Social Security Board, Box 322, Folder 710–1944 (Nov.).

68. Lewis Meriam, *Relief and Social Security* (Washington: Brookings Institution, 1946), 122, 111.

69. Edward D. Berkowitz, *Mr. Social Security: The Life of Wilbur J. Cohen* (Lawrence: University Press of Kansas, 1995), 341.

70. On the 1950 amendments see Edward D. Berkowitz, *Robert Ball and the Politics of Social Security* (Madison: University of Wisconsin Press, 2003).

71. Edward D. Berkowitz, *Mr. Social Security: The Life of Wilbur J. Cohen* (Lawrence: University Press of Kansas, 1995), 80.

72. Dwight Eisenhower to E. F. Hutton, October 7, 1953, Central Files, File 156-C, Box 848, Eisenhower Library, Abilene, Kansas.

73. Edward Berkowitz, *Disabled Policy America's Programs for the Handicapped* (New York: Cambridge University Press, 1987).

74. David Stockman, *The Triumph of Politics: Why the Reagan Revolution Failed* (New York, Harper-Collins, 1986), 197.

# CHAPTER 3

## Education Policy from the New Deal to the Great Society: The Three Rs—Race, Religion, and Reds

*Gareth Davies*

When they voted for the No Child Left Behind Act of 2002 (NCLB), conservative members of Congress embraced an extraordinary intrusion by the federal government into the affairs of the nation's school districts, which for most of American history had largely governed themselves. The new law instructed states to ensure that *all* public school children achieve competency in English, math, and science by the year 2014, and threatened them with penalties should they fall short. That conservatives should have supported NCLB reflected, among other factors, the degree to which the politics of education in the early twenty-first century were framed by a civil rights paradigm, according to which arguments about local control, or about the constitutional propriety of a particular federal initiative, or about the capacity of the federal government to achieve its stated objectives, were easily trumped by arguments about the fundamental rights of all children to educational opportunity.

The ultimate origins of that paradigm lie in the tremendous changes in the American political system that occurred during the 1960s and 1970s, some of which are considered in the next essay. The present essay, by contrast, explores the previous world of conservative education politics, a world now long gone. Now, conservatives as well as liberals embrace tough federal mandates and penalties in the name of educational opportunity. Back then, liberals as well as conservatives protested their devotion to the hallowed principle of local control. In that environment, the challenge for liberals was to persuade conservatives that federal aid was compatible with this principle, or that a pressing national emergency compelled Washington to intervene. Generally, though, they failed.

During an era when a conservative coalition of Republicans and Southern Democrats dominated Congress, that failure had a good deal to do with racial politics, especially once the 1954 *Brown v. Board of Education* decision had declared school segregation to be unconstitutional. In other cases, meanwhile, religious controversy helped to sink federal aid. Existing historical accounts have tended to highlight these two aspects of the story, and they are not ignored in the account that follows.[1] However, if there was any single factor that was salient in every single battle, and which allowed congressional majorities to form against general aid, it was the continuing opposition of antistatist conservatives to the specter of federal intrusion. For that reason, and because it throws the "big government conservatism" of today into such dramatically sharp relief, it is this aspect of the problem that receives the greatest consideration here.[2]

## The Federal Role in Education in the 1940s

As the long presidency of Franklin D. Roosevelt drew to a close, many aspects of American political life had been utterly transformed by the successive traumas of the Great Depression and World War II. In such politically contentious areas such as social welfare, financial regulation, labor relations, economic management, and black civil rights, the federal government had assumed responsibilities hitherto reserved to the states, or outside the public realm altogether. That claim, however, could certainly not be advanced in the case of American education, to the frustration of those who had been making the case for an enlarged federal role throughout the late 1930s and the war years.

Reflecting their failure, the federal government contributed only 1.4 percent of total spending on schools in 1945–1946. Even *within* the states, those who wished to restructure the traditionally decentralized American school system had made comparatively little progress: the state governments still provided only one-third of the funds, while fully 64 percent was raised locally. And there were still over 100,000 school districts, the great majority of which served fewer than 6,000 children. These figures present a vivid contrast to the early twenty-first century, by which time the federal share of spending had increased sixfold, while the state contribution substantially exceeded that of the localities. By this time, moreover, the number of school districts had shrunk to 14,000.[3]

In the case of education, then, traditional American federalism remained intact. There was, it is true, a United States Office of Education (OE), and indeed it was one of the older federal agencies, having been created soon after the Civil War. But with the federal government spending only $41 million on schools in 1945, and with much of that being administered by other agencies, OE was in no position to have much influence on the direction of American education, even if it had the will to do so, which it did not. It had hardly any programmatic responsibilities, Congress having refused to entrust it with responsibility for the Progressive-Era Vocational Education program, which was the only substantial federal school program at this time.[4] Instead of administering programs, as did the Bureau for Public Assistance (which administered some of the programs established under the Social Security Act), OE staff spent the bulk of their time collecting education statistics and research, and disseminating them to the states, all the while striving to avoid giving offense to their suspicious paymasters on the Hill, who resented any indication of greater initiative.[5] One of their other challenges was to live in Washington on the ungenerous salaries that they received: the longstanding Commissioner of Education, John W. Studebaker, finally had to resign in 1948, because he was no longer able to afford to live in the nation's capital.[6]

The federal role in education remained small throughout the period under review in this essay. As of 1964, the federal share of education spending had only crept up to 4.4 percent. Not surprisingly, OE remained at the end of the period what it had been when Studebaker left office: a sleepy backwater. When the ambitious and accomplished Francis Keppel became commissioner in 1962, he found that it resembled "a kind of faculty of education, spewing reports on topics like a leaky boiler."[7] His predecessor's approach to the job, he surmised, had been to "sit back and think high thoughts," and Keppel gained an insight into the challenge facing him as a more activist and ambitious agency head when the normal repose at OE was unexpectedly interrupted by a call from the White House. Guessing that "the President hadn't called since before Franklin Roosevelt," he recalls that John F. Kennedy "damn near frightened the office to death."[8]

Even in 1945, the lack of a substantial federal role in elementary and secondary schooling had stood out, given not just the broader expansion and centralization of government, but the longstanding tendency within the

United States "to regard education as the keystone of the American democratic experiment"; the chronic inability of the poorer states to support their schools; and the pressure for an expanded federal contribution that these factors had periodically created on the Hill during the past three-quarters of a century.[9] It was not for want of trying: federal aid proposals had been before Congress, on and off, since the 1870s. Reviewing the almost complete failure of these efforts, in 1948, Senator Lister Hill (D-AL), who was the foremost supporter of federal aid in Congress at this time, observed that "If we were to bring into the chamber from the Committee on Labor and Public Welfare the many volumes of hearings" that had been compiled during this period, "they would be piled high on our desks. Year after year the committee has held hearings. Year after year the committee has spent many weeks… attempting to reconcile differences, attempting to wipe out inequities, attempting to bring forth the best possible bill to provide Federal aid, with the primary responsibility for education still continuing in the States."[10] Yet almost nothing had happened.

Why should this have been? In part, it reflected the fact that federal aid to education had not been a priority for the Roosevelt administration during the 1930s. True, the Depression had greatly exacerbated the fiscal plight of the nation's school districts, prompting lengthy federal reports and all manner of ambitious reform proposals.[11] But the administration had chosen to address the emergency via other means: cash grants for teacher salaries from the Federal Emergency Relief Administration, basic skills training through the Civilian Conservation Corps, aid to help poor youngsters to stay in school through the National Youth Administration.[12] That had diminished pressure for a more permanent extension of the federal role, and so too had the nation's subsequent entry into World War II, which greatly dissipated an already weakening liberal reform impulse, and precipitated an economic recovery that bulged the coffers of states and school districts.[13]

Also, the very scale of the changes in American federalism that had occurred in other areas of national life only redoubled the determination of mid-century conservatives to protect this one remaining bastion of Americanism from the red tide of collectivism. Take Senator Kenneth Wherry, a sometime Progressive Republican from Nebraska who had moved sharply to the Right since the advent of the New Deal. He told colleagues in 1948 of his opposition to any measure that might result in federal influence on what was taught in the nation's public schools. "What we need," he proclaimed, "is Americans, and we want educational systems which will teach Americanism." He did not trust a centralized system to preserve this threatened credo; the only hope lay in "the patriotism that comes from the little old red schoolhouses."[14]

Many conservatives of the 1940s felt that "their" America—an individualistic republic of limited, decentralized government—had been virtually obliterated by the New Deal, and by the vast expansion in governmental power and debt that had taken place during the war. For some such conservatives, federal aid to schools was all that was necessary to kill off Republican ideals altogether. Senator Eugene Millikin of Colorado opened his critique of Lister Hill's 1943 bill by remarking that it meant "one more death among the people's liberties through the creeping paralysis of Federal intervention—a mortal illness rendered almost pleasant by the continual and always enlarging doses of that beguiling narcotic, Federal money." In his peroration, he went further, warning that its enactment "would blot out all pretense of Federal solvency, blot out the sovereignty of our States, the sovereignty of home rule, and individual sovereignty."

> We would then have the equalized squalor of communism. It would be the final, lethal blow to what is left of the American system of government. Because this bill is the premise in action to that conclusion and because I want to help to preserve and restore the American system, I must oppose the bill.[15]

Lest one think that such views were confined to entirely unreconstructed Coolidge Republicans who dreamed of rolling back the damage wrought by the New Dealers, it should be noted that versions of the same argument were also not uncommon among more moderate conservatives. Senator Robert Taft of Ohio (a strong conservative but, as we shall see, by no means as inflexible as Millikin) told a colleague at the close of the war that "there is only one fundamental domestic issue in this country today. That is whether we maintain reasonable freedom in this country or turn quickly to an all-powerful Socialist State."[16] And when Dwight Eisenhower, then president of Columbia University, was asked in 1949 what he thought about federal aid to schools, he disclosed the same anxiety. "Unless we are careful," he told House members, "even the great and necessary educational processes in our country will become yet another vehicle by which the believers in paternalism, if not outright Socialism, will gain still additional power for the central government." He was not opposed to *all* federal aid, he went on, but in a time of growing Cold War tension he "firmly believe[d] that the army of persons who urge greater and greater centralization of authority and greater and greater dependence upon the Federal Treasury are really more dangerous to our form of government than any external threat that can possibly be arrayed against us."[17]

As some of these examples suggest, conservative hostility to federal education aid during the 1940s was not just influenced by the growth of government that had occurred in recent times. It was also shaped by the belief that schools played a decisive role in determining the health of American democracy. As one Congressional witness put it in 1945, "our nation includes 50 or more nationalities and races, and some 250 religious sects and cults." In so heterogeneous a nation, he believed, the public schools were "the bulwark of our free institutions," responsible among other things for "impress[ing] upon the minds of the pupils the ideals and traditions of our country."[18] Speaking on the floor of the Senate three years later, the normally sober Senator Taft told colleagues that education "has been, after all, the foundation of all progress in the United States."[19]

## Postwar America: New Momentum for Federal Aid?

But if the perceived centrality of schooling to American democracy helped to mobilize conservative opposition to federal education aid during the 1940s, it inspired precisely the opposite reaction in Americans less preoccupied with the collectivization of national life. Indeed, it even had that effect on some conservatives, including Taft, whose conversion to the cause of federal aid helped to galvanize a strong legislative push during the immediate postwar years.[20] In 1943, when he led the opposition to the Hill-Thomas Educational Finance Act, "Mr. Republican" had indicated that this was too important a function to go the same way as social welfare, highways, and farming. "I should rather extend Federal aid to other fields than education," he explained, "because I am less afraid of the Federal control that ultimately comes from any kind of Federal aid."[21] When he spoke of the importance of education in 1948, though, the context was his strong *support* for Lister Hill's latest proposal. He was now persuaded that the poorer states simply had no way of raising adequate funds for schooling from their own taxpayers.[22] Acknowledging that he still worried about federal control, he told colleagues that this was no longer his *primary* concern:

> I simply decided that the danger of Federal control can be guarded
> against...I would rather stand on that ground than stand on
> the ground...that the Federal Government has no concern with
> education, has no concern with housing, has no concern with health;
> that those are matters solely for the States to take care of, and if there
> are poor States which are unable to give its citizens what they need,
> why that is too bad; those people cannot have equal opportunity.
> I do not think that is a defensible position.[23]

Although Taft was by far the most influential conservative to come out in support of federal aid to education during the 1940s, he was by no means the first. Reflecting the fact that the poor states to which he referred were disproportionately located in the former Confederacy, many Southerners had long supported federal aid, so long as they were convinced that it posed no threat to Jim Crow. What was more, they had been not just moderate Southerners such as Lister Hill, his Senate colleague Pat Harrison (D-MS), and Congressman Robert Ramspeck (D-GA), but such strong conservatives as Walter George (D-GA) and Alan Ellender (D-LA). Now, at the end of the war, they were joined by a number of other Republicans and Southern Democrats who were generally suspicious of the growth and centralization of government, but who also worried about the unevenness of educational provision in the United States. In 1946, when the National Education Association assembled a House Committee for the Support of Federal Aid for Public Schools, its members included a number of highly conservative young congressmen, including Karl Mundt (R-S.D.), Everett Dirksen (R-IL), and Jamie Whitten (D-MS). In their founding statement, the leaders of the coalition explained that "the national interest in the education of American children is of grave concern to federal government," and that "it is the responsibility of national government through grants-in-aid to assist the states that lack financial strength to provide adequate public school facilities." To those who mourned the passing of Coolidge's America, they noted that "the duties of citizens of the nation have steadily mounted as compared with those long established in state and local offices. The hour is now at hand when federal government must recognize that youth must be prepared for a different world than the one that existed a short decade ago."[24]

The willingness of conservatives to put their name to this sort of statement in 1946 owed much to the recent war, and to the belief that one of its taproots had been the gullibility and ignorance of the ordinary German citizen. Writing as tensions with the Soviet Union were beginning to rise, but at a time when the Cold War was not yet set in stone, Everett Dirksen and his colleagues issued a stark warning: "We have two choices. . . . We can either select for the future the way of war, and perish; or we can select the way of peace, and survive." In the latter case, "the great task is that of finding a way to educate the youth of the world to the tasks of lasting peace. Ignorance is a catastrophe."[25]

Clearly, the support of conservatives such as Taft, Dirksen, and Ellender increased the likelihood that federal aid to schools would finally come to pass. There were other reasons for optimism too, during the postwar period, foremost among them being the great difficulty that school districts were having in funding their operations. During the Depression and the war years, school construction projects across the nation had been put on hold. To that backlog was now added a new set of challenges: the baby boom; the expansion of suburbia; the difficulty of recruiting teachers—a traditionally underpaid profession—in a booming economy; the desperate effort by Southern governors such as James F. Byrnes (D-S.C.) to stave off the dread threat of court-ordered integration by equalizing spending on black schoolchildren. With local property taxes rising and bond issues proliferating, public support for federal aid reached high levels: in opinion polls, between two-thirds and three-quarters of respondents approved of the idea.[26]

One final source of postwar momentum for federal aid to education deserves comment. The importance that Americans had always attached to education, as the key to individual opportunity and national strength, had already been increased by the experience of war: Lister Hill observed in 1946 that 2 million draftees had been rejected "because of educational deficiencies...which for the most part could have been prevented through an adequately supported public school program."[27] Now, its importance was further accentuated by postwar economic change: the mechanization of Southern agriculture; the growth in white-collar employment; the automation of industry. While the economy was booming as never before, opportunities for those who lacked even a basic education were arguably declining.[28] When Supreme Court Chief Justice Earl Warren handed down the historic *Brown* decision in 1954, that was one of the principal rationales that he advanced for reversing *Plessy v. Ferguson*:

> Today, education is perhaps the most important function of state and
> local governments. Compulsory school attendance laws and the great
> expenditures for education both demonstrate our recognition of the
> importance of education to our democratic society. It is required in
> the performance of our most basic public responsibilities, even service
> in the armed forces. It is the very foundation of good citizenship.
> Today it is a principal instrument in awakening the child to cultural
> values, in preparing him for later professional training, and in helping
> him to adjust normally to his environment. In these days, it is
> doubtful that any child may reasonably be expected to succeed in life
> if he is denied the opportunity of an education. Such an opportunity,
> where the state has undertaken to provide it, is a right which must
> be made available to all on equal terms.[29]

## Dashed Hopes

For all this, supporters of federal aid to education achieved very little between 1943 and 1964, despite four or five moments of optimism. At the beginning of the period, it was something of a breakthrough when Senator Hill's salary-aid bill was debated on the floor of the Senate (this had not happened since the 1880s). But the measure died when members approved a motion by Taft to send it back to committee, by a vote of 53 to 26. Then, during the later 1940s, following Taft's conversion, federal aid was *approved* by the Senate. On this occasion, though, it got bottled up in the House Education and Labor Committee, and was not reported to the floor. A third moment of hope came in the mid-1950s, at the height of the baby boom, by which time the focus had shifted from unrestricted general aid to categorical aid for school construction. Encouragingly, the principle of construction aid was backed by the Eisenhower administration, and also enjoyed strong support in the House of Representatives, which held floor debates on federal aid to education in both 1956 and 1957 (the first time that this had happened in the twentieth century). Each time, though, construction aid was defeated, the second time by the agonizingly close margin of 203 to 208. Next, in the election year of 1960, broad general aid bills passed both the House and the Senate (the first time that each body had voted for federal aid in the same year), only to fall at virtually the last hurdle, when the House Rules Committee refused to schedule a conference. Finally, in 1961, the first year of the Kennedy administration, another general aid proposal ran aground in the Rules Committee. Reviewing the overall legislative record of the previous two decades in 1964, veteran reporter Robert Bendiner observed that the defeat of general aid "has become almost as much a tradition as bean soup in the Capitol restaurants and free haircuts in the Senate."[30]

What was the explanation for this record of failure? There was no great mystery. As the contemporary quip went, when it came to the *politics* of education, the "three Rs" were race, religion, and Reds. There were comparatively few American politicians by now who opposed federal aid in *any* form, but the support of most was constrained by one or more of those combustible factors. In the case of religion, some opposed aid to parochial school in any form, while others insisted on "parochaid," and it was disputes between these factions that played the largest role in defeating general aid during the Truman and Kennedy administrations.

As for race, supporters of African American civil rights were reluctant to endorse general aid bills that benefited segregated school districts, but even comparatively liberal Southerners could not support measures that contained an antisegregation amendment, which they generally did during the Eisenhower administration. The crucial turning point was the *Brown* decision. Stewart McClure, who was chief clerk to the Senate Labor and Public Welfare Committee at the time, recalls its dramatic impact on Lister Hill:

> [Before 1954] his real interest in legislation, other than things for Alabama, and TVA, and changing the basing point in steel pricing and that sort of thing, was education: vocational education and any other kind of education. And just about the time he was to inherit the Labor

Committee, which handled all the legislation affecting education, the *Brown* decision came down and the segregationists went mad. George Wallace wasn't governor, but the mood in Alabama was that it was no time for the federal government to put its fingers into public education. He was driven off of it, except for the NDEA, which was wrapped in the flag and safe. That's why he turned to health[;] it afford[ed] him a vast field of action that supplanted what he would have preferred, I think, the field of education.[31]

The third "R," Reds, was shorthand for continuing conservative concern about federal control.[32] Despite all of the fiscal challenges facing school districts in mid-twentieth century America, "schoolmen" (the contemporary term) continued to prize local control and to fear federal encroachment. As Thomas Shannon has noted, "school board members were skeptical that the federal government would provide the funds and then passively back off when decisions about actual programming would have to be made. They viewed federal guidelines, policies, rules and regulations, conditions, and suggested operating approaches...as nothing short of pre-emption of local authority and a subversion of the American institution of local representative governance of the schools."[33] The National School Boards Association (NSBA) voted at its 1962 delegate assembly to oppose any general federal aid legislation. "Our task is not to stop or obstruct the splendid efforts to provide excellence in education," its president insisted. The key to success, though, lay not in federal aid, but "in re-awakening our local communities to the importance of the principle of self-autonomy."[34] With little interest in appealing to Washington for help, the Evanston, Illinois–based NSBA did not even establish a branch office in the nation's capital until 1966.

Many conservatives also believed that states and school districts were quite capable of rising to the challenges that faced them, and did not need federal aid. When President Eisenhower appointed a study committee to examine the issue in 1955, its members acknowledged that enrollment in elementary and secondary schools was poised to increase from 29 million in 1952 to 44 million in 1965, that 40,000 new classrooms were needed every year, and that this put a strain on state and local finances. But the solution was not federal aid. To the contrary, the best thing that the federal government could do was to "reduce its tax bill," making it "easier for State and local governments to raise additional funds for the schools without increasing the total tax burden of their citizens." Even with the growing federal tax burden, they were doing a remarkably good job: between 1951 and 1953, 50,000 classrooms per year had been constructed. The study committee concluded that "federal aid is not necessary either for current operating expenses for public schools or for capital expenditures of new school facilities. Local communities and States are able to supply both in accordance with the will of their citizens."[35]

A decade later, when the Elementary and Secondary Education Act (ESEA) was being put together, the bureau of budget would be telling Lyndon Johnson that this prediction, remarkably, had been borne out: the incipient "crisis" identified by advocates of construction aid had not materialized.[36] For some liberals, though, the inability of the states to handle their problems seemed transparent, and the tenacity with which groups like NSBA, the Council of Chief State School Officers, and the U.S. Chamber of Commerce continued to defend the principle of local control was vexing. Democratic staffer Stewart McClure recalls an attitude that to him was almost inexplicable:

> [T]hey clung on to some mythical constitutional principle: the last thing that could happen in the United States was for the federal hand to be laid on local education, which belongs to the hands of the school boards and local council of education or whatever they're called—which, of course, are all controlled by the Chamber of Commerce....Now what all this was supposed to prevent or forestall I never could figure out, but it was a religious faith. They'd get white and scream and wave their hands in the air about the *horrible* prospects of this vicious, cold hand of federal bureaucracy being laid upon these pristine, splendid local schools that knew better than anyone what needed to be done, and so forth and so forth....I don't know, it's a real mythology, but it was real and senators and congressmen had to deal with it.[37]

Some congressional conservatives—Jeffersonian Democrats such as Sen. Harry Flood Byrd and Rep. Howard W. Smith, both of Virginia; Old-Guard Republicans such as Sen. Styles Bridges of New Hampshire, and Congressmen H. R. Gross (Iowa), John Taber (New York), and Clare Hoffman (Michigan)—continued to oppose almost all federal education proposals on these grounds, and on grounds of economy.[38] In the case of Byrd and Smith, of course, these positions often had a racial subtext, and one might reasonably consider their hostility to federal aid under the heading of "race" rather than "Reds." However, it should be noted that their opposition to the encroachment of Washington long preceded *Brown* (each had been an early opponent of the New Deal), and that they opposed almost *all* forms of federal aid to education, including some that did not invoke the specter of race (such as the National Defense Education Act, library aid, and aid to the handicapped). While people like Byrd and Smith were racists, they were not *just* racists, something that is often lost in contemporary writing on the postwar politics of social policy.[39] Southern congressional delegations indubitably contained plenty of crude race-baiters such as Senators James O. Eastland (D-MS) and Herman Talmadge (D-GA), but they also included legislators whose anti-statism persisted independently of race.[40]

While their numbers were comparatively small, the political influence of these rock-ribbed antistatist conservatives in both parties was greatly enhanced when "Judge" Smith became chairman of the House Rules committee in 1955. To be debated on the floor, legislation had to win a "rule" from Smith, and while it was theoretically possible to bypass him, the practical barriers to that happening were formidable, in the hierarchical world of the mid-century Congress.[41] With the chairman deeply committed both to small government and to racial segregation, Rules acquired the reputation for being the "graveyard of reform." That owed something to his exceptional knowledge of parliamentary procedure and his canny political brain. In the case of federal aid to education, he was aided by the fact that the committee's membership featured blocs of conservative Republicans, Southern Democrats, and (from 1961) Northern Catholic Democrats.[42] Just like on the floor of the House, any two of these three elements was sufficient to defeat federal aid, and there were few cases where neither race nor religion raised its head (the leading two examples are considered below).

Far more numerous, especially in the House, were those conservatives who acknowledged *some* national and hence federal interest in education, but who nevertheless approached even modest legislative proposals with deep scepticism, worrying that they might create irresistible pressure for massive federal aid. That was true, for example, of the GOP leadership in the House during the debate over school construction. Formally, Minority Leader Charlie Halleck of Indiana, and Minority Whip Leslie Arends of Illinois, supported the Eisenhower administration's bill, but their reservations were strong, and when they had an opportunity to kill it without appearing disloyal to their president, they took it.[43]

Despite his rhetorical advocacy of modern Republicanism, and his disdain for unrealistic paleoconservatives who sought to roll back the New Deal, President Eisenhower shared Halleck's doubts about even limited school aid.[44] When reporters suggested to him that he could have pushed the 1957 construction bill harder, and forced it through, he demurred. At the same time, though, he made it clear that he was not entirely unhappy about the outcome:

> [I]f you try to make every State believe that they are getting something for nothing out of such a bill, then I would doubt your ability to terminate the operation of the bill at the end of the five-year period. At least, I would be fearful, and certainly at the end of that time I am not going to be around to veto any extension of the thing....I am getting

to the point where I can't be too enthusiastic about something that I think is likely to fasten a sort of an albatross, *another one,* around the neck of the Federal Government—I don't believe it should be done.[45]


## Threading the Needle: The Cases of Impact Aid and NDEA

There were two important exceptions to the general record of success that opponents of federal aid to education enjoyed during the postwar period. The first was the impact aid program, which was enacted in 1950 as P.L. 815 and P.L. 874. The second was the National Defense Education Act (NDEA), which passed in 1958. The circumstances surrounding their enactment, and their early years in operation, suggest that Eisenhower was quite right to worry that even seemingly limited extensions of the federal role, justified on impeccably conservative grounds, might ultimately serve to advance the cause of general aid. With the advantage of hindsight, each of these two measures can be seen to have helped pave the way for the subsequent passage of the historic Elementary and Secondary Education Act of 1965.


### *Impact Aid*

Impact aid, enacted in 1950, distributed federal grants to "school districts overburdened with enrolments resulting from defense and other Federal activities."[46] Aid was provided both for school construction (P.L. 815) and for maintenance and operations (P.L. 874), on the grounds that the presence of a large federal installation in a school district, especially a rural district, placed an intolerable burden on local taxpayers. In part, that was because federal property, unlike commercial property, was not subject to local property taxation, while government employees who lived on such property (such as military personnel living on base) were similarly exempt.[47] In further part, it was because the influx of federal employees increased the number of school-age children in the district. The combination of a reduced tax pool and an expanded school population could be highly disruptive.

Take the example of Midway City, Oklahoma. Its superintendent, Oscar V. Rose, told senators in 1949 that the number of public school children in his district had increased from 104 to 2,648 since the start of the World War II defense build-up. Before the Tinker Field Air Force Base came to town, he observed, the district's children had all been housed in "four permanent modern brick classrooms." Now, though, most of them were educated in unsatisfactory temporary accommodation. (Some, according to Rose's congressman, Mike Monroney (D-OK), "had to be educated in a firetrap at an airplane take-off location.") Rose emphasized that this did not reflect any lack of local effort: to the contrary, Midway City taxpayers had repeatedly voted to increase their contribution during the past decade, to the point where they had now reached the legal limit permitted by the state of Oklahoma. Rather, the problem was that "the fiscal economy of the Midwest City School District is thrown completely out of balance through the large percentage of federally owned, tax-exempt property located within the district." Since the federal government employed 70 percent of the district's employment, Rose asked, did it not have at least some responsibility to provide financial assistance?[48]

The answer to that question seemed obvious to members of Congress, who gave the two impact aid measures their unanimous support. During the House floor debate, there were references to districts being "overrun by the government," "suffering from the impact of federal activities," and enduring a "miserable situation brought about by the United States government." Children in these districts, the principal House sponsor of the measure remarked, were forced to "bear the marks of governmental maladministration and governmental neglect."[49] As these excerpts suggest, impact aid was if anything *particularly* to appealing to strong conservatives, whose natural tendency was to view most federal activity in such terms. Also increasing its acceptability to this group was the fact that P.L.815 and P.L. 874 were presented as being emergency, temporary measures, with the first expiring after three years, and the second after four.[50] And it was not a big program: it was estimated that only 600 or so of the nation's 80,000 districts would be eligible for aid.

These reassuring aspects of the impact aid program, however, do not explain the striking absence during the debate over impact aid of the usual conservative argument that even *small*, seemingly unexceptionable federal aid proposals should be viewed with suspicion, on the grounds that they would inevitably expand. At similar moments in other aid to education debates, some conservatives would detect beneath the veneer a nefarious liberal plot to hoodwink Congress, as when the Midwestern radio commentator, Clarence Manion, charged that school construction aid, "under the guise of 'do-goodism,'" was "a Socialist scheme to subvert the minds of American youths."[51] More frequently, they would accept the sincerity of those who felt that the level of federal aid could be contained, and local control preserved, but would doubt their political realism. Federal administration, they often observed, would *inevitably* result in centralization, as officials quite properly sought to ensure that federal funds were used for the intended purpose.[52] And, they went on, the strong political appeal of education spending was such that initially limited federal aid measures would *inevitably* expand out of all recognition, as clientele groups got to work, and politicians competed for their approbation.[53]

Perhaps these arguments did not appear in the case of impact aid for the reason that conservatives did not believe that P.L. 815 or P.L. 874 constituted federal aid to education. Rather, they told one another, it was an arrangement for making payments in lieu of taxation, as this colloquy between two of the flintiest Republicans illustrates:

> Mr. [CHARLES] JONAS [R-N.C.]:    What I am personally interested in is whether or not this is in any sense of the word, intentionally or unintentionally, directly or indirectly, a step toward Federal aid to education?
>
> Mr. [CLARENCE] BROWN [R-OHIO]:    No; this is not a bill to provide Federal aid to education. If it were, I would oppose it.... This is simply a matter wherein the Federal Government is to pay its fair share of the cost of maintaining schools in areas where the Government itself has a specific interest, land, property, or where the number of Government employees are overcrowding the public schools.
>
> Mr. JONAS:    In other words, the Federal Government is merely being put in the position of a local taxpayer or business concern.
>
> Mr. BROWN of OHIO:    That is correct.[54]

It is ironic that conservative opponents of federal aid to education should have been so enthusiastic about impact aid, for the subsequent development of the program during the 1950s presents a classic case study of the kind of pork-barrel politics and expansion by stealth that they deprecated in other contexts. By 1960, impact aid had become a *de facto* form of general aid to some 4,000 districts that educated one-third of the nation's public school children. While liberals such as Rep. Frank Thompson (D-NJ) supported it as a useful proxy for their preferred solution of large-scale federal aid, conservatives such as Senator Barry Goldwater (R-AZ) and Rep. Clarence Brown clung stubbornly to the idea that it continued to comport with their principles.[55]

As to why Goldwater and Brown adhered so tenaciously to this fiction, the inconspicuous process by which it was transformed permitted them to do so, while the popularity of the enlarged program among their constituents would have made any other course politically hazardous. Almost every year during the 1950s, eligibility requirements were loosened. For example, in 1953 the definition of "federal property" was expanded to include buildings that were leased to the private sector, even though they were subject to state and local taxation. In the same year, the requirement that recipient districts maintain a certain local contribution rate was dropped. Later in the decade, legislators endorsed amendments that allowed school districts to continue to receive benefits for an additional two years, in the event that they ceased to be eligible. And another revision expanded the definition of a "federally connected child" to include Indian children, who had hitherto been excluded on the ground that they already received federal support under the Johnson-O'Malley Act of 1934.[56]

Many of these modifications were highly technical and seemingly trivial (the above examples have been selected because of their comparative simplicity), and few of them attracted any significant debate. Typically, one member of Congress whose district would become eligible for funding under a proposed amendment would speak in its support, and a bipartisan succession of similarly placed colleagues would then rise to compliment him for his perspicacity. Sometimes, an amendment would be designed simply to help one member, as when the powerful but politically embattled Carl Elliott (D-AL) won inclusion of a measure that counted private flight training schools as "federal property," so long as they provided training to the occasional member of the U.S. Air Force.[57] In such situations, however difficult it might be to justify the change in terms of the original rationale of the act, colleagues would go along, presumably either out of collegiality, out of self-interest (perhaps they wanted Elliott's support for *their* special provision), or out of sheer inattention.

The inspiration for many of these amendments came from school superintendents, ably led by Oscar Rose, the Oklahoma school chief whose 1950 testimony was excerpted above. While Rose was, of course, particular interested in changes that would protect or expand the flow of federal dollars to Midway City, he was also keen on any amendment that would increase the number of legislators with a stake in the program. Tactful, precise, and exceptionally well-informed about "his" program, Rose's real power resided in the close ties that he developed with congressional staffers on the authorization committees, and with the mid-level bureaucrats who administered the program at HEW.[58] Also, he worked hard to develop a good relationship with the members and staff of the House appropriations subcommittee whose deliberations played the biggest part in determining impact aid funding levels. One of his closest allies was Rep. John E. Fogarty (D-R.I.), chairman of that subcommittee, who regularly told colleagues that they had a moral obligation to fund the program in full, given that these were moneys "in lieu of taxes." As for those colleagues, they equably went along with this claim, even in years when they were generally eager to slash spending, such as 1957.

At the other end of Pennsylvania Avenue, these programmatic developments were viewed with consternation. Both the Eisenhower and Kennedy administrations tried to cut impact aid, highlighting how detached eligibility had become from fiscal need, and how problematic it was to view the federal government's presence in a district as a burden. A congressman like Mendel Rivers (D-S.C.) would fight tooth-and-nail to have big military installations located in his district, and then, when he succeeded, would protest at the fiscal burden that they created, and demand compensation. How could such a claim be justified, given the jobs and purchasing power that came with the influx of federal employees into a district? And how could one defend the fact that the biggest beneficiaries of impact aid included the prosperous suburban districts that ringed the District of Columbia? To be sure, Fairfax County, Virginia, and Montgomery County, Maryland, were federally impacted, but their federal employees invariably paid property taxes and had been largely responsible for the tremendous boom that the Washington metropolitan area had enjoyed in recent years. Were they really a burden? Finally, was it right that a district should qualify for aid because it was home to a manufacturer of adhesive coating that happened to sell some of its products to the federal government?[59]

With ammunition such as this, Kennedy was able to make an intellectually powerful critique of impact aid.[60] On the Hill, however, his arguments counted for little, when set against the elemental political fact that 115 school districts in Barry Goldwater's Arizona received funding under P.L. 874, and that a dozen of them would lose a third or more of their revenue if it ceased to exist.[61] When ESEA was being assembled, Hugh Davis Graham observes, "virtually the entire senior bureaucracy" at HEW and the budget bureau saw an opportunity to reform P.L. 874: already hard to defend as a payment in lieu of taxes, it would now be difficult to justify even on pragmatic grounds, as a de facto form of general aid.[62] Such was its appeal in Congress, however, that Johnson ultimately elected to package ESEA as an expansion of the entirely unreformed impact aid program.[63]

It would be wrong to attach too much significance to this device: it is hard to imagine that too many legislators in 1965 were persuaded by the idea that ESEA was an extension of impact aid, and that they should vote for it on that basis.[64] Rather, the significance of the program's development since 1950 lies in the way that it illustrates the natural tendency of members of Congress, irrespective of ideology, to support established, clientele-oriented programs that distribute funds to their constituents, and enjoy the backing of a politically sophisticated lobby group. The development of ESEA after 1965 would illustrate the same pattern, as is revealed in the next essay in this volume.

However, the most direct legislative precedent for ESEA was not impact aid, but NDEA. With the passage of this Cold War education measure in 1958, the federal government was injected into the day-to-day operations of American schools for the first time.

## National Defense Education Act

During the fall of 1957, prospects for federal aid looked particularly gloomy. First, the House had just defeated the Eisenhower administration's modest school construction bill. Second, the House more generally was in a conservative mood, a fact that had been illustrated particularly vividly by a recent economy drive.[65] Third, momentum for school aid in the Senate had slackened greatly since *Brown,* with the majorities of the late 1940s melting away as Southerners shied away from measures that might be interpreted back home as promoting integration. School construction had not even made it out of committee in the Senate.

In these circumstances, the cause of federal aid to education received an enormous boost when the Soviet Union succeeded in sending the Sputnik satellite into orbit around the earth in October of 1957, stirring an intense wave of anxiety within the United States about the adequacy of its education system. Why had the Soviet Union succeeded with Sputnik, anguished commentators inquired, while the American Vanguard rocket had been a flop? Why was the United States not producing engineers and mathematicians capable of sending a satellite into orbit? What could be done about the problem?[66]

This reaction boosted the prospects for federal aid in two ways. Most obviously, it could be presented as an act of national defense, making it hard for Republicans to oppose, and possible for moderate Southerners to support. Also, conservatives were likely to be well-disposed to one of the central charges of post-Sputnik alarmists, namely that in the course of trying to make schooling relevant to the nonacademically gifted majority of children, American educators had succumbed to a fundamentally anti-intellectual doctrine of "life-adjustment," according to which—as Admiral Hyman Rickover complained—instruction in science and mathematics had yielded to courses on fly-fishing, "rest," and "how to tell when you are in love."[67] This sort of charge was not new, and indeed by the time of Sputnik, the critics of Progressive Education had already largely won the battle.[68] Still, it was helpful to supporters of NDEA that they were able to harness the passions stirred by this debate to the cause of federal aid to education. Congressmen learned from one witness that 56 percent of U.S. high schools offered no foreign languages, and that the number of newly qualified science and mathematics teachers had declined by 50 percent between 1950 and 1954. Meanwhile, the purposeful, grim Soviets had been forging ahead. As this same witness (a journalist who had been studying Soviet education for the past two years) put it, if "the battle of Waterloo was won on the playing fields of Eton, . . . it might be that the battle of survival for the West is being lost in the high schools of America."[69]

Quite apart from their genuine concern about the implications of American educational underperformance for national security and their authentic regret that American schooling had become so unscholarly, many conservatives felt politically constrained to respond to this furore. At the same time, though, these same conservatives worried about where the Sputnik-inspired scare might lead, in terms both of federal aid to education and (in Eisenhower's case) in terms of defense spending. Eisenhower tried to strike a balance, attempting to calm what he took to be inflated fears about national preparedness, while also presenting to Congress a $1.6 billion, four-year defense education bill that emphasized scholarships for needy high school graduates interested in studying science and mathematics at college. For groups like the National Association of Manufacturers, the Chamber of Commerce, and the American Farm Bureau Federation, however, that was going too far. A spokesman for the NAM regarded defense education as a "Trojan horse" for general aid, and detected "grave danger" of federal control, while the Chamber of Commerce questioned whether federal scholarships were "either necessary or desirable." The solution, for them, lay in local and state initiative, in private scholarships, and in changes in the way that education schools taught American teachers, rather than in federal action.[70]

Faced with such arguments, Stewart McClure recalls how supporters of broad federal aid confounded their opponents. First, they came up with the title "National Defense Education Act." Privately, McClure considered this to be a "God-awful title," exclaiming to an interviewer a quarter century later that "if there are any words less compatible, really, intellectually, in terms of what is the purpose of education—it's not to defend the country; it's to defend the mind and develop the human spirit, not to build cannons and battleships. It was a horrible title." Still, he went on, "it worked. It worked. How could you attack it?" Second, they arranged for "the cream of the brains of this country" to give testimony, including such noted Cold War figures as Wernher von Braun, who headed the U.S. rocket program, and the physicist Edward Teller, father of the hydrogen bomb. McClure recalls the ammunition that liberals could hurl back when a Barry Goldwater or a Strom Thurmond criticized the committee bill on the floor:

> When we went on the floor we could say, "Well, now, does the senator mean that he challenges the distinguished leader of the National Council on Science, Detlev Bronk, who says...." We hammered them into the ground. And, of course, if anybody brought up socialism or something like that, the dreadful specter of Socialism, we had Edward Teller and the Hydrogen Bomb to clobber them with! Well, hearings...really can shape the form of anything. You get the right witnesses and ask the right questions and they give the right answers,

your opposition is slaughtered before they can open their trap. That's one of the tactical secrets of functioning on this Hill. Well, I really pulled together an incredible array of talent, of not only Ph.D's but Nobel Prize winners and so forth. And, of course, the press was paying a great deal of attention to this. We were getting headlines every day, and all of that has an impact, too.[71]

In the face of this onslaught, conservatives on the Hill did succeed in cutting back the expansive bill that Lister Hill and Carl Elliott had proposed in place of Eisenhower's more modest measure: whereas the Hill-Elliott bill authorized $3 billion in expenditures over seven years, Congress approved only $1 billion over four years, after which time it was hoped that the emergency would have passed. And they won a number of pleasing amendments: converting the scholarship program to a loan program, for example, and requiring recipients of federally financed loans to sign a loyalty oath. Appeased by those small victories, and perhaps worried about the prospect of looming midterm elections (the nation was in recession, and the GOP was getting the blame), a majority of Republican congressmen voted in favor of NDEA.

It is clear, though, that they did so with mixed feelings: before voting in favor of NDEA, they had voted to recommit it (a move that, had it succeeded, would have allowed them to kill the bill, without explicitly voting against it).[72] Senator Barry Goldwater captured their anxiety when he appended the following, succinct minority views to the Labor and Public Welfare's report on the Hill-Elliott bill:

> This bill and the foregoing remarks of the majority remind me of an
> old Arabian proverb: If the camel once get his nose into the tent,
> his body will soon follow.
>     If adopted, the legislation will mark the inception of aid, supervision,
> and ultimately control of education in this country by Federal authorities.[73]

The bulk of NDEA funds were allotted to higher education. In this area, the federal government's role was comparatively uncontroversial: the precedents went back as far as the Morrill Act of 1862, which had distributed federal land for the establishment of land-grant universities. More recently, the G.I. Bill of 1944 and the establishment of the National Science Foundation in 1947 had attested anew to the willingness of even conservative legislators and interest groups to endorse federal aid to higher education, so long as it could be tied to a compelling national interest.[74]

It is likely that Goldwater was more worried by the small but precedent-setting provisions that concerned elementary and secondary education. One title of NDEA, for example, awarded funds to the states for improving the teaching of science, mathematics, and foreign languages in American high schools. Others allotted $60 million to state education agencies for establishing better record-keeping procedures, and for testing student achievement. A fourth provided matching grants to states for the purchase of educational equipment. Eisenhower, approving NDEA, expressed the view that "the Federal Government having done its share, the people of the country, working through their local and State government and through private agencies, must now redouble their efforts." At the same time, though, he worried to reporters that "if you try to take it in such a sweeping way that the whole country is looking merely to the Federal Government to do this now for the coming years, I think we have lost a very great and vital feature of our whole free system."[75]

The subsequent trajectory of the program must have disappointed Eisenhower. Far from being a temporary measure, NDEA became, like impact aid, an enduring and popular addition to the federal role in education, enthusiastically backed by lobbyists for the American Council of Education (the umbrella group for higher education), the land-grant colleges, librarians, and manufacturers of audiovisual equipment. When it was amended in 1961 and 1964, its connection to national defense became considerably attenuated. In 1961, the definition of what constituted a "modern foreign language" under the terms of the act was broadened to include English (on the grounds that it *was* a foreign language to some Americans); and the list of subjects deemed essential to national defense was extended with the inclusion of physical fitness. At the same time, a new title was added to the act providing federal funds for library provision in schools and colleges. In 1964, meanwhile, the list of subjects for which equipment could be purchased was broadened to include history, civics, geography, and remedial reading. Commending this change to the Senate, the Labor and Public Welfare Committee urged the Commissioner of Education to construe these terms broadly: history, for example, "stretches from today to embrace the emergence of man from the caves and forests."[76]

## The Persistence of Local Control

Alarmed by the implications of the 1964 amendments, four of the more conservative members of the House Education and Labor Committee reminded colleagues of Barry Goldwater's 1958 warning about the camel, and suggested that he had been prescient. "This bill," they suggested, "represents a considerable part of the body of the camel of Federal control of education; it would begin the conversion of the act into a program of general Federal aid and supervision of education."[77] On the strength of the legislative histories of it and the impact aid program, one could conclude that the cause of federal aid to education had gained important momentum during the seemingly unpropitious years that preceded the launch of the Great Society. A solid platform had been constructed, precedents had been established, and the supporters of general aid had learned important political lessons both from their frequent defeats, and from their less common victories. If antistatist conservatives had managed to stave off large-scale federal aid to education in the name of economy and federalism, their capacity to continue to do so for much longer looked uncertain.

How were these albeit limited advances for federal aid to be explained? In the familiar language of the American Political Development school, they owed something to both ideational and institutional considerations.[78] In terms of the former, supporters of impact aid and NDEA found ways of framing federal aid that appealed to conservatives; the popularity of federal aid in the country at large forced Eisenhower to give at least tepid support to construction aid; and the passage of these foot-in-the-door measures diminished the political force of constitutional objections to subsequent, larger proposals such as ESEA. As for the institutional dimension, the early years of both impact aid and NDEA illustrate the usual pattern of path-dependency, whereby once-bold policy innovations rapidly bed down in the constituency- and clientele-dominated world of Capitol Hill politics and become very hard to challenge.

But if some important foundations had been laid for ESEA, it would be harder to argue that the events considered in this chapter in any way anticipated the massively intrusive character of the federal role in education today. To encounter conservative perspectives on elementary and secondary education circa 1950, in light of the knowledge of what was to come half a century later, is to stumble across a lost world, one that is extremely remote from modern American conservatism. Eisenhower-era conservatives worried about an enlarged federal presence in the nation's schools, believing that localism was essential both to the survival of the federal system (which they cherished), and to educational excellence. What would Charles Halleck or Clarence Brown think of the No Child Left Behind Act of 2002? To ponder this enormous transformation in American conservatism is, in larger terms, to recognize the continuing force in American politics of the revolutionary changes in government that occurred not just during the Johnson presidency, but (perhaps more especially) during the Nixon-Ford years, when "regulatory federalism" utterly transformed the federal-state relationship.[79]

In 1964, all that lay in the future. In this sense, what needs to be explained is the success of pre–Great Society conservatives in resisting the considerable momentum for federal aid to education that sometimes existed during the years considered in this essay. This was a time when most Americans supported federal aid, when the centrality of education to individual and national success was increasingly acknowledged, when plausible Cold War rationales could be advanced, and when school districts across the nation were struggling to cope with the effects of the baby boom. Yet construction aid and general aid always failed. Again, it is helpful to think about this failure in relation to the ideational/institutional dichotomy. Doing so, we find the institutional dynamic to be especially powerful, especially the disproportionate power that the hierarchical, committee-centered midcentury Congress gave to numerically outnumbered antistatist conservatives such as Howard Smith and Graham Barden (the choleric North Carolinian who chaired the House Education and Labor Committee until 1961).

At the same time, there were also powerful ideational barriers to anything resembling federal control of schools. It is not just that conservatives continued to adhere to the principle of local control. Additionally, they controlled the agenda. If education politics today are framed to some extent by a civil rights paradigm, then during the period under review here, they were framed by a local control paradigm. Throughout the period considered in this essay, even *liberals* asserted their undying devotion to the hallowed principle of local control. Let us close, where we began, with Francis Keppel, John F. Kennedy's second commissioner of Education. When ESEA was being put together, he recalls, "a good many" of his colleagues "felt that the state departments of education were the feeblest bunch of second-rate, or fifth-rate, educators who combined educational incompetence with bureaucratic immovability." For Keppel, though, the solution to that problem lay not in federal mandates or penalties. "Having sat on that educational bureaucracy in Washington," he recalls, "the last thing in the world I wanted was all those 25,000 school districts coming in with plans with my bureaucrats deciding whether to approve them or not. I wanted that stuff done out in the states." The key, therefore, was to stimulate improvements in the state departments of education, and Title V of ESEA was designed to achieve that purpose.[80]

Only in an extremely limited and indirect sense, then, could one claim that the seeds of contemporary education politics were sown during the period from 1943 to 1964. Neither is it easy to say that they are to be found in the passage of the 1965 act, whose draftsmen deferred to the principle of local control to a degree that would be unthinkable today. It is probably more accurate to say that those seeds are to be found in ESEA's failure to achieve its goals, as well as in the exogenous changes in American governance that came about during the later 1960s and the 1970s. As of 1965, the really revolutionary change in the federal politics of education still lay in the future.

## Acknowledgments

The author would like to thank Edward Berkowitz, Martha Derthick, Larry DeWitt, Robert Mason, and James T. Patterson for their responses to an earlier version of this essay.

## Notes

1. For accounts that treat them in greater detail, see Frank Munger and Richard Fenno, *The National Politics of Education* (Syracuse, NY: Syracuse University Press, 1962), Robert Bendiner, *Obstacle Course on Capitol Hill* (New York: McGraw-Hill, 1964), James L. Sundquist, *Politics and Policy: The Eisenhower, Kennedy, and Johnson Years* (Washington, DC: Brookings Institution, 1968), 155–220.

2. On big government conservatism, see, for example, David Broder, "So, Now Bigger is Better?," *Washington Post,* January 12, 2003, B1; Fred Barnes, "A 'Big Government Conservatism,'" *Wall Street Journal,* August 15, 2003, 20; Paul Peterson, "The Changing Politics of Federalism," in *Evolving Federalisms: The Intergovernmental Balance of Power in America and Europe,* ed. Craig Parsons (Syracuse, NY: Maxwell School, 2003), 19–36.

3. All statistics for the 2002–2003 school year, drawn from National Center for Education Statistics, *Digest of Education Statistics: 2005* (Washington, DC, 2006), Tables 152 and 84, available online at http://nces.ed.gov/pubsearch/pubsinfo.asp?pubid=2006030.

4. Three-quarters of OE's meager budget was earmarked for the education of Eskimos in Alaska. Vocational education was not *very* significant in terms of its budget, which stood at $21 million, but was popular on the Hill, having put down strong roots since its establishment in 1917. It was administered by a separate Board of Vocational Education, located in the Federal Security Administration. See Rufus E. Miles, *The Department of Health, Education, and Welfare* (New York: Praeger, 1974), 141.

5. Stephen K. Bailey and Edith K. Mosher, *ESEA: The Office of Education Administers a Law* (Syracuse, NY: Syracuse University Press, 1968), 18.

6. He had been in position since 1934.

7. Francis Keppel, Oral History for the Lyndon Baines Johnson Library (LBJ OH), 15.

8. Ibid., 2, and Keppel Oral History with John F. Kennedy Library, 7.

9. Quote from Hugh Davis Graham, *Uncertain Triumph: Federal Education Policy in the Kennedy and Johnson Years* (Chapel Hill: University of North Carolina Press, 1984), xvii.

10. *Congressional Record* (March 23, 1948), 3290.

11. For a contemporary account of the fiscal strain, see William G. Carr, *School Finance* (Stanford, Calif.: Stanford University Press, 1933).

12. See Gilbert E. Smith, *Limits of Reform: Politics and Federal Aid to Education, 1937–1950* (New York: Garland, 1982).

13. On the weakening of the reform impulse during the late 1930s, the best source remains James T. Patterson, *Congressional Conservatism and the New Deal* (Lexington: University of Kentucky Press, 1967).

14. *Congressional Record* (March 24, 1948), 3557.

15. Ibid., October 19, 1943, 8490.

16. Letter, Taft to Bruce Barton, November 12, 1945, in Barton Papers, Box 67, State Historical Society of Wisconsin, Madison.

17. Letter, Eisenhower to Cong. Ralph Gwinn (R-NY), June 7, 1949, in *Public School Assistance Act of 1949*, Hearings before a Special Subcommittee of the Committee on Education and Labor, House of Representatives, 81st Cong., 1st sess. (Washington, DC: GPO, 1949), 888.

18. The witness was Colonel John H. Cowles, Southern District Grand Commander of the Scottish Rite Masons, and he was appearing before the Senate Committee on Education and Labor on January 31, 1945. His remarks are reproduced in *Congressional Digest* 25, 2 (Feb. 1946): 49.

19. *Congressional Record* (March 23, 1948), 3289.

20. On the evolution of Taft's thinking, see James T. Patterson, *Mr. Republican: A Biography of Robert A. Taft* (Boston: Houghton-Mifflin, 1972).

21. *Congressional Record* (October 18, 1943), 8424.

22. In 1942, affluent Massachusetts and Connecticut were able to spend $130.73 per pupil on education, despite spending only 0.3 percent of their total income on schools. By contrast, the poor states of Mississippi, Arkansas, and Alabama spent 1.3 percent, 1.5 percent, and 1.4 percent of their incomes, respectively, on education, yet were only able to raise $31.52, $38.59, and $39.75 per pupil with that greater tax effort. See *Congressional Digest* 25, 2 (February 1946): 42, for a table comparing per pupil spending and tax effort in all 48 states.

23. Ibid., April 1, 1948, 3931. Taft's change of heart had taken place earlier, immediately after the end of the war. See the speech, "A Republican Program for Progress," that he delivered on October 19, 1945, at a conference of the Ohio Federation of Republican Women's Organizations. Copy in Barton Papers, Box 67.

24. *NEA Journal*, March 1946, 127. The coalition had 89 members. For their names and photos, see ibid., March 1946, 125–8; ibid., April, 1946, 184; ibid., May, 1946, 233; and ibid., September 1946, 307.

25. Ibid., March 1946, 125–8. The other signatories to this declaration were Dirksen's coalition cochair Jennings Randolph (D-W.V.), and George P. Miller (D-Calif.), who served as secretary. The tone of the coalition statement strongly recalled Wendell Willkie's wartime book, *One World* (New York: Simon and Schuster, 1943).

26. For poll data, see Munger and Fenno, *National Politics*, 91–92. For a useful survey of the financial pressures facing the states during the postwar period, see Peter Veillette, "State and Local Efforts to Finance Schools since 1945," *Current History* (June 1972): 293–7.

27. *Congressional Record* (August 1, 1946), 10619.

28. For the political uses of this argument, see the debate accompanying the launching of the war on poverty in 1964. Although the postwar boom was now nearing its zenith, Congressman Philip Landrum (D-GA) remarked that "the frontiers such as existed for our forbears and for us as young men simply do not exist any more." Senator Ralph Yarborough (D-TX), meanwhile, fondly recalled "the early days when the will to work and a strong back, or a fertile imagination and a great deal of energy, were all that one needed to get

ahead." Cited in Gareth Davies, *From Opportunity to Entitlement: The Transformation and Decline of Great Society Liberalism* (Lawrence: University Press of Kansas, 1996), 37.

29. *Brown v Board of Education, Topeka* 347 U.S. 483.

30. Bendiner, *Obstacle Course*, 36.

31. Interview with Stewart McClure, Senate Historical Office Oral History Collection, Interview No. 3, January 1, 1983, 76, Manuscript Reading Room, Library of Congress. The reference to NDEA is explained below.

32. Sometimes it also referred more directly to McCarthyite fears about communist penetration of the American education system. See Diane Ravitch, *The Troubled Crusade: American Education, 1945–1980* (New York: Basic Books, 1983), 81–113.

33. Thomas A. Shannon, *The National School Boards Association: Reflections on the Development of an American Idea* (Alexandria, VA: NSBA, 1997), 30. (Shannon was executive secretary of NSBA during the 1970s and 1980s.)

34. Shannon, *National School Boards Association*, 30.

35. Study Committee, *Federal Responsibility in the Field of Education* (Washington, DC: Commission on Intergovernmental Relations, 1955), 8–9, 48–49. The chairman of the study committee was Adam S. Bennion, who was chairman of the Utah Public School Survey Commission. It is likely, though, that the report was prepared by Roger A. Freeman, a leading conservative critic of federal aid, who served as research adviser to the committee. For his other writings on this subject, see Freeman, *Financing the Public Schools* (Washington, DC: Institute for Social Science Research, 1958), and Freeman, *Federal Aid to Education: Boon or Bane?* (Washington, DC: American Enterprise Institute, 1955).

36. In a memo to LBJ aide Bill Moyers, the bureau observed that: "A crisis was forecast in the 1950's in meeting the burdens of the post World War II baby boom; yet State and local governments somehow increased their 1950 school expenditure of $6 billion to $16 billion in 1960 and to $20 billion in 1963. In 1957 a 'shortage' of 336,000 classrooms was announced; after a year the estimate was revised to 159,000 and it has remained at about 125,000 for the past several years; yet classroom construction has approximated 70,000 units annually (despite annual predictions of a reduction)." Cited by Graham, *Uncertain Triumph*, 60.

37. Interview with Stewart McClure, Senate Historical Office Oral History Collection, Interview No. 4, January 28, 1983, pp.110–111, Manuscript Reading Room, Library of Congress. McClure was chief clerk to the Labor and Public Welfare Committee.

38. Gross was by temperament a contrarian and a backbencher, and the same might be said of Hoffman (although, in the case of education politics, his seat on the House Education and Labor Committee gave him a useful base from which to fight federal encroachment). The other three were highly influential individuals: Bridges and Taber were top Republican on their

respective Appropriations committee, and Byrd chaired the Senate Finance committee.

39. See Robert C. Lieberman, *Shifting the Color Line: Race and the American Welfare State* (Cambridge, Mass.: Harvard University Press, 1998); Ira Katznelson, *When Affirmative Action Was White: An Untold History of Racial Inequality in Twentieth-Century America* (New York: Norton, 2005).

40. Of Smith, Patterson observes that "no man was more stridently opposed to the New Deal. A member of the Glass-Byrd machine, he considered himself the true descendant of Thomas Jefferson in the House; indeed, Monticello was in his home district. Safe from defeat at the polls, [he] opposed...almost all ventures of the national government into the social and economic life of the nation." Byrd, meanwhile, opposed the New Deal primarily on economic grounds: "There was no more determined exponent of fiscal orthodoxy," says Patterson. "Affable, soft-spoken, even-tempered, even a little cherubic-looking with his pink complexion and moon-face, he had on the subject of deficit spending the 'peculiar, angry, dry pertinacity more typical of New England than the easy-going South.'" Patterson, *Congressional Conservatism*, 180, 30 (quoting a 1939 Washington *Star* column by Stewart Alsop and Robert Kintner).

41. On the institutional sources of Smith's power, see Richard Bolling, *House Out of Order* (New York: Dutton, 1965). On the broader institutional character of the midcentury Congress, see Julian Zelizer, *On Capitol Hill: The Struggle to Reform Congress and Its Consequences, 1948–2000* (New York: Cambridge University Press, 2004).

42. The Northern Catholics were Thomas P. O'Neill (D-MA), John Delaney (D-N.Y.), and Ray Madden (D-IN). For the role that O'Neill and Delaney played in defeating federal aid in 1961, see Graham, *Uncertain Triumph*. For a recent analysis of the Republican-Southern Democratic alliance, see Nelson Polsby, *How Congress Evolves: Social Bases of Institutional Change* (New York: Oxford University Press, 2004), 8–16.

43. See Sundquist, *Politics and Policy,* 172–3.

44. See, in particular, his remarks at a 1959 cabinet meeting, during which he told colleagues that he had been "dragged into supporting" construction aid, and that he saw it as being part of "a world trend toward socialism." Maybe, though, he mused, "we cannot get out of it. Perhaps we are like the armed guard with rusty armor and a broken sword, standing at the bridge and trying to stop progress." Eisenhower's secretary, Ann Whitman, prepared a transcript of the meeting, and it is partially reproduced in James C. Duram, "'A Good Growl': The Eisenhower Cabinet's January 16, 1959 Discussion of Federal Aid to Education," *Presidential Studies Quarterly*, VIII, 4 (Fall, 1978): 441, 438.

45. Remarks at press conference, July 31, 1957, in *Public Papers of the Presidents: Dwight D. Eisenhower: 1957*, 575 (emphasis added). The administration bill had been presented not as a permanent extension of the federal role, but as a five-year emergency measure.

46. *School Construction in Areas Affected by Federal Activities,* House Report No. 2810, to accompany S.2317, 81ˢᵗ Cong., 2ⁿᵈ sess. (1950), 1.
47. In most states, the bulk of school spending was raised from the property tax.
48. *Federal Assistance for Construction of Public Schools,* Hearings before a Subcommittee of the Committee on Labor and Public Welfare, U.S. Senate, 81ˢᵗ Cong., 1ˢᵗ sess., June 14, 1949, 273–81; *Congressional Record* (August 22, 1950), 13049.
49. The speakers were Rep. Mendel Rivers (D-S.C.), whose district included Charleston Naval Base; Frank Chelf (D-KY), whose district was home to Fort Knox; and Cleveland Bailey (D-W.V.), who was a senior member of the House Education and Labor Committee and principal draftsman of P.L. 815. The second quote comes from *Operating Expenses of School Districts Affected by Federal Activities,* House Report No. 2287, June 20, 1950, 81ˢᵗ Cong., 2ⁿᵈ Sess., to accompany H.R. 7940. The others come from *Congressional Record* (August 22, 1950), 13043, 13045, 13047.
50. The emergency was occasioned by the slower-than-expected pace of postwar reconversion, and the massive Cold War defense buildup that began in 1948. By the time that the House debated impact aid, moreover, the Korean War was just under way.
51. Manion, the former Dean of the Notre Dame Law School, presented a monthly broadcast over the Mutual Broadcasting System, devoted to decrying the socialization of American life. The quote is from the 4ᵗʰ anniversary edition of his newsletter, *Manion Forum* (October, 1948), 4.
52. See Robert Taft's remarks in *Congressional Record* (October 18, 1943), 8424–7. He cited unemployment compensation, agricultural subsidies, and highway construction as other areas where an initial commitment to "home rule" had yielded to central direction. See also the remarks of Sen. Harry F. Byrd (D-Va.), Ibid., April 1, 1948, 3927–9.
53. See the remarks of Senator Edward Martin (R-PA), ibid., March 31, 1948, 3777; also, Byrd, loc. cit.
54. Ibid., July 13, 1950, 10093.
55. Thompson was an influential member of the House Education and Labor Committee. For a candid statement of why he supported impact aid, see *Public Laws 815 and 874, 81ˢᵗ Congress (Administration's Proposal For Modifying Existing Legislation),* Hearings before a Subcommittee of the Committee on Education and Labor, House of Representatives, 86ᵗʰ Cong., 1ˢᵗ sess., on H.R. 7140, June 9, 1959, 13. For Brown, see *Congressional Record* (March 7, 1961), 3380; for Goldwater, see ibid., September 11, 1961, 19055–56.
56. For a summary of these changes, see "Liberalizing Amendments to P.L. 874 and Fiscal Year in Which They Became Effective," attached to Memo, Peter Muirhead to Wilbur Cohen, August 24, 1962, in Papers of Wilbur Cohen, Box 119, State Historical Society of Wisconsin, Madison. For a more detailed account, see I. M. Labovitz, *Aid for Federally Affected Public Schools* (Syracuse, NY: Syracuse University Press, 1963).

57. Elliott was chair of the House Education and Labor Committee's education subcommittee. Post-*Brown,* he—like his fellow Alabamian, Lister Hill—was embattled back home because of his comparative racial liberalism.

58. Interview with Charles W. Radcliffe, Washington, DC, August 8, 2005. (Radcliffe was a congressional relations specialist at HEW during the 1950s.)

59. This and other entertaining incongruities were highlighted by Wayne Morse, *Congressional Record* (September 11, 1961), 18924. By this time, Morse and other liberals were making a strong push for massive, general federal aid and were worried that some colleagues might prefer to expand impact aid again, instead.

60. For one such critique, see Labovitz, *Aid for Federally Affected Public Schools,* 87–88.

61. *Administration of Public Laws 874 and 815: Eleventh Annual Report* (Washington, DC: HEW, 1961), 34–5.

62. Graham, *Uncertain Triumph,* 76. It was proposed that Title I of ESEA would distribute $1 billion in federal funds to almost every school district in the country, dwarfing P. L. 874, which distributed $150 million to about one-third of the districts.

63. See Gareth Davies, *See Government Grow: Education Politics from Johnson to Reagan* (Lawrence: University Press of Kansas, 2007), chap. 2.

64. Whereas House Republicans voted unanimously for the renewal of impact aid in 1961 and 1964, almost 80 percent of them would vote against ESEA.

65. Early in the year, Treasury Secretary George Humphrey predicted a "depression that will curl your hair" unless the federal government curtailed its profligate habits, and observed that there were "a lot of places" in his own budget "that can be cut." House conservatives took up the challenge with relish, forcing through a series of cuts to the Labor-HEW appropriations bill. See Richard Neustadt, *Presidential Power: The Politics of Leadership* (New York: John Wiley, 1961), 67–75, and Richard F. Fenno, *The Power of the Purse: Appropriations Politics in Congress* (Boston: Little, Brown, 1966), 478–87.

66. For a flavor of the reaction, see *The Challenge of the Sputniks,* ed. Richard Witkin (New York: Doubleday, 1958), and the widely noticed series of articles headed, "Crisis in Education," which began in *Life* Magazine on March 24, 1958. The opening story began with a front cover that depicted an earnest, purposeful-looking "Alexei Kutzkov of Moscow" and a relaxed, casual-looking "Stephen Lapekas of Chicago," and went on to feature more "exclusive pictures of a Russian schoolboy and his U.S. counterpart."

67. *Scholarship and Loan Programs,* Hearings before a Subcommittee of the Committee on Education and Labor, House of Representatives, 85th Cong., 1st sess., 972. Admiral Hyman Rickover was head of the Division of Reactor Development at the Atomic Energy Commission.

68. On Progressive Education, and the reaction against it, see Ravitch, *Troubled Crusade,* chap. 2.

69. *Scholarship and Loan Programs,* 293, 300, 301.

70. Ibid., 1498, 1501, 1525.

71. McClure OH No. 4, 116–7.

72. Support for recommital was especially strong among Midwestern Republicans: 6 of the 7 GOP congressmen from Illinois voted to kill the bill, while the figures for other states in the region included: Indiana, 9 of 9; Iowa, 6 of 7; Nebraska, 4 of 4; Ohio, 15 of 17.

73. *National Defense Education Act of 1958*, Senate Report No. 2242, August 8, 1958, on S. 4237, 55.

74. See Nancy Diamond and Hugh Davis Graham, *The Rise of American Research Universities: Elites and Challengers in the Post War Era* (Baltimore: Johns Hopkins University Press, 1997).

75. Remarks at NDEA signing ceremony, February 9, 1959, *Public Papers: Eisenhower: 1958*, 243.

76. *Amendments to National Defense Education Act and Impacted Areas Legislation*, Senate Report No. 1275, July 31, 1964, to accompany S. 3060, 10.

77. *National Defense Education Act Amendments, 1964*, House Report No. 1639, July 30, 1964, to accompany H.R. 11904, 56.

78. For a helpful analysis of these approaches to APD, see Brian J. Glenn, "The Two Schools of American Political Development," *Political Studies Review* 2 (2004): 153–65.

79. Davies, *See Government Grow*.

80. Keppel, LBJL OH, 13.

PART II


The Great Society to 1980

# CHAPTER 4

## Environmental Policy from the Great Society to 1980: A Coalition Comes Unglued

*Richard Harris*

Environmentalism burst upon the American political landscape in the late 1960s, posing a new and straightforward
challenge to an emerging conservative consensus. Drawing their intellectual
sustenance from the civil rights and antiwar movements, environmentalists
had far loftier ambitions than those of the conservation advocates involved
in Marc Eisner's narrative of postwar natural resource policy. Animated by a
New Left critique that viewed New Deal liberals and Eisenhower Republicans alike as in league with an almost omnipotent corporate establishment,
they saw environmental degradation as perhaps the ultimate indictment of
a soul-crushing and materialistic American economy. For environmental
activists, saving the planet required not merely preservation of natural beauty
and resources, but a radical reorientation of values from individualism and
subordination of nature to collectivism and harmony with nature. Moreover,
their political analysis required not merely fighting for stronger regulations to

protect the environment, but a radical reorientation of policy-making institutions from a pluralistic system hospitable to corporate influence to a more open and directly participatory one.

Predictably, the challenge of environmentalism evoked a strong reaction from conservatives and their business allies in the 1970s. Despite their indignation, however, they failed to halt the enactment of environmentalist policies that imposed billions of dollars of compliance costs or the creation of new regulatory institutions that altered the role of the courts and administrative agencies in the policy process. The astonishing success achieved by environmental advocates in remaking the regulatory regime would set the stage for the "Reagan Revolution" and its program of "regulatory relief" that Judith Layzer takes up in the following chapter. The Reagan Revolution was, therefore, as much a response to the new regulatory ideas and institutions implanted by environmentalism as it was a reaction to the measurable burdens new environmental policies placed on the economy and on business. Insofar as environmentalism was a program designed to infuse the policy process with the values of participatory democracy, collectivism, and post-materialism, conservatives were impelled to confront environmentalists ideologically as well as politically.

By the time of Ronald Reagan's election in 1980, environmental policy had become a salient liberal-conservative fault line defining American politics, and Reagan's promise of "relief" from environmental regulation generated enthusiastic support from business interests that had been on the defensive ever since Earth Day in 1969. At one level, this observation seems unremarkable. Between 1969 and 1977, Congress enacted no fewer than 18 major pieces of legislation aimed, in one way or another, at conservation and pollution control.[1] This tide of legislative activity imposed significant regulatory costs and established a number of new government agencies to oversee business compliance: predictably, the National Association of Manufacturers (NAM), the U.S. Chamber of Commerce, and countless industry lobby groups and individual firms reacted with strident resistance. This negative business response received academic support in the late 1970s as economists' and policy analysts' critiques questioned environmental regulation in terms of cost-benefit and efficacy criteria. What could be more natural than business interests finding common cause with a conservative presidential candidate in opposition to intrusive new regulation and in regaining the initiative from liberal politicians and environmental advocates?

At a deeper level, however, Reagan's animus toward environmental regulation was rooted in core precepts of post–World War II conservatism in America that were in sharp conflict with environmental principles. In particular, environmentalists' implicit, and at times explicit, advocacy of collective values and planning posed a direct challenge to conservatives' commitment to

individual freedom and property rights. This underlying philosophical fric-
tion was exacerbated by the environmentalist movement, which advanced its
policy objectives under the banner of a more fundamental critique aimed at
institutional transformation of the policy process. As Bruce Ackerman and
William Hassler observed,

> The passions of Earth Day have marked our law in deep and abiding
> ways. Statutes passed in the early 1970s did more than commit
> billion of dollars to the cause of environmental protection in the
> decades ahead. They also represent part of a complex effort by which
> the present generation is revising the system of administrative law
> inherited from the New Deal.[2]

Thus, the environmentalists of the 1970s, like advocates of other new social
regulations, from consumer protection to affirmative action, had concluded
that the "privileged position of business" necessitated a thorough remaking
of the policy process if reform objectives were to be secured.[3] They not only
shifted attention from the traditional regulatory focus on particular markets
(e.g., securities, banking, railroads, or communications) to broader, postma-
terialist quality-of-life concerns, but also sought to make the policy process
more hospitable to public interest groups and less susceptible to industry
capture and business dominance.

In the postwar period, historians, sociologists, and political scientists taught
environmentalists that despite a half century of reform, beginning with the
Progressive Era and culminating in the New Deal, the public interest had
really made little headway in its struggle with business interests and corporate
power. America was portrayed as under the sway of a power elite that, according to revisionist historians and radical sociologists, ensured business dominance of American politics and public policy through its ultimate control of
the legislative processes and its occupation of interlocking directorates.[4] For
their part, political scientists showed that the administrative institutions that
Progressive and New Deal reformers had constructed to regulate business in
fact created a symbiotic relationship between regulators and the regulated,
presided over by senior legislators such that industry capture of regulatory
agencies was the logical result. They also asserted that those same institutions
raised barriers to meaningful participation that business rather than the public was best equipped to surmount.

Environmentalism, born in the milieu of activism and protest during
the 1960s, accepted this critique and aimed not only to save the ecosystem
but also to open up administrative and policy processes to more democratic
impulses that proved hostile to individualism, liberty, and property rights.
For conservatives like Reagan, the fundamental challenge of environmental

policy therefore lay not in business complaints about rising compliance costs or economists' concern about market inefficiency, but in its animating ideas and its institutional objectives. It is important to understand that these challenges were born, not of the older conservationist policies that many conservatives could support, but rather of the post-1970 variant of environmental policy that sought to democratize the policy process and supplant individualism and liberty with collectivism and planning. An effective response would require a conservative counterrevolution in the policy process that directly addressed the ideational and institutional bases of environmental policy.

That response would flow from the confluence of three distinct streams of conservative thought: *libertarianism, traditionalism,* and *anticommunism.* The discussion below describes how the fusion of these distinct elements of postwar conservative thought formed the basis for a vigorous and visceral conservative reaction of environmentalist programs. With a clear understanding of the intrinsic conflict between environmentalism and conservatism as a foundation, we will turn to an appraisal of two landmark pieces of environmental legislation of the 1970s, the Surface Mining Control and Reclamation Act of 1977 (SMCRA) and the Clean Air Amendments Act of 1977 (CAAA), both of which clearly illustrate the ideational and institutional challenges that environmental policy posed for conservatives.

## Conservative Intellectual "Fusion"

While the seeds of conflict between environmentalism and conservatism were sown in the triumph of modern liberalism, the conflict only came to full flower when environmentalism turned from the effort, championed by Theodore Roosevelt and Gifford Pinchot, to preserve our natural heritage to a project aimed at altering the exercise of influence in public policy and well-established American values. The implacable opposition of conservatism toward environmentalism was unmistakable by the mid-1970s. Explaining why anti-environmentalism became a defining characteristic of the conservative movement, however, requires a clear understanding of the precise makeup of postwar conservatives' ideas as well as an appreciation of those underlying the environmentalist challenge. We turn first to the conservatives.

As Marc Eisner intimates in chapter 1, the ideological divide on regulation in general, and on environmental regulation in particular, can be traced to a post–World War II coalescence of libertarian and traditional conservatism formed around a common animus toward the New Deal and its practical manifestation, the administrative state. Yet the intellectual history of this period also demonstrates that a third philosophical position, namely the anticommunism championed by James Burnham and Frank Chodorov, was paramount in uniting traditionalist followers of Russell Kirk and Richard Weaver with the libertarian followers of Ludwig von Mises and Fredrich Hayek. If libertarian and traditionalist thought stood as two distinct elements bonded together to form conservatism, the catalyst for this chemical reaction was undoubtedly anticommunism. The postwar conservative angst over Soviet and, later, Chinese expansion tended to overwhelm any philosophical tensions between libertarians' commitment to rationality and individual freedom on the one hand and traditionalists' commitment to transcendent principles of virtue and the need for social order on the other. Although the individualism of libertarians and the opposition to moral relativism of traditionalists seeded the tension between conservatism and environmentalism, it was the anticommunist strain of conservative thought that animated their deeper hostility to environmentalism. Conservatives, already alert to perceived socialist tendencies of modern liberalism, found a deeply disturbing confirmation of their fears in environmentalists' vision, rooted in collectivist arguments about the need to subordinate property rights and individual freedom to societal needs and ecological laws. The conservative suspicion of environmentalism as a particularly virulent manifestation of socialist tendencies seemed all the more plausible given its direct linkages with 1960s-style New Left radicalism.

As early as 1947, conservatives articulated their fear of Western societies retreating from the challenge of collectivism. The Declaration of Principles issued at the formation of the Mont Pélerin Society avers that:

> The central values of civilization are in danger.... The position of the individual and the voluntary group are progressively undermined by extensions of arbitrary power.... Even the most precious possession of Western Man, freedom of thought and expression is threatened by the spread of creeds which...seek only to establish a position of power in which they can suppress and obliterate all views but their own.[5]

These fears definitely informed the anti-environmentalism of the conservative movement. Environmental policy, more than any other area of the new social regulation introduced in the Great Society and its aftermath, became a lightning rod for conservative reaction because environmentalists had, to use the terminology of the Mont Pélerin Society, introduced a "creed," established their own position of power in policy subgovernments, and, through the federal courts, sought to "obliterate all views but their own." As deep as the philosophical divisions ran and as sharp as the debates between the libertarian and traditional conservatives were, the two schools' common apprehension of collectivism, manifest in both the modern liberal administrative state and communist expansion, provided a powerful incentive to work out a coherent position from which to oppose such challenges.

The central figure in forging a coherent conservative message was Frank S. Meyer. Like many intellectual leaders of the postwar conservative movement, Meyer was a former socialist. Indeed, he was a loyal member of the Communist Party in the 1930s who ultimately rejected the oppression and statism he came to see as the inevitable logic of the Left. In his treatise, *In Defense of Freedom,* Meyer insisted that using state power to promote virtue was both wrongheaded and romantic. "Unless men are free to be vicious they cannot be virtuous."[6] Nevertheless, as adamant as he was that true conservatives could never advocate employing the state to promote public morality (as environmentalists clearly advocate), he was equally uncomfortable with the perceived moral relativism that Dewey, Holmes, and their modern liberal disciples promoted. What Meyer sought, perhaps quixotically, was a position in which universal moral principles were rooted in a rational analytic defense of freedom rather than in metaphysical arguments for public virtue backed by police power. It was precisely this objective that he maintained could integrate the philosophical positions of the libertarian, traditional, and anticommunist strains of conservative movement.

According to Meyer, conservatives believed, above all, that individual human beings were the basis of any desirable social or political order, and that society was organized to promote their freedom and well-being. He contended that all conservatives understood that freedom and individual responsibility defined human beings as human beings, distinguished them as more than merely another species occupying a niche on planet earth. Freedom thus was inherent in the human condition, not simply a value to be supported by a utilitarian calculus. This understanding was the basis, he claimed, for libertarians, traditionalists, and anticommunists to oppose social engineering in whatever guise and however well-intentioned. Communism, socialism, and the welfare state, as well as post-1970 environmentalism, all undermined the dignity and freedom of human beings, even if they varied in the degree of their overt intrusiveness on the individual. Meyer also discerned that a coherent conservatism rejected cultural relativism and embraced a set of universal principles, including the rule of law, private property as a bulwark against the state, and Judeo-Christian morality. The sanctity of property and the centrality of man to a definition of civilization inherent in Judeo-Christian theology, as I demonstrate below, were principles strongly contested by environmental advocates. Conservatives, in Meyer's estimation, were unified perhaps above all else in their implacable opposition to international communism. Beyond an abstract hostility to core values of Western civilization, communism trampled on the rights of millions of individuals living behind the iron curtain.[7]

Meyer's fusionism did take hold, if for no other reason than the over-whelming reality of the threats that conservatives of all persuasions perceived: the unchecked expansion of a centralized administrative state; the attacks on private property in the cause of unconstrained egalitarianism; and the ineffec-tual American response to communist expansion. By 1964, all of these appar-ent challenges impelled conservatives to adopt Meyer's fusion thesis, even if they did not do so with complete enthusiasm. Barry Goldwater's candidacy, moreover, stood as a testament to the practical application of fusionism.

Ronald Reagan's nominating speech at the 1964 Republican Convention in San Francisco reads as a tribute to fusionism. In tracing the lineage of con-servative thought, it is worth quoting this speech at some length, for it serves as a bridge between the intellectual development of postwar conservatism and the beginnings of its practical adaptation to politics and policy. The most basic tenet of fusionism, a conviction that freedom is inherent in the human condition, runs throughout Reagan's speech:

> You and I are told increasingly that we have to choose between a left
> or right, but I would like to suggest that there is no such thing
> as a left or right. *There is only an up or down—up to a man's age-old*
> *dream, the ultimate in individual freedom consistent with law and*
> *order—or down to the ant heap totalitarianism, and regardless of*
> *their sincerity, their humanitarian motives, those who would trade*
> *our freedom for security have embarked on this downward course...*
> Senator Clark of Pennsylvania, another articulate spokesman, defines
> liberalism as "meeting the material needs of the masses through
> the full power of centralized government." Well, I for one resent it
> when a representative of the people refers to you and me—the free
> man and woman of this country—as "the masses." This is a term we
> haven't applied to ourselves in America. However, beyond that, "the
> full power of centralized government"—this was the very thing the
> Founding Fathers sought to minimize. They knew that governments
> don't control things. A government can't control the economy without
> controlling people. In addition, they know when a government sets
> out to do that; it must use force and coercion to achieve its purpose.[8]

The centrality of freedom to man's humanity is readily apparent, as is its connection with the Constitution and the original intent of the Founders. As Reagan announced these key components of fusionist conservatism, the quarrels between libertarians and traditionalists seemed small and irrelevant.

No less apparent in Reagan's rhetoric were the universal principles Meyer associated with conservatism. With respect to rule of law and private prop-erty, Reagan was direct and unapologetic in identifying modern liberalism as a threat to these core American values. More than liberals' record of advocating ever-increasing state power at the expense of individual freedom, the problem with liberalism was its real impacts on the institutions of property and rule of law:

> Now it doesn't require expropriation or confiscation of private property or business to impose socialism on a people. *What does it mean whether you hold the deed or the title to your business or property if the government holds the power of life and death over that business or property?*[9]

Neither Milton Friedman nor William Buckley could find much to quibble with in these sentiments. Reagan was offering a clarion message that "fused" essential elements of libertarian, traditionalist, and anticommunist thought. His message, that the modern liberal project of constructing a strong state to protect an ever-expanding list of "rights," posed a fundamental threat to our core political values, also proved effective in attacking the command and control regulation as well as the collectivist values that underlay environmental policy. We turn now to an examination of the environmentalist movement and an exploration of why its views aroused such a strident conservative response.

## The Environmentalist Challenge

The advent of extensive environmental regulation in the 1970s posed a multidimensional challenge for conservatism. In a very basic sense, the myriad environmental laws enacted after 1970 imposed tremendous regulatory burdens on business enterprise that could limit economic growth and investment at the macro level and impinge on managerial discretion at the micro level. From a partisan, political perspective, it was obvious that conservative business interests would be spurred to action. However, for conservatism, contemporary environmental policy constituted a double-edged sword. In addition to transferring wealth from the private to the public sector and swelling the size of federal bureaucracy (the classic conservatives' complaints about modern liberalism), the new environmental laws had, in their view, institutionally remade the policy process to promote an ideologically radical critique of American capitalism as well as an assault on core values of individual freedom and private property. This dual nature of the environmentalist challenge suggests a strong basis for the conservative countermobilization that helps to account for the advent of the Reagan Revolution taken up by Judith Layzer in the next chapter. Both the cost of environmental regulation and the ideational/institutional challenges of environmentalism help to explain the centrality of anti-environmentalism in the modern conservative movement.

In a widely publicized study, Murray Weidenbaum and Robert DeFina claimed that by 1976 environmental and energy-related regulation was costing $8.372 billion annually, far more than the $6.610 billion and $4.498 billion attributable to consumer protection and worker safety, respectively.[10] A few years later, the Business Roundtable released a study it had commissioned from the accounting firm of Arthur Anderson that analyzed social regulatory compliance cost impacts of the Environmental Protection Agency (EPA), the Occupational Safety and Health Administration (OSHA) and the Federal Trade Commission (FTC) on the top 48 U.S. corporations in 1978. The findings revealed that EPA imposed $2.018 billion, while OSHA accounted for $217 million and the FTC $26 million.[11] Moreover, studies by students of the policy process showed that environmental regulation significantly affected business behavior, not only by imposing higher costs, which might be justified by externality arguments or by the value of social benefits identified, but also by inflexible implementation that was driven more by compliance procedures than policy outcomes.[12] These claims about the economic impacts of new social regulation, and environmental measures in particular, were amplified by the energy crisis and cost push inflation of the late 1970s that focused attention on the macroeconomic impacts of environmental policy. Even under the Carter administration, the EPA was beginning to examine alternatives to the standard command/control approach to regulation that liberal as well as conservative economists attacked as inefficient and anticompetitive. With respect to air pollution control, for example, emissions trading programs sought to adopt more efficient, marketlike approaches to environmental regulation. As interesting as these measures were, they constituted reform efforts intended to make environmental regulation more "rational"; they did not attack the ideational or institutional bases of environmental policy.

While conservatives agreed that environmental regulation imposed unacceptable financial costs and inefficiencies on business and on society, they pressed for a more aggressive and more fundamental response than Democratic reformers were willing to pursue. This aggressive posture, revealed in Ronald Reagan's eschewing the concept of "regulatory reform" for the more confrontational concept of "regulatory relief," reflected the conviction that environmentalism posed a more fundamental challenge. Conservatives viewed the environmental movement as a small, ideologically motivated elite that had foisted its collectivist worldview and no-growth vision of ecology on the American people at the expense of freedom, prosperity, and energy security. More worrisome to conservatives, environmentalist organizations appeared to subvert democratic processes and the rule of law by establishing an undue and unhealthy influence within regulatory agencies such as the

Environmental Protection Agency (EPA) or Department of the Interior (DOI). As Jeffrey Berry noted in his path-breaking study of public interest groups, they had ushered in an essentially new regulatory regime.

> These organizations are slowly changing the overall environment within which government officials formulate public policy...public interest groups have been consistent and enduring actors, aggressively trying to influence governmental decision makers.... The opinions they can arouse, the bad publicity they can generate, the lawsuits they can file are all factors relevant to the deliberations of those who must make policy decisions.[13]

In addition, by transforming the courts into agents of policymaking and implementation, as one conservative critic put it, the courts had become, "full managing partners in the administrative state."[14]

The accomplishments of this regulatory regime transformation appear remarkable, given the broad academic consensus at the end of the 1960s that business interests held sway in the policy process generally, and most particularly in rule making and administrative procedure.[15] In spite of this scholarly agreement, or rather based on their appreciation of the scholarship, environmental advocates succeeded in establishing myriad programs that not only imposed significant costs on business but also essentially remade the American regulatory process into one that conservatives deemed deeply threatening.[16]

The conservative reaction to environmental regulation, moreover, reflected all three elements of fusionism—libertarianism, traditionalism, and anticommunism—at least in its broad, antistatist guise. Environmental policy aroused libertarians by challenging the morality of the market, interposing bureaucratic analysis for managerial prerogative, and saddling the economy with unjustifiably high regulatory costs. It aroused traditionalists by challenging the very concept of private property and substituting judicial policy making for the representative functions of Congress. Finally, it aroused antistatists by challenging freedom and individualism with a collectivist New Left vision of society in which ecological principles trumped individual rights and in which natural law would be subordinated to the laws of nature—as articulated by environmental activists.

The first Earth Day in 1969 proclaimed a new environmentalist order with a manifesto, *The Declaration of Interdependence*, which asserted:

> Nature has instituted certain principles for the sustenance of all species, deriving these principles from the planet's life support system...whenever any behavior by the members of any one species

becomes destructive of these principles, it is the function of the other members of that species to alter or abolish such behaviors and to reestablish the theme of interdependence of all life . . . cultural values long established should not be altered for light and transient causes, that man is more disposed to suffer from its asserting a vain notion of independence than to right themselves by abolishing that culture to which they are now accustomed.[17]

These assertions left no doubt that the core values of environmentalism challenged individualism and traditional concepts of freedom or that environmentalists, the "other members of that species," arrogated to themselves the right to determine what behavior and culture were legitimate. Most importantly, though, the Earth Day manifesto rejected universal principles of private property and rule of law in favor of a collectivist, statist vision of the future. Indeed, Mary Douglas and Aaron Wildavsky argued that only an anthropological analysis could explain environmentalism, since it challenged the cultural bases of American society.[18]

Congressional testimony of environmental organizations that had become fixtures in the Washington policy community reinforced the perception that environmental policy was rooted in a public philosophy at odds with core conservative values. Speaking before Henry Reuss's (D-WI) Subcommittee on Conservation and Natural Resources, David Brower, president of Friends of the Earth, called for the 1970s to be a "decade of renunciation" in which Americans would abandon their "cowboy economy," which was incompatible with existence on "spaceship earth."[19] Even more chilling for conservatives was the view expressed by Garrett de Bell, director of Zero Population Growth:

> To get at the root of our problem [the environmental crisis], the goal of production and consumption for its own sake must be changed . . . We can put the highway people and the detergent industry out of business if we just don't buy their products. We can adopt life-styles that require less material goods and leave us more time for enjoyment.[20]

The conservative response ultimately articulated by President Reagan in 1980 was aimed at confronting this ideological and cultural challenge posed by environmentalism as much as it was aimed at easing the regulatory burden of environmental policy.

While one may disagree with the depth of dangers that Reagan and his conservative fellow travelers diagnosed, an honest analysis of environmentalism and its impact on federal regulation suggests that many environmentalists harbored a deep suspicion not only of the established liberal policy processes developed under the New Deal, but also of the capitalist system FDR had sought to make more human. Environmentalists' values clearly clashed with those of free enterprise, and environmental advocates viewed the regulatory institutions constructed in earlier periods as a democratic sham, a view that grew out of the New Left philosophy and the movement politics of the 1960s.[21] Environmentalists, therefore, demanded both policy changes to protect the American people from the ecological degradation and negative public health effects of a market economy and process changes to protect them from corporate power. Conservatives, for their part, saw that environmental policy was part of that "broader effort," as Ackerman and Hassler put it, to impose new regulatory ideas and to reconstruct administrative institutions. Environmentalists "recognized" that the New Deal formula of passing laws and creating agencies to implement them left the critical policy space of implementation open to excessive business influence, and accordingly proposed to democratize administrative decision making. Their misgivings about the New Deal regulatory model naturally drew environmental organizations to the New Left concepts of participatory democracy, procedures, and institutional mechanisms to assure a genuine voice for citizens throughout the policy process.

The animating idea for New Left critics was that American democracy had been supplanted by corporate liberalism, a big government–big business condominium that morphed from the New Deal effort to control "economic royalists" into a policy system that systematically catered to organized corporate interests and excluded citizens. Accordingly, public interest groups, including environmental lobby groups, organized to provide a measure of countervailing power to the organized corporate interests the New Left decried. To be sure, the Natural Resources Defense Council (NRDC) and Sierra Club were a far cry from community action projects organized by the Student Nonviolent Coordinating Committee (SNCC) and Students for a Democratic Society (SDS)—though Green Peace and the Friends of the Earth certainly employed the concept of direct action pioneered by the New Left. Nevertheless, environmental leaders clearly saw their groups as consistent with the objectives of participatory democracy. A director of litigation for Public Citizen, Alan Morrison, saw in his work a strong "democratic participatory aspect" of public interest activity: "A framework was established *in which people other than industry have a significant role to play,* and this is not only true in regulatory agencies, but also in terms of going to court to assure compliance with the law...In the mid-sixties, agencies could do anything not strictly prohibited by law."[22] In words strikingly similar to New Left calls for participatory democracy, Daniel Becker, the legislative affairs director for Environmental Action (EA), explained that:

One of the most significant achievements brought about by the
public interest groups has been the development of the grass roots...
EA is concerned with how to get people involved in the movement
and to learn how to help themselves, *equipping local citizens to
protect their interests against corporate power.*[23]

Environmental advocates such as Morrison and Becker, with their emphasis on the
use of the courts as a means of enforcing regulatory laws, posed a double challenge
to conservatives. Not only did they promote regulation that conservatives saw as
undermining property rights and the free market, but they also used the rule-
making process and administrative law to enlist federal courts in the enforcement
of regulation and the obstruction of development projects and economic growth.
This approach was especially objectionable to conservatives because it interposed
the judicial branch in a decisive policy-making and policy-implementation role, in
direct conflict with what they held to be its original constitutional responsibilities.

The central importance, for environmentalists, of changing decision-
making processes in our regulatory regime is suggested by the fact that perhaps their most significant achievement was the enactment of the National
Environmental Policy Act (NEPA), a procedural law. Passed in 1970, NEPA
was the inaugural piece of modern environmentalist legislation and articulated the essential principles of environmentalism that galvanized conservative opposition by the end of the decade. Moreover, it fundamentally changed
the way the federal government did business, explicitly embedding environmental considerations in all federal activities and requiring a documentary
and evidentiary trail for all decisions that environmental activists could follow to hold businesses and regulatory agencies accountable. Reflecting the
notion of interdependence expressed in the Earth Day Declaration, NEPA's
statement of basis and purpose acknowledged "the profound impact of man's
activity on the interrelations of all components of the natural environment,"
and declared it to be federal policy to "create and maintain conditions under
which man and nature can exist in productive harmony."[24] The most far-
reaching effect of NEPA, however, was section 102-c, its requirement for
environmental impact statements. This section directs all federal agencies to:

C) Include in every recommendation or report on proposals for
legislation and other major Federal actions significantly affecting
the quality of the human environment, a detailed statement by the
responsible official on—

(i)   the environmental impact of the proposed action,
(ii)  any adverse environmental effects which cannot be avoided should
      the proposal be implemented,

(iii)   alternatives to the proposed action,

(iv)   the relationship between local short-term uses of man's environment and the maintenance and enhancement of long-term productivity, and

(v)   any irreversible and irretrievable commitments of resources which would be involved in the proposed action should it be implemented.

At a stroke, this provision established a basis for federal environmental review of all laws and projects with any federal involvement. In practice, section 102-c also imposed significant costs in terms of the time value for environmental impact statement (EIS) preparation and the actual dollar outlays for these reports. More importantly, EISs provided both a means of engaging environmental organizations in the approval of projects and a paper trail that environmental lawyers like Alan Morrison could bring to court to monitor performance in the name of the public. Once in court, the EIS record provided a basis for public interest groups to participate more effectively in the implementation process. Even though the courts themselves are hardly a democratic arena, judicial review of administrative action and corporate compliance proved to be a most effective weapon in the environmental organizations' arsenal for blasting open the insular politics of subgovernments.

An interesting, albeit contemporary, example of how far-reaching NEPA's effect could be is the use of its EIS requirement in the context of contesting implementation of the North American Free Trade Agreement (NAFTA). Ralph Nader's public interest group, Public Citizen, led a challenge to NAFTA, contending that the Federal Motor Carrier Safety Administration (FMCSA), a bureau in the Department of Transportation, was required under NEPA to develop an EIS, particularly with respect to potential effects on air quality, in order to open up the United States market to Mexican trucking firms. FMCSA contended that an environmental assessment (EA), a far less thorough evaluation tool, would suffice, and the agency prepared to issue a "Finding of No Significant Impact" (FONSI) to implement NAFTA with respect to the trucking industry. Public Citizen, joined by the International Brotherhood of Teamsters, the California Labor Federation, the Environmental Law Foundation, the NRDC, and the Planning and Conservation League, employed NEPA to challenge this action in court. The Ninth Circuit Court ruled in *DOT v. Public Citizen*[25] that, in refusing to require an EIS, the FMCSA had acted in an "arbitrary and capricious" manner, thereby violating the rule-making standard of the Administrative Procedures Act. Although the Supreme Court ultimately granted DOT a *writ of certiorari* and reversed the decision, the case demonstrates the significance of NEPA in providing access to administrative decision making, even in the area of international trade.

Following the enactment of NEPA, environmental laws, including the 1977 Clean Air Amendments Act and the 1977 Surface Mining Control and Reclamation Act, not only mandated extensive new environmental protection policies but also reinforced the role of public interest and environmental activists in the regulatory process. The new laws, which are examined below in more detail, included provisions that expanded efforts to counter the influence of business interests and advance the goals of participatory democracy. Most notably, these and other environmental measures enacted in the 1970s mandated public permitting processes that required projects—ranging from highway and power plant construction to the opening of surface mines or logging operations—to provide opportunities for public interest group participation. These permitting requirements are very precise about where and how frequently notice of public hearings had to be provided. They maximize the prospects for citizens affected by projects to have their voices heard, on the record, thereby providing official documentation that could be useful in Congress, in regulatory agencies, and in court. Environmental laws also granted, in some instances, automatic standing to sue to "interested parties," thereby facilitating lawsuits by which environmentalists could intervene in regulatory approvals or challenge implementation even if they did not have a direct economic interest. Perhaps most galling to many conservatives, court decisions appeared to incentivize public interest lawyers by providing for their recovery of fees in successful lawsuits against regulated firms. As Dick Ayers, a lawyer with the NRDC explained, the courts were a key to environmental organizations providing a counterweight to industry influence:

> The basic formula for public interest activity is for the public to form a balance against industry. In the past, business had the advantage in administrative settings, but now the courts are a lever against the agencies...I live in terror of the present [Supreme] Court shutting down the avenue of litigation as a means of asserting balance in the administrative process.[26]

Ayers, a graduate of Yale Law School in the late 1960s, explained how he and a few dedicated young environmental activists launched the NRDC with seed money and continued early support from the Ford Foundation. Their intent was to leverage their legal expertise to create a channel for citizens' voices to be heard in the implementation of environmental regulation. As the Ford Foundation proclaims in its mission statement:

> The fundamental challenge facing every society is to create political, economic and social systems that promote peace, human welfare and the sustainability of the environment on which life depends. *We*

*believe that the best way to meet this challenge is to encourage initiatives*
*by those living and working closest to where problems are located;* to
promote collaboration among the nonprofit, government and business
sectors; and to ensure participation by men and women from diverse
communities and at all levels of society.[27]

This view reflects one of the key messages of the New Left critique, that
success in getting a set of issues on the national agenda, or even enacting
landmark legislation, was no guarantee of achieving one's aims unless people
directly affected by policy choices had a seat at the table and a voice when
decisions were made. For environmental policy, Ford's support of the NRDC
and other organizations was intended to level the policy playing field by guaranteeing that, when it came time to write regulations and oversee their execu-
tion, competent challenges to business interests could be made—in court, if
necessary. In a legal venue, a few good environmental lawyers could have a
more predictable impact on regulatory implementation than environmental
organizations participating in electoral or congressional politics, where business held sway through campaign contributions and organizational resources.
This perceived business dominance, echoing the academic and ideological
critiques that shaped environmentalism, provided a powerful populist rhetorical resource for environmentalists. Business leaders and conservatives, for
their part, correctly perceived that the environmentalist narrative had moved
considerably beyond the New Deal project of saving capitalism from its own
excesses and providing a helping hand to the forgotten man. It had become
a frontal attack on capitalist culture and the standing of corporations in
American society.

When environmental protection emerged on the national agenda in the
late 1960s, it did so in the context of a particular policy narrative that made
the rhetorical case for action.[28] The narrative, developed by environmental
advocates, wove time-honored egalitarian arguments about business dominance and citizen disenfranchisement, albeit recast in a distinctly New Left
motif, with the classic Progressive approach of compiling data about the social
and public health effects of business practice, especially the effects on children
and the aged. As it had in the opening decades of the twentieth century, this
narrative provided a potent set of arguments for major legislative and judicial
action. Its potency was enhanced by the introduction of modern epidemiological analyses as well as scientific and engineering studies that highlighted
risks to humans and endangered species. By focusing the public's attention
on how corporate behavior undermined our "rights" to clean air and clean
water and by emphasizing the particular vulnerabilities of the very young and
the very old to environment-based cancers and respiratory diseases, public
interest advocates were able to mobilize voters and financial supporters (both

individuals and foundations). This message resonated very well politically because the public perceived that measures to protect the environment would force corporations to be "socially responsible" by complying with new programs that guaranteed a healthy environment and would create new government agencies to guarantee environmental rights for all citizens. Moreover, environmentalists proved especially adroit at using the media, particularly television and film, to dramatize the ecological and, more importantly, health effects of irresponsible business behavior or lax government regulation. For example, *In Our Water,* a classic environmental advocacy film funded by the Geraldine R. Dodge Foundation, portrayed the plight of several New Jersey residents who lived adjacent to a landfill that was leaching toxic pollutants into their well water.[29] The film effectively shows crops devastated by irrigation from the polluted wells, discolored tap water in family kitchens, and interviews with parents of sickly children. The film strikingly juxtaposed these images with scenes of state and local regulators providing bureaucratic justifications for why they could do nothing to alleviate an unconscionable situation and with interviews of corporate officers of the landfill denying that there is any "scientific" proof of a problem. As effective as such documentaries were, their political impact paled in comparison to evening news stories about asthma, emphysema, carcinogens in food and water supplies, and airborne toxins, or Hollywood films such as the *China Syndrome* that depicted how corporate interests, in their immoral pursuit of profit, were only too willing to expose ordinary people to life-threatening risk. In the face of this policy narrative, business complaints about regulatory burdens or conservative admonitions about substituting judicial activism for congressional deliberation appeared self-centered and small-minded.

A particularly telling indicator of the success environmentalists had in winning the hearts and minds of the public was the consistent appearance of environmental protection at the top of surveys asking which policies citizens would be willing to fund. A recent survey of public opinion polling on environmental issues from the early seventies to the present asserted that, "public awareness of environmental problems and support for environmental protection is higher now than in the early 1970s. Since most problems fade from the public agenda rather quickly, the persistence and recent renewal of environmental concern might be termed the second miracle" of public opinion.[30] According to the Gallup Organization, in March of 1970, 63 percent of Americans polled (compared to 79 percent in 1990) answered "yes" to the question, "Would you be willing to pay the slightly higher prices for your goods and services business would have to charge to control pollution?" The same study also reports an NBC/*Wall Street Journal* poll that tracked Americans' responses to the question, "Which do you think is more important: Protecting the environment or keeping prices down?" The results show that from 1975 through 1981, a period of severe stagflation, over 50 percent consistently thought protecting the environment was more important (note: the figure jumped to 80 percent in 1990). In this political setting, debates about environmental policy took shape, not around *whether* the federal government should protect the environment (and public health), but around *how extensive* those efforts should be.

Clearly, by the end of the decade of the 1970s, environmentalists had accomplished a remarkable reversal of political fortunes *vis a vis* conservatives and business interests. In the period from the first Earth Day to the presidential election of 1980, the environmental movement created new federal agencies, the Council on Environmental Quality (CEQ), EPA, and the Office of Surface Mining (OSM), enacted landmark legislation that established not only new policy mandates but also new policy processes, mobilized millions of citizens, organized new interest groups, and raised millions of dollars in support of their agenda. Their success was predicated on a challenge to traditional ideas of individual freedom and private property as well as a critique of traditional institutions of policy making. Their extraordinary accomplishments present what might be termed the enigma of environmentalism: How can we explain not only their initial victories but also their sustained success in Congress and the courts over the money and organizational capacities of purportedly dominant business interests as well as the determination of an aroused conservative opposition? The following policy cases of the Surface Mining Control and Reclamation Act (SMCRA) and the Clean Air Amendments Act will demonstrate how the ideas of environmentalism combined with institutional and process changes to establish a beachhead for environmental programs. These cases will also show how that beachhead was subsequently solidified to a genuine occupation of the policy-making apparatus such that conservative opposition might win specific battles, but would never dislodge environmentalism.

## Environmental Regulation in Practice: SMCRA and the CAAA

When Reagan used his 1980 inaugural address to characterize environmentalists as "obstructionists" and a "tiny minority," he gave voice to the widespread belief among conservatives that modern environmental policy posed not only an immediate economic challenge but also, and more importantly, a threat to the core ideas and institutions that defined American political culture. As Reagan prepared to meet the environmentalist challenge, he and his supporters faced a stern test. At the end of the 1960s a student of American politics would have been hard-pressed to predict that by the middle of the next decade environmentalists would have overcome the well-documented political and organizational advantages of business interests, not to mention the political inertia of the Washington establishment, to enact landmark legislation and essentially remake the regulatory process. Yet they did. These achievements testified to the success that environmentalists achieved in reframing policy discourse in terms of their own narrative and in redesigning policy institutions to redress what they saw as the undue influence of business interests. Their success derived from four critical factors that conservatives would have to address with respect to environmental policy:

1. The environmental movement had changed the terms of debate by introducing scientific analysis and public health issues into a policy arena that had been dominated by questions of natural resource development versus conservation;
2. The movement also succeeded in embedding collectivist arguments and ecological principles in policy discourse and more specifically in legislative language, and in doing so effectively trumped traditional values of individual freedom and private property that had served as ideological firewalls against the kind of intrusive and costly regulation implicit in environmentalism;
3. Public interest groups, especially environmental organizations, had become permanent players in Washington issue networks, while their role in the policy process was enhanced by institutional and process changes they won in statutes and court cases;
4. Business interests proved to be far less than monolithic and, in some instances, far more open to finding common ground on environmental regulation than portrayed by post–World War II political science.

The enactment of SMCRA and the Clean Air Amendments Act (CAAA), both of which developed between 1970 and 1977, clearly reflect these four factors specifically, as well as the ideational and institutional transformation of the regulatory process brought about in the area of environmental policy more generally.

In their 1981 classic, *Clean Coal/Dirty Air,* Bruce Ackerman and William Hassler documented the emergence of an unholy alliance between environmental activists, committed to reducing emissions in all coal-fired power plants regardless of marginal benefits, and eastern coal producers, intent on protecting their market position against lower-sulfur western coal. Together, they conspired to insure that the 1977 Clean Air Amendments Act would require costly and inefficient "scrubbing" of coal at each power plant. As Ackerman and Hassler indicated in the subtitle to their study, this was really the story of "how the Clean Air Amendments Act became a multibillion dollar bailout of high-sulfur coal producers" rather than an effective pollution control measure. A contemporaneous policy history reveals how environmental activists first abandoned their intention to regulate all surface mining in favor of a focus on coal and then how, ironically, they aligned themselves with western producers of low sulfur coal to insure that the 1977 Surface Mining Control and Reclamation Act severely constrained the production of "dirty" coal in the East. To achieve their legislative goals, environmentalists relied on not only their analysis of ecological impacts and the broad public support for environmental protection but also divisions among business and regional interests represented in Congress. These two landmark statutes also illustrate the dual aims of environmentalists: they were willing to work with eastern coal producers on the CAAA and western coal producers on SMCRA because each statute coupled compromises on overall policy substance with noteworthy progress on their efforts to remake the policy process. This assessment of environmentalism's impact on the policy process applies with equal force to the Surface Mining Control and Reclamation Act and the Clean Air Amendments Act.

## The Surface Mining Control and Reclamation Act of 1977

SMCRA clearly bears the ideational and institutional as well as the policy imprint of environmentalism. In fact, six years before Ackerman and Hassler published their analysis, Carl Bagge, president of the National Coal Association, concluded that, "Politically, the consumer movement, the environmental ethic, the drive toward participatory democracy...are all pushing regulatory agencies to adopt policies that were regarded as irrelevant a few years ago."[31] His observation is important not only insofar as it took note of new legislative initiatives (such as SMCRA), but also because it associated these policy initiatives with key ideas that animated the new social regulation. The "environmental ethic" overrode considerations of higher prices (How can one put a value on human life or scenic beauty?) and property rights (What was private property but a legal refuge for business obstinacy?). Similarly, "the drive toward participatory democracy" impelled congressional allies of environmentalist "elites" to write specific provisions into the law that guaranteed easier access for public interest advocates to both the rule-making process and the courts, institutional venues where they could participate in the implementation of SMCRA. Among the thirteen specific purposes enumerated in the law, three are particularly noteworthy reflections of environmental policy's ideational and institutional bases:

1. Establish a nationwide program to protect society and the environment from the adverse effects of surface coal mining operations;
2. Assure that appropriate procedures are provided for the public participation in the development, revision, and enforcement of regulations, standards, reclamation plans, or programs established by the Secretary or any State under this Act;
3. Wherever necessary, exercise the full reach of Federal constitutional powers to insure the protection of the public interest through effective control of surface coal mining operations.[32]

The surface mining law, then, promised more big government, a commitment to embedding environmental elites in all phases of policy making, and an obligation to protect society against depredations of private enterprise. Thus, SMCRA embodied essentially the canon of the new social regulation and exemplified critical environmental challenges to libertarian, traditional, and anticollectivist streams of conservatism.

SMCRA's complex and detailed requirements for obtaining a permit to surface mine coal illustrate the triumph of environmental ideals over economic efficiency and a competitive market. They also demonstrate how environmentalists changed the terms of policy debate by introducing scientific analysis and data requirements, thereby neutralizing to a degree the political and resource advantages of business lobbies. In order to operate a surface mine, SMCRA directed coal firms to produce 25 separate sets of information for OSM to review. Some of the more onerous and expensive requirements mandated include:

1. Maps of the permit area, including cross sections of mining pits indicating soil types, siltation ponds, storage pile locations segregated into topsoil and overburden;
2. A study of climatology and ambient air quality along with a "fugitive dust" control plan and monitoring system;
3. A study of hydrology on the site with analysis of sources and quality of water, a restoration plan, and long-term impacts on surrounding water supplies;
4. Studies of flora, fauna, and geology on the site, along with a thorough restoration plan.

When President Carter signed SMCRA into law, the economics of coal production changed instantly. In particular, compliance with its pre-mining information provisions compelled firms under its provisions to allocate significant resources to meeting these requirements before moving a cubic yard of earth. Each of these measures reflects another of the Act's objectives, providing "a means for development of the data and analyses necessary to establish effective and reasonable regulation of surface mining operations."[33]

Like other environmental statutes, including the CAAA, SMCRA shifted discussions of policy development from traditional concerns about stakeholder influence and economic growth to the realm of science, engineering, and public health data. In the legislative process, environmentalists produced data in support of their goals. In the regulatory phase, individual coal firms were responsible for developing all information necessary for permitting. For larger firms with in-house scientific and engineering resources, SMCRA increased their cost of capital insofar as the studies demanded could take a considerable amount of time (years in the case of flora and fauna analyses). Mid-sized firms without the necessary expertise on staff had to allocate additional funding to contract out for acquiring the necessary information. Smaller firms, operating with low cash reserves and higher relative labor costs, often faced insurmountable financial challenges to comply with informational requirements, a result that did not displease environmentalists and that reduced competition. In fact, SMCRA exacerbated the financial burden on smaller firms, primarily located in the East, by establishing minimum bonding fees far above the levels to which they were accustomed and on which their profitability depended. In testimony before Congressman Morris Udall's Subcommittee on Energy and Environment, B. V. Cooper, executive director of the Virginia Surface Mine and Reclamation Council, a regional trade association, summed up the views of small eastern mining firms: "[SMCRA] is not a reclamation bill. It is purely and simply a land use bill and a ban strip mining bill. The word 'ban' is never used, but the result is just exactly that—a ban.... There are literally dozens of impractical, shortsighted, punitive, harassing, and otherwise unreasonable requirements in this bill."[34] This position, shared by most small and medium-sized coal operators and supported by state governments and regional banks as well as power companies that enjoyed lower coal prices from smaller producers, proved to be of no avail. The environmentalist arguments and the divisions with larger firms tended to isolate or even marginalize such strident opposition.

By tying these information requirements to regulatory permits, moreover, the law provided environmental lawyers with an evidentiary basis to sue firms for noncompliance. SMCRA, in clear anticipation of environmental organizations' use of the federal courts to play a supplementary enforcement role, endowed "interested parties" with automatic standing to sue noncompliant coal firms or even to sue OSM for non-enforcement. Along these same lines, the law provided explicit instructions for alerting interested parties of permitting proceedings for any new surface mining project, specifying the media and frequency of public notice. These arrangements represent the law's clear attempt to move away from the New Deal regulatory regime and put teeth into the promotion of participatory democracy throughout the policy process. Subsequent regulations in fact guaranteed that private citizens could request that OSM perform spot inspections of a duly permitted surface-mining operation if they had "reason to believe that a violation exists."[35] The authors of the regulations well understood that local, state, or even national public interest groups would support private citizens in such activities. Moreover, to guard against the coal industry's capturing OSM, implementing regulations prohibited the agency from hiring of any federal employee from a department or bureau that had any "legal authority, program or function in any Federal Agency which has as its purpose promoting the use or development of coal."[36] Thus, SMCRA and its regulations positioned environmental advocates to augment the enforcement capacity of OSM and sought to ensure that the agency would remain hospitable to them. These institutional measures embedded citizens and public interest groups in the implementation of the surface mining law, thereby altering subgovernmental politics to fit the new social regulation's goal of participatory democracy and underscoring the fact that environmentalists saw that remaking regulatory processes was as important an objective as passing legislation if they were to achieve their environmental goals.

As significant as was environmentalists' success in enacting SMCRA, it did not represent a total triumph. Indeed, even with public opinion in support of environmental protection overwhelmingly on their side, public interest groups fighting for SMCRA had to find ways to adapt to and exploit differing business interests. As SMCRA took shape in the mid-1970s, the deep divisions in the broader mining industry help to explain why the law, originally intended to control all surface mining, came to regulate only coal. Although environmentalists initially sought a comprehensive federal law to regulate all surface mining, by the time Congress passed SMCRA all that remained of this sweeping goal was a brief title that allocated funds to study the feasibility of regulating noncoal operations. This outcome of environmental policy making clearly illustrated how divisions among business could facilitate the enactment of major regulatory programs. It also shed light on the limits of translating broad public support into tough environmental laws, on the transformation of subgovernmental politics, and on the political maturation (some might say "aging") of the environmental movement. While there was legislative precedent for treating coal separately from so-called hard rock mining, the former being governed by the Coal Leasing Act of 1928 and the latter by the Mining Act of 1872, environmental organizations were not likely to be persuaded that reclamation should be bound by laws intended to promote mining operations. Rather, the explanation lies in congressional and subgovernmental politics.

From the outset of the struggle to enact a surface mining law, hard rock mining interests within the American Mining Congress (AMC) strove to dissociate themselves from coal, and several factors helped their effort along. The coal surface mining historically located in the East and the lower Midwest had ravaged Appalachia as well as farmland in Ohio and Indiana. The results of surface mining in these regions and the surface effects of extensive underground mining (also controlled by SMCRA) created a visceral impression that environmentalists adeptly translated into effective political material. Harry Caudill's influential *Night Comes to the Cumberlands* served as the surface mining equivalent of Rachel Carson's *Silent Spring,* exposing the deleterious impacts of eastern surface mining on water resources, on local communities where erosion and landslides had proved devastating, and on the scenic beauty of the region. Congressional hearings included tragic photographic evidence of these natural and human effects. In addition, environmentalists were keenly aware that coal, unlike other mining, produced fossil fuel that contributed to air pollution and serious public health problems for children and seniors. Environmentalists also worried that the development of mining technology suitable to vast coal deposits in the West, combined with the energy crisis following the Arab oil embargo, would create a "second Appalachia" in Wyoming, Colorado, and Montana. The public understanding of surface mining issues, therefore, provided dominant AMC members such as the National Limestone Institute, the National Crushed Stone Association, Phosphate Lands Conference, the American Iron Ore Association, the Copper Development Association, the National Land and Gravel Association, and the Industrial Sand Association with the perfect scapegoat, coal mining. The fact that the sand and gravel mining industries were integral to road construction and, by extension, the National Highway Trust Fund, created an additional powerful incentive for legislators to accept hard rock arguments that coal ought to be treated separately and that a more comprehensive treatment of surface mining should be postponed. Just as importantly, key legislators represented western hard rock mining interests. In the House, Morris Udall (D-AZ) chaired the Subcommittee on Energy and Environment, while, on the Senate side, Henry Jackson (D-WA) chaired the Interior Committee and John Melcher (D-MO) chaired the Subcommittee on Mines and Mining. Each of these lawmakers was a strong supporter of environmental regulation, especially Udall, whose brother Stewart, as secretary of the Interior, had issued a major study of surface mining impacts in Appalachia. However, all were sympathetic to hard rock mining, which was critical to their state economies. In particular, Udall was a strong supporter of major copper interests based in Arizona. The National Coal Association (NCA) and the National Independent Coal Operators Association (NICOA) complained bitterly, but to no avail, that these congressional leaders acquired national credentials as environmental advocates while catering to mining firms back home. Once it became clear that the law would be about coal, AMC lent its support to the efforts of its coal members to minimize the negative economic effects, even forming a joint AMC-NCA legislative task force to work on SMCRA. A divided business community made it impossible to defeat or significantly amend SMCRA and illustrated a key lesson for opponents of the new social regulation; because it was not industry specific (all mining interests were initially involved), like classic price and entry regulation of the Progressive Era or the New Deal, business would face significant collective action problems. While railroads might have enough of a clear interest in their interactions with the ICC to coalesce on common ground[37] or provide an opportunity for a trade association to organize and represent that interest effectively,[38] the mining industry was too variegated to realize these benefits, and its fractured policy stance helped to undercut opposition to SMCRA.

Environmentalists, recognizing political reality, decided to seek as aggressive a coal surface mining law as possible. Notwithstanding the AMC-NCA task force, the regional and economic diversity of the coal industry itself facilitated their strategy. By the time the struggle to enact a surface mining law commenced, the coal industry was very diverse. This diversity owed, in part, to the consolidation of large segments of the industry as major oil companies acquired coal firms. It also reflected the different nature and scale of surface mining operations in the East, the Midwest, and the West. In the East, relatively small surface mines unearthed narrow coal seams among the steep slopes of the Appalachians, where they impinged directly on the quality of life in many rural communities. In the Midwest, medium sized companies, so-called "captive firms" owned by coal-burning power companies, operated on rolling terrain in southern Ohio, Indiana, and Illinois, often clashing with farming interests. In the West, huge surface mining projects employed gigantic earthmoving equipment to excavate wide coal seams, many of which lay on public lands in Wyoming, Colorado, and Montana. These differences were magnified by the fact that coal in each of the regions varied substantially in its BTU rating and its sulfur content, eastern coal yielding the highest heat content but also the most sulfate pollution, and western coal providing both the lowest heat and the lowest sulfur content. This industry diversity created major collective action problems for lobby groups representing the coal industry, and spawned the formation of alternative organizations to advocate for particular segments of the industry. The four most important business groups involved with SMCRA, in descending order of size and scope, were the American Mining Congress (AMC), the National Coal Association (NCA), the National Independent Coal Operators Association (NICOA), and the Mining and Reclamation Council (MARC). The AMC represented all mining industries, including hard rock mining as well as coal. NCA organized mostly larger coal firms with operations in several states, while NICOA essentially represented smaller eastern firms and a few like-minded ones from southern Ohio and Indiana. According to its vice president, Dan Jerkins, MARC organized in 1977 to speak for firms committed to "expansion of the coal industry through environmentally sound practices."[39] The difficulty businesses encountered in speaking with one voice opened the door for environmentalists to pursue a divide-and-conquer strategy. As it suited them, they forged alliances with firms more congenial to environmental policy, ordinarily larger ones interested in legislative certainty and uniform national regulatory policies, and confronted more ideologically conservative firms, ordinarily smaller ones unaccustomed to Washington Beltway politics and for whom SMCRA's compliance costs could spell economic ruin.

With respect to congressional politics, western domination of the critical committees and subcommittees again came into play as Udall, Jackson, and Metcalf were disposed to write a law that included particularly draconian requirements on returning surface mined lands to their "approximate original contour" and banning any mining in areas adjacent to farmland or slopes of greater than 20 degrees. These provisions clearly targeted Appalachian mining in the East, rather than the rolling terrain of the western coal reserves. In addition, when President Ford had vetoed an earlier version of SMCRA in 1975, he had attempted to head off further legislative efforts by authorizing the Bureau of Land Management (BLM) to regulate surface mining on public lands, almost all of which were in the West. Once BLM promulgated its surface mining rules, most western operations moved into compliance with reclamation practices on original contour, and they reprised the role of hard rock mining firms, characterizing older, eastern firms as the real culprits in despoiling the land. As an environmental bonus, they and their congressional allies highlighted the fact that lower sulfur western coal promised to help abate pollution from power plants (though the CAAA eliminated that advantage with its rules requiring scrubbing technology). To make matters worse for the majority of coal firms operating in the East and the Midwest, the United Mine Workers (UMW) joined this "alliance" of environmental advocates and western coal. Since the enactment of the 1969 Mining Safety and Health Act, underground mining in the East and the Midwest lost significant market share to nonunion surface mining, and a tough surface mining law held out the prospect of leveling the economic playing field in favor of unionized underground operations. The UMW also reasoned that SMCRA would reduce the comparative advantage of the emerging nonunion western coal market. Although the persuasiveness of this view evaporated when OSM wrote rules to treat surface effects of underground mining as severely as surface mining, the UMW did provide valuable legislative support for enacting SMCRA.

In sum, SMCRA typified the environmental policies that provoked conservatives and animated the Reagan Revolutionaries. In their view, SMCRA's detailed "command and control" approach to regulation supplanted free enterprise with bureaucratic direction. Its costly federal requirements undermined state authority while increasing the price and decreasing the supply of a key energy resource. Its concept of environmental ethics trumped individualism with a collectivist vision. Finally, conservatives saw its institutional reforms as endowing elite liberals with undue influence on the policy process while bastardizing the constitutional role of the courts. Just as dismaying to conservatives, the business response to SMCRA appeared feckless and short-sighted. Neither business lobbies nor conservative critics could stop SMCRA or other environmental laws that they opposed.

## The Clean Air Amendments Act of 1977

The other major environmental law of 1977, the Clean Air Amendments Act provided no less a disheartening outcome for conservatives. As Ackerman and Hassler explained, the CAAA of 1977 exemplified the ideas and institutions typical of the new social regulation in general and environmental policy in particular. Indeed, it was § 304 of the CAAA that pioneered the inclusion of citizen suit provisions in environmental protection laws. While their analysis of the law's attempt to regulate power plant emissions is highly instructive, many observers agree that the major legislative engagement occurred around the CAAA's efforts to control automobile emissions. As with the case of SMCRA, the battle to regulate auto emissions under the CAAA reveals the bases of conservatives' frustration with both environmental policy and the business community.

In discussing the genesis of the CAAA, one of its key architects, Senator Edmund Muskie (D-ME) identified the three pillars of the law:

> Three fundamental principles shaped the 1970 law. I was convinced that strict federal air pollution regulation would require a legally defensible premise. Protection of public health seemed the strongest and most appropriate such premise. Senator Howard Baker believed that the American technological genius should be brought to bear on the air pollution problem, and that industry should be required to apply the best technology available. Senator Thomas Eagleton asserted that the American people deserved to know when they could expect their health to be protected, and that deadlines were the only means of providing minimal assurance. *Over a period of several markup sessions, those three concepts evolved into a proposed Clean Air Act that*

*set deadlines, required the use of best available technology, and established health-related air quality levels.*[40]

These three principles, enshrined in the 1970 Act, drove the confrontation between the auto industry and environmentalists when the CAAA came up for reauthorization in 1977. In particular, § 202 of the 1970 Act required a 90 percent reduction in automobile emissions by the 1975–1976 model year, while prescribing the best available control technology to achieve that goal. The law's supporters readily acknowledged that they were not banking on the precise achievement of the 90 percent reduction by the deadline. (Note: As a compromise, the Senate amended its original bill to extend the deadline by one year.) Rather, as many legislators made clear in hearings on the 1970 and 1977 Acts, these "technology forcing" measures were intended to hold the auto industry's feet to the fire and allow Congress to directly monitor progress, rather than following the New Deal model of tasking regulatory agencies with that responsibility. Epidemiological evidence of the negative public health effects of emissions, especially as they affected children and the elderly, provided the political lever that environmentalists and their congressional supporters used to enact these ambitious measures over the considerable clout of the Big Three auto manufacturers and the Automobile Dealers Association. In public debates and congressional testimony, environmentalists allied themselves with the National Cancer Institute, the American Heart Association, and the American Lung Association in order to hammer home the public health threat, which Muskie had identified as the "legally defensible premise" of the law. The Senate bill passed unanimously, a testament to the political efficacy of the environmental/public health nexus. The House of Representatives, however, passed a far less stringent bill for two principal reasons. First, the automobile industry had a powerful ally on the Commerce Committee, John Dingell (D-MI), representing the Detroit area. Second, members of the House were more susceptible to electoral pressure than Senators, not only because they ran every two years instead of six but also because almost every congressional district in the nation had an automobile dealership and some ancillary industry to automobile manufacture. While a spirited fight ensued in the Conference Committee, the Senate conferees ultimately prevailed and the stronger CAAA passed both houses. This initial victory in 1970 set the stage for a dramatic clash between the auto industry and environmentalists in 1977.

Between 1970 and 1977, a number of significant developments framed the context for amending the CAAA. Most notably, the oil embargo and accompanying economic stagflation posed an effective political counterweight to the public support of environmentalism as well as the appeals to public health arguments advocates employed in Congress. In addition, corporations, Washington law firms, business lobby groups, and trade associations responded to the early successes of environmental policy by investing in their own scientific and analytic expertise in order to better participate in the new subgovernmental politics.[41] This investment had an important double-edged impact, on the one hand augmenting the capacity of these interests to contest the scientific and engineering data adduced in support of environmental laws, but on the other hand reinforcing the terms of debate and the authority of environmental ideas. To the chagrin of conservative critics, building this capacity focused the political debate on how much environmental protection we could afford rather than on the legitimacy of the policies' underlying ideas and institutions. Thus, the question for the CAAA was what the deadlines should be for achieving automobile emission targets, not whether the framework for regulating them under the CAAA was appropriate. As with SMCRA, conservative and business opponents lost the fundamental disputes and were relegated to negotiating the most advantageous terms of surrender.

Nevertheless, the increased capabilities of business interests did reshape the character of environmental-issue networks and establish limits on the sway of environmentalism. In this same period, the first analytic and economic critiques of environmental policy emerged, providing important evidence of the attendant opportunity costs. Finally, after several years of opposition to reauthorization by Gerald Ford, the first Democratic presidential victory since 1964 brought to the White House an individual who was committed to signing a new Clean Air Amendments Act, Jimmy Carter. Within this political milieu, the effort to reauthorize the Clean Air Act began in mid-1970s, and it quickly became clear that the auto emissions provisions would be the major battleground.

The initial engagement would be in Subcommittee on Health and Environment, chaired by Paul Rogers (D-FL), widely known as "Mr. Health." Closely allied with Senator Muskie and a mentor to another strong environmental advocate in the House, Henry Waxman (D-CA), Rogers faced off against Dingell, the second-ranking Democrat on the Subcommittee. With Rogers representing Palm Beach, Florida (whose senior citizens were interested in promoting public health), and Dingell representing Detroit (where the auto industry was interested in preserving jobs), the CAAA was vigorously contested. Environmentalists, angered by the fact that the auto industry had not come close to achieving the 90 percent emissions reduction mandated by the 1970 Act, were intent on achieving a stringent bill and on Congress holding business to account precisely as the CAAA framework had intended. Unlike seven years earlier, though, car manufacturers, reeling from Japanese competition as well as the trebling of oil prices, enjoyed the support of the United Auto Workers (UAW). When Leonard Woodcock, President of the UAW, testified as part of a panel including executives of the Big Three automakers, Rogers, Waxman, and their allies in the environmental and public health communities understood that they would have to moderate their objectives. By the time Rogers's Subcommittee passed the bill on to the full Commerce Committee, Representative Joel Broyhill (R-VA) had openly aligned with John Dingell, signaling that opposition to a strong set of auto emission provisions would come from a formidable coalition of business, labor, a united Republican Party, and a powerful Democrat. Also, in contrast to the 1970 enactment, the Senate had to overcome a filibuster that delayed passage until 1977. Indeed, by the time the law emerged from conference this time, the CAAA provided an additional four-year extension on achieving the original 1970 emissions targets. As Muskie reviewed the 1977 struggle, he concluded, "Fortunately, most of the special interests' political capital was exhausted in the fight for the auto industry amendment, and we were able to avoid a number of other special industry efforts."[42]

In retrospect, it appears that a unique set of political and economic circumstances explain why Congress relented on the Clean Air Amendments Act's auto emissions standards. The economic distress of the 1970s, an uncharacteristically unified business front, and an unprecedented opposition alliance doomed the environmentalists' effort to bring the auto industry into compliance with the ambitious 1970 standards. The legislative history on National Ambient Air Quality Standards (NAAQS) and power plant emissions reflects a more predictable "substantive" outcome of environmental policy, a strong command and control regulation pursued regardless of effectiveness or efficiency. With respect to administrative "process," however, the auto emissions provisions of the 1977 CAAA remained consistent with the rest of the Act, with SMCRA, and with the new social regulation in general. Both SMCRA and the CAAA demonstrate the ideational and institutional transformation effected in the realm of environmental policy, as well as the limits of this transformation. By introducing participatory reforms such as public permitting and citizen suits, changing the terms of debate to require scientific and engineering information, relying increasingly on courts as policy partners, rooting policy arguments in concerns about public health, and effectively promoting a collectivist ethic, the environmental movement helped to remake both the policy agenda and the regulatory process.

While these successes could not purge business or conservative influence from congressional politics, as both SMCRA and the CAAA show, they did bring about the enactment of landmark legislation and advanced a public philosophy that conservatives viewed as incompatible with American democracy. In fact, conservatives began to respond in the 1970s, organizing the Pacific Legal Foundation in 1973 and Mountain States Legal Foundation in 1976 to combat environmental lawyers and advocates. The American

Enterprise Institute launched *Regulation,* a magazine devoted to a market-based critique of government regulation and focused its much of its attention on the environmental laws that took shape in the 1970s. Yet all this activity failed to avert the formation of an essentially new regulatory regime built largely around the ideas, institutions, and policies advanced under the banner of environmentalism. Indeed, the mobilization of resources to create counter-vailing legal foundations signaled that conservatives acknowledged that they would need to find ways, at least in the short run, to operate effectively in the new regime.

## Conclusion: David Slays Goliath

By the late 1970s, the ideational and institutional development of environ-mental policy presented Ronald Reagan and the fusionist coalition he helped to forge with both a *raison d'être* for mobilization and significant barriers to overcome. Resurrecting America's commitment to individualism, freedom, and patriotism, while forcefully rejecting collectivism and a defeatist foreign policy, proved effective in constructing a conservative electoral consensus. The problem conservatives would face, though, was that their electoral con-sensus organized around opposition to modern liberal statism would con-front a powerful alternative consensus in support of a powerful federal role in support of environmental policies. Laws and regulations aimed at limiting exposure to carcinogens or protecting children and the elderly from air pol-lution had convinced Americans that environmental policies were a good thing. Conservative critics of environmentalism were speaking to an elec-torate over 60 percent of whom consistently asserted that they would pay higher taxes for a cleaner environment. By the 1970s, moreover, environ-mental organizations became permanent players in the Washington policy community and were very adroit at nurturing the consensus in favor of envi-ronmental protection.

Notwithstanding opposition from well-organized business interests to environmental regulation and the critiques of well-financed conservative ideologues that environmentalists had perverted the role of courts and regula-tory agencies, not to mention the drumbeat of criticism from economists that environmental policy was costly and inefficient, SMCRA, the 1977 CAAA, and a host of other landmark environmental laws poured out of Washington. Over strenuous objections from business lobbies and conservative-funded legal foundations, these new laws established judicial and institutional mech-anisms, such as automatic standing to sue and public permitting that per-manently changed the regulatory process to constrain the post–New Deal subgovernmental politics in which those lobbies had thrived. Environmental laws, moreover, reflected a political philosophy that moved beyond New Deal efforts to make the market work better so that capitalism might be saved from itself to a more radical vision in which the market economy itself was fundamentally flawed. In hindsight, the achievements of environmental advocates in less than a decade seem astounding and clearly beg the question of how they could accomplish so much in the face of established corporate interests and a growing conservative movement.

Business and conservative resistance never gained sufficient traction to mount an effective political counterattack precisely because environmentalists succeeded in changing the regulatory institutions to reflect their ideas about the primacy of both ecological and participatory values. By the mid-1970s, the argument that capitalism should trump environmentalism was essentially lost. It was lost in part because Americans were persuaded that the negative environmental effects of business activity posed a genuine threat, particularly when those effects were tied to advocacy and evidence focused on public health. The argument also failed because corporate businesses were never as convinced as their conservative allies of the efficacy of a true libertarian model. In a sense it became graceless, if not implausible, to argue against environmental policy, except to rail against environmental extremism. At the same time, corporate interests, in contrast to smaller firms and libertarians, were more concerned with establishing regulatory rules of the game within which they could prosper, rather than taking on an ideological fight against environmental policy. For larger firms it was simply more rational to pursue certainty in regulatory policy than to commit the political and legal resources necessary to reverse the tide of environmentalism. The logic of accommodation rather than confrontation, of course, proved all the more persuasive because the triumph of environmentalism imbued the regulatory regime with new participatory values as well. With aggressive and vigilant public interest lawyers at the ready to participate in rule makings, to sue business firms for noncompliance with regulations, or to sue the EPA itself for non-enforcement of environmental laws, many in the business community concluded that discretion was the better part of valor. The upshot would be that conservatives would have to contest regulatory policy on the terrain established by environmentalists: using arguments grounded in science and engineering; control of the administrative and rule-making apparatus; disputing the best way to achieve environmental protection.

Thus, at the beginning of the 1980s, the stage was set for a clash between conservatives who opposed environmentalist ideology and a popular consensus that supported environmental policies. The former helped to elect a Republican president with a vision of relieving business and the nation of overbearing and overly expensive environmental regulation. The latter provided a staunch barrier to the policies essential to realizing that vision. This clash would be played out in the administrative and judicial institutions that environmental organizations and their congressional supporters had built into the regulatory process. Those institutions, as we have seen, included important procedural "safeguards" that assured environmental advocates an ongoing role in implementing policy as well as entrée to the courts, where they could hold federal regulators as well as private firms accountable. In addition, by 1980, those institutions had been operating for almost a full decade, and businesses, trade associations, congressional committees, public lobby groups, and federal agencies had developed a familiarity with these processes. This new regulatory regime bred an inertia that would require extraordinary resources to break. Environmental policies, then, had become embedded in American politics in both an ideational and an institutional sense. While these policies were open to a reformist critique aimed at protecting the environment in the most efficient way possible, it would take a huge investment of political capital to build a legislative coalition effective enough to change environmental laws and rein in environmental regulators through the congressional oversight process. The consensus on environmental policy had taken deep root in the nation's legal and regulatory institutions, as well as in the popular mind, and would constrain President Reagan's efforts at regulatory relief.

## Notes

1. Richard Harris and Sidney Milkis, *The Politics of Regulatory Change: A Tale of Two Agencies* (New York: Oxford University Press, 1989), 80–96.
2. Bruce Ackerman and William Hassler, *Clean Coal/Dirty Air or How the Clean Air Act Became a Multi-Billion Dollar Bail-Out for High-Sulfur Coal Producers and What Should Be Done about It* (New Haven, CT: Yale University Press, 1981), 5.
3. Charles E. Lindblom, *Politics and Markets: The World's Political and Economic Systems* (New York: Basic Books, 1977).
4. Gabriel Kolko, *The Triumph of Conservatism: A Reinterpretation of American History, 1900–1916* (New York: Free Press of Glencoe, 1963); C. Wright Mills, *The Power Elite* (London: Oxford University Press, 1971); E. E. Schattschneider, *The Semisovereign People: A Realist's View of Democracy in America* (Hinsdale, IL: Dryden Press, 1975); Marver Bernstein, *Regulating Business by Independent Commission* (Princeton, NJ: Princeton University Press, 1955); Theodore Lowi, *The End of Liberalism: The Second Republic of the United States,* 2nd ed. (New York: W.W. Norton, 1979).
5. Quoted in George H. Nash, *The Conservative Intellectual Movement in America since 1945* (New York: Basic Books, 1976), 26.
6. Frank S. Meyer, *In Defense of Freedom: A Conservative Credo* (Chicago: Regnery Press, 1962).
7. Meyer, *In Defense of Freedom,* 228–231.

8. Ronald Reagan, "A Time for Choosing," delivered at the 1964 Republican National Convention, San Francisco, July 1964. Emphasis added.

9. Ibid., emphasis added.

10. Murray L. Weidenbaum and Robert DeFina, *The Cost of Federal Regulation of Economic Activity*. Reprint No. 88. (Washington, DC: The American Enterprise Institute, 1978).

11. Business Roundtable, "The Incremental Costs of Regulation," A Report Prepared by Arthur Anderson & Co., 1979.

12. George C. Eads and Michael Fix, "The Prospects for Regulatory Reform: The Legacy of Reagan's First Term," *Yale Journal on Regulation* 1 (1985): 293–318.

13. Jeffrey M. Berry, *Lobbying for the People* (Princeton, NJ: Princeton University Press, 1977), 289.

14. Jeremy Rabkin, "The Judiciary in the Administrative State," *The Public Interest* 71 (Spring 1983): 62–84.

15. Grant McConnell, *Private Power and American Democracy* (New York: Knopf, 1967); Bernstein, *Regulating Business by Independent Commission;* Lowi, *The End of Liberalism*; Schattschneider, *The Semisovereign People.*

16. Harris and Milkis, *The Politics of Regulatory Change.*

17. http://www.rexweyler.com/resources/green_declaration.html#5.

18. Mary Douglas and Aaron Wildavsky, *Risk and Culture: An Essay on the Selection of Technical and Environmental Dangers* (Berkeley: University of California Press, 1982).

19. U.S. House Hearings, Committee on Government Operations, *The Environmental Decade: Action Proposals for the 1970's,* 91st Cong., 2nd sess. (February 2–6, 1970), 182.

20. U.S. House Hearings, *The Environmental Decade,* 185.

21. Harris and Milkis, *The Politics of Regulatory Change,* 53–91.

22. Personal interview with Alan Morrison, June 12, 1986, emphasis added.

23. Personal interview with Daniel Becker, June 11, 1986, emphasis added.

24. *National Environmental Policy* Act, P. L. 91–190, *U.S. Statutes at Large* 83 (1970), codified at *U.S. Code* 42 (1982), sec. 101-a.

25. *Department of Transportation, et. al. v. Public Citizen, et. al.* No. 03–358. Argued April 21, 2004—Decided June 7, 2004, Slip Opinion.

26. Personal Interview with Dick Ayers, July 21, 1986.

27. Ibid., emphasis added.

28. Deborah Stone, *Policy Paradox and Political Reason* (New York: Norton, 2002).

29. Meg Switzgable, *In Our Water* (Franklin Lakes, NJ: New Day Films, 1981), Video 44.

30. Riley E. Dunlap and Rik Scarce, "The Polls—Poll Trends: Environmental Problems and Protection," *Public Opinion Quarterly* 55 (1991): 651–672.

31. Quoted in *Business and Society on Change,* ed. Daniel Patrick Moynihan (New York: AT&T Press, 1975), 187.

32. 30 USCS 102, SMCRA Federal Regulations (http://www.osmre.gov/regindex.htm).
33. Ibid.
34. U. S. House Hearings, *Reclamation Practices and Environmental Problems of Surface Mining*. Subcommittee on Energy and Environment, 95–1, 1977, 370.
35. 30 U.S. Code of Federal Regulations 842.12.
36. 30 U.S. Code of Federal Regulations 1211.
37. Mancur Olson, *The Logic of Collective Action: Public Goods and the Theory of Groups* (Cambridge, MA: Harvard University Press 1965).
38. Robert H. Salisbury, "An Exchange Theory of Interest Groups," Midwest Journal of Political Science 13 (1969): 1–32.
39. Personal Interview with Dan Jerkins, February 2, 1981.
40. Edmund S. Muskie, "The Clean Air Act: A Commitment to Public Health," *The Environmental Forum: NEPA to CERCLA* 6 (January/February 1990): 23–28. Emphasis added.
41. D. Vogel, *Fluctuating Fortunes: The Political Power of Business in America* (New York: Basic Books, 1989).
42. Muskie, "The Clean Air Act."

# CHAPTER 5

## Social Security from the Great Society to 1980: Further Expansion and Rekindled Controversy

*Nancy Altman and Ted Marmor*

By the middle 1950s, as chapter 2 suggested, Social Security seemed no longer a vulnerable program. Republican critics like Carl Curtis might well have wished to turn the program back, but neither the Eisenhower administration nor the bulk of the congressional Republicans were ready to take on that task. Indeed, by the election of 1960, a clear policy threshold on Social Security—understood as retirement, survivors' and disability insurance—had arrived. The program so understood was an established part of the political landscape.[1] The social insurance question for the early 1960s was expansion, not contraction. It involved whether what was labeled Medicare, medical care for the elderly, seen by its supporters as the first step to national health insurance, would be added to the cast of income protections already enacted.[2]

From today's vantage point, though, the late 1950s to the mid-1970s, appears to have been a watershed for Social Security. As chapter 2 describes, before this period, ideological opponents in the business community, in the Congress, and, most dramatically, in the presidential election of 1936, challenged the concept of social insurance directly. In the subsequent period, described in chapter 8, opponents of social insurance did not attack the concept directly, but nevertheless organized, worked to undercut confidence in the viability of Social Security, and championed substituting private accounts for a part of Social Security's guaranteed protection.[3]

Two sets of questions cry out for answers: First, what caused the domestication of what had been an ideologically inflammatory matter, so that during this period, the Social Security vision became so acceptable that the mainstream of both parties came to support it? Put differently, how can we explain the fact that from the mid-1950s until the early 1970s, expansive amendments to Social Security came to legislative fruition regularly? If Social Security amendments were routinely enacted every two years on a bipartisan basis, generally right before elections, what happened to conservative opposition?[4] Why did it fall victim to the mainstream presumption that to attack social insurance in principle risked political ridicule or, worse, suicide?

The second set of questions concerns what was transpiring below the surface. Though opposition to the basic concept of social insurance seemed to have been vanquished after the mid-1950s, it was, in reality, simply sleeping. What caused it to awaken? In other words, what developments led opponents of Social Security to believe that they could take on the issue safely? Furthermore, what did opponents learn about how to tackle the issue safely, lessons hard-learned during this period and the one before?

We seek to answer the first set of questions in the next section. The answer involves the bifurcations of a once-solid conservative coalition, and the ascendancy of what we call traditional conservatives, those who held positions of leadership, who worked through consensus and compromise, and who believed in the conservation of popular government programs that worked.[5] In the final section, we describe the multiple factors that led to a renaissance and reinvigoration of those we label radical conservatives, those who remained adamantly opposed to Social Security, despite its success and relative longevity. It was this part of the political opposition that would reemerge, in full bloom, in the period described in chapter 8.

## The Bifurcation of the Conservative Coalition

As chapter 2 makes clear, the conservative coalition opposing the old-age and survivors' protection of Social Security had, for a variety of reasons, begun to break apart in the 1950s. First, conservatives had been successful during the start-up period in influencing the design of Social Security. Receipt of benefits was conditioned on work, with no requirement of tests of need. Consequently, Social Security was viewed as a middle-class program, not welfare, despite its redistributive and antipoverty qualities. Furthermore, its financing—a dedicated tax in the form of mandatory contributions from wages, matched by equal employer contributions—provided a built-in check on unbridled growth. Similarly, the program's low administrative costs and self-sufficient financing, kept separate from the overall federal budget, instilled a sense of confidence in the prudent and careful management of the program. The perception that Social Security was a well-managed program embodying traditional American values gave it wide-based support among both mainstream politicians and the electorate.

The contributory financing of Social Security provides, ironically, both constraints on growth and sources of cultural support for the program. Since deductions from wages are highly visible funding, any program reductions are, in turn, salient. After all, the specific payments to Social Security that legitimate benefits put pressure on government to honor the program's promised pensions. This cultural pressure is stronger because most American workers have the idea that they are contributing toward their own retirement. To the extent this contributory design provides a sense of having "earned" an entitlement to benefits, it stabilizes American Social Security. Not based on means tests, Social Security benefits are part of a worker-saver ethos, not a poverty-charity conception. Thus, while conservative insistence on self-financing provided an upward limit on benefit growth, it also provided a check against undoing benefits once promised.

By the end of the last period, Social Security was beginning to play an increasingly important role in providing financial security in old age. As chapter 2 details, the Social Security Amendments of 1950, known by historians as Social Security's third start, substantially expanded the coverage of the program and raised its benefits. Perhaps more importantly, in 1952, Congress discovered that, as a result of the method of forecasting program costs, which almost guaranteed surpluses, incumbents could increase benefits every two years, right before elections, without the necessity of substantial tax increases to pay for them.

The 1950 Amendments expanding coverage, together with the discovery two years later of the opportunity for politicians to enact pain-free, biannual expansions in benefits, catapulted the program to its status as the most popular domestic program in the nation. The low-cost, popular, pre-election vote became a staple of Congress for the next two decades.[6]

In addition, as Social Security became an established part of the social structure, General Motors and other major employers, in concert with unions to which their workers belonged, integrated their employee pension plans, either explicitly or implicitly, with Social Security. These powerful business interests thus began to have a substantial stake in the continuation of Social Security.

These developments—the perception that Social Security embodied traditional American values, the electoral rewards that support for the program brought, and the vested interest that business began to have in a strong Social Security program—led to the bifurcation of conservative opposition. Virtually all conservatives opposed Social Security's enactment at the outset because it greatly expanded the role and power of the central government, it afforded no role for state and local governments, and it was not narrowly targeted to the needy. Once Social Security had been in existence for decades, though, was the conservative position to conserve or maintain it, while preventing its expansion, or to seek its overthrow? On that, conservatives differed.

Perhaps the best example of a conservative who advocated the program's overthrow was Senator Barry Goldwater (R-AZ). Because of his radical stance, he never evinced any interest in the program's maintenance and, consequently, never played any direct role in its shaping. In contrast, conservative congressional figures who took the opposing view with respect to Social Security—that is, they desired to halt or limit its growth but, given its established nature, not dismantle it—were reinforced in their position because they came to receive credit for expertise in social insurance and gained power from helping to shape a popular institution.

The biannual Social Security bills meant that members of the relevant tax committees of the Congress, those serving on the House Ways and Means Committee and the Senate Finance Committee, acquired valuable and hard-earned expertise in the complicated legislation, expertise that had reputational value and that translated into power. Representative Wilbur Mills (D-AR), who became chairman of the House Ways and Means Committee in 1958 and retained that powerful position until a scandal forced him out in 1974, presents perhaps the best example of this dynamic. He studied the details of the program and every proposed amendment, and presented himself as a guardian and protector of Social Security.

Mills inherited the role of chair in a committee that over time institutionally celebrated prudence, fiscal caution, and control. Mills in particular was prepared to compromise his policy preferences for greater control over the level, structure and reach of pending legislation. (This will later be evident in his role in Medicare's legislative history.[7])

Other scholars have portrayed the distinctive operating style of the finance committees of the Congress in the 1950s and 1960s. The picture they paint is relatively straightforward. Ways and Means had until 1965 a 3-to-2 ratio of Democrats to Republicans, but the combination of Republican and conservative Southern Democrats on the committee was the most reliable, predictable coalition.[8] That coalition's leaders, Mills and John Byrnes (R-WI), were hardly ideological enthusiasts for either the New Deal or classic social insurance. They were, though, institutional protectors of the program's pace and scope after that program had become politically invulnerable to outright assault. They supported expansion (controlled by them) of the retirement program not because they were zealots but because that was the condition of their control and the source of power. Put another way, as was the case with Medicare as well, they were expansion-minded to the extent that brought with it conservative dominance of the boundaries and pace of the expansion, as well as electoral success.[9]

The stance of Mills, Byrnes, and others we term "traditional conservatives," presented a huge problem for those we label "radical conservatives," whose preference was for no social insurance whatsoever. To add to the troubles of the radical conservatives in Congress, large business enterprises with employee pension were no longer in their camp either. These powerful business enterprises might, depending on their plans' structures, even favor benefit increases, because increases in Social Security reduced their liabilities with respect to their own plans.

If the pace and extent of expansion was dominated by finance leaders within the broader conservative coalition, and was backed, or, at least, not opposed, by large and powerful segments of the business community, what were the more radical-conservative critics of Social Security to do? The answer for most of the 1960s was to join forces with their traditional conservative brethren and concentrate on opposing Medicare, rather than fighting to stop cold the growth of retirement pensions. And, in that decision, there were ironies we will now highlight in connection with the fight over Medicare.

## *The Coalition United: The Fight over Medicare*

By the mid-1950s, readers should recall, the battleground over Social Security was over whether to expand the program to cover other kinds of benefits. Once disability insurance was added in 1956, that benefit also rapidly became established. By the time of the 1960 election, the debate over social insurance concentrated on whether health insurance for the elderly should be added to the Social Security package of benefits.[10]

Medicare became the battleground for the expansion of the American version of a welfare state concentrating on social insurance principles. The main outlines of that story have long been available. It is one of determined efforts of the conservative coalitions in the finance committees to limit the expansion of social insurance to the cash benefit programs, old age, disability and survivors' insurance, and not to adopt the health insurance model favored by the stalwarts of expanded social insurance—Wilbur Cohen, Robert Ball, Nelson Cruikshank, to name but three, all of whom had been advocates either inside government or out, in the successful addition of disability insurance and other program expansions.

The formal Democratic leadership in Congress, which included Senate Majority Leader Lyndon Johnson (D-TX), favored a federal Medicare proposal in 1960 that would provide hospital insurance as part of a worker's retirement benefits. The Republican administration proposed a modest alternative, which provided for federal grants to states in order that states could provide low-income residents with subsidies for private insurance. As a compromise, Representative Wilbur Mills and Senator Robert Kerr (D-OK) proposed increasing federal funds for old age assistance, establishing a new category of recipients under the program—the "medically indigent"— and permitting states to provide medical services under the program. The so-called Kerr-Mills Amendment was enacted as part of the Social Security Amendments of 1960.

This was the "conservative" position on governmental financing of medical care. The role of government was to be limited, extending no farther than helping veterans and, if forced, financing state programs to care for those who might be considered the "deserving poor." This position was conceptually at odds with social insurance doctrine. It was a position regularly identified with a conservative conception of the role of government generally. So, the American Medical Association was willing to accept, and even facilitate, the enactment of the Kerr-Mills "welfare approach" legislation, in an effort to avoid social insurance legislation that the organization viewed as far worse. So would other expected conservative opponents—the Chamber of Commerce and the National Association of Manufacturers, for example—of the Democratic agenda identified with the soon-to-be Kennedy Administration. Illustrative of the once-united but now bifurcated coalition of conservatives, in the Senate, only ten Democrats and only one Republican, Senator Barry Goldwater, voted against the bill's passage.

President John F. Kennedy made enactment of Medicare a top domestic priority of his new administration. As the new administration envisioned it, Medicare would be a part of Social Security, financed by workers and their employers from a tax on wages, just like Social Security, and providing payments for hospital costs, once those workers reached age 65. Kennedy's first message to Congress on the issue came just three weeks into his term. With his assassination and the succession of master strategist and politician Lyndon Johnson, the fight over Medicare accelerated. At this point, the politics surrounding Social Security took an unusual twist.

Supporters of Medicare had, at the start of the fight, decided to refrain from seeking increases in the levels of cash benefits, and instead concentrate their resources on the enactment of Medicare. Their strategy was one of leg-islative innovation in medical care and fiscal restraint in Social Security's cash programs. Mills, Byrnes, and other opponents of Medicare took the converse tack. Concerned that the appeal of helping retirees with hard-to-afford hos-pital insurance would be difficult to counter over time, they came to see that their best chance of defeating Medicare was to increase the cash benefits, and the concomitant payroll tax supporting them, and thus make a health insur-ance program supported by a payroll tax politically impossible.

In other words, their legislative strategy was to make Medicare appear fiscally unworkable. Payroll tax hikes to fund the increases in cash benefits would, they reasoned, make a Medicare program appear fiscally irresponsible and thus less politically attractive. This was, it turned out, a naïve tactic in the short run and a good example of how vulnerable the conservative coalition in these years was to an expansionary social insurance vision promoted by knowledgeable and able policy advocates.

The Social Security Amendments of 1964 vividly illustrates the play of these conventional politics, but by contrast. On August 31, 1964, after three years of intense and deadlocked debate, the Senate took the historic step of passing Medicare's hospital insurance program. To counter this development, the House conferees—reflecting the conservative coalition's strategy—pressed for a large increase in the cash benefits.

Such a proposal, as noted, had become the normal pre-election pattern: just prior to an election, both sides would agree to a benefit increase and, at least, enact that. That pattern of pre-election increases reflected what ana-lysts now would describe as the locking in of expansionary momentum in a policy.[11] Regardless of ideological premises, ordinary members of Congress had come to see cash benefit increases at election time as useful for reelection purposes. As an indication of Social Security's political invulnerability in this stage of its policy history, this mode of expansion is crucially important.

In this particular 1964 instance, the story unfolded in an illuminating, inter-estingly different way. Though the Senate conferees had been sympathetic to increasing cash benefits, they nevertheless refused to go along this time. Presi-dent Johnson, supported by the AFL-CIO and the National Council of Senior Citizens, feared rightly its negative implications for Medicare's appeal, and urged the Senate conferees to refuse the bait. Hopelessly deadlocked over what was really a fight over Medicare, Wilbur Mills, the House leader in Congress's conservative hesitancy about Medicare, announced on October 2, 1964, that the conference committee was unable to reach agreement and, as a result, fore-went the pre-election opportunity to take a Social Security increase home for that year's November elections. This conservative play was a losing tactic from the beginning, but few realized that October just how decisive the election of 1964 would be for social insurance expansion with Medicare.

The landslide Democratic victory, an election in which enactment of Medicare was a prominent campaign issue, produced a two-to-one party ratio in the House and a liberal majority in the Senate as well, and overwhelmed the conservative coalition's capacity to delay or dilute any of the Great Society's legislative reforms. Medicare passed overwhelmingly in June of 1965, with its former critic, Wilbur Mills, turning from an agent of delay to an architect of measured expansion. But that story was one of a congressional control artist outfoxing the liberal reformers, not a change in conservative strategy over Social Security generally.[12]

## Odd Bedfellows: Automatic Indexation of Benefits

After Medicare's enactment was certain, the majority of Congress returned to the political pattern of constrained increases in cash benefits. Mainstream congressional conservatives supported increases that could be understood as keeping the program up to date with cost of living and wage increases, but opposed what they viewed as unwarranted or excessive expansions. For example, since no across-the-board increases had been enacted since 1958, it was easy for Congress, without controversy, to improve cash benefits in 1965 by 7 percent. In 1967, another move in the game revealed how the conservatives in Congress assumed they could both take credit for expansion and limit it at the same time. President Johnson had requested a 15 percent increase, together with more targeted adjustments, but Congress responded with a slightly lower increase of 13 percent.

The Johnson administration's chief strategists in this period were social insurance professionals of long standing, not White House managers. Robert Ball, the longtime civil servant, had become, in 1962, commissioner of Social Security, the top position in the agency. He worked daily with Wilbur Cohen, who since 1961 had moved from Health, Education and Welfare (HEW) assistant secretary for legislation to undersecretary by 1965 and, by 1968, was the secretary of the department. They were the leaders of an extensive social insurance brain trust, but they were also sensitive to executive branch hierarchy.[13] Accordingly, they made sure that important White House assistants— like Douglas Cater and Joseph Califano—were kept informed of HEW's strategic judgments about what expansion the Congress would tolerate and how the Democrats could take credit for it without offending influential conservative coalition leaders like Wilbur Mills. These two veterans were central to the strategic calculations of the liberals within the Kennedy-Johnson administrations, having been ceded tremendous autonomy by Presidents Kennedy and Johnson on how to deal with congressional actors.

Ball and Cohen were aided by Robert J. Myers, the respected professional civil servant who, while indisputably devoted to social insurance, was concerned about undue expansion of it. He was respected as a straight shooter, recognized as a conservative Republican, and relied on by Mills and the other mainstream conservatives. Consequently, when he gave his imprimatur to limited expansions and championed their adoptions as sound and fiscally responsible policy, his support for and defense of the changes helped convince other conservatives of the appropriateness of the reforms.

Once conservative congressional leaders had accepted the legitimacy of Social Security's cash benefits, their strategic options were limited. They could constrain the levels of cash increases to some extent, but not challenge the appropriateness of adjusting benefits to cost of living changes. They could resist across-the-board upward adjustments in benefit generosity, but not attack the conceptual foundations of social insurance. (That was largely the role of ideological critics outside Congress, after Goldwater left the Senate to run for president in 1964. Examples outside the government include Goldwater adviser Professor Milton Friedman of the University of Chicago or, in the case of Medicare, the American Medical Association and its counterparts among conservative interest groups like the National Association of Manufacturers. Inside Congress, attacking the premises of Social Security had long become the special preserve of libertarians and free-market zealots, the group we call radical conservatives, few of whom, other than Curtis and Goldwater, achieved prominence during these years for antisocial insurance advocacy.[14])

Legislation to expand Social Security's cash benefits culminated in calls for automatic annual adjustments, which would obviate the need for regular, periodic congressional action. In 1968, both parties included in their platforms planks proposing automatic adjustments in Social Security's benefit levels, the policy that would in time become technically and politically problematic. But then, the cross-party agreement reflected the manifest consensus that keeping real benefit levels constant was not ideologically problematic. That Democrats differed on the question of the basic benefit levels themselves showed where party and ideological differences remained. Their platform of 1968 urged that the Social Security basic levels first be increased "to overcome present inadequacies."[15] In short, one could count on self-identified liberals to demand improvements in the scope and scale of social insurance, while conservatives were predictably hesitant about the size of the expansion and were guarded concerning whether the expansions were merely keeping pace or were benefit improvements in real terms.

Emblematic of just how mainstream, well-accepted, and consensual Social Security had become, the replacement of eight years of Democratic control of the White House with a Republican president in 1968 made little change with respect to Social Security policy making. In the first year of the new

Republican administration, President Nixon proposed an ad hoc 10 percent increase in Social Security benefits and automatic adjustments thereafter. "This nation must not break faith with those Americans who have a right to expect that Social Security payments will protect them and their families," the president's legislative message stated, arguing that the "impact of an inflation now in its fourth year has undermined the value of every Social Security check."[16] One could not have imagined a more telling example of how conventional the idea of maintaining Social Security benefits in real terms had become than this message from a Republican president.

An examination of the administration's 1969 legislation also offers interesting insight into the way that Social Security policy making was separated from issues of wealth and poverty. Social Security was, to repeat, understood as a middle-class program primarily. It prevented workers from falling into poverty as a result of old age, but it was not seen as a program for the poor. Rather, it was recognized to be insurance. In contrast, two welfare programs also enacted as part of the 1935 legislation, Aid to Dependent Children, and Old Age Assistance, programs administered at the state level but supported by the federal government, were very much seen as antipoverty programs and were very controversial. With stereotypes, broadcast by the media, of promiscuous mothers and welfare cheats, the programs played on prejudices concerning the dichotomized "deserving" and "undeserving" poor. The Nixon administration decided to tackle the controversial issue and recommended that Congress enact its Family Assistance Plan, which would have provided a completely federal, uniform benefit to all low-income people. FAP was self-consciously wrapped together in the same legislative package as the Social Security increases in hopes of making the welfare reform proposal more appealing.

Keeping Social Security benefit levels up to date was by now an uncontroversial concept among all but the radical conservatives. Making those adjustments automatic, independent of congressional credit taking, was controversial, but not along the normal liberal/conservative fault line. Despite the fact that the platforms of both parties had proposed automatic adjustments, the idea was in fact controversial both in the specialized world of social insurance experts and in the more general world of elected officeholders. Liberal Robert Ball was one proponent. He favored this nondiscretionary mode for substantive reasons, reasoning that automatic increases would prevent beneficiaries from experiencing declines in their standards of living while waiting for Congress to raise benefit levels. The obvious rationale was that Social Security's beneficiaries were mostly elderly, with many in their 80s and 90s facing relatively short life expectancies. The Ball case, in short, was against delay in the accepted practice of updating benefits to deal with price inflation.

This form of automatic expansion of Social Security had the support as well of the conservative Robert Myers, but for completely different reasons. Myers had long worried about the congressional tendency to respond to election-year pressures by significantly expanding benefits rather than just updating them. Social Security benefits, in his view, should be kept up to date, but not casually increased. Automatic adjustments, to this kind of conservative supporter of Social Security, would perform an important restraining function.

But not all social insurance experts agreed with the assessments of Ball and Myers. Wilbur Cohen, who, like Myers, had begun working on Social Security matters in 1934, disagreed with his long-time colleagues. It was helpful to the program, he thought, to have frequent congressional action. The assumption here was clear. Consistent attention by Congress was expansionary in the main, Cohen was arguing, and he was right from the standpoint of the expansionists. After all, in the course of making adjustments to deal with inflation, Congress generally enacted other improvements in the same legislation. Attention to what was noncontroversial increased attention to expanding Social Security more generally. Constant legislating had other benefits. It not only produced more knowledgeable members, but also gave leaders, like Chairman Mills, opportunities to wield influence on the form and pace of adjustments. Automatic adjustments would remove a noncontroversial legislative vehicle for measured expansion and would remove the credit claiming that had become part of Social Security's allure.

On this question, Cohen was more prescient than his colleagues Ball and Myers. As later developments would illustrate, the automatic inflationary adjustments would not only bring substantive concerns in the fiscal setting of the 1970s, but also meant that Social Security would come to congressional attention more because of troubles rather than as welcome opportunities for credit taking. And in those times of trouble, as chapter 8 reveals, the institutional expertise, in the form of knowledgeable members, would be largely nonexistent.

There were other grounds on which to be concerned about automatic cost of living increases. Economists like Arthur Burns, a Nixon adviser who would become chairman of the Federal Reserve Board, worried about the impact on the economy of larger benefits in inflationary times, when spending should be curbed, and no increases in deflationary times, when spending should be encouraged. The irony of this concern is that Social Security was moving in two directions at once in the late 1960s. On the one hand, its separate budgetary treatment—the trust fund accounting convention—was replaced in at least the economic calculations of the president and his budget staff by unified fiscal accounting. (We will return to this matter in later reflections.) Surpluses held by the Social Security trust funds and generated by annual income in excess of benefit payouts were linked to demand management in the sense that they were part of the overall balance of revenues and expenditures in macroeconomic plans. On the other hand, the ultimate decision to increase benefits automatically in line with inflation in 1972 decreased oversight of the program's actual management. This may have contributed over time to the sense that the program was effectively autonomous, with an internal dynamic that made it seem out of the control of budgetary authorities and, in that sense for some, a fearful "entitlement."

Elected officials were no more uniform in their views about the wisdom of automatic adjustments. Representative John Byrnes, the ranking minority member on the Ways and Means Committee, and Representative Melvin Laird (R-WI), the ranking member on the Social Security subcommittee of the House Appropriations Committee, both favored the idea of automatic adjustments for the same reasons Myers did: namely, its restraint on the impulse to add improvements to adjustments for mainly Democratic gain. Wilbur Mills did not share their policy conclusion, though he had more in common with their political philosophies than he did with Democratic liberals. Mills enjoyed the combination of political control and credit that came with legislating increases. And, as a powerful chairman, he rightly believed he could keep the improvements within acceptable bounds.

The story of how and when the United States came to adopt automatic inflation increases in Social Security benefits is one of great surprises. It took four years of effort and persuasion for Congress to enact the automatic increases in 1972. It involved the jettisoning of the Family Assistance Plan, and the enactment of the Supplemental Security Income program, a federal takeover of the welfare programs for the aged, blind, and disabled—the so-called "deserving" poor.[17]


## The Transformation of Social Security's Politics

When automatic adjustments were enacted, the policy had the broad support of members of both parties. Yet, within a year, many of them will have no doubt wondered about their decision. The Social Security Trustees reported in July of 1973 that for the first time in the program's history, the actuaries projected a long-range deficit. Never before had the nation undergone simultaneously double-digit inflation, sluggish wage growth, and high unemployment. Stagflation, an unexpected new development, meant that Social Security would generate benefit increases from inflation at the very time its revenues would fall from reduced levels of employment. So the context for automatic increases suddenly changed.[18]

The economic news was worse within months. An already-sluggish U.S. economy and already-high inflation intensified when, on Yom Kippur,

October 6, 1973, Egypt and Syria attacked Israel. The Organization of Petroleum Exporting Countries (OPEC) announced that its members would ship no oil to the United States or any other country supporting Israel in the war and would quadruple the price of oil worldwide. The price of food jumped 20 percent. Inflation climbed to 11 percent, in some months reaching annualized rates of over 16 percent. At the same time, unemployment rates soared. External events produced stagflation and that in turn fueled the assumption that Social Security was on some automatic pilot of expansion.

The arithmetic was simple. Inflation caused benefit levels—outgo—to increase more rapidly than anticipated, while increased unemployment and slower wage growth produced lower levels of Social Security income than projected. To make matters worse, the formula enacted in 1972 was extremely sensitive to the exact economic conditions the country was experiencing. The formula worked for adjusting the benefits of those already retired. It would have worked adequately for workers just starting to retire had the same conditions that obtained over the past continued. But that was not the case in this period of rapid inflation and lethargic wage growth. For those just applying for benefits, the formula indexation produced larger and larger benefits as a percentage of final pay. If the formula were unchanged and the economic conditions remained what they were, eventually it would have provided people more in monthly Social Security benefits than they took home in paychecks while working. This represented a reversal of Social Security's reputation for technical competence and an opportunity for complaint by those who had always thought the program inappropriate for American beliefs and practices.

Nonetheless, there was lethargy in response to the flaw in the formula. Despite the obvious need for corrective legislation, a distracted Nixon administration took no action in response to the 1973 Trustees Report. Why this is so remains something of a mystery. Watergate is obviously one part of the explanation, as the White House was soon absorbed with defending itself against serious charges of wrongdoing. In addition, it was difficult to transform a technical error into an ideologically appealing opportunity for fundamental reform. The Nixon administration had backed the automatic indexing, Congress had approved, and everyone was surprised at the "mistake." Perhaps most important, the politics of Social Security had shifted overnight from one of credit claiming to one of blame avoidance: however the problem was solved, it would necessarily include higher taxes or lower benefits or both. For perhaps all of these reasons, this problem persisted despite its recognition and gave opportunities for radical conservatives to question whether Social Security should continue to play so prominent a role, much less an expansionary one, in American public life.

Two months before the trustees' report, the Senate Watergate Committee convened its hearings before a nationally televised audience. Three days before the trustees' report, Alexander Butterfield, the former presidential appointments secretary, testified that President Nixon had installed a recording system in the Oval Office and, since 1971, had recorded all conversations and telephone calls.

The subsequent year's trustees' report, issued on June 3, 1974, projected a considerably larger deficit. Two months later, on August 8, 1974, President Nixon resigned and Vice President Gerald Ford took over as the new president. The following year's trustees' report, dated May 6, 1975, showed a still-larger projected deficit. In response to the projected deficit, President Gerald Ford sent a Special Message to Congress on February 9, 1976, proposing a correction to the benefit formula, so that it mirrored what had been done historically on an ad hoc basis every few years, but without the problems of the one enacted in then-current law. In addition, the Ford proposal recommended a modest increase in the Social Security payroll tax contributions of 0.3 percent on employers and employees each—an amount costing workers, at most, $1 a week—but Congress took no action on the legislation. With the unveiling of the Ford proposal, the politics of Social Security flipped, a reversal not likely to be lost on the politically attuned members of Congress. Social Security had always been an election-year bonanza, the chance to send larger pre-election checks to numerous constituents—federal largesse that they and their families undoubtedly appreciated and routinely rewarded at the voting booth. This election year, the choice was anathema: to enact even the small payroll tax increase and to remedy the indexation problem by the scaling back of promised benefits was not likely to garner any incumbent a single vote and might have cost him the election. Indeed, never again would a Social Security bill be enacted in an election year. Rather, the only chance of passage—and even then odds were against it—was if the bill were passed and signed into law in an odd-numbered year.

## A Changed Landscape: The Social Security Amendments of 1977

The last half of the 1970s was largely devoted to playing catch-up on Social Security's problems. Jimmy Carter defeated President Ford that November and became the 39th president of the United States. The following May, he sent a message to Congress outlining proposals to correct the flawed benefit formula. That President Carter recommended the same change to the benefit formula that President Ford had called for indicates that widespread consensus across political parties and ideologies existed about the value of social insurance, together with the desirability of keeping benefits current.

In addition to correcting the formula, policy makers confronted two other problems in the 1977 legislation. Additional short-term revenue was needed to get Social Security out of the hole in which the economy, the flawed formula, and congressional delay had put it. Also, by this time, the demographic shift in the population was clear. The baby boom generation, brought into being by the high birth rates following the end of World War II, had all been born by 1964. In the decade since then, fertility rates had dropped substantially, resulting in a baby bust. In addition to the short-term deficit, Social Security forecasts projected a long-term shortfall as a result of the projected aging of the population.

To make up the shortfall, the administration proposed two fundamental changes in the program. President Carter proposed taxing employers on the entire payrolls, while employees still paid taxes up to a maximum taxable wage base. In addition, the administration proposal provided for general revenue financing in times of high unemployment. Both of these ideas came from within the Social Security establishment; neither of them reflected the views of ideological opponents of Social Security. Notably, though, they were departures from two aspects of the basic structure that the program had embraced since its inception: parity in taxes paid by employees and employers, and self-contained financing. Neither of the reforms passed.

Congress rejected the new ideas for dealing with understood problems and instead stuck with the approach that had worked so well from the program's start. Standard operating procedures (SOPs) dominated in short, allowing politicians of all stripes (except eliminationists or, as we term them, radical conservatives) to get rid of a problem in a familiar way. Members of Congress bit the bullet and enacted unpopular Social Security legislation to avoid the fate of an even greater catastrophe: the failure of checks to go out at all. It chose to finance Social Security's shortfall through the traditional method of increasing the maximum taxable wage base and raising the payroll tax rate equally on employers and employees. This was a tax increase that would be much more visible to working men and women, one they would see every payday, than those proposed by the Carter administration. Whether Congress was acting in a statesmanlike manner in rejecting more hidden taxes or simply believed the new policy instruments, especially those coming from the expansionist side of the policy community, to be even more controversial, it stuck with the design of the founders.

The familiar instruments went a significant way toward eliminating the long-range deficit identified by the trustees. But, in a break from the past, the adjustments did not put the program in actuarial balance for the subsequent 75 years, the estimation period consistently employed since 1965 by the trustees in their reports assessing the long-term health of the program.

Having bitten the bullet hard, Congress left to future legislators the matter of dealing thoroughly with problems that might arise in the next century.

The 1977 Social Security legislation was the most controversial ever enacted, but experts believed the changes would solve the short-term financing problem. Accordingly, the 1978 annual trustees' report stated, "The Social Security Amendments of 1977 ... restore the financial soundness of the cash benefit program throughout the remainder of this century and into the early years of the next one."[19]

But they were wrong. Congress had bitten the bullet hard, but not hard enough. Based on past experience, the actuaries had projected rates of inflation, unemployment, and wage growth that were much more optimistic than those that actually materialized. Instead of improving, the economy had grown worse since the 1977 amendments. Inflation ran in double-digits consistently, hitting 13.5 percent in 1980. Wages decreased, declining 4.9 percent in 1980, and unemployment climbed close to 8 percent. Contributing to the program's short-term woes, Congress, uncomfortable with the unpolitic action of scaling back already-enacted benefit increases, had delayed the effective date of the benefit formula change. The delayed effective date, together with the combination of high inflation, negative wage growth, and high unemployment, caused Congress's fix to not be a fix at all.

In the Social Security annual report issued on June 19, 1980, the trustees forecast that the program unexpectedly was once again in financial trouble in the short term. The trustees projected that the trust funds would be exhausted, unable to pay benefits on time, starting in 1983. On the heels of news stories complaining about Congress's enactment of the largest tax increase in history came a new, headline-grabbing shortfall in Social Security. Unsettling stories began appearing in the press. The *New York Times* ran one on November 30, 1980, headlined "Social Security Is Still Not Secure," in which it reported that Social Security "remains in deep financial trouble."

The story of the 1977 Amendments is a watershed moment and a crucial backdrop to understanding Social Security's fate in the next quarter century. Congress sought to act responsibly by enacting huge tax increases and addressing, at least in part, a problem not predicted to materialize until the next century. Mainstream, traditional conservatives once again controlled the contours of the legislation, this time in rejecting more hidden taxes, which would have fallen more heavily on business. But all that those responsible members got for their troubles were accusing headlines and voter wrath. This was a window of opportunity of a sort, but it closed in ways that rewarded no one in the short run and program opponents in the longer run. The reputational halo came off Social Security as a program that could handle itself without much outside scrutiny, that always dispensed golden eggs, and that could expand in relatively painless ways. It surely could not be adjusted in painless ways when in trouble.

Supporters of Social Security received a painful lesson. They suddenly found themselves burned by the program that had always worked for them in the past and by the experts who had smoothed the way. Instead of moving ahead to other issues, Congress found itself confronted with what was beginning to feel like a chronic ailment: insufficient funds to cover the short-run costs of benefits, not to even mention the long-range deficit caused by the demographic shifts looming on the horizon.

Those radical conservatives fundamentally opposed to social insurance received an education, as well. Though still without a developed strategy to attack Social Security, they began to see and hope that the economic realities the country faced then and the demographic changes forecast in the future would provide them with an opportunity that had not been available since the early days, decades before.

By the end of the period this chapter addresses, Social Security was both a settled feature of American political and economic life and a source of anxiety about the future. It was shortly thereafter that Speaker of the House of Representatives "Tip" O'Neill famously described Social Security as "the third rail of American politics," which electrocutes all those who "touch" it with hostile intention.[20] There was a good deal of apparently solid support for this judgment. Social Security, polls reported, had overwhelming approval from most Americans, and the nation's mainstream political figures took for granted the program's continuation, if not its precise level of benefits. Congress had improved benefits every few years to keep pace with inflation and wage growth and thus insulated the elderly from some of the inflationary misery of the period. This ad hoc legislative activity had by 1972 culminated in automatic increases, which, once corrected, made unnecessary any action by politicians to keep Social Security benefit levels current with inflation and growth in wages. This was the apparent state of affairs, an established institution that seemed invulnerable to fundamental reconsideration. But from today's vantage point, that assessment captured only some of the underlying realities of the period. We now turn to those more elusive developments in a series of reflections of the period as a whole.

## Reflections on Social Security in Transition

Political actors who tried to challenge Social Security's fundamental bases had little to show for themselves throughout this period. Those like Congressman Curtis found themselves isolated as libertarian cranks in the 1950s. Senator Barry Goldwater's presidential bid in 1964 provides an object lesson in how not to win friends in this policy arena. A supporter of a so-called "voluntary" conception of social insurance programs, Goldwater faced nothing but difficulty trying to explain his position. In response to a reporter's question about Social Security in the midst of the New Hampshire Republican primary, Goldwater had responded unguardedly: "I would like to suggest...that Social Security be made voluntary, that if a person can provide better for himself, let him do it."[21] The costs of suggesting a major change in the architecture of Social Security were immediately apparent. The headline the next day in the *Concord Monitor* read, "Goldwater Sets Goals: End Social Security."[22] Though Goldwater eventually won the Republican nomination, he not only failed to win the New Hampshire presidential primary but, more importantly, lost the 1964 election itself by a landslide. What does this episode reveal, over this entire period, about the strategic posture of conservatives opposed to Social Security or, at least, its expansion?

The central point is that radical conservatives, Republicans with strong free-market and/or libertarian beliefs, and no compunction about overthrowing well-established programs, did not have a coherent, basic strategy for dealing with either Social Security's popularity or the logic of expansion. Among liberals, expansion was a matter of faith, but their faith was buttressed by an identified set of policy intellectuals, a base of committed civil servants with long experience in the program, and a plan of incremental expansion risk by risk, period by period.

These actors faced three sets of potential obstacles. One was within the Left of the Democratic Party, those who thought Social Security was not redistributive enough. Well-intentioned liberal academics complained that Social Security's payroll tax was regressive, and that a means test would assure more efficient, targeted use of benefits. Supporters of Social Security rejoined that programs for the poor made poor programs, a shorthand way of arguing that to tilt Social Security too far toward the poorest workers risked weakening its support among average and higher-paid employees. No serious challenge to Social Security's structure was ever mounted during this period, and the attacks on Social Security about its rates of return at the beginning of the next period, by conservative critics, emphasized the delicate nature of Social Security's balance. As chapter 8 describes, however, some of these well-meaning critics increased the noise level by joining the cacophony of criticism produced mainly by those we have termed radical conservatives.

More relevant for present purposes is a distinction between those conservatives—both Republican and Democratic—who had by 1960 accepted the program's continuation but sought to constrain its growth, and those who harbored dreams of substantial transformation. Wilbur Mills typified the former type; Goldwater represented the latter. Neither had a way of unraveling the expansionist trajectory, though Mills had a much clearer idea of how to slow the pace of expansion.

The costs of confronting Social Security directly were evident throughout our period, but well illustrated by the Republican presidential primary of 1976. Ronald Reagan, at that time the governor of California, had decided that year to challenge President Gerald Ford for the Republican nomination. In the end, Ford barely won the nomination with a delegate count of 1,187 to Reagan's 1,070. The important point for present purposes is how Ford went about winning the Florida primary. There his campaign made a prominent issue of Reagan's supposed hostility to Social Security. Here was a Republican president chastising his opponent for statements that Reagan, like Goldwater, had made in the 1960s about a voluntary form of Social Security.[23] During that hotly contested battle, Ford committed himself to "preserve the integrity and solvency of the Social Security system."[24]

That episode no doubt influenced Reagan's thinking about how to talk about Social Security, which would be important during the 1981–1983 period of crisis; perhaps it influenced Vice President Dick Cheney's thinking as well, during the 2004–2005 privatization battle. (Cheney was President Ford's campaign manager at the time of the Florida primary.) More generally, conservative thinkers who fundamentally disapproved of Social Security, but recognized political realities, were given a lesson in how not to talk about Social Security. Certainly, avoid the language of ideology, voluntarism, or restrained growth, as had been tried in the past. A better tactic, they likely realized, lay in more recent developments from the 1970s, concerning anxieties about Social Security's fiscal soundness.

In electoral terms, the place of Social Security actually solidified over this period. In his successful campaign for president in 1980, Reagan distanced himself from, and implicitly rejected, his earlier statements about Social Security. By the 1980s, the program had been championed by every president since its enactment, which included five Democrats and three Republicans. Underneath the supportive surface, though, were ground-shifting changes that would dramatically affect the politics of Social Security.

## The Emergence of a Radical Conservative Movement

From Social Security's start, a small group of conservatives outside the mainstream—a group President Dwight Eisenhower had labeled, "a tiny splinter group"—opposed Social Security on ideological grounds.[25] One of their number, Senator Goldwater, had, as we noted, won the Republican presidential nomination in 1964. Despite his election loss, he inspired a new generation of like-minded conservatives.

Goldwater had published *Conscience of a Conservative* in 1960. The 120-page volume, ghostwritten by *National Review* editor and speechwriter L. Brent Bozell, set out the senator's philosophical premises and expressed a version of American conservatism that sharply differed from the views of either Southern Democrats like Wilbur Mills or Northern Republicans like Leverett Saltonstall or Jacob Javits. The Goldwater book became an overnight hit, selling millions of copies and attracting an army of followers.

Goldwater's nomination as the Republican candidate for president was itself the culmination of an extensive grassroots political movement that had begun in the summer of 1961, soon after *Time* magazine featured Goldwater on its cover. Discontent with the Republican Party's response to the Kennedy administration, a group of men who had been leaders of the nationwide Young Republicans organization formed what would become the Draft Goldwater Committee. Also actively supporting Goldwater was another organization of young conservatives, the Young Americans for Freedom (YAF), which had been created in the fall of 1960 on the Sharon, Connecticut, estate of William F. Buckley, Jr., conservative founder and publisher of the *National Review*. In 1962 the YAF had held a rally in Madison Square Garden at which Goldwater addressed a crowd of 18,500 people.

Advising Goldwater was Milton Friedman, who helped give shape to the candidate's visceral opposition to a New Deal program like Social Security. There were in every part of the country nodes of general discomfort with the legacies of the New and Fair Deal. The composition of the Kennedy administration's domestic cabinet made certain that unfinished Democratic business from the Roosevelt/Truman years would be addressed. Though the universities at the time had the reputation for Democratic sympathies, in many economic departments and some law schools there were free-market opponents of governmental regulation, fiscal conservatives, and libertarians skeptical about the growth of government responsibilities. The common ground for such conservatives was the idea that government's proper social role was, at most, to help those who could not help themselves, a view incompatible with Social Security's expansionist vision of pensions or social health insurance. In the academy, Professor Milton Friedman was perhaps the most vocal advocate of this view and was important in legitimating the Goldwater approach to public policy among some Republicans.[26]

The Goldwater campaign is, on the surface, an emblem of conservative failure. Unlike earlier Republican conventions where the winning candidate sought to unify the party, Goldwater made no such effort, picking fellow conservative Bill Miller for his running mate rather than a more moderate member of the party. The Republican ticket went down in flames, with a landslide victory for President Johnson and equally impressive Democratic congressional wins. Nonetheless, the political ground of American politics was shifting in ways that few connected to Social Security in the 1960s, but that would prove important over the longer run.

Without attention to these shifts in American sentiment about government's proper role and its capacity to deliver on its promises, the transformation of Social Security's political trajectory in the 1980s and 1990s is almost incomprehensible. These changes—both in circumstances external to public control like stagflation and distant from Social Security, like the Vietnam war—call for attention in understanding Social Security's history.

By 1968, the Vietnam War had become increasingly unpopular, and the mood of the country had shifted. On March 31, 1968, President Johnson announced that he would not run for another term as president. Later that year, Republican nominee Richard Nixon was elected with 43.2 percent of the popular vote. The same army of supporters who had championed the Goldwater candidacy in 1964 worked, two years later, to elect Ronald Reagan to the office of governor of California. During the 1968 convention, these Young Americans for Freedom had mounted a losing campaign to nominate Governor Reagan for president.

Notwithstanding the loss, these young conservative activists were gaining valuable political expertise. It is important to distinguish two roles in the development of a cadre of conservative activists opposed fundamentally to social insurance. The Goldwater movement and the transition of much of that support to the political career of Ronald Reagan gave continuity to a powerful, small-government voice in the nation's political dialogue. But there were other developments that gave intellectual heft to that movement that are easily missed. We have in mind here the development of policy advocates and think tanks in which their advocacy was able to draw upon research, links to the media, and to influential conservatives in the American academic world. So, one could rightly pay as much attention to the 1973 forming of the Heritage Foundation and the 1977 forming of the Cato Institute in Washington, D.C., as to the support Goldwaterites gave to the gubernatorial elections of Ronald Reagan in California during that same period.

Those young Goldwaterites remained in politics, some following Reagan to Washington, and would in time become some of the supporters of the think tanks just mentioned. In 1969 the Young America's Foundation was formed to become, in its words, "the principal outreach organization of the Conservative Movement."[27] In addition, the Intercollegiate Society of Individualists, whose first president, back in 1953, had been William Buckley, now renamed the Intercollegiate Studies Institute, channeled money to conservative students who were starting and running college newspapers with a conservative slant.

Moreover, during the decade of the 1970s, as this undercurrent of conservatives was gaining strength, public confidence in the future of Social Security dropped sharply, even as approval of its purposes remained high. Public confidence in the future of Social Security, so high in the past, fell precipitously and remained low. The magnitude of the change in public perception was substantial. In 1975, 63 percent of those polled answered that they felt very confident or somewhat confident in the future of Social Security; 37 percent replied that they felt not too confident or not at all confident. In just three years, the numbers had just about reversed, with only 39 percent responding in 1978 that they felt very or somewhat confident and 60 percent answering that they felt not too confident or not at all confident.

Some of this reflected a drop in confidence in government generally. In 1964, 75 percent of Americans claimed they trusted the government in Washington. The numbers started to slip into the low 60s and 50s along with the escalation of the Vietnam War. Watergate caused the numbers to take a nosedive, from which they have never recovered. In 1974, only 36 percent of those polled responded that they trusted their government. (Opinion polls showed a new all-time low in 1995, when only 15 percent reported that they trusted the government.)

The drop in public confidence in the future of Social Security was not simply an unvarnished fact of life, a product of simple public reflection. Throughout the troubled story of indexation, there was amplification of an emboldened conservative perspective on Social Security's future. Here is where events internal and external to Social Security had combined effects on the conservative movement's posture. The previously described "mistake" in the indexation formula, combined with the obvious impact of stagflation on fiscal forecasts, gave program opponents a new opportunity. They could for the first time switch from simply opposing the basis or the pace of Social Security expansion to one of prudent dismay. If the program appeared unaffordable over the long term, if the trust funds were "forecasted" to be "insolvent," then opposition—and ideas about private accounts—suddenly seemed less impossible to suggest.

The point of having annual trustees' reports provide 75-year forecasts of Social Security's inflow and outflow was, from the standpoint of expansionists, at least in part, a way to reassure Americans that the program was prudently managed. The very idea of "trust funds"—one of the oldest arrangements in Anglo-American jurisprudence, dating back centuries—was to accord special responsibility to Social Security's administrators and congressional overseers to make sure promises were kept and the flow of contributions made adequate to promises offered for pensions decades hence.

A promise to provide a benefit 40 years in the future requires trust. In the 1930s, most Americans appeared to trust the national government. By the late 1970s, after the experiences of Vietnam and Watergate, many citizens no longer were so trusting. Whether that distrust extended to the Social Security Administration fully is not a settled matter. What evidence there is suggests that SSA managed to escape the harshest of critical assessments, maintaining a reputation for reliable treatment of its beneficiaries. But, for long-run promises, the decline of governmental trust was relevant, and doubly so when joined to the view that the talk of trust funds was dishonest.

There is much more to say about this strategic shift in the 1980s and beyond. But it had its roots in the 1970s and its carriers located in policy communities that transformed the discussion of what trust Americans ought to have in Social Security's trust funds. In short, there were intellectual entrepreneurs capable of taking advantage of Social Security's plight to damage its reputation and thus try to change the debate about its future.

## The Decline of Private-Sector Defined-Benefit Plans and the Rise of Defined-Contribution Arrangements

There were, in addition to the diminished confidence in the future of Social Security, other changes in the environment that opponents of Social Security would be able to use increasingly. During the 1970s, simultaneous with Social Security's financing woes, the world of private pensions was changing in ways that would over time also affect the discussion of Social Security. The universe of pension plans, public and private, can be divided into two broad categories, defined-benefit plans and defined-contribution plans. Social Security exemplifies a defined-benefit plan, one which promises a monthly percentage of pay as a lifetime benefit. Defined-contribution plans, like 401(k)s, make no promises down the road, and in some cases, do not even involve employer contributions. Employers who do contribute might, for example, transfer 5 percent of a worker's salary into an account, but make no promises about—and bear no responsibility for—the funds that might (or might not) be available at retirement. These arrangements are called retirement plans because they do provide income in retirement. But they are more appropriately thought of as savings plans with tax advantages.

The traditional rationale for American Social Security pensions was that they constitute the base leg of a three-legged stool. Private pensions are the second leg for those whose work setting provided them, and the third leg is family savings. Although private defined-benefit plans are better as vehicles of retirement planning because their benefits are pegged to final pay, the amount needed to maintain a certain standard of living, they are not as secure as their private defined-contribution counterparts. The employer making the promise can, for example, go bankrupt or inadequately fund the plan. These and other concerns were a major reason that Congress passed pension reform legislation in 1974. The Employee Retirement Income Security Act (ERISA) of 1974 addressed many of the insecurities, requiring, for example, that employers set aside in trust sufficient funds in advance to satisfy the future promises and that the plans purchase insurance in the event of insufficient funds to pay promised benefits.

ERISA was an important reform, but all the safeguards imposed substantial additional costs on employers—and private pensions are voluntary arrangements. Defined contribution plans are much cheaper for the employer to provide. Employers largely stopped establishing defined-benefit plans after pension reform was enacted, and switched to offering defined-contribution plans instead.

Employer-provided defined-contribution plans had been around for a century, but they got a big boost as a by-product of the new costs now imposed on defined-benefit plans. Despite the many weaknesses of defined-contribution plans as a mechanism for accumulating retirement income, many workers preferred them, or at least did not object to the change. Defined-contribution plans are often better for the young, mobile worker. A 30-year old who quits Employer A for a job with Employer B will not get much retirement income from Employer A's pension plan, no matter how generous it is, when he or she is ready to retire in 35 years upon turning age 65. Even if Employer A were to provide 80 percent of final pay, the 80 percent would be calculated on the unindexed salary that the retiree had earned as a 30-year-old, three and a half decades earlier. As part of the pension reform law, Congress provided individual retirement accounts for those who had no pension plan, and the new device introduced even more people to the concept of savings accounts as retirement-income vehicles.

Defined-contribution plans—already exploding as a result of the added costs the pension reform legislation had imposed on defined-benefit plans— went through the roof when Congress added subsection (k) to section 401 of the Internal Revenue Code. Here is where policy action in one sphere— the IRS and the regulation of private pension arrangements—spills over in time to another programmatic sphere like Social Security. As chapter 8 will explain, the ideological opponents of Social Security made a powerful link between the appeal of private pensions of the defined-contribution type and the argument that Social Security should embrace this popular vehicle, especially when Social Security's future could be represented as uncertain. Individualization and reliability were potential vehicles for policy arguments in ways not imagined in the pre-1974 period.

Although section 401(k) was enacted in response to a seemingly narrow question raised by some proposed regulations promulgated by the Department of the Treasury, employers quickly saw the possibilities in the new section, which permitted employees to elect whether to take cash wages or tax-deferred compensation placed in an account. Section 401(k), which took effect on January 1, 1980, became an overnight sensation. Within two years, almost half the large companies in the country had either started a 401(k) plan, often as a supplemental plan, or were actively exploring doing so. These new investment vehicles became familiar to many Americans. Employees with 401(k) plans and everyone with individual retirement accounts received regular statements and could watch their contributions and earnings grow.

It is important to understand that the development of these private investment vehicles was totally unrelated to the world of Social Security. They were not orchestrated by Social Security opponents; they simply provided a fortuitous, from the perspective of radical conservatives, opportunity. For all the talk of a three-legged stool and the desirability of an overarching retirement income policy, the worlds of Social Security and private pensions are quite separate and apart. Experts tend to specialize in one field or the other, rarely both. Historically, different members of Congress claimed expertise; different congressional committees and different executive branch agencies had jurisdiction. Indeed, the histories of the development of Social Security and private pensions are separate, with only rare intersection. The development of the new private sector vehicles was totally separate and independent from anything going on in the world of Social Security policy making. Yet, once these vehicles existed, Social Security opponents imported them into the debate, as chapter 8 highlights.

## The Blossoming of a Conservative Intelligentsia and Other Environmental Changes

To summarize then, the combination of anxiety over Social Security as a result of the projected shortfalls, general distrust of the government, and the growth in individual retirement accounts and, later, 401(k) plans thus presented new opportunities for opponents of Social Security. The libertarian Cato Institute, founded as we noted only in 1977, began publishing books and articles critical of Social Security. In 1979 it published a piece by Carolyn L. Weaver advocating Social Security "choice," with the provocative title "Social Security: Has the Crisis Passed?" The following year, it published a book by Peter Ferrara, *Social Security: The Inherent Contradiction,* and two years after that, his *Social Security: Averting the Crisis.* Both books claimed that Social Security was a bad deal and should be privatized. Whereas earlier analytical attacks on Social Security were intermittent and their dissemination haphazard, the development of conservative think tanks, especially in Washington, would be an important new factor in the evolution of the Social Security debate. Cato, the American Enterprise Institute, the Heritage Foundation—these were leading examples of institutions that would shape the conservative response to Social Security in different ways.

Indeed, attacking Social Security became a more common—even, in some settings, fashionable—pursuit among academic economists and their counterparts in law and public policy schools. This development cannot be separated from the more general shift in trust about the capacity of government to do the right thing. From airline deregulation to trucking, from attacks on agricultural price supports to revelations of Pentagon sweetheart contracts, the volume of writing critical of an expansive role of government increased. Criticism of Social Security was a modest part of that development at the outset, but by 1980, the engagement of free-market microeconomists in critiques of Social Security was no longer much of a surprise.

Professor Martin Feldstein, for instance, sparked a cottage industry by his research asserting that Social Security depresses national savings. Michael Boskin of Stanford was another young economist with similar views, as would later be the case with the Boston University economist, Lawrence Kotlikoff, who embedded his critique in what he called "generational accounting." Other academics began to publish analyses comparing how much beneficiaries got from Social Security in contrast to what they might have received if they had invested their contributions in private investment accounts. Along with these analyses of whether Social Security beneficiaries got their money's worth, critics also began to publish plans to privatize Social Security.[28]

During these same years, General Augusto Pinochet and Chile became part of the American Social Security debate. On September 11, 1973, General Pinochet had launched a bloody coup d'état against the democratically elected Salvador Allende, who died in the government takeover. Two years later, Milton Friedman traveled to Chile, where he delivered lectures at the university in Santiago and met privately with Pinochet.

With Friedman's encouragement, Pinochet employed the Chicago-based private sector approach to fix the serious economic problems confronting his country. A group of Chilean exchange students had done graduate work in economics in the United States, mainly at the University of Chicago, where they had studied with Friedman. Known as the Chicago boys, they returned to Chile after their studies. Pinochet appointed the Chicago boys to high-level positions in his government and gave them the green light to work their private-sector magic.

Pinochet appointed one of the Chicago boys (although so-labeled, he had actually studied at Harvard), José Pinera, to be his minister of labor. During his tenure from 1978 to 1980, Pinera substituted a system of private accounts for Chile's Social Security system. As soon as it was in place, Pinera and his supporters in the United States began to write articles about its wonders.

Another seemingly unrelated fiscal policy development in the late 1960s came to have a substantial impact on perceptions about Social Security as well. Because President Johnson continued to push for and expand his Great Society programs at the same time he waged the Vietnam War, the federal deficit had ballooned and had become a major source of controversy. In an effort to mask the size of the deficit, Johnson implemented a modification in the presentation of the budget—a seemingly innocuous change, which shifted the perceptions of some about Social Security.

In 1968, as we noted in the opening part of this chapter, President Johnson altered the presentation of the federal budget, so that all receipts, irrespective of source, and all expenditures, irrespective of destination, would be combined in one unified budget. The seemingly technical accounting decision, which followed the recommendation of a blue-ribbon commission, had the felicitous result, for Johnson, of diverting attention away from the size of the deficit in the general fund, out of which most expenditures, including those to support his budget-busting Vietnam War, were drawn. As Johnson intended, the new presentation combined that deficit, for presentation purposes, with surpluses in the Social Security trust funds. In addition to the recognized consequence of masking the size of the general fund deficit, however, the change in how the budget was presented had the unintended consequence of altering perceptions about Social Security. These altered perceptions were to blossom into full-blown policy fights by the late 1970s.

Throughout its history, Social Security was generally understood to be similar in spirit to a private pension trust established by an employer.[29] In contrast, after the shift in the budget presentation, increasing numbers of policy makers began to portray Social Security like any other entitlement program of the government. From that perspective, it was a small step to the view that Social Security had no greater claim on federal revenue than any other program. On this conception of public finance, federal receipts were fungible, and all claims had to be justified in competition with every other national need.[30]

While many of the policy elite in Washington and in academia embraced this public finance view of Social Security, most Americans continued to view the program as separate and apart from other government spending. They saw the visible withholding not merely as a tax but as a payment that gave them a political claim on future benefits. The perception of the program's benefits as an earned right, a perception held by all supporters at the outset but increasingly rejected by some policy analysts, historically had given those conservatives who wanted to curtail the size of the program an uphill battle. The shift in perception by the policy elite made the uphill climb not quite so steep.

Making the battle even a bit easier was another development. Social Security had lost its stability at the top. Robert M. Ball had been Commissioner of Social Security from 1962 until 1973. During the subsequent eight years, between 1973 and May 6, 1981, when President Reagan appointed Jack Svahn to be commissioner, Social Security experienced fully seven leadership transitions at the top. On the congressional side, Wilbur Mills served in Congress from 1939 until 1977 and had been chairman of the House Ways and Means Committee from 1957 to 1974. Russell Long (D-LA), who chaired the Senate Finance Committee during most of this period, began his career in the Senate in 1948. Each man had developed expertise as a consequence of the frequent Social Security legislation during their tenures in office. With the automatic indexation of benefits and the need to legislate only when the trustees' reports projected deficits, future members of Congress would never have the opportunity to develop such intimate knowledge and shrewd expertise of this complicated institution.

Coupled with the loss of members with expertise were other institutional changes that made consensual decision making, particularly over difficult issues such as benefit cuts and tax increases, much harder to achieve. The post-Watergate reforms, with their limitations on closed-door sessions, reduction in the power of seniority, and other changes designed to make government more democratic and open, arguably made responsible compromise more rare.


## Conclusion: Looking Back and Looking Forward

These various changes—falling confidence in the future of Social Security and in government more generally, growth in private investment vehicles, an academic rationale for fundamentally altering Social Security, a Republican Party less inclusive of moderates and liberals with a pragmatic focus, and changes in both the organization of Congress and the composition of the Democratic leadership—were to set the stage for what was to follow.

Mills, Byrnes, and other traditional conservatives were extremely successful in slowing the size, scope, and growth of social insurance. Benefits never reached the levels that liberal supporters of social insurance desired, nor was general revenue or other progressive financing introduced. While Medicare was enacted, liberal supporters thought it would be the first step to national health insurance. After four decades, no major expansionary steps had been taken.

But the election of President Nixon, in 1968, was the end of the solid Democratic South, and the beginning of party realignment. In the decades that followed, the only Democratic presidents elected—Jimmy Carter and Bill

Clinton—were those who were Southerners themselves. And the 1964 nomination of Goldwater, with the convention's demonizing of Nelson Rockefeller and energizing of extremists ("Extremism in the defense of liberty is no vice..."), brought major changes to which faction held the power in that party.

At the same time, ordinary Americans continued to support the idea of Social Security for the reasons they always had, even though a substantial proportion of them feared the program might be unable to fulfill its promises. Social Security came to have a reputation for political invulnerability for a variety of reasons. Most importantly, its leaders had constructed a rationale for its operation that expressed widely shared American values. It reputation for reliable administration provided additional grounds for regarding the program as one of American government's great successes. Whether the program unambiguously embodied consensual American values is a matter of debate in the scholarly literature. Social Security, its advocates maintain, is conservatively structured. But that does not correspond to what others regard as a core value in the American version of conservatism: namely, sharp limits on the programmatic and financial reach of government. Advocates treat a dedicated tax in the form of equal contributions from employers and employees as a "conservative" way to keep costs in check. The fact that Social Security proceeds from the premise of work surely appeals to a widely shared norm in America. It is true that only those who have worked long enough to gain insured status and those workers' dependents are eligible for benefits, and that does constitute another broad appeal. Likewise, Social Security has been prudently and conservatively managed, with low administrative costs. From a critic's standpoint however, doing the wrong thing prudently does not count as the right thing to do.

More fundamentally, many libertarian conservatives have argued throughout the program's history that it restricts freedom. While most Americans believe that Social Security has given them increased economic independence, there is no doubt about the continuing ideological disagreement about Social Security's place in American political thought. The broad political agreement about the basic stability of Social Security by the end of the 1970s appeared to be unraveling. Certainly the emergence of the Cato Institute, the Heritage Foundation, and the coming Reagan Revolution bolstered that view. But another new actor came on the scene at the beginning of this period. Founded in 1958, the American Association of Retired Persons (AARP) established its Washington presence in 1963. Begun to offer services like health benefits to older Americans, it expanded, over the subsequent decades, to include educational and advocacy work. Though Cato and Heritage might, in the next period, offer insight into the thinking of conservatives, particularly those determined to undo social insurance in this country, the AARP, with its millions-strong membership, would arguably become the better bellwether of where the majority of Americans stood on the issue of Social Security.

## Notes

1. For a comprehensive discussion of the meaning and fundamental logic of social insurance, see Theodore R. Marmor and Jerry L. Mashaw, "Understanding Social Insurance: Fairness, Affordability, and the Modernization Of Social Security And Medicare," *Health Affairs*, March 21, 2006, Web exclusive.

2. As chapter 2 showed, this was by no means the case from the inception of the program. Republicans had challenged Social Security forcefully in the presidential election of 1936; American entry into World War II had brought the program to a standstill with frequent postponements of already scheduled tax increases and frozen benefit levels. The Republican-controlled Congress of 1946 had rolled back the coverage of the program, and the U.S. Chamber of Commerce and Congressman Carl Curtis had sought to convince the Eisenhower administration, the first Republican presidency since the enactment of Social Security, to champion their proposal, which supporters of Social Security believed would unravel the social insurance design of the program.

3. For a brief description of the philosophical underpinnings of social insurance, see Theodore R. Marmor, Jerry L. Mashaw, and Philip L. Harvey, *America's Misunderstood Welfare State: Persistent Myths, Enduring Realities*, (New York: Basic Books, 1990), 26–8.

4. Because Robert J. Myers, Social Security's Chief Actuary from 1947 to 1969, employed conservative assumptions, including static wage growth, prior to the indexing of benefits, the program projected sizable surpluses, paving the way for Congress to enact biannual increases in a fiscally responsible manner. For a more detailed explanation of this point, together with how the relationship of the assumptions and benefit increases was brought to the attention of the politicians, see Nancy J. Altman, *The Battle for Social Security: From FDR's Vision to Bush's Gamble* (Hoboken, NJ: Wiley, 2005), 167–9.

5. It is both obvious and deserving of explanation that the term "conservative" in the common usage lumps various divergent, and sometimes conflicting, ideologies under one label. As Professor James Ceaser has rightly emphasized, "American conservatism is a remarkably disparate movement." He distinguishes four variants found today: traditional conservatives, libertarians, neoconservatives, and the religious right. See James Ceaser, "Four Heads and One Heart: The Modern Conservative Movement in America," paper presented March 30, 2006, at a conference, Conservative Predominance in the United States: A Moment or an Era? University of Montreal, Montreal, Canada (unpublished draft of paper on file with authors).

6. The adoption of the 1950 Amendments and the subsequent biannual legislation raising benefit levels was, as chapter 2 describes, in large part the handiwork of a liberal civil servant, Robert M. Ball. Ball had been, as described in chapter 2, the extremely successful executive director of the 1948–1949 advisory council, whose recommendations led directly to the enactment of the Social Security Amendments of 1950. After his service as executive director of the council, Ball worked for the Social Security Administration in a position that called for him to work closely with Congress. Concerned that benefits, not large to begin with, could keep pace with inflation and gains in the standard of living only if Congress acted, Ball studied the projections of Robert J. Myers, the conservative Chief Actuary of the Social Security Administration. Myers chose to employ conservative, static assumptions in projecting the long-range financial status of Social Security. These conservative assumptions almost guaranteed unanticipated surpluses in the program's funding. The surpluses, in turn, permitted Congress to increase benefits every two years, right before elections, without the necessity of substantial tax increases to pay for them.

Ball understood the natural proclivity of elected politicians to seek opportunities for credit-claiming and recognized the opportunity for this credit-claiming that Myers' method of making projections offered. In the spring of 1952, Ball had called Charlie Davis, the clerk of the Ways and Means Committee, and explained to him that the projected Social Security surplus made a benefit increase possible without raising taxes in an election year. Davis, in turn, informed his boss, the chairman of the Committee, Robert L. Doughton (D-NC).

7. The basis for this claim is the discussion in Theodore R. Marmor, *The Politics of Medicare,* (Transaction Books, 1973, 2000).

8. See Polsby, *How Congress Evolves: Social Bases of Institutional Change* (New York: Oxford University Press, 2003).

9. Whether Mills, Byrnes, and other, as we term them, nonradical, traditional conservatives favored the concept of social insurance, but simply did not want its expansion, or simply accepted it as a fixture in American life, too entrenched to turn back, is, we believe, unknowable, but more importantly, inapposite to our thesis. There is some, at least indirect, evidence that some in that group did indeed embrace the concept of social insurance. For example, Byrnes, in an oral history interview conducted in 1979, in explaining his opposition to Medicare, seemed to implicitly approve of other forms of social insurance: "There was just no justification for [putting a tax on wages to finance a health benefit.] You could justify unemployment compensation or [disability] insurance…" John Byrnes, Oral History Interview, recorded by Charles Morrisey, January 17, 1979. Manuscript Division, Library of Congress, 24–5. Whatever his views with respect to prior enactments, what is clear is that Byrnes did not champion expansions of social insurance.

10. The basis for this generalization is illustrated by the Social Security Amendments of 1958 and 1960, and events following the election. Social Security's

Amendments of 1960, for example, became law on September 13, 1960, less than two months before the upcoming election, a timetable that by now had become established practice. The legislation contained expansions of Social Security's retirement, disability, and survivor benefits, all enacted without controversy. See Altman, *The Battle for Social Security.*

11. Sed Paul Pierson, "Not Just What, but *When:* Timing and Sequence in Political Processes," *Studies in American Political Development* 14 (Spring 2000) "Increasing Returns, Path Dependence, and the Study of Politics," *American Political Science Review* 94, 2 (2000): 251–67; Kathleen Thelen, "Timing and Temporality in the Analysis of Institutional Evolution and Change," *Studies in American Political Development* 14, 2 (2000): 101–8.

12. See chapter 5 of Theodore Marmor, *The Politics of Medicare,* op. cit.

13. "Cabal" is a slightly pejorative term to describe these long-term reformers and their allies in the Social Security Administration, the labor movement, and other "liberal" interest groups who shared the expansionist aspiration; cf. Derthick. For a discussion of these reformers and their role that does not have the connotations of a "cabal," see Marmor and Feldman, "Policy Entrepreneurs: Robert Ball and Wilbur J. Cohen," *Public Policy.*

14. See chapters 9 and 10 of Altman, *The Battle for Social Security.*

15. Donald Bruce Johnson and Kirk H. Porter, *National Party Platforms 1840–1972* (Urbana, Chicago, London: University of Illinois Press, 1956, 1966, 1970, 1973), 736.

16. Altman, ibid. at 209, quoting Richard M. Nixon, Special Message to Congress, September 25, 1969.

17. For a more detailed discussion, see Altman, op. cit, 209–11.

18. See Marmor, Mashaw and Harvey, op. cit, for a discussion of the context in which stagflation transformed the environment for discussion of social policy in the 1970s.

19. 1978 Annual Report of the Board of Trustees of the Federal Old-Age and Survivors Insurance Aand Disability Insurance Trust Funds, (May 16, 1978), 2.

20. Rick Shenkman, "When Did Social Security Become the Third Rail of American Politics?" History News Network, available at http://hnn.us/articles/10522.html.

21. "The Man on the Bandwagon," *Time Magazine* (June 12, 1964), at http://www.time.com/time/magazine/article/0,9171,875856–6,00.html.

22. Theodore H. White, *The Making of the President, 1964* (New York: Atheneum Publishers, 1965), 104.

23. In 1964, Ronald Reagan explicitly voiced anti–Social Security sentiments, similar to those expressed by Goldwater. Speaking in a televised address in support of Goldwater, on October 27, 1964, Reagan criticized Social Security and called for making it voluntary. Toward the end of the speech, he summarized, "[I]n 1936, Mr. Democrat himself, Al Smith, the great American, came before the American people and charged that the leadership of his Party was taking the Party of Jefferson, Jackson, and Cleveland down the road under

the banners of Marx, Lenin, and Stalin. And he walked away from his Party, and he never returned til the day he died—because to this day, the leadership of that Party has been taking that Party...down the road in the image of the labor Socialist Party of England." Ronald Reagan, "A Time for Choosing" 10/27/64), at http://rncnyc2004.blogspot.com/2007/08/ronald-reagan-time-for-choosing-102764.html. By his successful run for the presidency, Ronald Reagan showed a different face. When accused by President Carter, during the second debate, of favoring making Social Security voluntary, Reagan implicitly disavowed his earlier position, stating, "I, too, am pledged to a Social Security program that will reassure these senior citizens of ours that they are going to continue to get their money." Second 1980 Presidential Debate, October 28, 1980, at www.pbs.org/newhour/debatingourdestiny/80debates/cart4.html.

24. Lou Cannon, *Governor Reagan* (New York: Public Affairs, 2003), 420.

25. Letter from Dwight D. Eisenhower to Edgar Newton Eisenhower, Document #1147, The Papers of Dwight David Eisenhower, *Volume XV—The Presidency: The Middle Way,*[0] available at http://eisenhowermemorial.org/presidential-papers/first-term/documents/1147.cfm.

26. Milton Friedman advised Richard Nixon on monetary policy, and Friedman's ideas about a negative income tax influenced Nixon's ultimately unsuccessful Family Assistance Plan. Nixon was extremely pragmatic in policy terms. He was less dominated by ideological appeals, as his administration's positions on both China policy and health reform showed. In particular, he does not appear to be influenced by Friedman about Social Security. Indeed, in an interview on PBS, Friedman claimed that "Nixon was the most socialist of the presidents of the United States in the 20th century." See "Commanding Heights," Milton Friedman on PBS (10/01/00, at http://www.pbs.org/wgbh/commandingheights/shared/minitext/int_miltonfriedman.html#8

27. Information about YAF Foundation at http://www.yaf.org/whoweare.asp.

28. See, for example, Martin Feldstein, "The Effect of Social Security on Saving," *Contemporary Economic Analysis III* (London: Croom Helm, 1981), Michael J. Boskin, Laurence J. Kotlikoff, Douglas J. Puffert, and John B. Shoven. "Social Security: A Financial Appraisal across and within Generations," *The National Tax Journal* XL, 1 (March 1987): 19–34. For a brief critique of some of the problems with these analyses, see Altman, *The Battle for Social Security*, 226.

29. Historically, Social Security was presented by its advocates to be a pension program, one to which people contributed with the expectation of receiving benefits in the event of an insured event—death, disability, or old age. The federal government was portrayed as a reliable, organizational instrument to collect, disburse, oversee, and make rules regarding Social Security's funds. Unlike general fund expenditures, Social Security has its own source of financing, contributions authorized by the Federal Insurance Contributions Act, whose use is restricted to payment for Social Security benefits.

30. David Stockman, President Reagan's director of the Office of Management and Budget, perhaps best exemplifies this perspective. Stockman saw Social Security, which he called "closet socialism," as simply one more part of the overblown welfare state. David A. Stockman, *The Triumph of Politics* New York: Harper & Row, 1986), 182.

As part of the 1980 Reagan transition, Stockman prepared a memorandum entitled "Avoiding a GOP Economic Dunkirk." He recommended that in Reagan's first 100 days in office, the president propose an economic package consisting of both tax reductions and substantial cuts to Social Security and other programs in the federal budget, which he claimed had "become an automatic 'coast-to-coast soup line.'" William Greider, *The Education of David Stockman* (New York: E. P. Dutton, 1981, 1982), 141.

A remark that captures perfectly the perceptual shift that occurred by including Social Security as part of the unified budget is one that Stockman made in private conversation with journalist William Greider. In analyzing alternative ways to squeeze money from Social Security, Stockman commented, "I'm just not going to spend a lot of political capital solving some other guy's problem in 2010." Rather, it was enough for him to worry four or five years down the road. To Ball, Cohen, and Myers, Social Security deficits in 2010 were not, in any way, "some other guy's problem." These are words that Cohen, Myers, or Ball would never have thought, much less uttered. They, like those who came before, saw Social Security on its own terms, a pension program that required balance over a period of decades.

Stockman's view was not limited to conservative Republicans. President Jimmy Carter, for example, was the first president to propose cuts to Social Security as part of a budget bill and not a Social Security bill. This did not mean Social Security had lost its programmatic autonomy, but it did suggest a less protected conception of its financing, which in turn was partly an unexpected consequence of the unification of the Federal budget in the late 1960s. On the other hand, this departure from separate accounting did not suddenly make Social Security vulnerable to cuts because of deficits in the rest of the budget. As the following chapter portrays, just about every effort to connect Social Security to the deficit politics of the 1980s failed.

# CHAPTER 6

## Education Policy from the Great Society to 1980: The Expansion and Institutionalization of the Federal Role in Schools

*Patrick McGuinn*

*The Proposed department [of education] is expressly designed to provide more money and more federal control of education.... It is not difficult to imagine this department establishing national "advisory" standards at some point in the future. Later, the department could require adherence to the compulsory standards if federal aid is to be continued. Next, standard tests, developed by the federal government, could be mandated to check whether the compulsory standards are being met. Last, State and local authorities will be coerced into acceptance of a standardized curriculum as the "only possible" guarantee of meeting compulsory standards.*
—Senator Harrison Schmitt (R-NM)[1]

America has a powerful tradition of limited government and local control in education; the federal government had little direct involvement in American education until the 1950s.[2] As Davies demonstrates in chapter 3, the widespread opposition to federal "intrusion" in education enabled conservatives to defeat most of the earlier proposals for new federal school programs or spending. Despite the New Deal's nationalizing effect on many areas of social policy, federal activism in education during that period was quite limited and was confined to a few small unconditional grants to the states and support for higher education through programs such as the G.I. Bill. The nation's school system remained extremely decentralized, and the day-to-day management of schools, including such matters as personnel, curriculum, assessment, and pedagogy remained in the hands of local authorities. The ability and willingness of conservatives to block proposals for greater federal involvement in education, however, began to change in the 1950s.

The Supreme Court's 1954 *Brown v. Board of Education* decision, together with the 1958 National Defense Education Act (NDEA) and the 1965 Elementary and Secondary Education Act (ESEA), initiated a new era of federal activism in education that continues to this day. At the heart of ESEA was a powerful equity rationale for federal government activism to promote greater economic opportunity through more equal access to more equally funded schools. Conservatives ensured that the original design of the program focused on providing targeted funds to disadvantaged students, with little federal involvement as to how the resources were utilized by state and local education authorities. Over time, however, federal legislative enactments, bureaucratic regulations, and court mandates in education became increasingly numerous and prescriptive, and federal influence over schools grew significantly, symbolized by the creation of the U.S. Department of Education in 1979. By the 1980s, policy feedback, and in particular the contentious politics of desegregation and growing skepticism about the intrusiveness and efficacy of federal education programs, led to a backlash against ESEA and provided an opening for conservatives to restrain and reform federal involvement in schools.

## Conservatives, the Great Society and the Passage of ESEA

ESEA was the big bang of federal education policy, the moment when national authority over schools grew suddenly and, in retrospect, decisively. How was ESEA able to overcome the many political and institutional obstacles that had stymied earlier attempts to expand the federal role in education? Why were conservatives unable to defeat this new proposal, as they had previous ones, or to prevent ESEA's rapid entrenchment and expansion in subsequent years?

### *The Opponents of Federal Aid to Education*

The political landscape of education at the national level in the 1960s was complex and contentious. The educational conservatives of the period came from many different corners of society and with very different interests, and as a result had very different reasons for opposing expanded federal influence in schools. The point that would prove crucial politically is that some conservatives were opposed to federal influence in education per se while others were opposed only to certain kinds of federal influence. The first group of opponents comprised those that might be considered "principled" conservatives and was composed of states' rights defenders, libertarians, and religious and social conservatives. Libertarians' focus on individual freedom and social and religious conservatives' focus on instilling values would at times come into conflict, but during most of the 1960s and 1970s they were united in their common opposition to the liberal policy agenda. For advocates of states' rights, opposition to federal intrusion in education was a matter of fundamental constitutional principle, and these folks rarely wavered in their defense of federalism. One of the most outspoken members of this group was Barry Goldwater, who once famously remarked that in the struggle to control our educational system, "I fear Washington as much as Moscow."[3]

The second group of opponents to federal influence in education was comprised of what might be called "co-optable conservatives." Members of this group were at times some of the most vocal opponents of a federal role in education, and their intervention was crucial to the defeat of federal aid proposals in the 1940s and 1950s. However, their opposition did not rest on ideological principle but rather on the content of particular bills, and their support could be bought. In this category were Catholics, represented by the U.S. Catholic Conference, who were willing to support federal aid to education, but only if parochial schools were included. State and local education officials, and particularly the influential Council of Chief State School Officers, could also be put in this group—while they remained adamantly opposed to federal mandates and regulations, they were quite supportive of federal programs that would deliver money to their schools.

The business community, in 1965 as in contemporary times, was another crucial wild card in the debate over federal involvement in education. It clearly had a keen interest in whether the country's schools were producing good workers and was a very powerful force in national education debates, as it was in public policy more generally. Some business groups, such as the U.S. Chamber of Commerce, the National Association of Manufacturers, and the American Farm Bureau, vigorously fought federal education aid during this period. Other business groups, however, were more inclined to see federal education funding as a subsidy—one that could potentially reduce both their corporate taxes and the amount of money they spent training workers.

A third group of opponents—and arguably the most important source of opposition to federal aid to education during the 1940s and 1950s—was segregationists, many of whom were conservative Southern Democrats. As

Davies discussed in his earlier chapter, many of these Democrats occupied powerful committee chairmanships in Congress because of Democratic Party strength in the South and the central position of this group within the New Deal coalition. During the first half of the twentieth century, these committee chairmen used their influence to block civil rights legislation as well as any federal program that might be used to force Southern states to integrate their public schools. The Democratic Party operated during the New Deal period under a fragile political dynamic—Southern conservatives in Congress would lend their support (or at least not oppose) liberal social welfare programs as long as they were not pushed too hard on the integration issue.

Prior to the 1960s, these different groups of conservatives were generally united in their opposition to proposals for an expanded federal role in education. By the late 1950s and early 1960s, however, a number of political developments had increased the leverage of proponents of federal education aid while simultaneously weakening the position of its opponents. These developments included a greater awareness of educational inequality by elites and the public, the passage of the Civil Rights Act, increased liberal strength in Congress, effective presidential leadership and tactics, and interest group mobilization and advocacy. Taken together, these developments served to strip away pillars of the conservative coalition and to undermine the public standing and the institutional influence of those that remained.

## A New Political Climate: Changes in Public and Elite Opinion on Education

Prior to World War II, education was not high on the national agenda (to the extent that it emerged on that agenda at all) and candidates for national political office generally ignored the issue. Progressives had fought doggedly to convince the public that schooling decisions ought to be entrusted to "nonpolitical" educational professionals,[4] and when education did emerge as a political issue, it was typically due to religious, ethnic, or racial tensions, rather than more abstract concerns about school quality.[5] During the New Deal, however, a tremendous increase in the breadth and depth of the activities of the federal government occurred, along with a profound change in public and judicial attitudes toward the responsibilities of government. Americans began to look to the national government for solutions to their economic and social problems to an unprecedented extent.

Education gained new prominence in America after World War II as high school completion became the norm and as the G.I. Bill spurred a dramatic increase in college enrollment.[6] For the first time, education became part of the lexicon of the working-class American and a key to economic and social mobility.[7] Local school districts were struggling with the demographic challenges presented by the baby boom as the number of students enrolled in K-12 schools in the United States doubled between 1940 and 1965, from 27 million to 53 million. In addition, during this period, expanding educational access became a central objective of the civil rights movement. The Supreme Court's *Brown v. Board of Education* decision in 1954 calling for the end of segregated schools dramatically altered the politics of educational policy making in the United States. The *Brown* decision would ultimately engage the federal government directly and forcefully in the effort to create a more equitable system of public schooling for the first time in the nation's history. The Court's powerful statement in *Brown* on the importance of equal educational opportunity also helped to give rise to a public conception of education as the birthright of a free citizenry and essential to social justice.[8]

These developments, together with the publication of a large body of social science research during the 1950s and 1960s, created a much greater public awareness of the economic and educational inequalities facing racial minorities and the poor in the United States. Work by Michael Harrington (*The Other America*), James Conant (*Slums and Suburbs*), and others highlighted the resource and achievement gap between students in poor schools on the one hand and students in middle- and upper-class schools on the other. Poor children, it was also recognized at the time, were concentrated in the inner cities and were often from racial minority groups. The consequence, as one observer noted, was that "beginning in the 1950's and continuing through the 1960's and 1970's, Americans generally were made keenly aware of the existence of a number of social injustices. Thus, there developed a climate of public opinion favorable to social reform efforts."[9] Federal and judicial pressure to integrate local schools would ultimately prove enormously controversial, particularly after the courts adopted a more aggressive approach and timetable for integration in the late 1960s (see below). But in the 1950s and early 1960s, the ultimate extent and cost of federal integration efforts was unknown, and the ideal of expanding educational opportunity for all citizens was quite powerful. As Davies noted in chapter 3, the local control paradigm that had long dominated the discourse over the federal role in education was replaced by a civil rights paradigm that emphasized the need to deploy national power in the pursuit of equality.

## New Rationales and Precedents: Education Aid as Defense Spending

Given the strength of conservatives in Congress and liberals' limited success in mobilizing support for increased federal education aid on purely educational grounds, proponents shifted tactics in the late 1950s and sought to tie such aid to other pressing domestic and international issues. In the 1950s, proponents used America's Cold War competition with the Soviet Union to provide a conservative justification for greater federal involvement in education with the National Defense Education Act (NDEA) of 1958, which provided categorical aid to states to improve math, science, and foreign language instruction in American schools. As Lee Anderson has observed: "The NDEA debate placed the education system at the center of federal efforts to solve non-educational problems. This strategy may have helped eclipse long-standing, bipartisan suspicion of federal involvement because schools were portrayed as one front in the broader ideological struggle against communism."[10] The NDEA passed 212 to 85 in the House and 66 to 15 in the Senate, and secured a majority of Republicans in each chamber. The program was an important political precedent and psychological breakthrough for advocates of federal aid to education, and it demonstrated that many Republicans were quite willing to expand the federal role in education in certain circumstances.

Even the opponents of federal involvement in education recognized the NDEA's significance, with Barry Goldwater writing during consideration of the bill that it reminded him "of an old Arabian proverb: 'If the camel once gets his nose in the tent, his body will soon follow.' If adopted, the legislation will mark the inception of aid, supervision, and ultimately control of education in this country by federal authorities."[11] Nonetheless, as of 1960, national support for education remained quite small in absolute dollars (less than $1 billion) and as a percentage of total education spending (around 2 percent). Due to fears of federal control, funding from NDEA and earlier programs was also fragmented into several categorical grants, with little direct federal oversight, and was generally devoted to narrow ends: statistics collection, specialized research and demonstration grants, vocational education assistance, the school lunch program, and impact aid.

The 1950s and early 1960s thus had a mixed legacy for the national politics of education. On the one hand, the Cold War demand for improved technical education, the greater number of Americans attending high school and college, and a growing awareness of the financial and racial inequities in the public school system combined to increase the salience of education and create significant momentum for expanded federal support for schools. Many citizens and political elites became convinced that states and localities were either unable or unwilling to address educational failures and inequities on their own. On the other hand, most conservatives in Congress, as well as most Americans, continued to believe that education policy decisions should be made at the state and local levels, and the period witnessed growing and often intense opposition to federal efforts to integrate public schools. As a result, as Graham has written in his classic work on the period, "to propose federal 'intrusion' into the sanctity of the state-local-private preserve of education was to stride boldly into a uniquely dangerous political mine field that pitted Democrat against Republican, liberal against conservative, Catholic against Protestant and Jew, federal power against states rights, white against black, and rich constituency against poor in mercurial cross-cutting alliances."[12] As Davies notes, conservatives succeeded in defeating a number of proposals for increased federal education spending by President Kennedy's administration in the early 1960s.

## LBJ's Extraordinary Leadership and Education Aid as Anti-Poverty Spending

A number of political developments converged in 1964 to create a more favorable legislative environment for an expanded federal role in education. Kennedy's successor, his vice president and the former Senate Majority Leader Lyndon Johnson, capitalized on the growing public awareness of school inequalities, the political goodwill for Kennedy's agenda following his assassination, and the large Democratic majority in Congress following the 1964 election to push again for an education bill. Johnson won the election by what was then the largest margin in American history—16 million votes. Johnson's popularity was widely credited with helping the Democratic Party significantly increase its control of Congress by expanding its majority to 36 in the Senate and 155 in the House. Equally important for the debate over education was the election of many liberals who favored greater federal involvement in education. As Eidenberg and Morey have noted, "Whereas in the Eighty-Eighth Congress, the coalition of southern Democrats and conservative Republicans held a working majority in the House, the Eighty-ninth Congress was tightly held by northern liberal Democrats."[13] One particularly important consequence of this shift was a series of procedural changes that limited the power of the House Rules Committee, which had been the graveyard for many education bills under the conservative leadership of Howard Smith of Virginia. The House Education Committee had witnessed a changing of the guard in 1961 when Chairman Graham Barden, a Southern conservative and opponent of federal aid to education, was replaced with Adam Clayton Powell, a liberal Northerner and an advocate of federal aid. The changes in these two powerful committees removed important institutional barriers to an expanded federal role in education.

As a former teacher, Johnson had a deep personal commitment to education, and he used the bully pulpit to talk about education more than any previous president in American history (see Table 6.1). Johnson also saw federal leadership in education as a logical—and essential—extension of the New Deal.

**Table 6.1.** Presidential Attention to Education (1789–1981)

| Years | President | Total Speeches with Word "Education" | Average Number of Speeches with Word "Education"/Year |
|---|---|---|---|
| 1789–1913 | Washington-Taft | 226 | 2 |
| 1929–1933 | Hoover | 148 | 37 |
| 1933–1945 | Roosevelt | 382 | 29 |
| 1945–1953 | Truman | 667 | 74 |
| 1953–1961 | Eisenhower | 771 | 96 |
| 1961–1963 | Kennedy | 777 | 259 |
| 1963–1969 | Johnson | 3,104 | 621 |
| 1969–1974 | Nixon | 1,428 | 238 |
| 1974–1977 | Ford | 830 | 277 |
| 1977–1981 | Carter | 2,055 | 514 |

Totals represent the number of public speeches and statements containing the word "education." Analysis conducted by author of the Public Papers of the Presidents of the United States, accessed online at http://www.gpo.gov/nara/pubpaps/srchpaps.html.

Johnson made education one of his administration's highest priorities and used his strong popular mandate and the gratitude of many Democratic senators and congressmen for the strength of his coattails to lobby for their support effectively. LBJ declared a "war on poverty" and thrust the quest for civil rights to the center of his domestic agenda. His education proposal became a central component of the broader antidiscrimination efforts begun with the Civil Rights Act of 1964 and of his antipoverty program, which had rejected an income-transfer strategy in favor of an emphasis on job training and education. In much the same way that liberals had linked NDEA to national security, Johnson hitched his federal aid proposal to another important national goal, aiding the poor, and adopted a rhetoric that appealed to conservatives as well as liberals. Johnson argued that "very often, a lack of jobs and money is not the cause of poverty, but the symptom. The cause may lie deeper—in our failure to give our fellow citizens a fair chance to develop their own capacities in a lack of education and training."[14] If education was the key to social mobility, however, it was clear that too many schools lacked the resources to provide the necessary skills to students from disadvantaged backgrounds.[15]

## Programmatic Design: Navigating the "Three Rs"

From the outset, Johnson and his advisors were cognizant of the political obstacles that had defeated previous attempts to expand the federal role in education. What had become known as the "three Rs"—race, religion, and the Reds (opposition to government support for integration, Catholic schools, and bureaucratic centralization)—remained a substantial barrier. The passage of the Civil Rights Act in 1964—and particularly Title VI, which outlawed the allocation of federal funds to segregated programs—would prevent federal education bills from becoming entangled with racial issues as they had in 1956 and 1960.[16] Johnson's Commissioner of Education Francis Keppel warned in a 1964 memo, however, that the other two Rs remained. Any plan to provide substantial new federal aid to schools, he observed, would still meet with intense opposition from states' rights and antigovernment conservatives as well as from two important Democratic constituencies, Catholics and the NEA.[17] Catholics opposed any bill that would direct federal money to public but not private schools, while the NEA opposed any diversion of federal education aid to private schools.

Keppel devised an ingenious compromise solution that provided the basis for the Elementary and Secondary Education Act (ESEA). His plan was to target federal aid to poor children, regardless of the type of school they attended (whether public or private). This plan had the advantage of spreading money around to a majority of congressional districts, to public and private school children, and to state education agencies for implementation purposes, thereby undercutting most of the potential political opposition to the aid. Keppel also recommended linking ESEA to the existing impact aid program, which had been established 14 years earlier and which enjoyed strong congressional support. Determined to prevent the bill from getting bogged down by endless public debates in congressional committees, the legislation was drafted in secret by a presidential task force and then passed through Congress quickly, with no amendments and with so little deliberation that it became known as the "Great Railroad Act of 1965."[18] By all accounts, President Johnson's legislative savvy and active lobbying on the bill's behalf were crucial to its passage. As Harold Howe (who succeeded Keppel as Commissioner of Education in 1965) remarked: "Johnson asserted a very personal influence...the 89th Congress voted all the new education legislation through, literally *pushed* by him."[19]

The bill was supported by large majorities in both chambers, passing by a vote of 263 to 153 in the House and 73 to 18 in the Senate. As had been the case with impact aid and the NDEA, the ESEA bill attracted a considerable amount of Republican support, with a majority of GOP Senators (18 of 32) and 35 of the 131 Republicans in the House voting for it.[20] A closer analysis of the vote on ESEA, however, demonstrates clear ideological divisions, as the mean ADA score of ESEA supporters was 61 in the House and 52 in the Senate and the mean ADA scores of opponents was 4.6 in the House and 1.8 in the Senate.[21] One way to understand why conservatives were unable to defeat ESEA or have greater influence on its provisions is to recognize that they were simply outnumbered in 1965—both inside and outside Congress. A number of important conservative groups—such as the Chamber of Commerce and the Daughters of the American Revolution—remained fundamentally opposed to federal aid to education and fought against the bill. But as one set of observers noted, these groups' "role and effectiveness within the education community and the Education and Labor Committee were negligible by the time the 1965 debate began."[22] In addition, while the initial parts of the liberal education establishment were already in place and were advocating passionately and effectively for federal aid, conservatives at the time lacked the grassroots organization or Washington infrastructure with which to counter their effort.

Eugene Eidenberg and Roy Morey, however, offer an additional hypothesis for why Republicans failed to mount more effective opposition to ESEA. They argue that after the Republicans' brutal electoral defeat in 1964, the House GOP leadership, under the direction of new Minority Leader Gerald Ford (R-MI), made a crucial change in legislative strategy. Convinced that the party had become negatively defined by its "blind opposition" to Democratic proposals, Ford pushed Republicans to become more constructive and to develop alternative proposals instead. "This new strategy prevented the minority members of the Education and Labor Committee from dismissing the school bill out of hand or from challenging the basic concept of federal aid. From the start, Republicans attempted to make it clear that they did not disagree with the majority on the need for school assistance but rather were taking issue with the means proposed."[23] Thus, while Republicans on the House Education and Labor Committee objected that the bill would transfer too much authority to the U.S. Office of Education (USOE), they also called for *more* federal spending on impoverished communities and for preschool training and aid to handicapped children.[24] At that time and later, the popularity of federal education spending among the general public—as well as its appeal as a major source of pork for congressional districts—presented a thorny political challenge for conservatives.

Many observers at the time remarked on the symbolic significance of ESEA for national education policy—an important threshold had been crossed and an important federal role in education policy cemented. President Johnson remarked at the time that in one year Congress "did more for the wonderful cause of education in America than all the previous 176 regular sessions of Congress did, put together."[25] And as both the supporters and opponents of federal aid to education acknowledged, the federal role in education was likely to expand after ESEA despite continuing opposition on some fronts. Congressman John Williams (R-DE), for example, remarked after the passage of ESEA that "Make no mistake about it this bill...is merely the beginning. It contains within it the seeds of the first federal education system which will be nurtured by its supporters in the years to come long after the current excuse of aiding the poverty stricken is forgotten.... The needy are being used as a wedge to open the floodgates, and you may be absolutely certain that the flood of federal control is ready to sweep the land."[26] The combination of the NDEA and the ESEA were to dramatically increase federal funding for education both in absolute terms and as a proportion of total education spending. Between 1958 and 1968, for example, federal spending on education multiplied more than ten times, from $375 million to $4.2 billion, and the federal share expanded from less than 3 percent to about 10 percent of all school funding.

ESEA was intended to be primarily a redistributive bill, to put a floor under spending in the nation's poorest communities and to lend federal muscle to efforts to innovate and improve educational services. The centerpiece of this effort and of the legislation itself was the Title I program, which received $1.06 billion of the initial $1.3 billion appropriated for ESEA.[27] The nature of the legislative process, however, meant that the redistributive edge of ESEA got rubbed off as money was spread around in exchange for political support. In the end, the funding formula was designed to maximize the number of school districts (and thus the number of congressional districts) that would be eligible. Ninety-four percent of the school districts in America ultimately received ESEA funds, which was an important reason for the program's popularity among liberals and conservatives, politicians and citizens alike. Because they were disproportionately poor, southern states received a disproportionately high share of Title I funds (42%), which helped diffuse potential political opposition from Southern conservatives. The restrictions on how ESEA money could be spent were also loosened considerably under pressure from conservatives. In order to assuage fears of federal control, the law specified that Title I funds could be used for a variety of purposes, including hiring additional staff, purchasing classroom equipment, or for classroom instruction.[28]

The design as well as the substance of ESEA was to have important consequences for the evolution of the federal role in education policy. One of the most significant features of ESEA was what it did *not* do—it did not provide general federal aid to public schools in the United States. Earlier liberal education proposals had typically called for such general aid because it was thought that this would result in a larger and more sustained federal commitment. It was for precisely those reasons that conservatives fought so hard to make ESEA programs categorical. While the political opposition to federal "control" in education had precluded the inclusion of any meaningful enforcement mechanism in the original ESEA legislation, as will be discussed in detail below, this would change in relatively short order. The categorical nature of ESEA thus ultimately opened the door to congressional and bureaucratic oversight of school districts and necessitated the creation of new federal administrative capacities to oversee the implementation of federal programs and ensure state compliance. This was a particularly ironic development given the insistence of many conservatives during the initial ESEA deliberations that any federal aid should be categorical in order to limit the size and intrusiveness of federal influence over states.

In addition to their role in administration, however, these federal educational institutions came to serve an important political purpose—as both defenders of existing federal education programs and advocates for new ones. As Terry Moe has noted, institutions are sticky—"they constitute an institutional base that is protected by all the impediments to new legislation inherent in separation of powers, as well as by the political clout of the agency's supporters. Most of the pushing and hauling in subsequent years is likely to produce only incremental change."[29] Increases in federal institutional capacity have thus not only enhanced the ability of the federal government to implement education programs, but have also contributed to a dynamic cycle of program creation and expansion. The NDEA and the ESEA had important consequences for the politics of ideas and the institutional structures that formed the context for future federal education policy debates. In a sense, it became path dependent. This did not mean that consideration of alternative arrangements was foreclosed, rather it made a rapid and sharp change of approach—such as was desired by many conservatives—exceptionally difficult and unlikely.

Once the federal role in education policy had been institutionalized, it became more difficult for opponents of that role to substantially reduce or change it. Any politician who proposed cutting federal education spending or eliminating federal education programs was labeled as being "against education" and suffered political consequences. The ideational and institutional legacy of ESEA, though it circumscribed the federal role in education in the short term, thus created many of the conditions that ultimately contributed to an expansion of the federal role. The focus on student socio-economic status and school resources enshrined an equal opportunity rationale into national education policy and created a federal education assistance entitlement for disadvantaged students. As more students were shown to be disadvantaged and as more and more disadvantages were claimed by social scientists and policy makers to impede children's learning, there was pressure for federal education aid to expand.

## The Growth and Institutionalization of the Federal Role in Education

The fundamental feature of the political environment of the Great Society era was the strength of the New Deal coalition—both in Washington and among voters at large. This enabled Democrats to dominate Congress for most of the 1960s, 1970s, and 1980s, and united the party in support of federal social welfare programs and efforts to equalize educational access and funding. While conservatives were unable to prevent the passage of ESEA, they succeeded in limiting the size and scope of the program and promised to remain vigilant to ensure that it remained so as it was implemented. As one observer noted, "the devotees of the 'religion of localism' were deeply suspicious of federal intentions. This meant that ESEA and especially Title I had to lean over backward to minimize the kinds of federal strings that were normally attached to categorical grants."[30] The original legislation gave the USOE little power to coerce states to comply with federal regulations or goals or to punish states and school districts that failed to do so. In another instance of irony, however, the successful efforts of conservatives in removing federal micromanagement from the initial ESEA funding increased the aid's popularity among states and made them less willing to join conservative efforts to repeal it.

The consequence of ESEA's initial flexibility was that federal funds were used in a wide variety of ways and for a wide variety of purposes, and local districts often diverted funds away from redistributive programs.[31] As Graham observed, "the upshot of all this is that when Title I was implemented, it produced not *a* Title I program, but something more like 30 thousand separate and different Title I programs."[32] The large amount of discretion accorded to states and school districts in spending the new federal money ensured that compliance with federal goals in the initial years of ESEA was spotty at best. In his examination of the implementation of ESEA, Berke noted that "federal aid is channeled into an existing state political system and pattern of policy, and a blend distilled of federal priorities and the frequently different state priorities emerges. . . . Federal money is a stream that must pass through a state capitol; at the state level, the federal government is rarely able—through its guidelines and regulations—radically to divert the stream or reverse the current."[33]

Initially the USOE relied on the assurances of state education officials that they were in compliance with federal guidelines.[34] But one of the fundamental premises behind the idea of compensatory education, and of ESEA more generally, was that state and local education authorities had failed to ensure equal educational opportunities for their students and that they could not be trusted to do so in the future without federal intervention. The distrust of local education authorities—and mounting evidence that states and localities were diverting federal funds to purposes for which they were not intended—ultimately led Congress and federal bureaucrats to increase the regulation and supervision of federal aid. By the 1970s, the additional resources available to the U.S. Office of Education and the agency's gradual adjustment to its new administrative role led the USOE to more aggressively enforce federal education mandates.[35] As Diane Ravitch has observed, "in this atmosphere of discord and distrust, those with grievances turned naturally to the courts and the federal government to enforce their rights against local school boards.... Programs, regulations, and court orders began to reflect the strong suspicion that those in control of American institutions were not to be trusted with any discretion where minorities, women, or other aggrieved groups were concerned."[36]

The implementation of ESEA also quickly became enmeshed in the highly charged struggles over integration and busing that were fought across the country during the 1960s and 1970s. While it was the 1964 Civil Rights Act that declared that federal funds could not be allocated to support segregated institutions or programs, it was ESEA funding that became a key carrot (and stick) for federal integration efforts. States that failed to comply with court integration decrees would lose their share of federal education funds, which as noted above were very sizable after the creation of ESEA. The original *Brown* decision in 1954, while declaring that states must integrate their public schools, was silent on the crucial issues of when and how this was to be accomplished. The court's 1955 *Brown II* decision declared that integration should proceed "with all deliberate speed," but the Court again declined to set firm deadlines or methods for integration. The following year, 101 congressmen and senators from the South signed the "Southern Manifesto," which denounced the *Brown* decisions as "contrary to established law and to the Constitution." Recalcitrant states such as Virginia engaged in "massive resistance" and were able to postpone large-scale integration efforts.[37] The initial flexibility and discretion that the Supreme Court accorded state desegregation efforts came to an end, however, with the 1968 *Green v. County School Board of Kent County, Virginia* case, when the court declared that school boards must develop integration plans that promise "realistically to work *now*."[38] In response to the decision, lower courts mandated the widespread busing of students, which engendered a great deal of disruption and opposition across the country.

Continuing opposition to federal involvement in the core functions of schooling and the lack of consensus on how to measure the effectiveness of school reform efforts led federal administrators to focus on school districts' spending patterns and administrative compliance. The result was that large numbers of bureaucratic regulations were created during the 1970s without any kind of concomitant focus on student or school results—everything was judged by procedure and process. In the 1980s, John Chubb would note that "in federal programs that are not explicitly regulatory, as well as those that are, policy has come to be carried out by increasingly detailed, prescriptive, legalistic, and authoritative means."[39] Between 1964 and 1976, for example, the number of pages of federal legislation affecting education increased from

80 to 360, while the number of federal regulations increased from 92 in 1965 to nearly 1,000 in 1977.[40]

One of the most significant consequences of ESEA was thus the bureaucratization and centralization of education policy making from the local level to the state and federal levels. From 1965 to 1975, federal funds for elementary and secondary education more than doubled (with a 210 percent increase in inflation adjusted dollars).[41] In addition, between 1960 and 1985, the percentage of total education spending provided by the national government grew from 8 percent to 16 percent. Over the same period, the share of local spending dipped from 51 percent to 31 percent, while the state share increased from 41 percent to 55 percent.[42] Eligibility for federal education funds was often conditioned on the provision of state matching funds, the creation of central implementing offices, and the collection of a variety of statistical information, which necessitated that state education agencies expand their size and activities and become more institutionalized. This was a clear objective of ESEA, as the original legislation contained funding for the agencies to build up their administrative capacity so that they would be better equipped to handle their new, federally imposed, responsibilities. The result, as Paul Hill has noted, was that state education agencies often became so dependent on federal funding and pliable to federal direction that they were effectively "colonized."[43]

Martha Derthick found, in *The Influence of Federal Grants,* that this was a crucial consequence of all federal grant-in-aid programs during the Great Society. She noted that "a state agency learns to accommodate its goals to federal ones. Where, as in Massachusetts before 1968, a state agency has little independent strength within the state political system, its dependence on federal patronage becomes very great. It must rely on federal action to create opportunities for action and on the justification of 'federal requirements' or the 'availability of federal funds' to rationalize and legitimize all that it does. Whatever power and autonomy the Massachusetts welfare department possesses derive very largely from the relationship with its federal patron."[44] It was through a similar process that state education agencies—which might have appeared to be a potential ally to conservatives—emerged instead as one of the greatest defenders of federal influence in education. Their national lobbying arm, the Council of Chief State School Officers, became a major advocate in Washington for strong categorical regulations on the use of federal funds and opposed reforms to give districts or schools more discretion. When the Nixon administration called for federal policy to give more flexibility to state officials, a planner from the Department of Health, Education and Welfare (HEW) observed that state education authorities "argued that such a percentage of discretion opened them up to battles from education interests they would rather not fight."[45] Paul Manna has also shown how as education rose on state agendas and governors and legislatures became more involved, they circumvented their own limited capacity and local resistance by pushing for federal policies (such as standards, testing, accountability, and choice) that would further their own educational goals.[46]

The number of independent school districts in the United States dropped from approximately 150,000 in 1900 to 15,000 in 1993, and this administrative centralization at the state level ultimately made education more susceptible to federal regulation.[47] In practice, centralization also meant that local decision makers had less and less flexibility in how they ran their schools. As Ravitch observed, "During the decade after 1965, political pressures converged on schools...in ways that undermined their authority to direct their own affairs....Congress, the courts, federal agencies, and state legislatures devised burdensome and costly new mandates. In elementary and secondary schools, almost no area of administrative discretion was left uncontested."[48]

## *The Rise of the Education Establishment*

Despite these developments and reservations about ESEA's implementation and effectiveness, federal education spending remained enormously popular. ESEA quickly developed formidable political constituencies and allies in Washington, which successfully pushed for incremental expansions in the size and scope of federal education programs. Federal spending for education— particularly when it was dispersed widely and came with few mandates or accountability measures—was very popular among state politicians and education agencies as well as powerful parent and education groups. These beneficiaries of federal aid to education quickly became a powerful political force in Washington, an "education-industrial complex" that fought hard to protect existing programs and to create new ones. As Graham notes, "by the end of the Johnson administration, the very proliferation of Great Society programs...reinforced the growing triangular networks with a vested interest in maximizing their benefits by pressing willing congressional authorizing committees to exceed by large margins the president's budget requests, especially in education."[49]

The increasing power of the National Education Association (NEA) during the 1970s and 1980s was a crucial driving force behind the expansion of the federal role in education. Liberal Democrats joined with the NEA in vigorously defending the equity regime at the heart of ESEA. They argued that the only education "reform" that was needed to improve bad schools was additional federal funding and new categorical programs to serve disadvantaged students. The NEA was the nation's largest teachers union and by 1976 had 1.8 million members (and an average of 4,000 in every congressional district), a staff of 3,000 in Washington, and a political action committee (created in 1972), all of which it used to become one of the most influential groups in national politics and in the Democratic Party. When Nixon proposed sharp cuts in education spending in 1969, over 50 education groups quickly formed the Emergency Committee on Full Funding for Education, which became one of the most powerful lobbies on Capitol Hill. As Orfield notes, "the programs involved were simultaneously able to rally local mayors and school boards, the huge teachers organizations, the book publishing and education materials industries, state school officials, the Catholic church leadership, and many other interests ranging from supporters of vocational education to defenders of children needing rehabilitation. Obviously, such constituencies had to be taken seriously by Congress."[50]

ESEA had been based on the idea that the federal government had the obligation to assist "disadvantaged" students and that such assistance would be efficacious. Once this rationale had been enshrined in federal law and court precedent, a number of education-related interest groups worked hard to protect it and to expand the number and type of students considered "disadvantaged" and thus eligible to receive federal Title I aid. These groups included the National Advisory Council for the Education of Disadvantaged Children, the National Welfare Rights Organization, the Legal Standards and Education Project of the NAACP, the Lawyers Committee for Civil Rights under Law, and the National Association of Administrators of State and Federally-Assisted Education Programs.

With the support of these and other organizations, a number of disadvantaged groups were able (often with the assistance of the courts and the U.S. Office for Civil Rights) to secure additional federal spending and protections in schools. Amendments to the ESEA in 1968 provided funding and new federal programs for disadvantaged students in rural areas, for dropout prevention programs, and for the support of bilingual programs. Congress strengthened the Act in 1974 and reauthorized it in 1978 by wide bipartisan margins. (The $50 billion five-year reauthorization of 1978, for example, passed 86 to 7 in the Senate and 350 to 20 in the House.) Education during the Nixon and Carter eras largely continued in the path established by LBJ in adding over 100 new categorical programs in education. Migrant children, children for whom English was a second language, delinquent and neglected children, and children with mental and physical handicaps would all eventually be added to Title I.

The evolution of the special education program within ESEA typifies the rapid growth of many federal initiatives and the expansionary role played by an activist judiciary. A 1966 amendment to ESEA created a new title (Title VI) to provide grants for programs for "handicapped" children. This new program—like ESEA itself—continued to expand over time as the definition of "handicapped" was broadened to cover more and more students. In 1970 Title VI was broken off from ESEA and expanded to form a separate Education of the Handicapped Act. In 1975 this became the Education for All Handicapped Children Act (EAHCA) and in 1997, the Individuals with Disabilities Education Act (IDEA). The vote on the EAHCA was almost unanimous (404–7 in the House and 87 to 7 in the Senate) and speaks to the political power of the educational equity rationale. Most conservatives voted in favor of the bill, despite of its significant expansion of federal authority and the enormous unfunded mandate it placed on states. Lee Anderson has argued that the power of the rights revolution of the 1970s combined with old-fashioned interest group politics to trump ideological reservations about the new policy. He notes that the willingness of conservatives to succumb to political pressures presaged their later support for No Child Left Behind in 2001. "Both episodes," Anderson writes, "teach us that long-standing ideological values in Congress can be either temporarily or permanently transformed."[51]

In *Between the Lines,* Shep Melnick demonstrates how the courts' expansive interpretations of the ambiguous language contained in the 1975 EAHCA and the subsequent broad determinations of eligibility by federal courts and administrators fueled the rapid subsequent expansion of federal funding and regulation.[52] The EAHCA mandated that all school systems provide a "free appropriate public education" to all handicapped children; that schools develop an "individualized educational program" for each handicapped child; and that schools provide "related services" to handicapped children. The Act did not, however, specify how the crucial terms—"handicapped," "appropriate," "individualized," or "related services"—should be defined. As Melnick notes, "legislators talked blithely about providing equal educational opportunity and allowing individuals to maximize their potential, without giving serious thought to what this might mean in practice."[53]

Because the legislation also granted parents the right to appeal school decisions to the courts, it ensured that judges would ultimately provide those definitions. And judges tended to interpret the EAHCA broadly in terms of protecting the individual rights of handicapped children. "The courts...insist[ed] on a literal interpretation of some phrases (such as the requirement that states educate all handicapped children) and [gave] a liberal interpretation to others (such as 'related services')."[54] These interpretations fueled an increase in federal, and particularly state and local, spending on special education—the federal share alone increased from $14 million in 1965 to $4.3 billion in 1999. The growth of spending on programs for the handicapped mirrored the growth of education spending for disadvantaged students more generally. Grants for the disadvantaged increased from $0 in 1965 to $6.7 billion in 1999; school improvement programs went from $72 million to $1.5 billion; Indian education went from $0 to $65 million; and bilingual education went from $0 to $385 million (all in inflation-adjusted dollars).[55] Despite a decline in the total public school population between 1968 and 1986, the number of children in special education programs in the United States during that period increased from 2.3 million to 4.3 million. The active role of the courts in education was not confined to handicapped children—the number of federal court decisions affecting schools grew from 112 during the 1946–1956 period, to 729 from 1956–1966, to in excess of 1,200 from 1966–1970.[56]

Democratic president Jimmy Carter continued the institutionalization of the federal role in education when he created a cabinet-level Department of Education in 1979. The move was widely regarded as a political payback for the endorsement and support of the NEA during the 1976 election—a recognition and further cementing of the powerful alliance that had formed between the Democratic Party and the education establishment. Legislation to create a new federal department for education had been introduced 130 times between 1908 and 1975, but the idea had always generated a great deal of political opposition from a variety of interests.[57] Conservatives and states' rights advocates opposed the new department on the grounds that education was a state and local responsibility and that the federal role had been intrusive and counterproductive.[58] But in 1975, the NEA—joined by its union allies in the Labor Coalition Clearinghouse—used its considerable influence to gain Democratic support for a department. Once created, it quickly became a powerful symbol to both proponents and opponents of federal involvement in education.

## Conservatives Regroup: The Backlash against ESEA and the Federal Role in Education

By 1980 federal spending and influence on schooling had expanded dramatically and ESEA had facilitated the centralization, bureaucratization, and judicialization of education policy making. The case of special education policy represented an extension of the ESEA logic—that the federal government needed to defend the worst off or most vulnerable from local majorities or inequities in the larger state and local systems. The result was increasing federal involvement in education but also increasingly inflexible and copious regulations and increasingly intrusive court involvement—by 1980 the Department of Education administered approximately 500 different federal education programs.[59]

Where was the conservative opposition during this major expansion of the federal role in education? As noted above, between 1965 and 1980 Republicans were overwhelmed by the Democrats' numerical advantage in

Congress—even had they so desired, they would have been unable to repeal ESEA or even substantially alter it. However, it is important to once again distinguish between *Republicans* and *conservatives*. In the years following the passage of ESEA, most Republicans in Congress did not work to repeal ESEA but instead sought merely to modify the amount or type of aid or the funding-allocation formula. In this sense, there were very few educational conservatives to be found in 1965 and during the subsequent 15 years. Those few that did exist (Republican and Democrat alike) fought unsuccessfully to minimize the conditions that were attached to federal aid or to convert it into unrestricted block grants for states. If the political conditions during the 1970s impeded conservative efforts in education, however, the decade witnessed a number of developments that would set the stage for the conservative revolution of the 1980s.

Beginning in the 1970s, there was a growing perception that federal education policy—like many other federal policies from the Great Society—had become more about providing entitlements and protecting rights than about enhancing opportunity or demanding responsibility. The federal focus was on access and equity issues rather than on improving schools' or students' academic performance, and there was little effort to measure the educational progress of students who received federal funds or protection. This situation led to growing discontent among Republicans, states' rights advocates and even some liberal Democrats about the nature and effectiveness of federal education aid and set the stage for a backlash against ESEA.

The renewed conservative attack against federal education policy coalesced around two different complaints—that it had become too prescriptive and intrusive and that it had been ineffective in improving school quality or student performance. The unpopularity of school busing during the late 1960s and 1970s also made education an attractive electoral issue for Republicans.[60] Opposition to the *Green* ruling and to busing was strong across the country, and the policy was bitterly attacked by conservatives George Wallace and Richard Nixon during the 1968 presidential election campaign. In this and subsequent elections, Republican presidential candidates would successfully use opposition to school busing and integration as a key part of their "Southern strategy" to appeal to conservative Democratic voters and their assault on federal government activism more generally. Several scholars have argued that race—and particularly the debate over school integration—became the decisive issue in American politics during the second half of the twentieth century and led to the unraveling of the coalition that had supported the Great Society and the war on poverty, and ultimately, to a partisan electoral realignment.[61]

Conservatives also seized on a number of prominent studies that were published during this period which argued that ESEA funds and programs had largely failed to improve educational opportunity for disadvantaged students.[62] Nixon's election in 1968 presented conservatives with their great-est chance of rolling back federal education policy during the 1965–1980 period. In a September 1970 speech whose themes would be widely repeated by conservatives in the following years, Nixon argued that increased spend-ing on education would not improve educational opportunity unless more fundamental changes in schools were required. Congress had been, he noted, "extraordinarily generous in its support of education... [and] much of this activity was based on the familiar premise that if only the resources available for education were increased, the amount youngsters learn would increase." It was time, Nixon argued, to recognize that existing education "programs and strategies...are...based on faulty assumptions and inadequate knowledge."[63] Lawrence McAndrews, however, has highlighted the inconsistency between Republican presidential rhetoric and presidential action on education. While Nixon and Ford entered office convinced of the need to alter the course of federal education policy, they were largely unable or unwilling to expend the political capital necessary to defeat the formidable groups with an interest in preserving the status quo.[64]

While Nixon's opposition to federal activism in education was clear, the issue ranked quite low on his policy agenda—in fact, in his 1969 message to Congress on domestic legislation, he did not even mention ESEA. Nixon's interest in education was largely instrumental—he focused on the integra-tion issue in the pursuit of electoral gain and on the funding issue in order to achieve broader fiscal restraint and tax cuts. As Table 6.1 (above) shows, Nixon (and later Ford as well) did not devote much attention to the issue of school improvement, in part because the issue (as opposed to integration and busing) remained quite low on the public agenda at that point, as Table 6.2 demonstrates. As a result, the education issue was one with high costs and little potential reward for conservatives. This dynamic—as well as the continued strength of the education establishment and the perpetual appeal of educational pork—was sufficient to ensure easy congressional reauthoriza-tions of ESEA during the 1970s. Opposition to ESEA was stronger in the House, but even there it generally was approved by wide margins with con siderable bipartisan support. ESEA was reauthorized in the House by a vote of 312 to 58 in 1970, 380 to 26 in 1974, and 350 to 20 in 1978. In the early 1970s, Congress rebuffed Nixon's proposals to consolidate or eliminate a large number of federal education programs, and instead created many new ones.

Nixon vetoed education appropriations bills that included large increases for education on several different occasions in 1970 and 1972. Nixon's vetos engendered bitter struggles with Congress in which many Republicans—including the GOP national chairman Rep. Rogers Morton (R-MD)—sided with the Democrats. Most of Nixon's vetoes were overturned, and on the two occasions that they were not, the president was still not able to cut education spending, only to slow its growth. In the end, Nixon felt compelled to sign what were then the largest education appropriations in American history. As Gary Orfield has observed: "the President came down strongly on the conservative side [of the education debate] ... The President pressed hard for a change of direction. In most cases, however, Congress resisted and Congress prevailed."[65]

Acknowledging the difficult post-ESEA political terrain for educational conservatives, President Nixon would eventually remark that "we will all have to be education presidents now."[66] Though Nixon failed to reduce federal influence or spending in education, he did introduce a number of proposals that would become an important part of the conservative approach to school reform in the 1980s and 1990s. These included a call for a National Institute of Education to develop better measures of school outputs, tax credits for private school tuition, and block grants. A major part of the challenge for conservatives during the 1960s and 1970s, however, was that they had not yet developed institutions that could develop and disseminate policy ideas and supporting research to the media, the public, or policy makers. Conservative ideas on education tended to emerge sporadically from journals such as *The Public Interest* and *Commentary* and in influential books such as Milton Friedman's *Capitalism and Freedom,* but there was no sustained conservative mobilization in the 1970s to counter the growing resources and activism of the liberal education establishment.

If conservative efforts to reduce federal influence in education during the 1970s were often weak and generally unsuccessful, however, by the end of the decade the broader political environment had become more fortuitous. As a

Table 6.2. Public Perceptions of the Nation's Most Important Problem in Presidential Election Years, 1960–1980

| Years | Candidates | Most Important Issue | Rank of Education |
|-------|------------|----------------------|-------------------|
| 1960 | Kennedy/Nixon | Foreign relations | 14th out of 20 |
| 1964 | Johnson/Goldwater | Civil rights | 24th out of 24 |
| 1968 | Humphrey/Nixon | Vietnam | 17th out of 17 |
| 1972 | McGovern/Nixon | Vietnam | 26th out of 26 |
| 1976 | Carter/Ford | Inflation | Not listed |
| 1980 | Carter/Reagan | Inflation | 23rd out of 41 |

*Source*: Roper Center at University of Connecticut, Public Opinion Online, http://web. lexisnexis.com/university/form/academic/s_roper.html. Accessed June 25, 2001.

*Note*: Respondents were asked, "What do you think is the most important problem facing this country today?" All surveys were conducted within two months of the presidential election.

result of the questionable benefits and unintended consequences of ESEA, public support for it and many of the other social welfare programs born during the Great Society began to wane in the 1970s and particularly in the 1980s. There was a growing perception that many programs that had begun as an effort to promote opportunity and self-reliance had morphed into entitlements that encouraged dependency—that opportunity liberalism had transformed into what Davies calls "entitlement liberalism."[67] As Kaplan and Cuciti have noted, "Although the very visible War on Poverty program appeared to be aimed at assisting the poor to find a competitive place in the system...the entitlement programs that evolved seemed premised on a commitment to assist a poverty population that could not, should not, or would not compete."[68] Typical of the growing backlash against the Great Society was Charles Murray's widely publicized book *Losing Ground: American Social Policy 1950–1980,* which argued that the poor were worse off after the Great Society than they had been before it, and which became a conservative touchstone.[69]

As ESEA continued to expand in size and to cover more and more disadvantaged groups despite its apparent failure to deliver on its promise to enhance educational opportunity, support for a fundamental reconsideration of the federal role in education gained momentum. Many conservative Republicans—who strongly opposed the growth of federal spending and influence in education as a violation of states' rights—seized on the reports as evidence that, far from providing constructive leadership, federal influence had contributed to the declining performance of America's schools. In the 1980 presidential election, Ronald Reagan, a champion of conservative Republicans, was able to seize on growing public opposition to the federal role in education and the expansion of the welfare state more generally to defeat Democratic incumbent Jimmy Carter. Reagan energized the Republican Party and mobilized it behind a conservative agenda that centered on cutting taxes and rolling back the size of the federal government and the scope of its activities.[70] The 1980 Republican platform called for "deregulation by the federal government of public education and...the elimination of the federal Department of Education." The platform fretted that "parents are losing control of their children's schooling" and that Democratic education policy had produced "huge new bureaucracies to misspend our taxes."[71] Reagan hoped to either eliminate the federal role in schools or to redefine the nature of the federal education policy regime by making privatization, choice, and competition—rather than equity—its guiding principles.[72]

States' rights advocates celebrated what they thought was the beginning of a new era (or, perhaps more accurately, a return to an old era) in which the federal government would leave education policy making to the states. As Graham observed at the time, however, "the Reaganite hostility to a strong federal role in education (beyond defense related R & D) is not shared by a congressional majority that clings with surprising tenacity to the consensus forged during the Kennedy-Johnson years, which survived and even prospered under the Nixon and Ford administrations, and which was strongly reinforced under Carter."[73] By 1980, ESEA and the federal role in education had been institutionalized and were vigorously defended by teachers' unions, state education agencies, and parent groups. The result was that, as Ravitch has noted, "the new politics of the schools rotated about a state-federal axis rather than a local-state axis."[74]


## Conclusion

Prior to the 1960s, conservatives were able to minimize federal involvement in education by relying on a general deference to the principal of federalism and the public and elite view of public schools as performing adequately and best when controlled by state and local governments. The Elementary and Secondary Education Act of 1965, though vigorously opposed in some quarters, established the ideational, political, and programmatic foundation for a dramatically more expansive federal role in schools. As Deborah Stone has argued, in policy debates the side that is able to gain public acceptance of its frame for understanding a problem gains an enormous advantage in the political battle over the content and scope of the governmental response.[75] During the Great Society, Democrats very successfully developed and disseminated an equity frame for federal education policy that built on the moral power of the civil rights and antipoverty movements. While the equity framing certainly enhanced the rhetorical appeal of ESEA, support for the expanded federal role in education in Congress and in the states was also bolstered significantly by something decidedly less idealistic: lots of educational pork. Scholars such as Theodore Lowi have frequently commented on the importance of programmatic design to the political viability of a government policy, with distributive programs tending to enjoy broader political support than redistributive ones.[76] As initially constructed, ESEA was politically untouchable because it could claim the mantle of redistributive idealism, even as it was designed and implemented in such a way as to maximize its distributional benefits. ESEA—like impact aid and the National Defense Education Act of the 1950s—began as a narrow, temporary categorical program but quickly morphed into a permanent mechanism for broadly distributing federal education dollars to a wide variety of purposes and beneficiaries. Even as conservative leaders struggled to combat the power of the liberal equity frame, they also had to confront the limitless desire of rank and file congressmen—Democrats and Republicans alike—and their constituents for federal education dollars.

Conservatives' efforts to challenge the liberal education frame during this period would be constrained by their reluctance to articulate a positive alternative agenda for federal power in education and their inability to break the universal addiction to educational pork. In particular, while Republicans began to cast doubt on the effectiveness of ESEA programs to achieve their goals, they were never able to reduce voters' or interest groups' demand for greater federal education spending. Those conservatives brave enough to call for cuts in the federal education budget quickly learned that such talk would carry a heavy political cost both on the campaign trail and in Washington, where education spending served as the glue that held together a powerful coalition of interests under the Committee for Education Funding umbrella. In this way, educational pork became a crucial mechanism for the entrenchment of federal education policy.

Another factor that contributed to the embedding of federal education programs was their gradual institutionalization at the state and national level. By the end of the 1970s, forty years of Democratic domination of Congress (and often the White House as well) had produced not only a legislative legacy but also an institutional legacy in the area of education policy. States expanded their education departments and created Title I offices that were dependent on federal funds. At the national level, as successive Democratic Congresses passed legislation broadening and deepening the federal role in education, they also created new bureaucratic agencies for research and oversight. Once created, these agencies had an incentive to justify their continued existence (and often their further expansion) by highlighting the failures of states to produce a quality and equitable public education for their citizens. As more information was collected and publicized by these federal agencies and commissions (and brought to the attention of national politicians and the public), pressure built for the federal government to take action to address newly documented educational problems. The National Center for Education Statistics (as well as the Office of Educational Research and Improvement), for example, provided policy entrepreneurs with a steady supply of information from which to make the political case for more federal government education spending and new programs. Legislators in Congress were often eager to initiate education proposals that allowed them to claim credit for addressing national problems, to bring federal money home to their districts or states, to establish a name for themselves in Congress, and to expand the influence and jurisdiction of their committees and subcommittees. The fact that much of the expansion of federal influence in education occurred through low-profile bureaucracies (as well as the courts) made it harder for conservatives to mobilize against, particularly since for much of the period they lacked the kind of organizational resources that liberals had developed in think tanks, academia, and public interest law firms.

Over time, however, the combination of legislative, bureaucratic, and judicial activism in education produced a large and complex web of federal mandates. If federal education spending was almost universally popular, busing and federal regulation were decidedly less so, and this presented a political opportunity for conservatives as ESEA evolved and its mandates expanded. Jennifer Hochschild and Nathan Scovronick have noted that Americans strongly support the principle of equal opportunity but are generally unwilling to support reforms that might bring it about in practice when they are seen as negatively impacting their families or communities.[77] During the 1960s and 1970s as the programmatic content of federal education policy changed, the issue of school reform became more and more entangled with bitter conflicts over racial integration and busing. Education politics became race politics, both on the streets of America and in partisan politics, and this had an enormous impact on conservative education strategy and ultimately on the nature of the Republican coalition.

As federal legislators, bureaucrats, and judges mandated more stringent (and more disruptive) integration remedies, Republicans seized on federal education policy as a powerful symbol of the dangers of centralized government power and its threat to individual liberty and states rights. As Edward Carmines and James Stimson have noted, it was a symbol that the GOP would use to great effect in splintering the New Deal coalition and building a new conservative majority in the 1970s and 1980s.[78] By the 1970s, conservatives had successfully reframed federal education policy; instead of promoting educational opportunity as originally intended, they argued, it had evolved into an expensive, intrusive, ineffective morass. In this sense, policy feedback played a crucial role in the emergence of a broader conservative coalition and a more effective political strategy in the area of education.[79] While Democrats argued that continuing achievement gaps revealed the need for additional federal spending and programs, Republicans countered that the data exposed the impotence of federal efforts, and some began to call for accountability, decentralization, and school choice. Herein lay the beginning of a positive national education agenda for the GOP, one that would shift from opposing federal power in education to redirecting it to conservative ends. Though as yet neither fully articulated nor fully embraced by a majority of party leaders, this alternative conservative vision would be fleshed out over the following two decades. The opposition of the Democratic Party to education *reform* (as opposed to education *spending*), meanwhile, would become increasingly problematic politically when federal activism across the board came under fire and when evidence of the continuing decline in public education mounted during the 1980s.[80]

With the ascension of Ronald Reagan to the presidency, conservatives seemed poised to eviscerate federal education policy and bring about a return to the pre-ESEA era of local control of education. While the moment appeared ripe, conservative efforts to roll back federal influence in education would continue to be stymied by several forces. The first was ideational—conservative rhetoric and strategy during the 1960s and 1970s had been focused on opposing the growth of federal educational influence as unconstitutional and criticizing its effectiveness rather than on offering a constructive vision for federal power, and many influential party leaders remained fundamentally opposed to *any* federal mandates for schools. In addition, many Republican political elites— and many in the conservative base nationwide—were more interested in education as a central battleground in the culture wars than in school reform. This presented a fundamental political challenge for Republican politicians in two ways: first it committed the GOP to high-profile positions on issues such as school prayer and sex education that many voters saw as tangential to more pressing concerns about school access and quality. It also pushed the GOP to center its educational platform for many years on school vouchers, which persistent majorities of Americans saw as a dangerous threat to public education.[81] Reagan would discover that while voters and states were eager to see the elimination of federal mandates, they were not prepared to forgo the federal largesse on which their school systems had become considerably dependent. And the issue of school quality, which Democrats had so effectively linked to the nation's Cold War and the war on poverty, would in the 1980s be connected to the emerging challenges of economic development and competition in the international marketplace. These developments shifted the terms of the school reform debate and ensured that the issue would receive increased attention in national politics even as they provided an opening for conservatives to advance an alternative vision for federal education policy.

*Notes*

1. Harrison Schmitt, *Congressional Record,* 1978, Vol. 124, 299.
2. As Hugh Davis Graham has noted, "Prior to the 1960s, one of the most distinctive attributes of America's political culture had been the tenacity with which the United States, unlike other nations, had resisted a national education policy." Hugh Davis Graham, *The Uncertain Triumph: Federal Education Policy in the Kennedy and Johnson Years* (Chapel Hill: University of North Carolina Press, 1984), xvii.
3. Eugene Eidenberg and Roy Morey, *An Act of Congress: The Legislative Process and the Making of Education Policy* (New York: W.W. Norton and Company, Inc., 1969), 11.
4. U.S. Department of Commerce, *Education of the American Population* (U.S. Census of Population. Washington DC, 1999): Table 8.
5. See, for instance, Paul Peterson, *The Politics of School Reform: 1870–1940* (Chicago: University of Chicago Press, 1985) 5–22; Michael Katz, *Reconstructing*

*American Education* (Boston: Harvard University, 1987) 16–20; or Diane Ravitch, *Left Back: A Century of Failed School Reforms* (New York: Simon and Schuster, 2000), 241–247.

6. Whereas in 1940, just 38.1 percent of 25–29 year olds had graduated high school and just 5.9 percent had completed four years of college, by 1970, 75.4 percent had finished high school and 16.4 percent four years of college (U.S. Department of Commerce, 1999: Table 8).

7. For more on this development see Diane Ravitch, *The Troubled Crusade: American Education 1945–1980* (New York: Basic Books, 1983), 10–16.

8. For an extensive account of the context and consequences of the Brown decision, see James Patterson, *Brown vs. Board of* Education (Oxford: Oxford University Press, 2001).

9. James Guthrie, "The Future of Federal Education Policy," *Teachers College Record* 84, 3 (Spring 1983): 674.

10. Lee Anderson. "Ideology and the Politics of Federal Aid to Education." Unpublished Dissertation, Stanford University, February 1997, 46.

11. As cited in James Sundquist, *Politics and Policy: The Eisenhower, Kennedy, and Johnson Years* (Washington, DC: Brookings Institution, 1968), 178.

12. Graham, 1984, xv.

13. Eugene Eidenberg and Roy Morey, *An Act of Congress: The Legislative Process and the Making of Education Policy* (New York: W.W. Norton, 1969), 35.

14. As cited in Julie Roy Jeffrey, *Education for Children of the Poor: A Study of the Origins and Implementation of the Elementary and Secondary Education Act of 1965* (Columbus: Ohio State University Press, 1978), 3.

15. As one observer noted, "the architects of the Great Society have found the school systems, for the most part, ill-prepared and ill-equipped to meet the educational challenges to be encountered in building the Great Society. Furthermore, they learned that most localities today are hard pressed to finance the schools on which success depends." Tinsley Spraggins, "New Educational Goals and Direction: a Perspective of Title I, ESEA," *The Journal of Negro Education* (Volume 37, Issue 1: Winter, 1968): 46.

16. Phillip Meranto, *The Politics of Federal Aid to Education in 1965* (Syracuse: Syracuse University Press, 1967), 132.

17. Joel Spring, *Conflict of Interests: The Politics of American Education* (Boston: McGraw Hill, 1999), 96–7.

18. Paul Peterson and Barry Rabe, "The Role of Interest Groups in the Formation of Educational Policy," *Teachers College Record* 84, 3 (Spring 1983): 717.

19. Howe, 1990, 101–102.

20. For a thorough discussion of the political context surrounding the passage of ESEA see Phillip Meranto, *The Politics of Federal Aid to Education in 1965* (1967), Eugene Eidenberg and Roy Morey, *An Act of Congress: The Legislative Process and the Making of Education Policy* (1969), and Hugh Davis Graham, *The Uncertain Triumph* (1984).

21. ADA scores are ratings calculated by the liberal group Americans for Democratic Action. Based on congressional voting records they estimate how liberal or conservative a member is with 100 being most liberal and 0 being most conservative. ADA scores cited in: Lee Anderson. "Ideology and the Politics of Federal Aid to Education." Unpublished Dissertation, Stanford University, February 1997: 72.

22. Eugene Eidenberg and Roy Morey, *An Act of Congress: The Legislative Process and the Making of Education Policy* (New York: Norton, 1969), 61.

23. Eugene Eidenberg and Roy Morey, *An Act of Congress: The Legislative Process and the Making of Education Policy* (New York: W.W. Norton and Company, Inc., 1969), 110–111.

24. Ibid., 113.

25. As quoted in Sundquist (1968), 16.

26. As quoted in Sundquist (1968), 215.

27. The text of Title I stated that "the Congress hereby declares it to be the policy of the United States to provide financial assistance...to expand and improve...educational programs by various means...which contribute particularly to meeting the special educational needs of educationally deprived children." Title I was designed to assist communities with a high concentration of low-income families (defined as families earning less than $2,000 annually) by raising per-pupil expenditures. The legislation contained four additional titles. Title II of the ESEA created a five-year program (funded at $100 million for the first year) to fund the purchase of library resources, instructional material, and textbooks by state educational agencies (which were then to loan them out to local public and private school students.) Title III created a five-year program of matching grants to local educational agencies to finance supplemental education centers and services. (It was also allocated $100 million for the first year.) Title IV gave the U.S. Commissioner of Education the authority to enter into contracts with universities and state educational agencies to conduct educational research, surveys, and demonstrations. This title received $100 million in funding for the five-year period. Finally, Title V provided $25 million over five years to strengthen state departments of education.

28. Eidenberg and Morey, *An Act of Congress,* 247.

29. Terry Moe, "The Politics of Bureaucratic Structure," in *Can the Government Govern?,* ed. John Chubb, and Paul Peterson (Washington, DC: Brookings Institution Press, 1989), 285.

30. Graham, 1984: 204.

31. See Paul Peterson, et. al., *When Federalism Works* (1986), 136–40 for a more detailed discussion of the local tendency to shift federal funds from redistributive programs to other purposes.

32. Graham, 1984, 204.

33. Joel Berke, *Answers to Inequity: An Analysis of the New School Finance* (Berkeley: McCutchan Publishing Corporation, 1974), 143.

34. The USOE was ill-suited to a compliance role—it had long been a small, passive organization which focused on collecting and disseminating

statistical data on education and did little else. The result, as John and Anne Hughes noted, was that "if USOE had limitations on its policymaking authority and capability—and these have been legion—its ability to enforce its policies has been even more limited. The state agencies and the local districts, by and large, were used to going their own ways, which often meant disregarding federal requirements." John Hughes and Anne Hughes, *Equal Education: A New National Strategy* (Bloomington: Indiana University Press, 1972), 50.

35. Hughes and Hughes, 1972, 57.

36. Ravitch, 1983, 271.

37. For more on the Supreme Court's Brown and Brown II decisions and southern desegregation efforts see J. Harvie Wilkinson, III, "The Supreme Court and Southern School Desegregation, 1955–1970," *Virginia Law Review*, Vol. 64, No. 4 (May, 1978): 485–559.

38. For more on the judicial and political context of this period see Gary Orfield and Susan Eaton, ed. *Dismantling Desegregation: The Quiet Reversal of Brown vs. Board of Education* (New York: The Free Press, 1996); David Armor, *Forced Justice: School Desegregation and the Law* (New York: Oxford University Press, 1995); and Marian Wright Edelman, "Southern School Desegregation, 1954–1973: A Judicial-Political Overview," *Annals of the American Academy of Political and Social Science* 407 (May 1973): 32–42.

39. John E. Chubb, "Excessive Regulation: The Case of Federal Aid to Education, *Political Science Quarterly* 100, 2 (Summer 1985): 287.

40. Ravitch, 1983, 312.

41. National Center For Education Statistics, *The Condition of Education 2000* (Washington, DC: 2000), 395.

42. Deil Wright, *Understanding Intergovernmental Relations* (Belmont, CA: Brooks Publishing, 1988), 195.

43. Paul Hill, "The Federal Role in Education," in Diane Ravitch, ed. *Brookings Papers on Education Policy* (Washington DC: Brookings Institution Press, 2000) 25–6. By 1993, state education agencies nationwide relied on federal funds for on average 41 percent of their operating budgets, with the federal share as high as 77 percent in some states.

44. Martha Derthick, *The Influence of Federal Grants* (Cambridge: Harvard University Press, 1970), 207.

45. Orfield, 1975, 168.

46. Paul Manna, *School's In: Federalism and the National Education Agenda* (Washington, DC: Georgetown University Press, 2006).

47. Michael Newman, *America's Teachers* (New York: Longman, 1994), 166.

48. Ravitch, 1983, 267.

49. Graham, 1984, 193.

50. Orfield, 1975, 137.

51. Lee W. Anderson, *Congress and the Classroom: From the Cold War to "No Child Left Behind"* (University Park, PA: The Pennsylvania State University Press, 2007), 98.

52. Shep Melnick, *Between the Lines* (Washington, DC: Brookings Institution Press, 1994).

53. Shep Melnick, "Separation of Powers and the Strategy of Rights: The Expansion of Special Education," in *The New Politics of Public Policy*, ed. Marc Landy and Martin Levin (Baltimore, MD: Johns Hopkins University Press, 1995), 37.

54. Melnick, 1995, 27.

55. National Center For Education Statistics, *The Condition of Education 2000* (Washington, DC: 2000), 409.

56. Ravitch, 1983, 312.

57. D. T. Stallings, "A Brief History of the U.S. Department of Education, 1979–2002," *Phi Delta Kappan*, May 2002, 83, No. 9, 677.

58. For more on the politics surrounding the creation of the department, see David Stephens, "President Carter, the Congress, and NEA: Creating the Department of Education, *Political Science Quarterly* 98, 4 (Winter 1983–1984).

59. For an extended discussion of the expansion of federal compensatory education programs and the accompanying increase in federal education regulations, see Paul Paterson's "Background Paper" in *Making the Grade: Report of the Twentieth Century Fund Task Force on Federal Elementary and Secondary Education Policy* (New York: Twentieth Century Fund, 1983).

60. In 1968 a majority (54%) of Americans thought that the Johnson administration was pushing integration too fast, and an equal number favored cutting government spending on domestic programs. Roper Center, Public Opinion Online, February 1968 (Accession number 0101680, question number 15) and September 1968 (Accession number 0041300, question number 24).

61. See, for example, Edward Carmines and James Stimson, *Issue Evolution: Race and the Transformation of American Politics* (Princeton, NJ: Princeton University Press, 1989).

62. See for example, those by Bailey and Mosher (1968), Berke and Kirst (1972), Berke (1974), McLaughlin (1975), Thomas (1975), and Jeffrey (1976).

63. As cited in Jeffrey, 1978, 143.

64. Lawrence McAndrews, *The Era of Education: The Presidents and the Schools, 1965–2001* (Urbana: University of Illinois Press, 2006), 122.

65. Gary Orfield, *Congressional Power: Congress and Social Change* (New York: Harcourt, Inc., 1975), 125.

66. As cited in Hugh Davis Graham, *The Uncertain Triumph: Federal Education Policy in the Kennedy and Johnson Years* (Chapel Hill: University of North Carolina Press, 1984), 215.

67. Davies, 1996, 1–9.

68. Kaplan and Cuciti, 1986, 217.

69. Charles Murray, *Losing Ground: American Social Policy 1950–1980* (New York: Basic Books, 1984).

70. For an in-depth examination of Reagan's political philosophy see James Ceaser, "The Theory of Governance of the Reagan Administration" in *The Reagan*

*Presidency and the Governing of America,* ed. Lester Salmon and Michael Lind (Washington, DC: Urban Institute Press, 1984).

71. *Historic Documents of 1980.* (Washington, DC: Congressional Quarterly, 1981) 583–4.

72. As D. T. Stallings has noted, "The new administration planned to move the Department of Education away from awarding categorical grants and toward the awarding of block grants, with the goal of eventually eliminating federal grants entirely, which would cause the federal role to revert to what it had been in 1838—nothing more than collecting statistics." D. T. Stallings, "A Brief History of the U.S. Department of Education, 1979–2002," *Phi Delta Kappan* 83, 9 (May 2002): 678.

73. Graham, 1984, 22.

74. Ravitch, 1983, 320.

75. Deborah A. Stone, "Causal Stories and the Formation of Policy Agendas" *Political Science Quarterly* 104, 2 (Summer 1989): 281–300.

76. Theodore J. Lowi, "American Business, Public Policy, Case-Studies, and Political Theory," *World Politics* 16 (1964): 687–713.

77. Jennifer L. Hochschild and Nathan Scovronick, *The American Dream and the Public Schools* (New York: Oxford University Press, 2004).

78. Edward Carmines and James Stimson, *Issue Evolution: Race and the Transformation of American Politics* (Princeton, NJ: Princeton University Press, 1989).

79. Paul Pierson, "When Effect Becomes Cause: Policy Feedback and Political Change," *World Politics* 45 (July 1993): 595–628.

80. *Time* wrote in a 1980 cover story, for example, that "like some vast jury gradually and reluctantly arriving at a verdict, politicians, educators and especially millions of parents have come to believe that the U.S. public schools are in parlous trouble." As cited in Thomas Toch, *In the Name of Excellence* (Oxford: Oxford University Press, 1991), 9.

81. L. C. Rose and A. M. Gallup, *The 38ᵗʰ Annual Phi Delta Kappa/Gallup Poll of the Public's Attitudes Toward the Public Schools* (Bloomington, IN: Phi Delta Kappa International, 2006).

# PART III

## 1980 to 2008

# CHAPTER 7

## Environmental Policy from 1980 to 2008: The Politics of Prevention

*Judith A. Layzer*

Shortly after its inauguration in early 1981, the Reagan administration set about instituting a host of reforms aimed at rolling back the environmental policy framework of the 1960s and 1970s. But the White House soon retreated in the face of congressional and popular resistance. Nearly two decades later, journalist David Mastio commented ruefully: "Conservatives have struggled to deal with the environment as a political issue. And with the exception of occasional tactical victories, we have failed miserably."[1] In some respects Mastio's despair was well founded; despite a sustained assault, between 1980 and 2008 conservatives failed to repeal or fundamentally revamp any of the nation's major environmental statutes. Furthermore, throughout this period public opinion on the issue barely budged; more than three-quarters of Americans consistently told pollsters they sympathized with the goals of the environmental movement, and nearly every year a majority claimed to support environmental protection, even at the risk of curbing economic growth.[2]

Conservatives' inability to enact wholesale reform belied their true impact, however. Beginning in the 1970s activists associated with the New Right disseminated a powerful story line to counter the environmentalist narrative, mobilized grassroots opposition to environmental regulations, and filed lawsuits challenging the basis for and implementation of environmental laws. They also worked tirelessly to elect allies to Congress and the White House. These activities did not have a single genesis but stemmed from similar ideological roots: distrust of the federal bureaucracy, admiration for markets, and disdain for environmental advocates.[3] Although activists touted these themes to mobilize the conservative base, they quickly ascertained that direct attacks on environmental laws provoked environmentalist mobilization, public criticism, and legislative resistance. So they adopted a subtler approach that effectively reduced the stringency of federal environmental protection without eliminating a single law.

Employing a strategy similar in nature and impact to the one they used in the realm of social welfare,[4] New Right conservatives prevented federal policy adjustments to mitigate environmental risk in several ways. First, despite the emergence of serious new problems and updated scientific thinking about existing ones, conservatives in Congress and the White House blocked the passage of any major new environmental legislation except the Clean Air Act Amendments of 1990. Second, conservative administrators employed procedural requirements—such as cost-benefit analysis, risk assessment, risk "balancing" and regulatory peer review—to discourage new regulations; they also changed the wording and interpretation of rules in ways that substantially weakened their environmental protectiveness. Third, an increasingly conservative judiciary retreated from its stance of holding regulators' feet to the fire: with increasing frequency, federal judges limited environmentalists' standing to sue, required agencies to consider economic and risk trade-offs when promulgating rules, and insisted that government compensate property owners when regulation reduced the value of their property. In short, New Right conservatives obstructed new legal mandates and capitalized on the relatively low visibility of bureaucratic and judicial decision making to weaken the implementation and enforcement of existing laws. New Right activism had indirect effects as well; it created a climate of distrust that stymied good-faith reform efforts supported by a broad coalition that included moderate conservatives.

## Creating a Conservative Context

To lay the groundwork for their deregulatory agenda, conservative activists emulated the tactics used by environmentalists in the 1960s and 1970s. Some sought to shape elite and popular opinion about environmental regulation by developing and disseminating an alternative story line to the one proffered by environmentalists. Others mobilized grassroots sympathizers by tapping into resentment of federal environmental restrictions among developers, farmers, ranchers, motorized recreationists, and small business owners. Still others filed lawsuits challenging existing regulations and their implementation. Conservatives hoped that by changing the political context, they could strengthen the hand of politicians, administrators, and judges who shared their antiregulatory views.

## Popularizing Conservative Ideas

In the late 1970s and early 1980s a handful of academics began criticizing the environmental regulation enacted in the preceding decade as inefficient, unduly burdensome for business, and fraught with unintended consequences.[5] Some went further, charging that environmentalists were simply promoting an elite, left-wing agenda.[6] Drawing on and embellishing these academic critiques, conservative writers popularized an antiregulatory story line in books, policy papers, and op-eds, as well as in publications such as *Regulation, Policy Review,* and *The Public Interest.* In addition, following the advice of prominent conservative intellectuals, conservation foundations and think tanks organized workshops and seminars for legislators, established programs for young journalists, and funded the work of students and academics interested in pursuing conservative environmental policy scholarship. The net effect of these activities was to legitimize a counternarrative to environmentalists' story about the devastating effects of industrialization and wasteful consumption.

Central to the narrative popularized by conservatives was a depiction of environmentalists as elitists and misanthropic extremists who routinely exaggerated the magnitude of environmental problems to scare the public into supporting policies that did more harm than good. For example, in *Progress and Privilege* (1982), freelance writer William Tucker argued that environmentalists were latter-day aristocrats who sought to preserve their own privileges by preventing economic growth.[7] Journalist Edith Efron's 1984 tome, *The Apocalyptics,* attributed the federal government's excessive focus on trivial cancer risks posed by chemicals in the environment to a coterie of prominent "apocalyptics" bent on imposing their anti-human, anti-American ideology on the nation.[8] Writing in the *National Review* in 1990, journalist David Horowitz depicted environmentalists as radicals motivated not by "compassion for the lost soul of mankind but the hatred of human beings as they are."[9] In their influential book *Trashing the Planet* (1990), Dixy Lee Ray and Lou Guzzo described environmental leaders as "determinedly leftist,

radical, and dedicated to blocking industrial progress and unraveling industrial society."[10] Ben Bolch and Harold Lyons, in their scathing indictment of
environmentalism entitled *Apocalypse Not* (1993), argued that "much of the
modern environmental movement is a broad-based assault on reason and,
not surprisingly, a concomitant assault on freedom."[11] Similarly, the main
theme of Michael Fumento's 1993 book, *Science under Siege,* was that irratio-
nal environmentalists were forcing government to focus on trivial risks and
ignore more serious ones.[12]

Extending this theme, conservatives argued that environmental regulations benefited narrow political and economic interests, not the public. For
example, Jonathan Adler, director of environmental studies at the Cato Institute, complained in *Regulation* that self-serving environmentalists were abet-
ted by rent-seeking industries that profited from strict environmental rules,
and by bureaucrats concerned primarily with maximizing their budgets and
job security.[13] Similarly, John Baden, founder of the Foundation for Research
on Economics and Environment, asserted that:

> The bureaucrats who...run the U.S. Forest Service, the National
> Park Service, the Bureau of Land Management, and the Bureau of
> Reclamation have been motivated by self-interest no less than private
> entrepreneurs. Their goal has been to maximize their organizations'
> work forces and budgets, and especially their discretionary budget
> authority. In collusion with elected politicians and special nterests
> representing business and labor, the federal bureaucracies have used
> taxpayer funds to subsidize economic activity that would never
> have taken place in the absence of subsidies. Perversely, as a result
> of public land ownership, American taxpayers have been financing
> the destruction of environments they increasingly value.[14]

Another element of the conservative story line was that although many environmental problems posed only marginal risks, the costs of policies to address
those risks were substantial. Conservative popularizers contended that regulations destroyed jobs, impeded growth, raised the prices of goods to consumers, and invariably produced harsh unintended consequences. For instance,
Bolch and Lyons pointed out that environmental protection required sacri-
fice, and they expressed amazement that "the cost of environmental improvements seems not to have sunk into the minds of voters and consumers."[15]
Journalist Warren Brookes disparaged environmentalists' "maniacally costly
pursuit of minimal health-risk reduction at maximum cost."[16] Fred L. Smith,
president of the Competitive Enterprise Institute, argued that efforts to attain
zero risk were paradoxical because taking risks ultimately enhanced safety,
and efforts to eliminate risk were expensive and often futile.[17]

Contrasting themselves with environmentalists, conservatives emphasized the need for "balance," "common sense," and "reason." Rather than challenging the goals of environmental policy directly, conservative activists insisted that they cared about the environment but wanted to protect it more efficiently and effectively. To this end, some echoed the academic prescriptions of devolving responsibility to state and local governments, requiring agencies to weigh the benefits of regulation against their costs and against the benefits of addressing competing risks, and using incentive-based mechanisms rather than rules to achieve environmental goals.[18] Others advanced a more radical fix, "free-market environmentalism," which entailed protecting the environment by establishing property rights in environmental amenities and relying on markets to allocate them properly. Proponents of free-market environmentalism contended that in response to price signals, markets would generate technological innovation to ameliorate any resource shortages that might develop; similarly, strengthening private property rights would lead to land and wildlife conservation if people truly valued nature.[19] On the rare occasion of market failure, they said, the common law of torts and contracts would provide a remedy.[20]

## Mobilizing the Grassroots

While some conservative activists focused on generating and disseminating ideas among opinion leaders, others mobilized grassroots support. Although connected only loosely to the intellectual edifice of the conservative movement, grassroots anti-environmental groups furnished a potent political complement. Particularly in the West, such groups helped elect and then vocally supported politicians proffering an antiregulatory message. Those politicians, in turn, wielded disproportionate influence among Republicans because the party's return to power in Congress in the 1990s was due largely to its strength in the West.[21]

The grassroots anti-environmental mobilization took off in the late 1980s, when conservative policy entrepreneurs rekindled the Sagebrush Rebellion of the 1970s by tapping into Westerners' resentment of environmental considerations in federal land management. In 1988 veteran political activists Ron Arnold and Alan Gottlieb hosted the Multiple Use Strategy Conference in Reno, Nevada, in order to bring under a single banner a disparate array of groups whose common objective was to remove environmental restrictions from public lands. The resulting amalgamation, which they dubbed the "Wise Use movement," included a handful of umbrella organizations, such as the Blue Ribbon Coalition, founded in 1987 to represent some 500,000 off-road vehicle users; the Center for the Defense of Free Enterprise, whose overarching goal was to promote and defend an unfettered capitalist economy; and People for the West!, formed by mining companies in 1989 to improve the industry's public image. These national or regional organizations, in turn, coordinated the activities of hundreds of smaller, local entities, such as the California Desert Coalition, the Oregon Lands Coalition, and the Washington Lands Coalition. Although most of these groups were heavily subsidized by industry, they boasted a substantial citizen following.[22]

Simultaneous with the birth of the Wise Use movement, Chuck Cushman, head of the National Inholders Association (later renamed the American Land Rights Association), coordinated a second grassroots movement that aimed to protect private property rights from incursions by the federal government. The property-rights movement's fundamental policy claim was that landowners must be compensated whenever government regulation reduces the value of their property. To promote this principle, Cushman forged alliances among groups with similar aims, such as the Washington, D.C.–based Defenders of Property Rights, a legal foundation created in 1991 to "bring about a sea change in property rights law through strategically filed lawsuits and groundbreaking property rights legislation."[23] Nancie Marzulla, president of Defenders of Property Rights, articulated her own motivation, saying: "Today, environmental regulations destroy property rights on an unprecedented scale. Regulations designed to protect coastal zone areas, wetlands, and endangered species habitats, among others, leave many owners stripped of all but bare title to their property."[24]

In 1991, 400 Wise Use and property-rights groups joined forces to form the Alliance for America, an umbrella organization whose objective was to rally public support for eliminating environmental regulations on both public and private land. Alliance leaders mobilized followers with populist appeals that cast environmentalists as elitists more concerned about plants and animals than people, and with anecdotes about the hard-working victims of government overreach. By contrast, they characterized themselves as defenders of freedom who sought a balance between human activities and the preservation of nature.

## Challenging Environmental Policy in Court

Conservatives activists also relied on a third tactic to advance their goals: undermining the legal basis for environmental regulation. Mimicking environmentalists' extremely effective litigation strategy, in the 1970s conservatives began establishing their own public-interest law firms.[25] The Pacific Legal Foundation, founded in 1973, was the first; by the mid-1990s there were at least twenty organizations—including the Competitive Enterprise

Institute, the Washington Legal Foundation, and the Mountain States Legal Foundation—whose purpose was to defend businesses and property owners against overreaching by government regulators. In addition to litigating, these organizations circulated newsletters and maintained web sites that contained conservative commentary on a variety of environmental laws, as well as on local land-use issues.

Conservative legal activists made a variety of arguments to advance their views. Their critique of the Endangered Species and Clean Water acts drew on reasoning laid out by Chicago law professor Richard Epstein in *Takings: Private Property and the Power of Eminent Domain,* according to which the takings clause of the Fifth Amendment to the Constitution guarantees compensation not only for property taken by eminent domain but for *any* loss in property value that results from government action. They challenged federal environmental laws on other constitutional grounds as well. For example, they charged that Congress had overstepped its authority to regulate commerce, as described in Article I, Section 8 (the Commerce Clause), and that state action that exceeded federal environmental standards violated the Supremacy Clause in Article VI.[26]

To increase the judiciary's receptiveness to these claims, conservative legal activists forged alliances among sympathetic lawyers and provided them with a common language. For example, in the early 1980s U.S. Attorney General Edwin Meese quietly initiated what Reagan's solicitor general Charles Fried dubbed the "Takings Project." Takings Project lawyers drafted President Reagan's Executive Order 12630, which required that "government decision-makers evaluate carefully the effect of their administrative, regulatory, and legislative actions on constitutionally protected property rights." Subsequently, they focused on promoting the appointment of libertarian judges to spots on the three federal courts—the U.S. Supreme Court, the Federal Circuit Court of Appeals, and the U.S. Court of Federal Claims—that control the direction of federal takings law.[27] The Federalist Society for Law and Public Policy, launched in 1982, brought together conservative and libertarian law students, practicing lawyers, and legal scholars in on-campus seminars and forums. Among the society's objectives were to recruit and train practitioners who could shepherd important cases through the legal system, and to advance the nomination of conservative judges. In 1992 a third organization, the Foundation for Research on Economics and Environment, began hosting all-expense-paid seminars for judges on property rights and the environment at resorts in Montana.[28]

Conservatives employed other tactics to thwart environmentalists' efforts to use the courts as well. Conservative lawmakers backed legislative provisions that limited judicial review of administrative decision making in order to prevent environmentalists from using the courts to hamper access by development interests to natural resources. In addition, conservative lawyers routinely disputed environmental plaintiffs' standing to sue, recognizing that the courts' liberalization of standing in the 1970s had enabled environmentalists to achieve prominence in the regulatory process. In late 1987 the Reagan White House issued a presidential directive requiring staff attorneys in the Department of Justice who were litigating cases involving the Environmental Protection Agency (EPA) and public interest groups to either challenge those groups' standing or get a section chief to prepare a memo explaining why no challenge was filed. As federal attorneys complied with this order, environmentalists were forced to expend enormous resources establishing their standing—something that had been largely assumed in the preceding decade.[29]

## Institutionalizing Conservative Principles in Legislative and Administrative Decision Making

As important as propagating ideas, mobilizing grassroots support, and filing lawsuits were complementary efforts by conservative activists to get their allies into positions of power. Thanks to a savvy and well-funded electoral strategy, they succeeded in electing a growing number of sympathizers to Congress and the White House beginning in 1980.[30] Although they were unable to repeal or substantially revamp laws enacted in the 1970s, conservative officials did succeed in reducing the federal government's ability to address environmental risks. Conservative lawmakers helped delay reauthorization of the Clean Air Act for a decade and, after 1990, prevented the enactment of new statutory mandates altogether; in particular, they turned back efforts to address environmentalists' most pressing concern, global warming. Conservative administrators slowed the proliferation of new rules by forcing them through a gauntlet of formal analyses and requiring extensive consultation with industry, and they implemented existing rules in ways that minimized constraints on industry and property owners.

### *The Reagan Administration, 1981–1989*

Conservatives' first real opportunity to enact their deregulatory agenda came with the election of President Ronald Reagan in 1980. As governor of California, Reagan had argued for subjecting environmental regulations to cost-benefit tests, claimed that environmental laws had crippled American business, and vowed to inject "balance" and "common sense" into environmental policy. Although Reagan rarely spoke about environmental issues during his presidential campaign, the Republican platform's environmental plank echoed many conservative themes, insisting that pollution control "must not become a cover for a 'no growth' policy and a shrinking economy." The platform also proposed revising the Clean Air Act's "cumbersome and overly stringent" regulations; called rules imposed on ranchers, farmers, loggers, and fishers "unrealistic and unnecessary"; and derided "excessive adherence to 'zero risk' policies" on pesticides, herbicides, and food additives.[31]

Once elected, President Reagan was more explicit about his own intentions, saying:

> To achieve a sound environmental policy, we should reexamine
> every regulatory requirement with a commitment to simplify and
> streamline the process. Moreover, we should return to the states
> the primary responsibility for environmental regulation in order
> to increase responsiveness to local conditions. In these ways, we
> can most effectively strike the delicate balance between protecting
> the environment and promoting economic growth.[32]

In its 1981 report, Reagan's Council on Environmental Quality (CEQ) laid out the administration's four guiding principles (the last of which it largely ignored): use cost-benefit analysis to determine the value of environmental regulations, rely as much as possible on the free market to allocate resources, decentralize environmental responsibilities to the states, and continue to cooperate with other nations to solve global environmental problems.[33]

Though firm in its convictions, the Reagan team faced a Congress in which "the bipartisan majority that had enacted most of the environmental legislation of the 1970s remained largely intact."[34] Therefore, following the advice of the conservative Heritage Foundation, the White House team declined to put forth deregulatory legislation. Rather, it adopted a strategy of cutting budgets and reinterpreting rules—an administrative approach that would enable the president to save his political capital for his larger agenda and minimize the repercussions of a public assault on the nation's popular environmental laws.[35]

To advance his administrative agenda, Reagan appointed high-level officials who shared his point of view. Among the most controversial was Secretary of the Interior James Watt, a founder of the Mountain States Legal Foundation, which filed actions throughout the West contesting regulation of public lands. Watt's primary goal was to shift federal natural resources policy from conservation toward development, and he made it clear that when in doubt he would "err on the side of public use versus preservation."[36] Watt pledged that he would remove impediments to energy development, saying: "The weakness of our energy system is centralist-type planning. There is no greater wisdom than the marketplace."[37] Reagan also appointed EPA administrator

Anne Gorsuch (later Burford), a firm believer in regulatory relief for business. Gorsuch's priorities were to negotiate regulatory standards with industry and dismantle the agency's enforcement apparatus. Another influential appointee, Office of Management and Budget (OMB) director David Stockman, warned of a "ticking regulatory time bomb" and argued that the EPA's rules "would practically shut down the economy if put into effect."[38]

A key element of Reagan's administrative strategy was to cripple agencies' ability to implement environmental legislation through budget and personnel cuts and bureaucratic restructuring. Therefore, the total amount of money authorized by the federal government for natural-resource and environmental programs fell from $17.9 billion in 1980 to between $12 billion and $15 billion (in 1987 dollars) per year for the next eight years. The declines were particularly steep in the area of pollution control, where spending fell 46 percent between 1980 and 1986.[39] Reinforcing these cuts, EPA Administrator Gorsuch laid off hundreds of staff and prompted the resignation of hundreds of others, so that by late 1982 the agency had lost close to 40 percent of its workforce.[40] In addition, Gorsuch reorganized the agency, dispersing its enforcement activities from a single office to the various media (air, water, land) offices, and transferred much of the pollution control burden to the states.

In the name of regulatory relief and economic development, Reagan's Interior Department eliminated barriers that impeded users' access to natural resources. For example, in response to complaints from coal companies about burdensome regulations, Secretary Watt suspended environmentally protective rules imposed by the Carter administration in its final days, eliminated many of the details of complying with strip-mining requirements, ordered his solicitor to settle industry lawsuits, moved to give the states more leeway in adopting their own strip-mining laws under federal statute, shut down the surface mining office's five regional offices, and reduced the agency's enforcement staff by 50 percent.[41] Similarly, John B. Crowell, assistant secretary of agriculture for natural resources and the environment (and former general counsel for the timber giant Louisiana-Pacific Corp.), announced his intention to double the harvest of trees from the national forests, saying he wanted to make the national forest system "contribute more to the economic well-being of the country."[42]

In addition to loosening existing rules, the administration adopted procedures to impede the flow of new regulations. In February 1981 President Reagan issued Executive Order 12291, which barred agencies from issuing any major rule unless the OMB's newly established Office of Information and Regulatory Affairs (OIRA) determined its benefits exceeded its costs. Shortly thereafter Reagan established the cabinet-level Task Force on Regulatory Relief, which reviewed hundreds of new and existing environmental regulations, rescinding some and remanding others to agencies for further study and modification.[43] To enhance the administration's ability to prevent the enactment of new regulations, Reagan's 1985 Executive Order 12498 required agencies to submit their regulatory plans for the upcoming year to the OMB.

In parallel with its aggressive administrative approach, the Reagan White House did its utmost to prevent the enactment of new environmental laws. Its primary target was a provision in the Clean Air Act reauthorization to address acid rain, which environmentalists claimed was killing lakes and forests, particularly in the Northeast. Throughout the 1980s the White House deferred action on acid rain, citing scientific uncertainty and requesting additional research.[44] David Stockman, head of the OMB, emphasized the prospective economic costs of sulfur dioxide emissions controls and minimized the environmental risk, asking, "How much are the fish worth in those 170 lakes that account for 4 percent of the lake area of New York? And does it make sense to spend billions of dollars controlling [sulfur dioxide] emissions from sources in Ohio and elsewhere if you're talking about a very marginal volume of dollar value, either in recreation terms or in commercial terms?"[45] The chairman of the CEQ, Alan Hill, also highlighted the costs of regulation, saying "we cannot, in good conscience, disregard or dismiss the fact that some of the proposed control programs will put Americans out of work."[46]

Itself riven by regional differences, Congress was unable to overcome presidential intransigence on acid rain, so reauthorization of the Clean Air Act languished throughout the 1980s. During Reagan's second term, however, Congress managed to reauthorize a handful of key environmental laws, including the Comprehensive Environmental Response, Cleanup and Liability Act, the Clean Water Act, and the Endangered Species Act. Furthermore, both Republicans and Democrats lambasted Secretary Watt's efforts to liberalize development interests' access to public lands, and a bipartisan majority repudiated EPA Administrator Gorsuch's steps to weaken enforcement of major environmental statutes. (In 1983, Watt and Gorsuch, as well as 20 other top EPA officials, resigned in disgrace, and Reagan appointed more moderate officials in hopes of softening the electoral impact of these upheavals.)

Although the Reagan administration adopted a more conciliatory posture on environmental issues over time, publicity about its antiregulatory activities sparked a resurgence in grassroots support for the environmental movement. Public opinion polls revealed that, after declining from its high in the early 1970s, concern about the environment jumped soon after Reagan took office and continued to climb thereafter.[47] Support for government action on behalf of environmental quality rose substantially in the 1980s as well; the public saw government as having primary responsibility for environmental protection and remained skeptical of the efficacy of efforts by individuals in the absence of government regulations.[48] Environmental groups benefited from the public's elevated concern: according to fund-raiser Roger Craver, the response to mail solicitations for three major environmental groups increased by about 30 percent immediately after Reagan's election.[49] As the Reagan era wore on, the membership and budgets of the top ten environmental organizations continued to rise. For example, the Sierra Club, which began the decade with 246,000 members and a budget of $9.5 million, had 378,000 members and a $22 million budget in 1985. The National Audubon Society's membership grew from 400,000 in 1980 to 500,000 in 1985, while its budget jumped from $10 million to $24 million.[50]

## The George H. W. Bush Administration, 1989–1993

During the 1988 presidential campaign, aware of the growing salience of environmental issues in several key states, Vice President George H.W. Bush's staff cast him as an environmentalist, notwithstanding his prominent role in the Reagan administration's antiregulatory efforts.[51] In a speech in Michigan on August 31, 1988, Bush laid out an ambitious environmental agenda, promising to address acid rain by cutting millions of tons of sulfur dioxide emissions by the year 2000. He also vowed to end ocean dumping of garbage and prosecute those who disposed of medical waste illegally. He advocated a major national campaign to reduce waste generation and promote recycling, committed himself to a program of "no net loss" of wetlands, and called for strict enforcement of toxic waste laws. He even vowed to address the emerging issue of global warming, saying: "Those who think we are powerless to do anything about the 'greenhouse effect' are forgetting about the 'White House effect.'"[52]

Once elected, President Bush began to follow through on his campaign promises. He met with representatives of 30 environmental organizations, who had submitted a "blueprint" containing more than 700 proposals for revamping the nation's environmental rules. He appointed William Reilly, the moderate former president of the Conservation Foundation, as EPA administrator. He injected new life into the dispirited Council on Environmental Quality by increasing its budget and staff. And he installed Robert Grady, who had written his environmental campaign speeches, as associate director of OMB. Bush also reversed his predecessor's course by raising spending on natural-resource and environmental programs; in particular, he increased the EPA's budget by more than 50 percent and its staff by about 22 percent.[53] Most important, shortly after taking office Bush created a task force to put together a clean air bill whose centerpiece was a sulfur dioxide emissions-trading system to curb acid rain. Largely thanks to the prominence of this market-based mechanism, which attracted the support of moderate conservatives, the president broke a decade-long stalemate, and in early 1990 Congress passed the sweeping Clean Air Act Amendments.

The revised Clean Air Act was President Bush's first and last legislative initiative on the environment, however. His administration was sharply divided on environmental issues, and by the end of 1991 conservatives had gained the upper hand. EPA Administrator Reilly found himself isolated, as the Interior, Agriculture, and Energy departments advocated policies to encourage resource consumption. Furthermore, three critical sources of counsel to the president—Chief of Staff John Sununu, OMB Director Richard Darman, and economic advisor Michael Boskin—vehemently opposed new environmental legislation, as well as international efforts to address issues such as worldwide biodiversity loss and global warming. In a sign of conservatives' ascendancy, during the 102nd Congress (1991–1992) the administration blocked action on most of the environmental statutes up for reauthorization.

These legislative victories were significant, but during the Bush era—as in the Reagan years—conservatives exerted their most substantial influence on administrative decision making. During his first year in office, Bush established the Council on Competitiveness, headed by Vice President Dan Quayle, to scrutinize environmental statutes and rules for ways to reduce the regulatory burden on the business. (The council, which comprised many of the administration's most vocal critics of regulation, got its authority not from executive orders but from less-publicized internal White House memos.[54]) In 1991, after a period of relative quiescence, the council began pursuing deregulation in earnest: it revised the federal manual that defines wetlands, removing as much as half of the land designated as wetlands from federal protection; it promoted rules limiting public appeals on timber cutting and other public-land management decisions; it scuttled an ambitious recycling program favored by the EPA; and it sought to weaken regulations for implementing the newly passed Clean Air Act Amendments.[55] Although the council did not always achieve its aims, it exacerbated environmentalists' already substantial distrust of and hostility toward their conservative adversaries.[56] Then, in his 1992 State of the Union address, the president announced his administration would temporarily bar new regulations and eliminate or weaken existing rules. He later extended the moratorium through the election—a move that supporters and critics believed helped to chill the regulatory climate, particularly with respect to the environment.[57]

The motive for these actions was pragmatic: the president wanted to solidify business support in the upcoming election. But in their public pronouncements administration spokespeople articulated a familiar conservative rationale: "What's driving this," said one White House official, "is simply that too much regulation does have the effect of decreasing economic growth and lowering the number of jobs."[58] In the fall of 1992, as the election loomed, Bush began adopting rhetoric favored by conservative activists even more conspicuously. He charged that regulations supported by Democratic candidate Bill Clinton would throw hundreds of thousands of people out of work and destroy the economy, and he ridiculed Clinton's running mate, Al Gore, as an environmental extremist, labeling him "Ozone Man."[59] In response to a controversy over logging the spotted-owl habitat in the Pacific Northwest that had dogged his administration, the president took a strongly anti-environmental stance. In a mid-September speech in a Washington timber mill town, he decried environmental "extremists" and depicted himself as an advocate of "balance." "It's time to make people more important than owls," Bush declared. He vowed to reform the Endangered Species Act, saying it and other laws were being used to bring about "the complete lockup of the most productive forest in the United States."[60]

## *The Clinton Administration, 1993–2001*

Although it was not the deciding factor, pre-election polls suggested that voters did not embrace President Bush's stance on the environment.[61] In fact, after ten years of Republican rule a 1990 Gallup poll found that 75 percent of Americans considered themselves environmentalists. A *New York Times*/CBS poll determined that 74 percent of Americans believed that "protecting the environment is so important that requirements and standards cannot be too high, and continuing environmental improvements must be made regardless of cost." Membership in the top ten environmental groups increased from 3.3 million at the beginning of the 1980s to 8 million in 1990, and donations rose from $218 million in 1985 to $514 million in 1990.[62] Grassroots environmental groups proliferated as well. For example, in 1986 the Citizens Clearinghouse for Hazardous Wastes oversaw the activities of 1,700 local organizations; by 1990 it was consulting for 7,000 groups.[63]

Hoping to capitalize on the pervasive public support for environmental protection, Clinton and Gore made a host of environmental pledges during the campaign, including promises to increase corporate average fuel economy standards for automobiles from 27.5 to 40 miles per gallon by 2000, encourage mass transit, support renewable energy development, create incentives for recycling, preserve old-growth forests, maintain the Arctic National Wildlife Refuge as wilderness, and limit the nation's carbon dioxide emissions to mitigate global warming. As important as its campaign vows, however, was the Clinton/Gore team's attempt to recast economic growth and environmental protection as complementary, not—as conservatives insisted—at odds with one another. Upon taking office in January 1993, President Clinton appointed a clutch of pro-environment officials, including EPA administrator Carol Browner and Interior Secretary Bruce Babbitt, all of whom repeated the no-trade-off language of sustainability. To demonstrate that environmental and economic health could be reconciled, Clinton replaced the antiregulatory Council on Competitiveness with a White House Office of Environmental Policy and orchestrated a summit at which he charged loggers, environmentalists, scientists, and administrators with resolving the controversy over protecting the northern spotted owl.

At the same time, Clinton and his appointees recognized that critiques of the conventional regulatory approach were not confined to academics and conservative activists but had, in fact, become widely accepted. After twelve years of hostility from the Right, many environmentalists were deeply suspicious of any efforts to reform the existing framework. On the other hand, some environmental groups had embraced incentive-based policy mechanisms and were routinely engaging in cost-benefit analysis. As journalist Margaret Kriz explained, "After years of arguing that environmental protection was morally right at any cost, environmental activists realized they had to fight economics with economics, particularly during a recession when industry groups charged that new global warming emissions controls would eliminate thousands of jobs."[64] Similarly, some environmentalists supported decentralizing environmental problem-solving on the grounds that states had become more professional and were better able to tailor policies to local conditions.[65] In addition, a number of environmental groups endorsed stakeholder collaboration as a way of enhancing civic engagement while reducing the polarization and gridlock that had accompanied the anti-environmental backlash.

Apparent agreement among conservatives and environmentalists on procedural principles concealed fundamental differences in goals, however. For example, whereas environmentalists hoped that collaborative decision making would facilitate the emergence of a precautionary consensus, conservatives regarded it as a way to enhance the regulated community's influence on decision making. For environmentalists, focusing on the most serious risks entailed devoting more resources to the threats posed by biodiversity loss and global warming; conservatives, by contrast, sought to reduce regulatory expenditures on *all* environmental threats. And finally, when environmentalists talked about the compatibility of economic and environmental health, they envisioned an economy powered by alternative fuels and environmentally oriented businesses. Conservatives imagined that a marketplace freed of cumbersome regulations would produce sufficient levels of environmental protection.

Despite these differences in underlying values and goals, agreement on means provided a powerful impetus for change—a trend amplified by the media. For example, shortly before Clinton took office journalist Phillip

Davis questioned the future of the environmental agenda, wondering in particular how the trade-offs between jobs and the environment would be managed. Davis suggested that "One-size-fits-all legislation may have to be superseded by innovative ways to get all sides in the big environmental battles to sit down and hash out solutions that are environmentally and economically acceptable."[66] Similarly, *New York Times* environmental writer Keith Schneider reported that "many scientists, economists, and government officials have reached the dismaying conclusion that much of America's environmental program has gone seriously awry."[67]

The idea of revamping the existing framework gained even more political traction in January 1993 when mayors from 114 cities in 49 states wrote to President Clinton urging him to focus on reforming environmental regulations. According to the mayors, "not only do we sometimes pay too much to solve environmental problems, we've been known to confront the wrong problems for the wrong reasons with the wrong technology."[68] Moreover, several Democratic members of Congress had been swayed by arguments that precautionary legislation sometimes had unintended consequences, including costly rules with little environmental benefit. Rep. Mike Synar (D-OK) and others hoped to inject into the reauthorization of major laws some moderate reforms, such as requiring consideration of costs before issuing a regulation, increasing spending on more important problems while reducing funding for low-risk problems, and giving businesses and cities more flexibility in complying with regulations.

Consistent with his political pragmatism and a strong desire to promote other aspects of his agenda, Clinton declined to depart as dramatically as many environmentalists had hoped from the regulatory approach established by Reagan and Bush. Determined to shrink the ballooning deficit, for fiscal year 1994 Clinton proposed only nominal increases in EPA spending (3.1 percent) and reduced overall spending for environmental and natural resource programs by 5 percent.[69] In response, the EPA scaled back its enforcement activities and devolved responsibility for numerous federal programs to the states.[70] On September 30, 1994, the president signed an executive order that continued the practice of centralized regulatory review by requiring agencies to demonstrate that the benefits of new regulations "justified" their costs and to submit all major regulations to OIRA for review (though minor regulations no longer needed OMB approval). Furthermore, agencies with jurisdiction over the environment adopted conciliatory postures in hopes of simultaneously improving regulatory effectiveness and defusing opposition. According to the head of the EPA's legislative unit, Tom Roberts, "The buzzwords around here these days are pollution prevention and market-based approaches and voluntary programs, and those have replaced the rigid, command-and-control, hard-core enforcement, fines-and-penalties approach."[71]

Attempts by the administration and some legislators to enact modest reforms did not appease an increasingly vocal group of New Right conservatives, however, and although Democrats controlled both the White House and Congress, antiregulatory efforts gained momentum.[72] In 1993 Democrats initiated an ambitious environmental agenda, but Republicans and conservative Democrats managed to squelch efforts to reauthorize a series of major environmental laws by tacking on provisions requiring cost-benefit analysis for every new rule. They easily derailed Clinton's highly touted proposal to reform mining, grazing, and logging practices on public lands, as well as his short-lived Btu tax proposal, by threatening to sabotage his legislative agenda. They also prevented Congress from establishing the National Biological Survey, forcing Secretary Babbitt to create it through administrative reorganization, and in early 1994 they torpedoed a bill to elevate the EPA to a cabinet-level department. Ultimately the 103rd Congress (1993–1994) passed only one piece of new environmental legislation, the California Desert Protection Act. By spring 1994 environmentalists and their legislative allies were on the defensive: in a March 1994 memo, they acknowledged that their opponents had forced them to change their strategy to "focus more sharply on a limited number of pieces of legislation and to put more substantial resources into winning that legislation."[73]

After setting environmentalists back on their heels, conservatives saw the prospects for advancing their own agenda brighten when the 1994 elections turned both the House (230–204) and the Senate (53–47) over to the Republicans, ending more than 40 years of nearly complete Democratic dominance. Furthermore, the new crop of Republicans—many of them from the West, where the Wise Use and property rights movements were in full swing—were thoroughly versed in the conservative antiregulatory philosophy. As John Shanahan of the Heritage Foundation explained, "The freshman class and a fair number of the sophomore class are fairly hard-core about the idea that the federal government has encroached on their lives. The idea that drives this movement is to dismantle the environmental laws."[74]

The top priority of these newly elected conservatives was to prevent legislation to address global warming—regarded by many scientists as the world's most pressing environmental problem. Reprising the approach Reagan had used to deflect acid rain legislation, opponents of global warming policies highlighted the uncertainty of the relationship between rising carbon dioxide levels and climate change, claimed that taking immediate steps to reduce greenhouse gas emissions would require huge and immediate economic sacrifices, and cautioned against following any course advocated by doomsaying environmentalists. Republican leaders enhanced the legitimacy of these arguments by inviting global warming skeptics to testify at more than a dozen congressional hearings. Reflecting the potency of conservative arguments, in

1997 the Senate voted unanimously to support a nonbinding resolution (the Byrd-Hagel Amendment) that it would not give its advice and consent to any international agreement that did not require developing countries to reduce their emissions or that would result in "serious harm to the economy of the United States." Reluctant to exert leadership in the face of such resistance, Clinton declined to submit the Kyoto Protocol (an international treaty calling for reductions in carbon dioxide emissions) to the Senate for ratification. Furthermore, he retreated from his Earth Day promise to fundamentally restructure energy use in the United States by converting it from fossil fuel to cleaner-burning renewable resources, instead proposing a global-warming package that consisted of tax incentives and voluntary programs, but no mandates.

In addition to preventing action on global warming, newly elected conservatives hoped to implement the "Contract with America," a set of regulatory reforms drafted by Speaker Newt Gingrich prior to the election. Although the 400-page contract did not contain the word "environment," its proposals had the potential to unravel decades of environmental law. Three provisions were crucial: one sought to reduce the federal government's preeminence in environmental regulation by prohibiting unfunded mandates to states and localities; another hampered federal agencies' ability to issue regulations by requiring them to conduct cost-benefit analyses and risk assessments before promulgating new rules; a third promised to curtail restrictions on land use by mandating that government reimburse property owners for reductions in the value of their land caused by regulations. Majority Whip Tom DeLay of Texas announced that the overarching goal of regulatory reform was to "make sure that American small business and the American taxpayer don't become the next endangered species."[75] Republican Thomas L. Bliley, Jr., of Virginia, chair of the House Commerce Committee, summarized what he regarded as the party's antiregulatory mandate, saying "The American people sent us a message in November, loud and clear: Tame this regulatory beast. Our constituents want us to break the Feds' stranglehold on our economy and to get them out of decisions that are best left to the individual."[76]

In the spring of 1995 a coalition of Republicans and conservative Democrats in the House easily passed an omnibus regulatory reform package (HR9, the Job Creation and Wage Enhancement Act) that—without amending a single environmental law—would have substantially weakened the nation's environmental protection framework. The bill required compensation for government limits on property owners' use of their land, outlined a procedure for detailed scientific and economic assessments of all proposed environmental rules, and required agencies to justify any new regulation by demonstrating that its benefits exceeded its costs and that it embodied the most cost-effective approach. During the House debates, supporters did not attack the goals of environmental laws directly; instead, they reiterated the conservative story line, according to which federal regulations impose a damper on the economy and burden small businesses with poorly designed, overly expensive rules and excessive enforcement; that federal agencies have imposed new rules without sufficient scientific evidence that they are necessary to prevent significant health or environmental hazards; and that the benefits of those regulations are often minimal and far less than their costs. The elaborate processes contained in HR9, they contended, were necessary to produce streamlined regulations that defined real hazards and provided protection without causing undue hardship. As Rep. Robert Walker (R-PA) explained, "It is time to use good science to ensure that the regulatory burden we impose on the American people provides them with the protection from real hazards, not the exaggerated risks of the zero-tolerance crowd."[77]

Despite the backing of a potent industry alliance that included the National Association of Manufacturers and trade associations representing plastics, electric utilities, and food manufacturers, conservatives' regulatory reform initiative fared poorly in the more divided Senate.[78] There, a strong mobilization by environmentalists galvanized Democrats and moderate Republicans who favored a greater reliance on tax credits, land exchanges, pricing policies, and other incentives, but not a complete regulatory rollback. Some big businesses, particularly those with long experience dealing with regulations, were also dubious about conservatives' most extreme deregulatory proposals.[79] As a result, Majority Leader and prospective presidential candidate Robert Dole (R-KS) failed on three back-to-back cloture votes to bring his companion bill to HR9 (S343) to a vote. In late December the Senate Judiciary Committee approved (10 to 7) a narrower proposal that would require the government to compensate people who lost 50 percent of more of the value of their property because of federal regulations. Senator Charles Grassley (R-IA) offered a conservative rationale for the measure, saying: "It seems to me that the people have grown tired of this government encroachment."[80] Because supporters lacked the votes to avert a filibuster, however, the full chamber did not consider that bill either. Similar fates awaited conservative rewrites of the Clean Water and Endangered Species acts, both of which fared well in the House but died in the Senate. Ultimately, the only stand-alone legislation conservatives succeeded in passing during the 104th Congress (1994–1995) was the Unfunded Mandates Act of 1995, a measure that reduced the federal government's ability to require state and local governments to pursue environmental goals.

Finding their direct, visible efforts at regulatory reform thwarted again, conservatives sidestepped debate by taking aim at environmental rules through the more arcane budget process. Among the 17 measures to relax environmental regulations added to the fiscal 1996 omnibus spending bill were provisions to impose a one-year moratorium on new listing under the Endangered Species Act, institute a 90-day moratorium on proposed grazing regulations, curtail the ecological assessment of the Columbia River Basin, dismantle the Energy Department's conservation programs, increase the harvest from Alaska's Tongass National Forest, and open up the Arctic National Wildlife Refuge to oil drilling. Partly in response to a massive publicity campaign by environmentalists, however, President Clinton vetoed the massive spending bill and—after a week-long government shutdown—forced Congress to remove most of the offending riders.

In fact, instead of revolutionizing environmental policy, conservatives' aggressive efforts to roll back protective rules inspired a publicity campaign that prompted another spurt in environmental group membership. The conservative attack also provoked dissent within the Republican Party, and many Republican freshmen took a beating back home for supporting anti-environmental provisions. Polls indicated that, by a more than two-to-one margin, voters trusted Democrats more than Republicans on environmental issues, and more than half of Republicans distrusted their own party on those issues.[81] Republican pollster Frank Luntz warned House leaders that 62 percent of all voters, and 54 percent of Republican voters, wanted to protect the environment more than they wanted to cut regulations.[82] "The public may not like or admire regulations, may not think more are necessary" he said, "but [they put] environmental regulations as a higher priority than cutting regulations."[83] In October 1995 the House Republican Conference sent out a tip sheet to its members on ways to counteract "the environmentalist lobby and their extremist friends in the eco-terrorist underworld,"[84] and in December, House Speaker Gingrich conceded that the Republicans had "mishandled the environment all spring and summer."[85]

During the remainder of the Clinton administration's tenure, conservative legislators moderated their language and maintained a lower profile on the environment. They also endured a postelection counteroffensive by President Clinton. In an effort to capitalize on the rebounding popularity of environmentalism, the president devoted an unusually long portion of his 1996 State of the Union address to environmental issues, deriding Republican efforts to roll back federal regulations. Then, in the midst of his reelection campaign, he infuriated conservatives by designating a 1.7-million-acre national monument in the red rock country of southern Utah. The administration also proposed strict new standards for tiny airborne particles and ground-level ozone and phased out the nationwide wetlands permitting process that gave virtually instant approval for developing wetlands of less than ten acres.

Congressional conservatives were not vanquished, however; instead they again resorted to an under-the-radar strategy. Within a year they were attaching dozens of antiregulatory riders to appropriations and budget bills, crafting their provisions more narrowly to avoid attracting attention. Furthermore, in 1998, 1999, and 2000 conservatives confounded the administration's efforts to address global warming by attaching riders to a variety of appropriations bill that prohibited spending any federal money to "develop, propose, or issue rules, regulations, decrees or orders for the purpose of implementation, or in contemplation of implementation, of the Kyoto Protocol."

Conservatives influenced administrative decision making during the Clinton era in more subtle ways as well. As part of the administration's overall regulatory reform effort, federal agencies began experimenting with regulatory negotiation and voluntary programs. For example, the EPA's Common Sense Initiative, introduced in 1995, enabled regulators to work with officials from six industries and outside groups to streamline regulations and eliminate inconsistent requirements. Project XL, initiated in 1996, aimed to facilitate cooperation between the EPA and individual companies in developing strategies for improving environmental performance. A small suite of "challenge" programs, such as Climate Leaders (2000), encouraged industry to act benevolently in the absence of regulatory clubs. The agency also adopted a more flexible approach to implementing Superfund that allowed cities to redevelop contaminated sites and return them to use without eliminating all pollution. Similarly, Interior Secretary Babbitt vigorously promoted habitat conservation plans, a mechanism that allowed developers to destroy endangered species' habitat in exchange for setting aside other tracts or buying permanent conservation easements.

The adoption of flexible, conciliatory approaches was not simply political retrenchment in the face of powerful opposition; it also reflected what some scholars have called "policy-oriented learning."[86] As policy scholar and EPA official Daniel Fiorino explains, experts were increasingly aware that the existing regulatory framework neglected important environmental problems and that some businesses would improve their operations if given positive incentives.[87] Pro-environment panels in the United States, including the National Academy of Public Administration and the President's Council on Sustainable Development, endorsed such innovations throughout the 1990s. In addition, other industrialized nations—such as Japan, Denmark, and the Netherlands—were experimenting with similar ways of achieving environmental protection. But federal regulators' more indirect approach was also a response to the polarization created by the anti-environmental backlash. As political scientist Peri Arnold observed, "The regulatory agencies have become much more cautious. Fewer rules have been generated. There are fewer new regulations. It's just self-preservation."[88] Regardless of their impetus, Clinton administration officials' reform initiatives encountered resistance from many environmentalists who worried that business would exploit them to gut environmental protections. As a result, few of these programs accomplished as much as their proponents had hoped.[89]


## The George W. Bush Administration, 2001–2008

Whereas the Clinton administration embraced moderate regulatory reform, the inauguration of George W. Bush in January 2001 heralded a return to governance that was more consistent with the values of New Right conservatives.[90] The Bush administration's environmental priorities mirrored those articulated by the Reagan White House: to reduce federal responsibility for environmental protection by cutting the EPA's budget and giving the states more control over implementation; to increase domestic energy production by providing subsidies and limiting environmental restrictions; and, more generally, to provide relief for businesses by eliminating burdensome regulations. Incorporating the lessons learned by his predecessors, President Bush aimed to achieve these goals primarily through an administrative strategy rather than a legislative campaign. Moreover, to avoid provoking the kind of pro-environment backlash triggered by previous antiregulatory initiatives, the administration and its allies made crucial adjustments in the way they talked about environmental issues. In response to advice from pollster Frank Luntz, conservative Republicans refrained from positing a choice between environmental protection and deregulation. Instead, they assured the public that they were committed to "preserving and protecting" the environment, but doing it more "wisely and effectively." Luntz urged Republicans to pepper their speeches on the environment with buzzwords such as "safer," "cleaner," "healthy," and especially "balance." In addition, he encouraged them to describe themselves as "conservationists," a word that conveys a "moderate, reasoned, common sense" perspective, whereas "environmentalist" connotes "extremism." In his speeches on the environment, the president appeared to be following Luntz's advice: for example, by summer 2002 he had replaced the words "global warming" and "environmentalist"—which appeared in a number of speeches in 2001—with "climate change" and "conservationist."[91]

Despite adopting a low-profile approach, the Bush administration rarely wavered in its efforts to roll back environmental rules. The president began by appointing officials with conservative credentials to a variety of top environmental posts, including Gale Norton, formerly of the Mountain States Legal Foundation, as secretary of the Interior, and J. Steven Griles, a former lobbyist for coal, oil, and gas interests, as deputy secretary; timber industry lobbyist Mark Rey as the nation's top forestry official; Don Evans, a former energy company executive, as secretary of Commerce; and James L. Connaughton, a former power company lobbyist, as CEQ chairman. (Bush appointed moderate Christine Todd Whitman to head the EPA, but she resigned after two years in the face of persistent disagreements with White House conservatives. Replacing her was Michael Leavitt, whose policy preferences more closely mirrored those of the president.) Immediately after taking office, the White House put a 60-day hold on the spate of rules instituted in the final months of the Clinton administration, subsequently weakening or eliminating many of them. For example, the administration dispensed with a rule phasing out snowmobiles in Yellowstone National Park, reversed a plan crafted by the U.S. Fish and Wildlife Service and local stakeholders to reintroduce grizzly bears in the Bitterroot-Selway Wilderness, and suspended a designation of more than 58 million roadless acres of Forest Service land as off limits to development. (In May 2005 the Bush administration replaced the roadless rule with a procedure whereby state governors could petition the Secretary of Agriculture for special rules to manage roadless areas in their states.) In addition, the Justice Department settled or declined to defend Clinton-era rules in court and, in some cases, encouraged legal challenges by industry. For instance, it invited a lawsuit against Clinton's Northwest Forest Plan and then agreed to a settlement favorable to the timber industry; it also settled several lawsuits over the Endangered Species Act by agreeing to shrink the areas designated as critical habitat. In response to environmentalists' complaints, Interior Secretary Gale Norton explained, "Many of the things we have done are to put in place common-sense approaches that we feel are a better balance."[92]

As time wore on, the administration adopted a variety of subtle tactics aimed at removing regulatory hurdles. As journalist Joby Warrick observed, "Rather than proposing broad changes or drafting new legislation, administration officials...[took] existing regulations and made subtle tweaks that carry large consequences."[93] For instance, in May 2002 the EPA rephrased a rule that prevented coal companies from burying Appalachian streams under wastes from mountaintop mining, thereby allowing the practice to expand dramatically. In 2003 the agency downgraded the "hazardous" classification of mercury emissions from power plants, giving affected utilities fifteen additional years to implement the most costly pollution controls. Similarly, to reduce the regulatory burden on industry, the administration rewrote the Clean Air Act's New Source Review rule to allow old, coal-fired plants to modernize without installing state-of-the-art pollution controls.

Federal agencies also reduced the impact of existing regulations simply by changing the way they were implemented. For example, a guidance document furnished by the Army Corps of Engineers and the EPA in early 2003 instructed field agents to minimize the application of the Clean Water Act to wetlands. (The administration also proposed new rules for managing wetlands that would remove 20 percent of swamps, ponds, and marshes, as well as up to 60 percent of rivers, lakes, and streams from federal protection, but it backed off after getting more than 133,000 comments opposing the change, many of them from hunters and state officials.) The Interior Department sharply limited the impact of the Endangered Species Act by recalculating the economic costs of protecting habitat, severely curtailing the number of species added to the threatened and endangered lists, and declining to protect listed species in the absence of a court order.[94] In addition, Interior streamlined the process to permit extracting minerals from federal land and constrained the ability of states to challenge dam licensure proceedings.[95] The EPA relaxed its enforcement of pollution control rules: civil enforcement penalties decreased by 45 percent in 2002 and criminal penalties decreased by 34 percent, prompting several high-level EPA enforcement officials to resign.[96] The EPA also reduced its reporting requirements for toxic emissions to air, land, and water.[97] CEQ chair James Connaughton defended the administration's actions with a conservative rationale, saying the president did not oppose environmental protection but did want to find new ways—such as personal stewardship and better technology, rather than regulation—to solve old problems.[98]

Perhaps the most controversial of the administration's deregulatory activities was its decision to accelerate oil and gas development across broad swaths of the Rocky Mountain West. After Vice President Dick Cheney's national energy policy group called for promoting energy development on federal lands, the White House wrote to cabinet officers asking them to "identify ways your agency could expedite the review of permits or other authorizations for other energy-related projects."[99] In addition, the administration set up a Task Force on Energy Policy Streamlining whose main purpose was to field complaints from and act as an "ombudsman" for the oil and gas industry. Finally, funding for the Bureau of Land Management (BLM) program to administer oil and gas exploration and development activities jumped 50 percent between 2001 and 2004. The combination was effective: in its 2005 review the U.S. General Accounting Office (GAO) found that the number of drilling permits approved by the BLM had more than tripled—from 1,803 in 1999 to 6,399 in 2004—but that, as a result, the BLM's ability to meet its environmental mitigation responsibilities for oil and gas development had declined.[100]

Beyond modifying and scaling back the implementation of environmentally protective rules, the Bush administration relied heavily on review by the OMB's Office of Information and Regulatory Affairs to prevent further growth in the regulatory apparatus. One of OIRA's most potent tools was the Data Quality Act, a 227-word provision that House Republicans inserted into the 2001 Treasury and General Government Appropriations bill that required all federal agencies to ensure "the quality, objectivity, utility, and integrity" of information they produced. As conservative lawyer James T. O'Reilly noted after the law's passage, allowing industry to challenge the data underlying regulations even before they were finalized erected a substantial barrier against such rules. "A prudent opponent of rulemaking," O'Reilly wrote in the *Administrative Law Review,* "will challenge the data accuracy first, before the notice of proposed rulemaking appears, so that the agency must be prepared to defend itself twice."[101] Shortly after the Data Quality Act became law, business groups led by the U.S. Chamber of Commerce began poring over regulations to find those that might be vulnerable. Bill Kovacs, the Chamber of Commerce's vice president for environment and regulatory affairs, declared the new mechanisms would be "huge, immense, a very big issue for straightening out the regulatory process."[102]

By the end of the Bush administration's first term, OIRA had succeeded in stalling, modifying, or derailing a variety of proposed regulations by challenging agencies to use more in-depth cost-benefit analyses, revise their methods for risk assessment, or respond in writing to critics of regulations. In the spring of 2004 OIRA director John Graham boasted before the Senate Small Business and Entrepreneurship Committee, "Even by conservative estimates, this administration has slowed the growth of burdensome new rules by at least 75 percent when compared with the previous administration, while still moving ahead with crucial safeguards."[103] In late January 2007 President Bush added another weapon to his administration's antiregulatory arsenal by signing an executive order requiring each agency to establish a regulatory policy office run by a political appointee. The office's purpose was to supervise the development of rules and documents providing guidance to regulated industries.[104]

Although they accomplished most of their objectives through administrative means, antiregulatory conservatives had a small number of legislative accomplishments during the Bush years as well. Most important, conservatives repeatedly fended off legislation to address global climate change.[105] Furthermore, early in its tenure, the Bush administration advanced two pieces of environmental legislation that garnered widespread support: the 2002 Small Business Liability and Revitalization Act, which accelerated the cleanup and redevelopment of brownfield sites by limiting liability for developers and small business owners, and the 2003 Healthy Forest Restoration Act, which streamlined and enhanced local control over timber sales in federal forests. Intense opposition to both laws surfaced during implementation, however, and the administration's subsequent legislative initiatives encountered fierce criticism.[106]

## Institutionalizing Conservative Principles in Judicial Decision Making

In addition to promoting legislative and administrative changes, conservatives used their dominance of the White House between 1981 and 2008 to appoint sympathetic federal judges. The changing composition of the federal judiciary, in turn, resulted in several shifts in the courts' treatment of environmentalists and environmental policy. Beginning in the early 1990s, the federal courts ruled with greater frequency than before that environmentalists did not have standing to sue, that agencies had failed to establish a scientific basis for regulations or to properly consider their costs, and that regulation constituted a "taking" of private property. As in the legislative and administrative arenas, the judiciary did not embrace conservative litigants' most direct assaults on environmental regulations; the Supreme Court, in particular, was reluctant to strike down laws that were broadly popular. The courts did, however, weaken tools formerly available to environmentalists and deter aggressive implementation and enforcement by regulatory agencies.

For conservatives, one of the most promising developments of the 1990s was the Supreme Court's propensity to deny environmental litigants standing to sue. In the 1990 case *Lujan v. National Wildlife Federation*, the Supreme Court refused to allow the National Wildlife Federation (NWF) to challenge a decision by the Bureau of Land Management to open up a tract of public land to development. In his opinion, Justice Scalia wrote that the two NWF members who filed the complaint had not demonstrated any specific injury, aside from asserting that they had recreational and aesthetic interests in the land under consideration. Two years later, in *Lujan v. Defenders of Wildlife* (1992), the court rejected (6 to 3) environmentalists' standing claim on the grounds that the plaintiffs would not suffer a "redressable" injury as a result of an Interior Department decision to forgo Endangered Species Act review of a U.S. government decision to fund two large overseas development projects. In a third case, *Steel Co. v. Citizens for a Better Environment* (1998), a six-justice majority again rejected plaintiffs' standing claim on the grounds that the injury was not redressable—in this case because any fine would go to the government and because the injunctive relief sought could not correct a past injury. (The plaintiffs had sued Steel Co. for failing to report its emissions for seven straight years, but the company began reporting its emissions upon receiving the notice of intent to sue.) Although significant, the conservative triumph on standing was circumscribed. In *Friends of the Earth v. Laidlaw Environmental Services* (2000), the defendants had been violating their permit under the Clean Water Act, and Friends of the Earth sought civil penalties that would be paid to the federal government. By a 7 to 2 majority, the Supreme Court upheld the lower court's decision to grant standing, and subsequent lower court decisions hewed to the standard established in *Laidlaw*.[107]

Conservatives were encouraged by a second judicial development as well: the increasing willingness of some judges to compel agencies to engage in cost-benefit analysis or risk balancing, even in the absence of a statutory mandate to do so. In the 1980s, after a decade of scrutinizing agency procedures according to a "hard look" standard of judicial review, the courts began to adopt a more deferential posture toward agency decisions. In the 1990s, however, the U.S. Circuit Court of Appeals for the D.C. Circuit, which hears the vast majority of environmental cases, adopted a third standard—conservative legal scholar Michael Greve called it "substantive review"—in which judges engaged in a probing analysis of the results of agency rule making.[108] As Greve noted, this kind of review relied not on hewing to the statutory language or trying to discern legislative intent, but instead imputed to Congress a willingness to consider trade-offs between environmental and other objectives. For instance, in February 1992 the court required the Department of Transportation to reconsider the 1990 fuel-economy standards for cars in response to an argument by two conservative organizations—the Competitive Enterprise Institute and Consumer Alert—that the agency had to evaluate risk trade-offs, particularly the claim that lighter, smaller cars were unsafe (*CEI and Consumer Alert v. NHTSA*). In May 1999, in *American Trucking Ass'n v. EPA,* the D.C. Circuit Court struck down the EPA's proposed National Ambient Air Quality Standards for ozone and small particulates, partly on the grounds that the agency should have conducted a cost-benefit analysis, even though the statute explicitly prohibits considering costs in setting air quality standards. This bold ruling did not hold up, however, and in 2001 the Supreme Court unanimously and decisively overturned it.

For conservatives, a third judicial trend also boded well: during the 1990s the federal courts became more hospitable to the argument that regulation infringed on landowners' property rights. In this regard, most observers viewed *Nollan v. California Coastal Commission* (1987) as a watershed event for property-rights advocates. The Supreme Court agreed with the Nollans that there was no relationship between the "exaction"—a requirement imposed in exchange for granting a development permit, in this case public access to the beach—required by the coastal commission and the applicants' request for a permit to build a new house on their beachfront property. A subsequent case affirmed the court's propensity to curb regulatory impositions on property owners: in *Lucas v. South Carolina Coastal Commission* (1992) the court held that because the plaintiff, David Lucas, had suffered a total loss of property value as a result of a state law passed after he acquired the land, he was entitled to financial compensation. Two years later, in *Dolan v. City of Tigard,* a 5-to-4 majority held that zoning officials could impose exactions on property owners only if they were related to the proposed development or were "roughly proportional" to any harms the development may cause. Then, in *Palazzolo v. Rhode Island* (2001), the court held that a landowner was not barred from asserting a takings claim by the fact that he acquired title to the property *after* a land-use regulation went into effect.[109]

Again, however, the Supreme Court resisted the most extreme conservative position. In *Tahoe-Sierra Preservation Council v. Tahoe Regional Planning Agency* (2002), the court held (6 to 3) that the enactment of a building moratorium by the regional planning agency while it devised a comprehensive land-use plan did *not* constitute a taking. Similarly, in the 2005 case *Kelo et al. v. City of New London et al.,* the Supreme Court upheld the City of New London's use of eminent domain as part of a comprehensive economic development plan. (In both cases, conservative Justices Rehnquist, Scalia, and Thomas dissented.)

Although the *Tahoe* and *Kelo* cases were setbacks for property-rights advocates, the Federal Court of Claims remained a friendly venue.[110] *Florida Rock Industry Inc. v. United States* (1994) exemplified that court's approach: the court found a "partial taking," with a potential federal liability of tens of millions of dollars, because the Army Corps of Engineers refused to grant Florida Rock a permit to extract limestone from the South Florida Everglades. The court found a taking even though Florida Rock had received offers for the property that would have allowed it to recover more than twice the purchase price. The claims court handed down a similar ruling in the 2001 *Tulare Lake Basin* case, finding that federal protections for salmon and delta smelt reduced the amount of water available to claimants under their contracts with the state of California. The court reasoned that "The federal government is certainly free to preserve the fish; it must simply pay for the water it takes to do so."[111]

Even as they succeeded in advancing some principles, conservatives suffered a variety of striking defeats between 1980 and 2008. The most prominent of these were the Supreme Court's 2007 "rebuke" of the Bush administration for refusing to regulate greenhouse gas emissions in *Commonwealth of Massachusetts et al. v. Environmental Protection Agency et al.,*[112] a 2007 Supreme Court decision requiring the agency to impose strict emissions limits on power plants and factories that add capacity or make renovations that increase their emissions (*Environmental Defense v. Duke Energy*), and a 2008 decision by the D.C. Circuit Court of Appeals striking down an EPA cap-and-trade rule on mercury emissions as insufficiently protective. Also disappointing for conservatives was the court's failure to embrace Commerce-Clause challenges of federal power to regulate wetlands in two closely watched cases: *Solid Waste Agency of Northern Cook County v. Army Corps of Engineers* (2001) and *Rapanos v. United States* (2006). The court was sharply divided on the Commerce-Clause question in these cases, however, and some observers believed that such challenges had the potential to eviscerate environmental regulation in the future.

To the extent there was a shift in judicial decision making during the era of conservative ascendance, what caused it? Greve opined that "while judicial appointments have played a role, judicial opinions evidence a learning process that transcends partisan political considerations."[113] Similarly, Fred L. Smith of the Competitive Enterprise Institute believed that judges came to understand that "regulations not only have the potential to do good, they have the potential to do harm, and not just economic harm but actual harm to public health and the environment."[114] But a spate of systematic empirical studies conducted in the late 1990s suggested a more prosaic explanation: the dominance of conservative judges on the bench. According to these investigations, a judge's ideology, although mitigated by panel effects, was the main determinant of his or her vote.[115] In particular, a study of appellate decisions conducted by legal scholar Cass Sunstein and his colleagues found that between 1970 and 2002, Democratic appointees voted more liberally than Republican appointees in environmental protection cases, and those effects were exaggerated if the panel was all-Republican or all-Democrat. As of 2008 trends in the composition of the bench suggested conservatives would continue to fare well in federal court for some time to come: when George H. W. Bush left office, 80 percent of all federal judges were Republican appointees, as were 75 percent of the members of the appellate bench, and Republicans dominated 11 of the 13 courts of appeals.[116] By the end of the Clinton administration, the federal bench was almost evenly split between Democratic and Republican appointees, but the balance tipped back in the Republican direction under President Bush. By 2008 most federal courts again had a majority of Republican appointees, and—with the 2005 and 2006 appointments of Justices John Roberts and Samuel Alito—conservatives needed only one more appointment to solidify their grip on the Supreme Court.

## Conclusions

Between 1980 and 2008 New Right conservatives sought to influence environmental politics and policy in two distinct but related ways. First, they tried to shape the political context by disseminating a multifaceted critique of environmentalism and environmental regulation, mobilizing grassroots groups, and filing strategic lawsuits. Second, they promoted the election of ideological sympathizers to Congress and the White House and the appointment of conservative judges to the federal courts. The main constraint on conservatives' ability to promote their agenda was public opinion, which remained broadly supportive of environmental protection throughout this period. After failing on several occasions to confront that consensus head on, conservative policymakers resorted to blocking new legislation; they also capitalized on the low visibility and arcane nature of rule making to make substantial changes in regulations and their implementation. These under-the-radar tactics were effective: although they failed to dismantle the statutory regime enacted in the 1970s, conservative policymakers inhibited the federal government's ability to promote new policies or make existing ones more protective, while quietly loosening administrative safeguards on the nation's natural resources.

By 2008, however, there were numerous signs that the dominance of U.S. environmental policy by New Right conservatives had run its course. Even within the conservative movement there were signs of growing restiveness. Some Christian groups had distanced themselves from the Bush administration on global climate change and protection of endangered species, and many businesses had endorsed federal regulations on greenhouse gases.[117] Moreover, in the face of rising energy prices and water shortages, states and municipalities were trying to address environmental sustainability issues despite the absence of federal leadership. What remained to be seen was how environmentalism itself would evolve; after enduring 30 years of rhetorical and tactical challenges, environmentalists were struggling to capitalize on the newfound salience of environmental issues without sparking yet another backlash.

## Notes

1. David Mastio, "The GOP's Enviro-rut," *Policy Review* 101 (June–July 2000), 19–34.
2. For instance, between 1984 and 2007 the Gallup organization asked: "With which one of these statements about the environment and the economy do you most agree—protection of the environment should be given priority even at the risk of curbing economic growth (or) economic growth should be given priority, even if the environment suffers to some extent?" With the exception of 2003 (47 percent) and 2004 (49 percent), more than 50 percent agreed with the first option. http://www.gallup.com/poll/1615/environment.aspx.
3. Although conservatives generally agreed on these three positions, they disagreed on others. The most important division concerned government support for business: libertarians were suspicious of concentrated political power, whereas "Hamiltonian" conservatives supported using the central government to promote business and economic growth. A third group of conservatives, the traditionalists, continued to support some government protection of the environment but were subordinate during this period to the more populist, antiregulatory New Right activists on whom this chapter focuses.
4. Jacob Hacker, "Privatizing Risk without Privatizing the Welfare State: The Hidden Politics of Social Policy Retrenchment in the United States," *American Political Science Review* 98, 2 (2004): 243–60.
5. See, for example, Eugene Bardach and Robert A. Kagan, *Going by the Book: The Problem of Regulatory Unreasonableness* (Philadelphia: Temple

University Press, 1982); Robert W. Crandall and Lester B. Lave, *The Scientific Basis of Health and Safety Regulations* (Washington, DC: Brookings Institution, 1981); R. Shep Melnick, *Regulation and the Courts: The Case of the Clean Air Act* (Washington, DC: Brookings Institution, 1983).

6. See, for example, Mary Douglas and Aaron Wildavsky, *Risk and Culture: An Essay on the Selection of Technical and Environmental Dangers* (Berkeley: University of California Press, 1982); Bernard J. Frieden, *The Environmental Protection Hustle* (Cambridge, MA: MIT Press, 1979).

7. William Tucker, *Progress and Privilege: America in the Age of Environmentalism* (Garden City, NY: Anchor Press/Doubleday, 1982).

8. Edith Efron, *The Apocalyptics: Cancer and the Big Lie* (New York: Simon and Schuster, 1984).

9. David Horowitz, "Making the Green One Red," *National Review* 42 (March 19, 1990): 39.

10. Dixy Lee Ray and Louis R. Guzzo, *Trashing the Planet* (Washington, DC: Regnery Gateway, 1990), 163.

11. Ben Bolch and Harold Lyons, *Apocalypse Not* (Washington, DC: Cato Institute, 1993), viii.

12. Michael Fumento, *Science under Siege: How the Environmental Misinformation Campaign Is Affecting Our Law, Taxes, and Our Daily Life* (New York: Quill, 1993).

13. Jonathan Adler, "Rent Seeking Behind the Green Curtain," *Regulation* 19, 4 (Fall 1996), 26–34.

14. John Baden, "Crimes against Nature: Public Funding of Environmental Destruction," *Policy Review* 46 (Winter 1987): 36.

15. Bolch and Lyons, *Apocalypse Not,* 2.

16. Warren T. Brookes, "Chaining the Economy: America Dragged Down," *National Review* 42 (October 15, 1990): 42.

17. Fred L. Smith, "Conclusion: Environmental Policy at the Crossroads," in *Environmental Politics: Public Costs, Private Rewards,* ed. Michael S. Greve and Fred L. Smith (New York: Praeger, 1992), 177–97.

18. John D. Graham, Laura C. Green, and Marc J. Roberts, *In Search of Safety: Chemicals and Cancer Risk* (Cambridge, MA: Harvard University Press, 1988); Robert N. Stavins, "Clean Profits: Using Economic Incentives to Protect the Environment," *Policy Review* 48 (Spring 1989): 58–63.

19. Terry L. Anderson and Donald R. Leal, *Free Market Environmentalism* (New York: Palgrave, 1991).

20. Jane S. Shaw and Richard L. Stroup, "Getting Warmer?" *National Review* 41 (July 14, 1989): 26–28.

21. Frank Clifford, "GOP Divided on Environmental Regulation," *Los Angeles Times,* September 25, 1995, 1.

22. Kate O'Callaghan, "Whose Agenda for America," *Audubon* 94 (September–October 1992): 80–91.

23. Nancie G. Marzulla, "The Property Rights Movement: How It Began and Where It Is Headed," in *Land Rights: The 1990s Property Rights Rebellion,* ed. Bruce Yandle (Lanham, MD: Rowman and Littlefield, 1995), 22.

24. Quoted in Kenneth Jost, "Property Rights," *CQ Researcher* 5 (June 16, 1995): 516.

25. Lewis Powell, a corporate lawyer and future Supreme Court justice, advanced the idea of a conservative litigation network in a 1971 memo to the United States Chamber of Commerce. Powell urged conservatives to embrace judicial activism, noting "Especially with an activist-minded Supreme Court, the Judiciary may be the most important instrument for social, economic and political change." Jeffrey Rosen, "The Unregulated Offensive," *New York Times Magazine,* April 17, 2005, 46.

26. Conservative litigants also challenged federal environmental regulations based on the Tenth Amendment, which reserves powers not explicitly granted to the federal government to the States, and the Eleventh Amendment, which formed the basis for claims that states have immunity from private lawsuits (including citizen suits under various federal environmental laws).

27. Jon Margolis, "The Quiet Takings Project Is Trespassing on Democracy," *High Country News,* August 2, 1999, 193.

28. Ruth Marcus, "Issues Groups Fund Seminars for Judges," *Washington Post,* April 9, 1998, A01.

29. Richard A. Harris and Sidney M. Milkis, *The Politics of Regulatory Change: A Tale of Two Agencies* (New York: Oxford University Press, 1996).

30. Richard Viguerie, *The New Right: We're Ready to Lead* (Falls Church, VA: The Viguerie Company, 1981); Sidney Blumenthal, *The Rise of the Counter-Establishment: From Conservative Ideology to Political Power* (New York: Times Books, 1986).

31. Kathy Koch, "Philosophical Split Divides Candidates on the Environment," *Congressional Quarterly Weekly Report* 38 (October 18, 1980): 3161–3.

32. Quoted in Lawrence Mosher, "Reagan and Environmental Protection— None of the Laws Will be Untouchable," *National Journal* 13 (January 3, 1981), 17.

33. Michael E. Kraft and Norman J. Vig, "Environmental Policy from the 1970s to 1990," in *Environmental Policy in the 1990s: Toward a New Agenda,* 2nd ed., ed. Norman J. Vig and Michael E. Kraft (Washington, DC: CQ Press, 1994), 3–29.

34. Norman J. Vig, "Presidential Leadership and the Environment," in *Environmental Policy: New Directions for the Twenty-First Century,* 5th ed., ed. Norman J. Vig and Michael E. Kraft (Washington, DC: CQ Press, 2003), 107.

35. Melissa Martino Golden, *What Motivates Bureaucrats? Politics and Administration during the Reagan Years* (New York: Columbia University Press, 2000).

36. Pamela Fessler, "A Quarter-Century of Activism Erected a Bulwark of Laws," *Congressional Quarterly Weekly Report* 48 (January 20, 1990): 156.

37. Quoted in Lawrence Mosher, "Reagan and the GOP are Riding the Sage-brush Rebellion—But for How Long?" *National Journal* 13 (March 21, 1981), 476–481.

38. Quoted in Constance Holden, "The Reagan Years: Environmentalists Trem-ble," *Science* 210, 4473 (November 28, 1980): 988.

39. Kraft and Vig, "Environmental Policy from the 1970s to 1990."

40. Marc K. Landy, Marc J. Roberts, and Stephen R. Thomas, *The Environmen-tal Protection Agency: Asking the Wrong Questions,* expanded ed. (New York: Oxford University Press, 1994).

41. Lawrence Mosher, "Regulatory Striptease—Watt Takes Aim at Surface Min-ing Regulations," *National Journal* 13 (May 30, 1981), 971–973.

42. Quoted in Lawrence Mosher, "The Nation's Ailing Timber Industry Finds It has a Friend in Washington," *National Journal* 13 (July 11, 1981), 1237–1241.

43. Kraft and Vig, "Environmental Policy from the 1970s to 1990."

44. Michael Kranish, "Acid Rain Report Said Suppressed," *Boston Globe,* August 18, 1984, 1.

45. Quoted in Robert H. Boyle, and R. Alexander Boyle, *Acid Rain* (New York: Nick Lyons Books, 1983), 96.

46. Alan Hill, "Acid Precipitation and the Use of Fossil Fuels," Hearings Before the U.S. Senate, Committee on Energy and Natural Resources, 97th Cong., 2nd sess., August 1982 (Washington, DC: U.S. Government Printing Office, 1982), 161.

47. The most dramatic turnaround came on a question asking people to choose between one of three positions: (1) "We must relax environmental stan-dards in order to achieve economic growth." (2) "We can achieve our cur-rent goals of environmental protection and economic growth at the same time." (3) "We must accept a slower rate of economic growth in order to protect the environment." Between 1978 and 1981 the view that we should accept a slower growth rate to protect the environment dropped sharply from 58 percent to 15 percent, while the middle view—that we can achieve both objectives at the same time—went from 18 percent in 1978 to 59 percent in 1981. In the 1982 survey, however, 49 percent of the public expressed willingness to accept slower economic growth to protect the environment, while only 24 percent took the view we can have both at the same time (a shift from "balance" to protection). According to journal-ist Keith Schneider, "The reason seems to be that the Administration does pose the issue as a trade-off—a choice between economic growth and 'envi-ronmental extremism.'" Keith Schneider, "The Environment: The Public Wants More Protection, Not Less," *National Journal* 15 (March 26, 1983), 676–677.

48. Riley E. Dunlap and Rik Scarce, "Poll Trends: Environmental Problems and Protection," *Public Opinion Quarterly* 55, 4 (Winter, 1991): 651–72.

49. Bill Keller, "Environmental Movement Checks its Pulse and Finds Obituaries are Premature," *Congressional Quarterly Weekly Report* 39 (January 31, 1981): 211–216.

50. Christopher J. Bosso, *Environment, Inc.: From Grassroots to Beltway* (Lawrence: University Press of Kansas, 2005).

51. Bush's campaign team accurately discerned a bipartisan rejection of Reagan administration policies on the environment: a poll of 399 delegates to the Republican National Convention in August 1988 found a majority favored tough environmental regulations and disagreed with Reagan's positions on acid rain, public lands, and energy. Richard E. Cohen, Rochelle L. Stanfield, and Lane Williams, "GOP Delegates Willing to Pay for a Cleaner Environment," *National Journal* 20 (August 13, 1988).

52. Quoted in Norman J. Vig, "Presidential Leadership and the Environment: From Reagan and Bush to Clinton," in *Environmental Policy in the 1990s: Toward a New Agenda,* 2nd ed., ed. Norman J. Vig and Michael E. Kraft, (Washington, DC: CQ Press, 1994), 80.

53. Kraft and Vig, "Environmental Policy from the 1970s to 1990."

54. Robert J. Duffy, "Divided Government and Institutional Combat: The Case of the Quayle Council on Competitiveness," *Polity* 28, 3 (1996): 379–99.

55. John H. Cushman, "Federal Regulation Growing Despite Quayle Panel's Role," *New York Times,* December 24, 1991, A1; Keith Schneider, "Bush to Relax Air Pollution Regulations," *New York Times,* May 17, 1992, A12; Kirk Victor, "Quayle's Quiet Coup," *National Journal* 23 (July 6, 1991), 1676–80.

56. With respect to wetlands, the council's 1991 revisions to the Federal Manual for Delineating Jurisdictional Wetlands provoked a furor in the scientific community and were never approved. With respect to federal land management, both the Forest Service and the Bureau of Land Management instituted rules restricting appeals of agency decisions. (Congress subsequently reinstated citizens' right to appeal Forest Service timber sales but limited appeals to those who had participated in the rule-making process.) With respect to recycling, under pressure from the council the EPA dropped its proposal to require incinerators to recycle one-quarter of the waste they received. With respect to other Clean Air Act regulations, the council met with EPA officials 47 times but kept no records of those meetings, so it was impossible to document its impact. Congressional staff reacted vehemently to council initiatives, however, and managed to fend off some of them. Duffy, "Divided Government and Institutional Combat."

57. Robert D. Hershey, Jr., "Regulations March On, Despite a Moratorium," *New York Times,* September 21, 1992, D1.

58. Quoted in Keith Schneider "Courthouse Is a Citadel No Longer: U.S. Judges Curb Environmentalists," *New York Times,* March 23, 1992, B7.

59. Vig, "Presidential Leadership and the Environment."

60. Quoted in Joel Connelly, "Bush Blames Owl for Lost Jobs; State Campaign Speech Goes after the Blue-Collar Vote," *Seattle Post-Intelligencer,* September 15, 1992, A1.

61. Eugene Linden, "The Green Factor," *Time,* October 12, 1992, 57–60.
62. John B. Judis, *The Paradox of American Democracy: Elites, Special Interests, and the Betrayal of Public Trust* (New York: Pantheon Books, 2000).
63. Ibid.
64. Margaret Kriz, "The New Eco-Nomics," *National Journal* 24 (May 30, 1992).
65. Mary Graham, *The Morning after Earth Day: Practical Environmental Politics* (Washington, DC: Brookings Institution, 1999); DeWitt John, *Civic Environmentalism: Alternatives to Regulation in States and Communities* (Washington, DC: CQ Press, 1994).
66. Phillip A. Davis, "Environment—Protection, Costs Must be Reconciled," *Congressional Quarterly Weekly Report* 50 (September 26, 1992): 2908–10.
67. Keith Schneider, "New View Calls Environmental Policy Misguided" *New York Times,* March 21, 1993, A1.
68. Keith Schneider, "Second Chance on Environment," *New York Times,* March 26, 1993, A17.
69. Vig, "Presidential Leadership and the Environment."
70. By 1998 the EPA had given the states authority for over 757 federal environmental programs, up from 493 when Clinton took office in 1993. John H. Cushman, "Backed by Business, G.O.P. Takes Steps to Overhaul Environmental Regulations," *New York Times,* February 10, 1995, A22; Barry G. Rabe, "Power to the States: The Promise and Pitfalls of Decentralization," in *Environmental Policy: New Directions for the Twenty-First Century,* 5th ed., ed. Norman J. Vig and Michael E. Kraft (Washington, DC: CQ Press, 2003), 33–56.
71. Quoted in Jon Healey, "From Conflict to Coexistence: New Politics of Environment," *Congressional Quarterly Weekly Report* 51 (February 13, 1993): 309–12.
72. Ann Reilly Dowd, "Environmentalists Are on the Run," *Fortune,* September 19, 1994, 91–103.
73. Catalina Camia, "Legislators Draw in the Reins on Environmental Rules," *Congressional Quarterly Weekly Report* 52 (April 30, 1994): 1060–63.
74. Quoted in Margaret Kriz, "A New Shade of Green," *National Journal* 27 (March 18, 1995), 661–5.
75. Quoted in Scott Allen, " 'Contract' Reframes Issue of Environment's Worth," *Boston Globe,* February 6, 1995, 25.
76. Quoted in Bob Benenson, "GOP Sets the 104th Congress on a New Regulatory Course," *Congressional Quarterly Weekly Report* 53 (June 17, 1995): 1693–7.
77. Quoted in Bob Benenson, "House Easily Passes Bills to Limit Regulations," *Congressional Quarterly Weekly Report* 53 (March 4, 1995): 679–82.
78. Cushman, "Backed by Business."
79. Clifford, "GOP Divided on Environmental Regulation."
80. Quoted in Allan Freedman, "Property Rights Bill Advances but Faces Uncertainty," *Congressional Quarterly Weekly Report* 53 (December 23, 1995): 3884–5.

81. Jackie Koszsczuk, "Hard-Charging GOP Whip Seeks a Softer Image," *Congressional Quarterly Weekly Report* 54 (April 13, 1996): 977–9.

82. A July 1995 NBC News/*Wall Street Journal* poll found nearly 80 percent of those questioned wanted environmental laws and regulations to be strengthened or maintained at their current levels, and less than 10 percent favored making them more lenient. Margaret Kriz, "The Green Card?" *National Journal* 27 (September 16, 1995), 2262.

83. Quoted in Judis, *The Paradox of American Democracy,* 223.

84. Quoted in Tom Kenworthy, "Divided GOP Falters on Environmental Agenda," *Washington Post,* November 24, 1995, A01.

85. Allan Freedman, "Republicans Concede Missteps in Effort to Rewrite Rules," *Congressional Quarterly Weekly Report* 53 (December 2, 1995): 3645–7.

86. Paul A. Sabatier, "Policy Change over a Decade or More," in *Policy Change and Learning,* ed. Paul Sabatier and Hank C. Jenkins-Smith (Boulder, CO: Westview Press, 1993), 13–39.

87. Daniel J. Fiorino, *The New Environmental Regulation* (Cambridge, MA: MIT Press, 2006).

88. Quoted in Jonathan Weisman, "True Impact of GOP Congress Reaches Well Beyond Bills," *Congressional Quarterly Weekly Report* 54 (September 7, 1996): 2515–20.

89. Daniel J. Fiorino, "Environmental Policy as Learning: A New View of an Old Landscape," *Public Administration Review* 61, 3 (2001): 322–34.

90. Traditionalist conservatives continued to dissent from the New Right vision; moreover, during the George W. Bush administration the long-standing tension between libertarian and Hamiltonian conservatives became more evident, as libertarians dissented from the Bush administration's preference for using federal power to promote policies that advantaged business rather than to strengthen market competition.

91. Jennifer Lee, "A Call for Softer, Greener Language," *New York Times,* March 2, 2003, 24.

92. Quoted in Katharine Q. Seelye, "Bush Team Is Reversing Environmental Policies," *New York Times,* November 18, 2001, 20.

93. Joby Warrick, "Appalachia Is Paying Price for White House Rule Change," *Washington Post,* August 17, 2004, A01.

94. During Bush's first term the Fish and Wildlife Service added fewer than ten species per year to the list, compared to 65 per year under Clinton and 59 per year under George H.W. Bush. It also designated as "critical habitat" only half the acreage recommended by federal biologists. Juliet Eilperin, "Endangered Species Act: Protections Are Trimmed," *Washington Post,* July 4, 2004, A01.

95. Barry G. Rabe, "Environmental Policy and the Bush Era: The Collision between the Administrative Presidency and the State," *Publius* 37, 3 (2006): 413–31.

96. Richard J. Lazarus, *The Making of Environmental Law* (Chicago: University of Chicago Press, 2004).

97. Rabe, "Environmental Policy and the Bush Era."

98. Mary Clare Jalonick, "Environment Adviser Feels Industry's Pain, *Congressional Quarterly Weekly Report* 63 (January 24, 2005): 179–80.

99. Alan C. Miller, Tom Hamburger and Julie Cart, "A Changing Landscape," *Los Angeles Times,* August 26, 2004, A14.

100. U.S. Government Accountability Office, *Oil and Gas Development: Increased Permitting Activity Has Lessened BLM's Ability to Meet Its Environmental Protection Responsibilities,* 2005, GAO-05–418.

101. Quoted in Rebecca Adams, "Federal Regulations Face Assault on Their Foundation," *Congressional Quarterly Weekly Report* 60 (August 10, 2002): 2182–4.

102. Ibid.

103. Quoted in Rebecca Adams, "GOP Adds New Tactics to War on Regulations," *Congressional Quarterly Weekly Report* 63 (January 31, 2005): 224–6.

104. Robert Pear, "Bush Directive Increases Sway On Regulation," *New York Times,* January 30, 2007, A1.

105. Judith A. Layzer, "Deep Freeze: How Business Has Shaped the Global Warming Debate in Congress," in *Business and Environmental Policy: Corporate Interests in the American Political System,* ed. Michael E. Kraft and Sheldon Kamieniecki (Cambridge, MA: MIT Press, 2007), 93–125.

106. Rabe, "Environmental Policy and the Bush Era." For example, the White House failed on several tries to advance its Clear Skies Act, which sought to introduce cap-and-trade systems for several pollutants. Critics rejected the bill because it did not include carbon dioxide, weakened controls on mercury emissions, and instituted more permissive pollution caps than allowed under the existing Clean Air Act.

107. John Echeverria, "Standing and Mootness Decisions in the Wake of Laidlaw," *Widener Law Review* 183, 10 (2003), 183–204.

108. Michael Greve, *The Demise of American Environmental Law* (Washington, DC: AEI Press, 1995).

109. In 2005 the Rhode Island state court determined the wetlands regulations did not constitute a taking.

110. The Federal Court of Claims was established in 1982 specifically to deal with claims against the federal government of more than $10,000. The Federal Circuit Court of Appeals hears appeals from the Court of Claims.

111. Sharon Buccino, Tim Dowling, Doug Kendall, and Elaine Weiss, *Hostile Environment: How Activist Judges Threaten Our Air, Water, and Land* (New York: Natural Resources Defense Council, 2001), on-line at http://www.nrdc.org/legislation/host/hostinx.asp.

112. Robert Barnes and Juliet Eilperin, "High Court Faults EPA Inaction on Emissions," *Washington Post,* April 3, 2007, A01.

113. Greve, *The Demise of American Environmental Law,* 19.

114. Keith Schneider, "Counthouse Is a Citadel No Longer."

115. Very simply, the studies suggest that (1) a judge's votes in ideologically contested areas can be predicted by the party of the appointing president; (2) a judge's ideological tendency in such areas will be amplified if the panel

has two other judges appointed by a president of the same party; and (3) a judge's ideological tendency will be dampened if the panel has no other judges appointed by a president of the same party. Frank B. Cross and Emerson H. Tiller, "Judicial Partisanship and Obedience to Legal Doctrine: Whistleblowing on the Federal Court of Appeals," *Yale Law Journal* 107 (1998): 2155; Sidney A. Shapiro and Richard E. Levy, "Judicial Incentives and Indeterminacy in Substantive Review of Administrative Decisions," *Duke Law Review* 44 (1995): 1051; Richard Revesz, "Environmental Regulation, Ideology, and the D.C. Circuit," *Virginia Law Review* 83 (1997): 1717–72; Richard J. Pierce, "Is Standing Law or Politics?," *North Carolina Law Review* 77 (June 1999): 1741; Christopher H. Schroeder and Robert Glicksman, "Chevron, State Farm, and EPA in the Courts of Appeals During the 1990s," *Environmental Law Reporter* 31 (2001): 10371; Cass R. Sunstein, David Schkade, and Lisa Michelle Ellman, "Ideological Voting on Federal Courts of Appeals: A Preliminary Investigation," Chicago Public Law and Legal Theory Working Paper No. 50 (Chicago: University of Chicago Law School, 2003): 1–36, on-line at http://www.law.uchicago.edu/academics/publiclaw/resources/50.crs.voting.pdf.

116. Herman Schwartz, *Right Wing Justice: The Conservative Campaign to Take over the Courts* (New York: Nation Books, 2004).

117. Layzer, "Deep Freeze."

# CHAPTER 8

Social Security from 1980 to the Present:
From Third Rail to Presidential
Commitment—and Back?

*Steven M. Teles and Martha Derthick*

Conservatives have never been wholly reconciled to Social Security. Among other things, many conservatives contend that: the program rests on accounting fictions that mask its real liabilities and impact on the government's fiscal health; the program is fundamentally dishonest, because it has been sold as an insurance program when in operation its similarity to private insurance is weak or nonexistent; it is coercive, not voluntary; it is too large and insufficiently targeted; it suppresses private saving; and the dependence that it creates on the part of the public helps to maintain support for the Democratic Party. While not every conservative believed this entire litany (or even understood it), by the beginning of the 1980s most conservatives accepted enough of it to be very suspicious of the program.

Up to the point at which this chapter takes up the story, the position of conservatives on Social Security was fairly simple. They were for limiting the growth in program benefits, especially by ensuring that Social Security's supporters could not reap political gain (in the form of increases in monthly checks) without fiscal pain (increases in earmarked taxes).[1] In addition to this political motivation for programmatic restraint, conservatives sought to limit growth in benefits in order to allow space for private mechanisms for retirement savings to survive. As a political strategy, this approach was distinctly unattractive. It allowed supporters of the program, especially Democrats, to play a credit-claiming game with benefit increases at regular (electoral) intervals, while conservatives were put in the position of proposing present pain (or at least the withholding of pleasure) for the promise of fairly obscure long-term well-being. Even after benefits were indexed to cost-of-living increases, Democrats could make political hay with Social Security by taking credit for defending existing benefits from Republicans who, it was claimed, were looking for any opportunity to hack away.

The story of this period—from the early 1980s to the present—is how conservatives and Republicans adopted an alternative strategy of creating private accounts inside Social Security. This strategy, which came to be known as "privatization," became more attractive in the wake of the Reagan administration's botched attempt to cut Social Security benefits as part of a deficit reduction package. Reagan's failure—and the damage it caused to the Republicans' political momentum—created the idea that directly cutting Social Security was a "third rail," and thereby increased interest in alternative conservative approaches to the program.

At roughly the same time that the direct route to restraining Social Security went down to defeat, conservatives began to build the strategic and analytical infrastructure that they lacked in previous periods. While conservatives had made substantial electoral strides in the 1970s, culminating in the Republican victories in the 1980 election, they were continually frustrated at how Democratic strength in the universities, professions, media, and bureaucracy denied conservatives victories they believed they had won at the ballot box.[2] To rectify this imbalance, conservatives built a network of institutions to compete directly with liberals at the level of ideas, expertise, and long-term political strategy. The conservative infrastructure-building project in Social Security was especially intense, reflecting the deeply embedded character of the program. Conservatives took advantage of the slowly eroding Social Security establishment (discussed in chapter 5), and by building a counter-elite of their own, were able by the mid-1990s to transform the policy from one of monopoly to competition.

Not only did this rising conservative Social Security establishment have expertise that previous conservatives lacked, they also brought with them an idea that promised to transform the politics of the issue—privatized, individual accounts. Individual accounts seemed to have the potential to reverse the political dynamic of the previous period, moving conservatives to a sunny credit-claiming politics of programmatic transformation. Private accounts also drew on changes in tax policy that conservatives (and others) supported for other reasons—in particular the expansion of defined contribution savings plans, such as 401(k)s and IRAs—that had changed the public's relationship to the financial markets. The idea of privatization, combined with the new extragovernmental analytical capacity of the movement and the popularity of voluntary savings plans, allowed conservatives to attack Social Security's core premises and long-range projections effectively, while offering a positive alternative to the New Deal welfare state—one that promised all the security of the existing program, but in a new, market-friendly form. This new strategy was, in sum, "Janus-faced" in its relationship to the modern state—while conservatives declared a truce with the program's *present* promises to retirees, they were much more radical where the *future* of the program was concerned.

By the late 1990s, the idea of Social Security privatization, once the property of only the wildest-eyed libertarians, had become altogether mainstream. Starting with the historic Social Security Advisory Council report released in 1997, in which a plurality of members advocated a wide-ranging system of private accounts (reversing Advisory Councils' historical role of supporting the extension of social insurance), plans for major change in the program—including private accounts—began to fly in Washington. In a pattern that seemed to replicate that of other conservative policy victories, such as welfare reform, tax simplification, and deregulation, many of these partial privatization plans had bipartisan support. The election of President George W. Bush in 2000 on an openly pro-privatization agenda looked to be a sign that Social Security had definitively lost its "third rail" quality.

Despite what seemed like impressive momentum as the president took office in 2001, Social Security privatization gradually lost much of its bipartisan support in the first years of the Bush administration, and was then decisively routed when the president began a public campaign for the idea after his reelection in 2004. As we will argue, this failure was driven by three basic forces. First, the president made a fateful decision to devote the government's projected surpluses to tax reduction rather than Social Security reform. While this reflected the priority that tax cuts had in the modern Republican Party, it denied privatizers the opportunity to overcome the transition problem in private accounts, and ultimately caused moderate Democratic deficit hawks to abandon the idea as soon as the government's books went into the red. Second, a substantial number of the most significant Democrats sympathetic to private accounts retired, died, or were voted out of office in the administration's first term. This was especially damaging, given the cross-national evidence that major reform in public pension programs almost always requires supra-normal levels of political consent—in particular, cross-party support.[3]

Finally, Social Security privatization fell victim to party polarization and unified Republican control of Congress and the presidency. While these same
forces helped Republicans obtain major policy victories in the Bush years—in
particular large cuts in taxes—they also made it harder to create the cross-party
coalitions necessary for diffusing responsibility on issues of special political
sensitivity. Oddly enough, as we shall argue, the political stars were better
aligned for a major conservative victory in this area when Democrats held the
White House than when they attained unified national political control.

## Social Security in the Reagan "Revolution"

Ronald Reagan arrived in the presidency without a plan for Social Security
yet urgently in need of one. Social Security was quickly swept up with every
other federal program into the budget-cutting campaign of the Office of
Management and Budget (OMB) Director David Stockman, with political
consequences that would ramify for years to come.[4]

Mindful of the heavy price that Barry Goldwater had paid in 1964 for
seeming to oppose Social Security, Reagan's political advisers had steered him
away from the subject. During the campaign he said only that he would not
cut benefits, but the financial condition of the program in 1981 required a
response. Old-age and survivors insurance was running annual deficits on the
order of $3 to $4 billion, and the Social Security trustees' report for 1980 predicted that the trust fund would be exhausted late in 1981 or early in 1982.
Members of Congress were braced for action.

The new administration began, ironically, by taking the play away from
Republican senators, who were in the majority for the first time since 1954.
Senator Pete Domenici of New Mexico, chairman of the Budget Committee,
told the administration in March that he had a bipartisan majority within the
committee to revise the formula for automatic cost-of-living increases so as
to save $10 billion in the immediate budget and $25 billion by the fifth year.
With his advisers—both chief of staff James Baker, who feared the political
reaction to this proposal, and Stockman, who viewed members of Congress
cynically and preferred to design budget cuts himself—Reagan traveled to
Capitol Hill to quash this plan.

Meanwhile, an interdepartmental task force of the administration was at
work on its own proposal. Originating in the Department of Health and
Human Services (HHS) with Secretary Richard Schweiker, this group was
enlarged to include representatives from the departments of Treasury and
Labor, the White House Office of Policy Development, OMB, and the
Council of Economic Advisers. Schweiker, as a former senator, shared the
concern of members of Congress that action take place swiftly in order to

reassure the public. In his confirmation hearings, he had promised that Social Security would be his top priority. Within the work group, HHS advanced a conventional response to the fiscal problems of Social Security. Led by Deputy Commissioner Robert J. Myers, a lifetime veteran of the Social Security Administration, officials there would have expanded the program and brought fresh revenue to it by extending coverage to all new employees of the federal government in 1982 and to all state and local government employees, new and incumbent, in 1984. Because federal government employees had clung to their own pension system, while state and local governments had been free to participate in Social Security or not, public employees constituted a last frontier for expanded coverage. The Treasury Department, with support from the Council of Economic Advisers, advanced an alternative proposal for contracting the program by indexing promised benefits to prices (rather than wages), but they were unable to get support from the Reagan appointees in HHS. They did not press the fight at the level of the White House, given that their overriding goal was not Social Security reform but a tax cut.

The winner of this internal contest was a third party, OMB's Stockman, who was searching for ways to achieve the largest possible savings with the greatest possible speed. With Schweiker's acquiescence, Stockman settled on a package of cuts in disability insurance and in early retirement benefits. Since 1961, covered workers had had the option of retiring as early as age 62 with a reduction in benefits of up to 20 percent, and by the late 1970s, 60 percent of workers were choosing this option. Stockman proposed to reduce early retirement benefits to 55 percent rather than 80 percent of the full benefit, and he would have done it right away—on January 1, 1982. A worker retiring at age 62 on that date and expecting to get $247.60 a month would instead get $163.90. Reagan approved the package in May, but it was announced by Schweiker rather than the White House because Baker and his deputy, Richard Darman, correctly perceived its danger but were powerless to stop it.

Trying to make large and immediate cuts in benefits for early retirees was an extraordinary blunder. It was deeply embarrassing to congressional Republicans, who were angry and incredulous, and it was a windfall for Democrats, whose leadership in Congress seized on it as "a rotten thing to do…a despicable thing," in the words of Speaker Thomas P. ("Tip") O'Neill. Senator Daniel P. Moynihan of New York, ranking Democrat on the Social Security subcommittee of the Finance Committee, called it the Democrats' "best issue with the new president…. This was…our moment." The Senate unanimously repudiated the administration with a resolution promising not to "precipitously and unfairly reduce early retirees' benefits." Social Security politics had decisively shifted to blame avoidance mode.

The administration withdrew the proposal, and in December, acting at the suggestion of Senate Majority Leader Howard Baker, Reagan created the

National Commission on Social Security Reform. It had fifteen members chosen in equal numbers (five each) by Baker, O'Neill, and the president, and was charged with preparing a plan to assure the fiscal integrity of Social Security, with a deadline of December 31, 1982. In the meantime, Congress finessed the fiscal crisis in Social Security with borrowing among trust funds.

Known as the Greenspan Commission for its chairman, the conservative economist Alan Greenspan, the commission was unable to reach agreement on a plan by the end of 1982, but at the last minute, with the aid of two extensions of its deadline, it provided the cover for a negotiated agreement on Social Security between the administration and congressional Democrats, principally O'Neill. Wounded already by its blunder of early 1981, the administration was further weakened by the 1982 election, in which Democrats gained 26 seats in the House, giving them a majority of 269 to 166. In both parties it was believed that the administration's error on Social Security had contributed to this outcome. O'Neill and his artful, experienced representative within the commission, Robert M. Ball, a liberal Democrat who for three decades had been the dominant figure in building Social Security, therefore were able to get the result that Democrats wanted and Ball designed—a large infusion of revenue. This was accomplished by accelerating scheduled tax rate increases and by introducing taxation of the Social Security benefits of high-income persons, a policy change that Ball had long favored but that both political parties had opposed in 1980. The revenue increases were complemented by delaying the next automatic cost-of-living adjustment (COLA) for current beneficiaries from July 1983 to January 1984, and by timing all subsequent COLAs to the calendar year rather than the fiscal year. The Greenspan commission was, in effect, an ad hoc version of the centrist, system-maintaining politics that characterized Social Security in earlier decades. It was, in that sense, more the end of one era than the beginning of another.

The nearest thing to structural reform of the program at this time was achieved not by the Reagan administration but by Representative Jake Pickle, a Democrat from Texas who was chairman of the Social Security subcommittee of the House Ways and Means Committee. Pickle had set out in early 1981 to have a bill of his own for the financial relief of Social Security, and, while he failed in that, he ultimately succeeded in getting the approval of Congress for a gradual increase in the normal age of retirement from 65 to 67 by 2027. In a tribute to Pickle's persistence, and because organized labor was paying more attention to killing Social Security coverage of federal government employees, this measure was passed on the floor of the House, 228 to 202, without having been endorsed by the Greenspan Commission. Ball was opposed to it.

Reagan celebrated the outcome of 1983 as if it had been what he wanted. He said it reaffirmed "the commitment of our government to the performance and stability of Social Security." Ball thought of it as the apex of his career, "a moment for which [he] had been preparing all his life." The historian Edward Berkowitz, a leading student of Social Security politics, thought it possible to view the outcome "as a treaty of surrender in the conservative project to dismantle the welfare state."[5] Judging from the events of 1981–1983 under Reagan, this project had never amounted to much beyond David Stockman's desperate attempts to pay for the president's tax cuts. The real project of radical reform was, in fact, just beginning.

## The Rise of Privatization

The entire cycle of Social Security politics from 1981 to 1983 was quickly interpreted by many in the conservative movement as a decisive setback and a signal of the limits of Republican electoral power.[6] The failure of Reagan's gambit demonstrated the program's fiscal insularity, its immunity from purely executive-driven change, and the electoral consequences of touching what came to be called American politics' "third rail."[7] These events seemed to confirm that Social Security was, from a conservative point of view, uncontrollable.

While Republicans in elective office, with a few exceptions, concluded that Social Security was a hopeless cause, conservatives in the growing network of institutions outside government learned a very different lesson. Put simply, they concluded that the vulnerability of Social Security was a function of time. In the short term, it was true that the program's structure, the incentives it provided politicians, and its protective network inside and outside government made the program immune from direct attack. In that sense, the "structure of inheritance" in Social Security was, indeed, imposing. But if the program could not be assaulted directly, it *was* feasible to gradually eat away at its support over the long term. These think-tank conservatives concluded that they should shift away from the politically fruitless task of trying to cut benefits at the margins and concentrate their efforts on altering the conditions that would face subsequent generations of reformers.

Executing a strategy of this kind required an institutional apparatus almost completely absent just ten years earlier. For most of its history, the Social Security Administration held a monopoly on expertise and long-term strategic capacity. This monopoly allowed supporters of Social Security to marginalize criticism and take advantage of opportunities to incrementally expand the program. The conservative movement, on the other hand, contained few activists who genuinely understood how Social Security operated, could debate it in sophisticated terms, possessed the analytical tools to construct alternatives to those of the Social Security establishment, or were in a position to coordinate long-term strategic action. Reflecting the pattern seen in chapters 4 and 6, this imbalance between the non-electoral resources possessed by defenders of the modern administrative state and their conservative opponents was, up through the 1970s and in some areas even today, one of the most significant sources of the durability of liberal policy achievements.

By the early 1980s, conservatives had begun to develop a small but remarkably stable cadre of thinkers and policy entrepreneurs able to challenge the Social Security establishment. Beginning in the early 1970s, Harvard economist Martin Feldstein began to produce sophisticated critiques of the incidence of Social Security taxes and the program's effect on savings. Equally important, in the 1970s Feldstein was also training a generation of economists who would play key roles in the privatization movement in subsequent decades, such as Lawrence Kotlikoff and Jose Pinera. The Cato Institute, founded in 1977, made Social Security privatization one of its core issues from the beginning, publishing in 1980 the first sustained, comprehensive critique of the program, Peter Ferrara's *Social Security: The Inherent Contradiction*.[8]

The Heritage Foundation, founded in 1973, was also an early supporter of privatization, publishing an extension of Ferrara's ideas just two years after the Cato Institute. But the most significant role that Heritage played in Social Security was at the level of strategy and coordination, facilitated by the think tank's close links with congressional conservatives. Fatefully, in 1979 Heritage hired Stuart Butler, a British Ph.D. of libertarian instincts who brought to Heritage a detailed knowledge of the Thatcher government's reforms in social policy, close networks with British conservative thinkers, and a preference for playing offense on social policy. The combination of the growing critique of Social Security in economics, the Cato Institute's willingness to sustain a critique of the program despite its political popularity, and Heritage's strategic role gave conservatives a nascent Social Security counterestablishment.[9]

Seen from the perspective of this counterestablishment, Social Security had three fundamental advantages over any comprehensive alternative: existing Social Security recipients' mobilized expectations of unchanging benefits; taxpayers' expectations, rooted in experience, of future benefits; and uncertainty about the effects of any alternative. In order to uproot Social Security, conservatives needed to come up with answers to all three.

First, to avoid leaving themselves open to Democrats' attacks, conservative politicians accepted that the program, as it related to existing and soon-to-be retirees, was sacrosanct and separate from the rest of federal spending. In 1982, soon after the failure of the Reagan Social Security cuts, Peter Germanis of the Heritage Foundation concluded that, "Although it may have been highly irresponsible for the government to promise benefits that are becoming increasingly difficult to provide, these are, nevertheless, obligations that must be met. Rather than instilling widespread panic among our elderly, we should acknowledge these liabilities as a total write-off so that we can move on with reforming the system"[10] Long-term thinking was impossible until conservatives accepted the futility of changing the program in the present.

Second, conservatives recognized that waiting for the program to collapse under its own weight was not a viable strategy. As Butler and Germanis put it soon after the passage of the 1983 Social Security bailout, criticizing the program's "inherent flaws" would not necessarily open the way for structural changes:

> The public's reaction last year against politicians who simply noted the deep problems of the system, and the absence of even a recognition of the underlying problems during the spring's Social Security 'reform,' suggest that it will be a long time before citizen indignation will cause radical change to take place. Therefore, if we are to achieve basic changes in the system, we must first prepare the political ground so that the fiasco of the last 18 months is not repeated.[11]

"Preparing the political ground" meant raising doubts as to the certainty of future benefits, attacking the privileged status of social insurance, building up the social and political infrastructure for an alternative system, and undermining the financial accounting systems that create transition costs to a private alternative. In each of these cases, conservatives recognized the need to move from "normal" politics to a long-term strategy of disentrenchment.

Disentrenchment required that conservatives weaken the public's certainty that they would receive benefits (thereby reducing their belief that future benefits were a right to which they were entitled) while simultaneously increasing their certainty in and experience with an alternative. Conservatives could take advantage of the fact that well-known moderates were successfully convincing the public that Social Security would go "bankrupt" if radical changes were not made.[12] The *coup de grace* of this strategy was the poll by Third Millennium, a small conservative group, which claimed that 18 percent more young people believed that UFOs existed than that Social Security would pay benefits when they retired.[13] Despite the survey's serious methodological problems, it received enormous attention beyond the Washington policy community, suggesting how politically salient future expectations were to the program's political viability.

None of these steps were as important as a third and final innovation, the development of private alternatives. By supporting the move from defined-benefit private pensions to 401(k)s and tax-subsidized IRAs, conservatives were able to shift decisively from critiquing Social Security to building the foundations of their own preferred alternative. The alternative of Social Security privatization was simultaneously accommodationist and radical. It was accommodationist in that it explicitly consented to Social Security's "promises" in the present, and because it implicitly accepted a major role for the government in guaranteeing the retirement income of older Americans in the future. But it was radical in that it suggested that conservatives could turn back the program's momentum only by presenting an alternative, "market-based" approach that held out the promise of shifting conservative politics on the issue from blame avoidance to credit-claiming. No longer would conservatives simply stand athwart Social Security yelling "stop": they could pilot the program in a very different direction. Central to this effort to switch conservative strategy from defense to offense was getting the infrastructure of an alternative to Social Security up and running, and conservatives found this in the growth of defined-contribution savings and pensions plans.

It is always difficult, in hindsight, to distinguish between long-term planning and good fortune. Almost certainly, few members of Congress who voted to expand IRAs saw their decisions as part of a long-term strategy to uproot Social Security. But explaining elected officials' short-term motivations is not necessary for our purposes. What is important is that significant actors outside Congress did think about the policy in these terms, and organized their agenda-setting behavior accordingly. Almost immediately after the debacle of 1983, staffers at Heritage, led by Stuart Butler, recognized IRAs as the key to an alternative approach to reforming Social Security.

> IRAs can ease the transition toward structural reform of the Social Security system. This effort should begin with small legislative changes to make the present IRA system more comprehensive so that it becomes, in practice, a small-scale private Social Security system— supplementing federal Social Security.... The reason for designing a "Super IRA" law with these restrictions is primarily political. While in an economic sense, the current allocation of money for the various types of insurance may not be optimal, expanding the IRA system in this way would make it a mirror image of Social Security. Americans would be able to compare the two alternatives. As they gradually became more familiar with the parallel private sector option, they would find it easier to compare the private and public alternatives when deciding which plan to use as their principal guarantee of security.[14]

As Stuart Butler observes, "this was a long-haul strategy and involved the creation of a parallel system in Social Security. And it has clearly paid off and it was conscious at the time. We felt that as people became more familiar with these kinds of private retirement plans they clearly would feel less threatened with ideas of allowing people to privatize. When you say, 'you should be able to take some of your Social Security payroll taxes and put it into IRAs or 401(k)s,' they don't say, 'what's an IRA?' "[15] Widespread use of IRAs would reduce the uncertainty of privatization by allowing conservatives to analogize their alternative to programs that the public was already using, and encourage them to compare their returns from Social Security and their IRA. When combined with the increasing number of foreign nations that were experimenting with forms of pensions privatization—especially Chile, whose Secretary of Social Security, Jose Pinera, was trained at Harvard by Martin Feldstein—the increasing popularity of defined contribution pensions made the idea of privatizing Social Security seem considerably less off the wall.[16]

The fruits of these political investments started to ripen by the mid-1990s, when interest in Social Security reform—including private accounts—began to explode. While long-term trends and contingent factors helped get privatization onto the agenda in this period, the long-term strategic investments of the 1980s also played a significant role. The increasing salience of the deficit in the 1990s had the effect of shining a light on the government's long-term financial position, and in the process pushed Social Security higher on the political agenda. In addition, President Clinton had made fiscal discipline a keystone of the "New Democrat" public philosophy, along with a reconsideration of the means by which Democrats pursued their ideological commitments.

The issue of privatization went from fairly marginal to nearly mainstream in early 1997, when a plurality of the 1994–1996 Social Security Advisory Council proposed a far-reaching privatization plan that would have diverted 5 percent of the 12.4 percent payroll tax into private accounts.[17] Social Security Advisory Councils had typically been used to support the objectives of the program's establishment: the agency typically shaped the councils' membership, determined their agenda, and shaped the information they had to work with. Seen from this background, the 1994–1996 Advisory Council was a developmental break of the first order. Particularly striking was the inclusion on the Council of Carolyn Weaver (a member of Senator Robert Dole's staff), who had been an early and vigorous supporter of privatization. One measure of the intensity of Weaver's beliefs, as well as her strategic approach, can be seen in her 1983 observation that,

> Uncertainties…are what will make reform possible, even at a cost. Reforms that draw on non-familiar methods of supply (such as expanded use of IRAs) will be particularly attractive.…If the extreme (and costly) uncertainty about one's financial security in old age is

recognized by an administration that has concrete ideas for expanding the options for young people, then—despite the transitional costs of reform—we could see real changes in our social insurance system.[18]

By the time that the Council released its report, the preconditions for "reform" that Weaver had drawn attention to were well on their way to being established: IRAs had become widely popular, and "uncertainty" about the future financial prospects of the program had become widespread, in large part as a result of the program's conservative critics. The position of Weaver on the Council provided privatizers with the opportunity to put "concrete ideas" for change into the mainstream of policy discourse. Weaver took full advantage of this opportunity. In a letter to Milton Friedman sent right after the Council's report was made public, Weaver observed that, "I just wanted to reassure you that I agree 100 percent on the need to have full Social Security privatization on the table—both to enhance the public understanding and to improve the likely political outcome. The opportunity to get 5 members of the Social Security Advisory Council on board partial privatization—with real potential for garnering a majority—was, in my judgment, just too important to pass up."[19]

Equally as significant as the Council's plurality report was the proposal put forth by two of the other members of the Council, including its chairman, Edward N. Gramlich. Gramlich and Marc Twinney proposed integrating personal accounts into Social Security, albeit in indexed accounts managed by the government, and openly admitted the need for limiting the growth in the program's benefits. While the differences between the two plans were significant (because the latter proposal did not carve into the program's existing tax base, it could not in a literal sense be thought of as privatization), they both suggested the limits of the program's existing defined benefit structure.

In the years after the release of the Advisory Council's report, a wave of proposals for some form of individual accounts in Social Security poured forth—including many with support from prominent Democrats. Even before the Council released its report, the Bi-Partisan Commission on Entitlement and Tax Reform appointed by President Clinton (in order to get Senator Robert Kerrey's vote for the 1993 Budget Bill) proposed a personal account of 2 percent of payroll, and in 1998 Senator Daniel Patrick Moynihan proposed to cut the Social Security tax by 2 percent of payroll, and to divert the reduced taxes to individual savings accounts. The Progressive Policy Institute, the think tank of the Clinton-friendly Democratic Leadership Council, supported a plan very similar to Moynihan's, and stressed that individual accounts were consistent with "New Democrat" thinking. Finally, a commission established by the Center for Strategic and International Studies, whose members included Democratic Senator John Breaux and Representative Charles

Stenholm, also proposed diverting 2 percent of payroll into private accounts, as well as raising the retirement age to 70.[20]

This flurry of reports suggests that the idea of privatization was beginning to get the kind of support from moderate Democrats that had allowed other conservative ideas to become reality. This was especially significant, because while Stuart Butler and Peter Germanis had suggested that their strategy on Social Security was "Leninist," it was, in fact, Gramscian—designed to so alter the dominant conventional wisdom that their ideas could be championed by the opposing party. The ubiquity of privatization proposals suggested one final developmental phenomenon: the older Social Security establishment, so important in previous decades, had lost control of the program's agenda. Conservatives had developed the analytical resources and infrastructure to make the process of agenda-setting competitive rather than monopolistic.

In the end, no action on Social Security reform occurred at the end of Clinton's second term, for two reasons. First, the Lewinsky affair effectively stopped all major policy making in Washington (and poisoned the environment for bipartisan cooperation). Second, the Clinton administration concluded that the best way to counter the Republicans' drive to use the mounting surpluses for tax cuts was to argue that the money was needed to shore up Social Security's finances: hence the mantra of the administration's last years, "Save Social Security first." As a consequence, the issue was kicked into the next administration, where a governor from Texas was already thinking seriously about the issue.

## The Bush Administration and the Failure of Privatization

By the time George W. Bush became president in 2001, a reasonable observer might have concluded that Social Security privatization was an idea whose time had come. The president had run on the issue, making a number of high-profile speeches in which he openly called for the creation of individual accounts. For instance, Bush's acceptance speech to the Republican National Convention in 2000 reflected almost all the themes developed by the Social Security counterestablishment over the previous two decades:

> Social Security has been called the third rail of American politics, the
> one you're not supposed to touch because it might shock you. But
> if you don't touch it, you cannot fix it. And I intend to fix it. To
> the seniors in this country, you earned your benefits, you made
> your plans, and President George W. Bush will keep the promise of
> Social Security, no changes, no reductions, no way. Our opponents

will say otherwise. This is their last parting ploy, and don't believe a word of it. Now is the time—now is the time for Republicans and Democrats to end the politics of fear and save Social Security together. For younger workers, we will give you the option, your choice, to put part of your payroll taxes into sound, responsible investments. This will mean a higher return on your money in over 30 or 40 years, a nest egg to help your retirement or to pass on to your children. When this money is in your name, in your account, it's just not a program, it's your property.[21]

The 2000 Republican platform stated a similar position in the name of the party as a whole: "Personal savings accounts must be the cornerstone of restructuring."[22] The fact that a presidential candidate spoke these words at all was a significant victory for the conservative counterestablishment, for he was the first presidential candidate to support privatization openly and directly. Not only that, an increasing number of Republican candidates for Congress, such as Mark Sanford and Lindsey Graham of South Carolina, Pat Toomey of Pennsylvania, Nick Smith of Michigan, Jim Kolbe of Arizona, John Porter of Illinois, and Judd Gregg of New Hampshire, unapologetically supported private accounts. By 2000, privatization was close to the official position of the Republican Party. There is a significant difference, however, between a party changing the direction of its stated policy preferences, and the intensity with which those preferences are held. Bush and an increasing number of Republicans clearly believed in privatization strongly enough to risk whatever political heat might come their way for taking such a position. But were they willing to favor Social Security privatization when the issue was in tension with other party priorities?

Social Security privatization was not an issue on which George W. Bush seems to have been the captive of his advisors. Rather remarkably, given the marginality of the issue at the time, Bush ran for Congress in 1978 on a platform supporting privatization,[23] and his advisors describe him as actively interested in the issue early on in his governorship of Texas. In fact, "In Texas, before and during his years as governor, aides say, Mr. Bush learned about counties that had opted out of Social Security under an old federal provision and instead offered their employees investment accounts. As governor, his involvement in issues relating to Latin America piqued his interest in Chile's retirement system, which gave workers the chance to invest and became a prototype for other nations."[24] Starting in 1997, Bush held a series of meetings with conservative supporters of privatization, including Ed Crane, Jose Pinera, and Stephen Moore of the Cato Institute, who have all indicated that he had clearly thought about the issue and was interested in its potential. Moore in particular recalls that the president had no doubts about the merits of the issue, but "his thought process was, how do you overcome the political obstacles to this?"[25]

Bush repeatedly discussed the issue of Social Security with his economic advisors in the run-up to the 2000 presidential campaign. In April 1998, Bush participated in a meeting organized by former Secretary of State George Shultz with scholars at the Hoover Institution, including long-time supporters of privatization Michael Boskin, Martin Anderson, John Taylor, and John Cogan.[26] At that meeting, Cogan reports that the issue of Social Security's long-term solvency was "upper-most in his mind" and that he "asked about personal accounts as part of the solution."[26] By a meeting in April of 1999 with Cogan, Martin Feldstein, and others, the conversation had turned to the details of privatization. "Most of the discussion was substantive: the structure of personal accounts, the size of personal accounts, how you would finance personal accounts and transition costs, what you would do about the unfunded liability of Social Security independent of personal accounts, and how the two issues—personal accounts on the one hand, and insolvency on the other, go together."[27] In all of these meetings, it does not appear that the politics of privatization were actively discussed, but it is clear that, where Cogan is concerned at least, privatization was viewed not as a matter of political danger but as the honey that would help make the medicine of benefit cuts go down easier.

> My impression has always been that, Social Security accounting aside, personal accounts can be an important part of solving Social Security's financing problem, both from an economic standpoint and from a political standpoint.... [They would be a sweetener?] That was the political point... that still seems true to me. You have to ask yourself without personal accounts, is there anything attractive about Social Security reform? The answer is, unless you have a perverse mind and you think that cutting benefits is attractive or raising taxes is attractive for a politician, then the answer is no. Personal accounts on the other hand, gives some tangible benefit to a whole group of individuals in society. So there is a positive side to Social Security reform.[28]

Before taking office, therefore, Bush drew into his inner circle long-time advocates of Social Security privatization and put the issue near the top of his economic agenda. In this period, when advocates of privatization were given unprecedented access to and interest from a leading Republican presidential candidate, Bush seems to have denied them only one thing: priority over tax cuts. Unfortunately, given the structure of Social Security's financing, privatization required such a priority. Paul Pierson in particular has explained Social Security's durability by pointing to the "fiscal overhang" of the program's inherited commitments. As compared to the situation facing British conservatives, who introduced partial privatization into a program that had only been in existence for a decade, American conservatives faced a fully mature program, creating a "double-payment problem": advocates of privatization would have to find the funds for their new accounts, at the same time as they paid for existing Social Security commitments. This, in effect, established a large "tax" on innovation on the order of hundreds of billions of dollars. But the surpluses that appeared at the end of the Clinton administration promised a way out of this bind, since they could have been used to fund this transition, in the process neutralizing the concerns of deficit hawks in both parties.

In what appears to have been, in retrospect, a fateful decision, Bush chose to put a priority on tax cuts over Social Security privatization in using these surpluses. John Cogan recalls that:

> Certainly the projected surpluses that CBO and OMB were forecasting at the time led to a consideration of what was the best use of those surpluses, and the president, the governor at the time, made the decision that the priority use would be the tax cuts. I discussed it myself with the governor. . . . I recall one discussion with the governor [in the middle of 1999] where I said personal accounts were an alternative use of those surpluses, and the larger the tax cut proposal, the less room there would be for Social Security personal accounts. The governor made his policy decision that tax rate reductions would be the priority use that the surplus would be used for. Once he made that decision, we focused mainly on the tax reductions and secondarily on Social Security. . . . The president was fully aware that when he chose his tax plan as his major initiative, that would reduce the amount of money that would be available for the transition to Social Security reform.[29]

It is unclear what combination of substantive and political motivations drove this decision. From Bush's own statements, a desire to keep the surplus from being spent on programs supported by Democrats appears to have been one of his priorities, but if anything, using the surplus for private accounts would have been an even more secure way to lock up these projected funds.

Another possible motivation for prioritizing tax cuts was that these could be placed into the president's first budget fairly easily, whereas there would be a substantial delay, perhaps of over a year, in passing a Social Security overhaul, at which point the politics (as well as the budget projections) could have changed. But most persuasive as an explanation is simply the intensity of preference in the Republican Party on tax cuts. While this was the primary interest of a large swathe of the party, from grassroots activists to major business organizations, Social Security privatization was the number one issue only of a fairly small slice of the party's D.C.–based intelligentsia. The Cato Institute, in particular, was on the side of using part of the surplus for privatization: early in 2001, Cato's Michael Tanner opined that, "The question is going to be how they handle tax cuts…Does one prevent another from happening? I'd like to see some of the [political] capital that's being used on tax cuts go toward [Social Security], because the longer we wait, the more it gets into election year politics."[30] Similar statements were made later in the year by Representative Clay Shaw, the chairman of the House Ways and Means subcommittee that had jurisdiction over Social Security, and representatives of the Concord Coalition.[31] But while this tradeoff was actively considered before Bush was elected, by the time he took office it appears to have been a *fait accompli*. While Social Security privatization had certainly moved up the scale of party priorities dramatically over the course of the 1990s, it still did not rival the issue that Reagan had put at the core of the party's electoral strategy, tax cuts.

This decision points to the durability of the agenda that first brought conservatives to political power, the continuing low priority on welfare state restructuring, and the limitations on the power of the conservative Washington-based policy network. But it also shows the flip side of what some believe was the "starve the beast" motivation for tax cuts. While these tax cuts may, in the long term, limit the fiscal space for Democratic spending programs (although there is little indication as of this date that they have had such an effect), they also operate at cross-purposes to major conservative priorities like comprehensive tax reform and Social Security privatization, both of which require additional spending in the present in order to fund (or make politically palatable) structural changes in America's fiscal policy. And at the least, in a world of limited agenda space, tax cuts take up time and political will that could be deployed in other ways.

In effect, the decision to use the surplus for tax cuts pushed the issue of Social Security out of the president's first year, and eventually out of the first term entirely. Bush created a commission led by former Senator Daniel Patrick Moynihan and Time/Warner CEO Richard Parsons to design a proposal for reform, as well as to delay consideration of the issue. If nothing else, the following list of its commissioners demonstrated the growth in privatization's supportive network.

- Leanne Abdnor (R), former executive director of the Alliance for Worker Retirement Security (AWRS is the principal business-supported umbrella group supporting privatization);
- Sam Beard (D), founder and president of Economic Security 2000; long-time member of the Cato Social Security Privatization Advisory Board;

- John Cogan (R), former OMB deputy director; signer of Cato's privatization petition, long-time supporter of privatization;
- Bill Frenzel (R), former U.S. representative;
- Estelle James (D), consultant with the World Bank; author of *Averting the Old-Age Crisis,* the World Bank's major report supporting pension privatization;
- Robert Johnson (D), CEO of Black Entertainment Television; supporter of estate tax repeal as well as Social Security privatization;
- Gwendolyn King (R), former commissioner of Social Security under President George H. W. Bush;
- Olivia Mitchell (D), professor at the University of Pennsylvania's Wharton School; expert on pensions and supporter of private accounts;
- Gerry Parsky (R), former assistant secretary of the Treasury; chairman of George W. Bush presidential campaign in California;
- Tim Penny (D), former U.S. representative; member of Cato Social Security Privatization Advisory Board;
- Robert Pozen (D), vice chairman of Fidelity Investments; supporter of "progressive indexation" and moderate supporter of private accounts;
- Mario Rodriguez (R), Hispanic Business Roundtable; participant in numerous conservative Hispanic groups supportive of privatization;
- Thomas Saving (R), current Social Security public trustee; signatory of Cato privatization petition;
- Fidel Vargas (D), vice president of Reliant Equity Investors; member of 1994–1996 Advisory Council on Security, supporter of Weaver/Schieber privatization plan;
- Carolyn Weaver (R), (stepped down) member of 1994–1996 Advisory Council on Social Security; long-time supporter of privatization.

The composition of Bush's commission is in striking contrast to that of the Greenspan Commission. Where the Greenspan Commission was bipartisan not simply in terms of the nominal partisan affiliations of its members, but also in terms of their position on Social Security, Bush's commission was made up almost exclusively of long-time supporters of privatization—its membership would not have been dramatically different had it been chosen by the president of the Cato Institute. What is more, substantial parts of the commission's staff came directly out of Cato's Social Security privatization project.[32] Finally, the Executive Order establishing the commission established as nonnegotiable the two design features of any reform that were most likely to be the subject of partisan controversy:

"Social Security payroll taxes must not be increased. . . . Modernization must include individually controlled, voluntary personal retirement accounts, which will augment the Social Security safety net."[33] Given these principles and the Commission's composition, it was clearly not designed to discover a consensus that could form the basis of broad bipartisan support in Congress, but to help the president sort out the policy and political design questions in Social Security and to provide the impression that privatization had support in both parties.

Even a broader commission could not have concealed the fact that Democratic support for privatization was rapidly disappearing, a process that accelerated with each passing year of the Bush administration. This was a major obstacle to the passage of any form of privatization, for two reasons. First, a very large number of conservatives' most impressive policy victories, such as welfare reform, tax simplification, deregulation, and changes in policing and incarceration, came only because they were able to convince substantial numbers of Democrats of these ideas' merits. Even more important, declining Democratic support for privatization should have been worrying because comparative research shows that major reform of public pensions programs almost always requires a broader than normal political coalition.[34]

One source of the decline in Democratic support in Congress was retirements, both voluntary and involuntary. Both Senators Moynihan and Kerrey retired in 2000, and in 2004 Representative Charles Stenholm was removed from office as part of the Republicans' redrawing of Congressional district lines in Texas. These exits removed the Democrats most capable of building support for privatization in their caucus. Pushing in the same direction was the general trend toward the partisan polarization of Congress. As Republicans became more successful at defeating Democrats in more conservative states, they also removed precisely the kinds of Democrats needed to push privatization. As Peter Beinart presciently observed in early 2005, "By killing off the Democrats most susceptible to his influence, Bush may have created a political dynamic that works for his opponents, and against him. . . . On a major 'reform' like Social Security, one vote from across the aisle is worth more than one from your own side."[35]

But the decline in Democratic support for privatization did not come only from the diminishing number of Democratic moderates in Congress, but also from the decreasing willingness of those who remained to work with the Republicans. Indicative of this trend was the shift of the Progressive Policy Institute, and the members of Congress associated with it, who had been sympathetic to the idea during the Clinton administration. Will Marshall, PPI's president, suggests that the shift from a Democratic to a Republican president

decisively changed the context, because Democrats were not in a
position to lead the reform, and exercise veto power if they didn't like
the shape of it, as they had been in the 1990s. They'd also be more
willing to even consider the discussion if it was being led by a
reform-minded Democratic president.... But without Clinton there,
with a hated Republican president in the White House, particularly
with an even harsher right-wing regime controlling Congress, and
using their majority status there to the max, any support among
rank and file Democrats in Congress for radical changes in cherished
programs just evaporated.... Republicans have all the power, and
because they've abused the hell out of it, and because Bush after NCLB
[No Child Left Behind] and 9/11 decided to discard any notion of
center-out coalition building, a cohabitation, a regime that would allow
him to get big bipartisan achievements, he didn't go that way. Having
been on the receiving end of true abuse of power by the Republicans
in Congress, the passion to oppose took over any cooperative
spirit.... Many a time, Democrats were willing to sit down and try
to do deals with Republicans, only to see their issues stripped out in
Republican-dominated conferences and then get rolled in a majority
vote.... There's no upside and only pain for any iconoclastic Democrat
to say, 'I know Bush's Social Security plan is wrong, but we really need
to have a progressive modernization plan of our own.' You'd get accused
of collaborating with the enemy, making his job easier, and in the end
you don't have any ability to affect the ultimate result. Why bother?[36]

The shift away from support for private accounts among Democrats can
certainly be blamed, in part, on a shift in the composition of the Democratic
caucus, but the more interesting dynamic, as Marshall suggests, is the switch
by surviving moderate Democrats. When Democrats controlled at least one
branch of government, they were more willing to be flexible, because they
knew that they had enough power to protect their core interests. But without
that institutional veto, all the political incentives pointed in the direction of
ideological orthodoxy, and a concern that they would simply be used as props
for an agenda that was being driven by Republicans.

Finally, partisan polarization damaged the White House's search for moderate support by (as supporters of conditional party government theory
would predict) strengthening the ability of minority party leaders to set party
doctrine and threaten those who would break from it.[37] For instance, Ryan
Lizza has reported that, "Harry Reid has thus far been far more successful in
enforcing discipline among his shrunken caucus than his predecessor, Tom
Daschle. For instance, Reid has warned Senator Max Baucus, Bush's favor-
ite Democratic deal-maker and the ranking minority member on the Senate

Finance Committee, a crucial node in the coming debate, against cooperating with Bush."[38] When combined with the sour taste that was left in the mouths of many Democrats from their cooperation with some of Bush's first term policies (such as NCLB and Medicare Part D), by 2005 there was substantial support for this kind of leadership discipline over potential defectors.

Also important in drying up Democratic support for individual accounts was the explosion in deficit projections in the aftermath of the first term's tax cuts. For many moderate Democrats, especially those in the "Blue Dog Coalition," opposition to deficits was a defining issue. When the government was still projecting a surplus, the transition costs of private accounts were not an insurmountable obstacle to support from the Blue Dogs. But by 2005 the government's fiscal projections had changed dramatically, leading to tensions with the deficit issue that had not existed in the late 1990s, and that would have been unlikely to have arisen had Bush led Republicans to use the projected surplus to fund private accounts.

The increasing priority of the deficit caused defections not only by Democrats, but by many Republicans. Senator Lindsey Graham, a long-time supporter of privatization, insisted that any reform proposal not worsen the deficit—"If this debate is about deficits the reform movement is going to lose"—and proposed raising the cap on FICA taxes.[39] While such a proposal might have attracted Democratic support, it almost surely would have led to massive Republican defections, and would have been unlikely to attract support from a White House that had defined itself by opposition to tax increases. Finally, many moderate Republicans, especially those in Democratic-leaning states, were afraid of the electoral potency of opposition to Social Security privatization. As Graham pointed out, Bush "jumped out with a very big idea that he ran on, but he didn't lay the political groundwork in the Senate or the House. He ran on it. We didn't. He's not up for election again. We are."[40] In essence, the electoral logic of a second-term Republican president was at odds with that of the party's reelection-minded Congressional caucus—a caucus that, polarization notwithstanding, continues to have vulnerable members. To sum up, the combination of declining cross-party trust, and the deficit's effect of increasing the difficulty of the trade-offs (and their coalitional effects) in reform, led to defection by what remained of Congress' center.

The alignment of interests also disfavored Bush's 2005 Social Security gambit. While the more paranoid of liberal analysts have often seen Social Security privatization as a Wall Street plot, the truth has always been much more complicated. Business support for Social Security was nowhere near what it was for many of the administration's other priorities, especially tax cuts. First, most employers' key interest in Social Security is preventing an increase in the payroll tax, but especially after the surpluses dried up, it became clear that private accounts would make the job of eliminating the program's long-term funding shortfall *more* difficult without tax increases. Second, businesses that might have had a profit motive for supporting privatization, such as the financial services industry, are in fact faced with a complex political calculus. If private accounts are structured like 401(k)s and IRAs, with broad access to existing mutual funds, the possibilities for a substantial regulatory burden are significant, and the amounts of money, especially for low earners, may be unprofitable. But fairly early in the process of developing Bush's proposals (and in the thinking of many of the privatization network's members), it was decided that preventing moral hazard and having to create some form of minimum benefit required that the accounts be indexed, like the Federal Employee Retirement System (FERS). This had the effect of taking almost all the profit out of privatization and with it much of the benefit for financial providers to compensate for their regulatory risk.

Adding to the problems created by business ambivalence were labor union attacks on the few open business supporters of privatization. In 1999, unions sent letters to managers of labor pension funds, warning them that their continued investment of union money was threatened if they supported or contributed to groups pushing privatization. David John of the Heritage Foundation believes that this letter "scared away many potential supporters, and [continues to do] so to this day."[41] This points to one of the more peculiar consequences of America's private welfare state: the large sums invested in union-defined benefit pension funds give labor political leverage over their investment managers. Unions and supportive organizations also staged a number of high-profile media events attacking supporters of privatization, Charles Schwab in particular. The reason for targeting Schwab is not hard to fathom—despite labor's claims, even its own literature shows that Schwab was one of the only investment managers (along with Wachovia and Waddell and Reed) to support the Alliance for Worker Retirement Security, which was initiated by the White House to support Social Security privatization.[42]

Most other businesses have supported privatization in only the most hands-off manner possible, through larger business organization intermediaries. But the dependence of the privatization movement on such intermediaries, such as the Securities Industry Association, shows that most of the financial industry is in fact quite hesitant to be seen as openly supporting privatization. Even Schwab tried to downplay its support for privatization in the wake of attacks from unions. The modern Republican Party has, through the "K Street Project," placed ideological supporters in the leadership of major business groups, on the implicit condition that they support the party's positions. In particular, it appears that the White House made Social Security privatization one of the issues that business organizations had to support in order to get a hearing on matters of essential interest to them, thereby making it appear as if there was broader and deeper business support for privatization than there was. But the business organizations that are now a part of the Republican Party network got beyond the core interests of their members, and when the president's Social Security initiative began to wilt, the members in these organizations ran for cover.

The continuing power of the American Association of Retired Persons (AARP) also helped to doom the president's Social Security plans. While conservatives mercilessly criticized the AARP for decades, seeing it as the embodiment of the entrenched welfare state, they had never found a way to contain its power in defending the Social Security system. In 2005, the imbalance between the weak grassroots and limited resources of the privatizers and the power of the AARP was shown in sharp relief. The AARP's weak role in the campaign for national health care in the early Clinton years and the failure of the Medicare Catastrophic Coverage Act of 1988 showed that the organization was no longer very effective in helping to expand the welfare state. But 2005 showed that the organization still had impressive "negative capacity." In December 2004, right after the president was elected openly calling for Social Security privatization, the AARP called in its magazine (sent out to 35 million people) for complete opposition to the President's proposals.[43] The AARP backed up its opposition with a $5 million, two-week advertising blitz at the end of 2004, swamping anything that the privatizers—whose business support was already weakened by union mobilization—could muster.[44]

## The Sources of Social Security's Durability

What lessons does the experience of Social Security politics over the last quarter-century have for our understanding of American political development, and the role of conservatives in it? Put briefly, Social Security can be understood as the limiting case for conservatives' ability to transform the American welfare state. For some, explaining this outcome requires little more than pointing to the program's huge fiscal overhang.[45] But while the weight of inherited commitments in Social Security is surely critical to explaining the limits of conservatives' success, a closer examination of the issue renders this outcome significantly more contingent.

First and foremost, such a structural account would leave out the most remarkable shift in this period, the presence of privatization on the political agenda. Despite the widely acknowledged problem of transition costs, conservatives were able to transport the idea from the outer reaches of libertarianism to the official position of a two-term Republican president. This project of policy legitimation depended upon the existence of a dense network of organizations outside government—a network that simply did not exist in previous periods. The entry of privatization into mainstream policy debate took advantage of the weakening of the older Social Security establishment,[46] the broader concerns about the program that came from the deterioration in the program's long-term financial projections, and the existence of funding crises in the late 1970s and early 1980s, and the rise of defined contribution savings and pension plans. In short, the Social Security counterestablishment had developed the expertise, political sophistication, and networks to out-compete the defenders of the program in the arena of agenda setting. Regard-less of how the issue has turned out, this is a dramatic developmental shift from previous periods.

Shifting the agenda on Social Security required changing the dominant conservative position on the issue. Conservatives in previous periods sought to restrain the program's benefits, while simultaneously criticizing the notion that the program's benefits were "earned" and therefore "owed" to existing or prospective retirees. By the mid-1980s, conservatives had, in effect, sur-rendered on the current and near-term level of program benefits, declaring them a political lost cause. In a transformation quite similar to that described in chapter 9, conservatives switched from shrinking government to using it to achieve their own ends. In an even greater irony, as the idea developed over the past decade, it became ever more statist. Where conservatives in the mid-1980s modeled their privatization plans on the relatively freewheeling regulatory structure of IRAs, by the late 1990s, conservatives were pointing to the Federal Employee Retirement System, with its exceptionally compressed menu of choices, as their preferred option for investing private accounts. In order to get a hearing for privatization, conservatives had to show that their alternative was desirable even against the inherited, liberal standards of the existing program. The parallel with education, where conservatives have embraced concepts of educational equity and the idea that "education is a civil rights issue," is quite exact.[47]

The saga of Social Security privatization also points to the deep tensions between the components of the modern Republican Party's agenda. Given the limits on government finance that are a characteristic feature of modern American politics, the three big commitments of the Bush administration—Social Security privatization, a prescription drug benefit, and large tax cuts—could not be pursued simultaneously, even in the presence of large projected budget surpluses. This put the administration in the position of choosing between agenda items with substantial support among the Washington-based conservative policy establishment (Social Security privatization), one per-ceived as necessary in order to neutralize a prominent Democratic issue (pre-scription drug coverage) and another backed by the core components of the president's electoral base (tax cuts). In the end, the need to reward the party's base and liquidate the Democrats' issues won out over more transformational objectives. While the Washington-based conservative counterestablishment has certainly become an important player in Republican politics, when there is a zero-sum relationship between its goals and the electoral objectives of Republican politicians, the latter are still in the policy-making saddle.

The experience also demonstrates the importance of Democratic support for conservative victories in social policy. Over the last thirty years, whether in tax simplification,[48] welfare reform,[49] deregulation,[50] charter schools, or zero-tolerance policing and criminal sentencing, conservatives' victories beyond tax cuts and foreign affairs have come almost exclusively when they were able to attract significant support from Democrats. By the end of the 1990s, the pattern of increasing Democratic support climaxing in major policy reform seemed as if it might be replicating itself in the area of Social Security. But with the unification of Republican control of the federal government, combined with the increasing polarization of the parties, Democratic moderates—both in Congress and the broader New Democrat network—defected. The lack of Democratic support for privatization may also have contributed to the drying up of Republican ardor in Congress, since it signaled that the chances for bipartisan cover for reform were limited. At least where highly sensitive areas of social policy are concerned, Republican Congressional majorities still require substantial support from across the aisle, but partisan polarization means they are systematically less likely to get it.

The increasing support for privatization in the mid- to late 1990s and the decline in the Bush years suggests that, on issues with a large blame avoidance component, divided government may be more conducive to reform than unified government.[51] First, as suggested earlier, pension reform almost everywhere in the world has required cross-party support, for two reasons: (a) given the long-term impact of pension changes, legitimating them often requires support beyond a single party; and (b) pension reform under present conditions almost always involves loss imposition, and cross-party agreement is the best way to ensure risk-averse politicians that they will have electoral insulation against being blamed. Second, divided government provides the institutional control necessary for deliberation and bargaining. Parties may be willing to consider unorthodox ideas if they know that they have the institutional muscle to impose conditions on change necessary to make reforms palatable to their core constituencies and ideas. Under unified government, however, there is always the risk that the majority party will negotiate in bad faith, extracting concessions from the minority to give the impression of legitimacy, and then stripping them out in later stages of the process (such as conference committees). While bipartisan support for loss-imposing legislation may be possible in the United States under conditions of unified government, therefore, it may be considerably easier under divided government, since each party shares collective responsibility for governance, can evade blame at election time, and can protect their interests in negotiations.

Where conservative ends in Social Security are concerned, executive leadership seems even less of a panacea than unified government. In 1981, the president and his OMB director sidetracked a substantial cut in Social Security benefits that had been negotiated in Congress, for a politically reckless and poorly thought-through attack on early retirement. As a consequence, Social Security was spared in the early Reagan budget-cutting, and the fortunes of the Democrats resuscitated. A similar pattern recurred in 1985, when Senators Dole and Domenici believed they had put together a package of Social Security cuts that could get through Congress, only to see the White House undercut them. When a Republican president did make a Social Security reform supported by conservatives his top domestic priority, in 2005, he failed utterly to transform public opinion on the issue, attract Democrats into negotiations, or even persuade Congressional Republicans to support him. While it may very well be the case that Democratic presidents can take the lead in Social Security politics—because of the party's stronger public image on the issue—the same thing does not appear to hold for Republicans.

Finally, this period demonstrates the continuing power of the interests that grew up around Social Security, and the limits of the conservative counterestablishment. The AARP continues to dwarf anything that conservatives are capable of mobilizing against it, at least where protecting its existing policy turf is concerned. While conservatives have made an effort to mobilize alternative senior citizen organizations (such as United Seniors Association), none of them have the money, the reach into seniors' homes, or the policy infrastructure of the AARP. While years ago Stuart Butler and others dreamed that the financial industry, attracted by the opportunity to manage individual accounts, might be able to counter the AARP's power, a number of factors have militated against such a role. First and foremost, retail financial firms, like all businesses, are exceptionally sensitive about their public image, given that they sell to Democrats and Republicans. Second, large parts of the investment management industry manage money for union pension funds, making them very sensitive to political exposure on an issue near and dear to labor. Third, Social Security individual accounts are, at best, a mixed bag for the financial industry, and have become even less attractive to them as conservatives have tried to make them more attractive to the public and policy makers. In short, unlike tax cuts, which were a major, bottom-line priority of business, Social Security privatization continues to be a messy, complicated issue whose benefits to business are unclear. While some businesses have shown an interest in the issue, when the action got hot in 2005, most of them ran for cover. As has been the case enough to be a rule, business is, at best, a fair-weather friend of conservative efforts to restructure the welfare state.[52]

Finally, Social Security is popular, millions of seniors depend upon it for a large percentage of their income, it is in no short-term risk of financial collapse, and risk-averse, election-oriented politicians continue to see more downside than upside to changing it. The economic and political advantages of privatization are prospective and speculative, while the advantages of the status quo are contemporary and tangible. Privatizers, in short, faced an enormous structural challenge, against which their ability to get privatization on the agenda is an extraordinary accomplishment, and their failure to actually achieve their ends not much of a surprise.

## Notes

1. Martha Derthick, *Policymaking For Social Security* (Washington, DC: Brookings Institution Press, 1979), chap. 6.
2. Steven M. Teles, *The Rise of the Conservative Legal Movement: The Battle for Control of the Law* (Princeton, NJ: Princeton University Press, 2008).
3. Kent Weaver, "The Politics of Pension Reform: Lessons from Abroad," in *Framing the Social Security Debate,* ed. R. Douglas Arnold, Michael Graetz, and Alicia H. Munnell (Washington, DC: Brookings Institution Press, 1998).
4. This section is condensed from Martha Derthick and Steven M. Teles, "Riding the Third Rail: Social Security Reform," in *The Reagan Presidency: Pragmatic Conservatism and Its Legacies,* ed. W. Elliot Brownlee and Hugh Davis Graham (Lawrence: University Press of Kansas, 2003), 182–208. In addition to the sources cited there, we have drawn on Edward D. Berkowitz, *Robert Ball and the Politics of Social Security* (Madison: University of Wisconsin Press, 2003), which was not available when we wrote the earlier essay.
5. Berkowitz, *Robert Ball and the Politics of Social Security,* 270, 316, and 322–3.
6. This section is condensed from Steven M. Teles, "Conservative Mobilization Against Entrenched Liberalism," in, *Transformations of the American Polity,* ed. Paul Pierson and Theda Skocpol (Princeton, NJ: Princeton University Press, 2007).
7. The roots of the Social Security trust fund's insularity are carefully examined in Eric Patashnik, *Putting Trust in the Federal Budget: Trust Funds and The Politics of Commitment* (Cambridge, MA: Cambridge University Press, 2000).
8. Peter Ferrara, *Social Security: The Inherent Contradiction* (San Francisco: Cato Institute, 1980).
9. The term comes from Sidney Blumenthal, *The Rise of the Counter-Establishment* (New York: Harper and Row, 1988).
10. Peter Germanis, "Epilogue" in *The Heritage Lectures* 18 (1982), 80.
11. Stuart Butler and Peter Germanis, "Achieving Social Security Reform: A 'Leninist' Strategy," *Cato Journal* 3, 2 (Fall 1983): 545–6.
12. Peter Peterson, *Facing Up* (New York: Simon and Schuster, 1993).

13. Third Millennium, *Social Security: The Credibility Gap,* 1994, *http://www. thirdmil.org/media/releases/ufopol.html.*

14. Peter Germanis, "Increase the IRA Advantage," *Heritage Foundation Backgrounder,* (August 24, 1983), 11.

15. Personal interview with Stuart Butler, 1998.

16. The dynamics of libertarian transfer of policy ideas across borders—both from the United States to abroad and back, in a form of "policy reimportation"—is discussed in detail in Steven Teles and Daniel Kenney, "Spreading the Word: The Diffusion of American Conservatism in Europe and Beyond," in Jeffrey Kopstein and Sven Steinmo, *Growing Apart? America and Europe in the 21st Century* (New York: Cambridge University Press, 2007).

17. All details on the Council's report can be found at http://www.ssa.gov/ history/reports/adcouncil/report/toc.htm.

18. Carolyn Weaver, "The Economics and Politics of The Emergence of Social Security: Some Implications for Reform," *The Cato Journal* 3, 2 (Fall 1983): 361–91.

19. Letter from Carolyn Weaver to Milton Friedman, March 18, 1997.

20. http://digitalcommons.ilr.cornell.edu/cgi/viewcontent.cgi?article=1006& context=institutes.

21. George W. Bush, "Address to the 2000 Republican National Convention," August 3, 2000. http://www.cnn.com/ELECTION/2000/conventions/ republican/transcripts/bush.html.

22. Republican Platform 2000, http://www.cnn.com/ELECTION/2000/ conventions/republican/features/platform.00/#25.

23. Richard Stevenson, "For Bush, A Long Embrace of Social Security Plan," *New York Times,* February 26, 2005, 1.

24. Ibid.

25. Ibid.

26. Personal interview with John Cogan, January 19, 2006. Another interesting participant in the meeting was T. J. Rogers, the CEO of Cypress Semiconductor and perhaps the most stridently libertarian leader of a major publicly traded American company. Rogers has also been a long-time supporter of and participant in the Cato Institute's programming.

27. Ibid.

28. Ibid.

29. Ibid.

30. Rebecca Adams, "Politics and Priorities," *Congressional Quarterly Weekly,* 59 (January 13, 2001): 110.

31. David Nather and Anjetta McQueen, "Social Security Overhaul Pane's Report Lands With a Thud," *Congressional Quarterly Weekly,* 59 (December 15, 2001): 2982.

32. Randy Clerihue and Andrew Biggs had both been at Cato immediately before working on the commission. The staff also included experts who were not members of the Social Security privatization network, such as David Richardson of George State University (then at the Treasury Department),

Jeff Brown of the University of Illinois and Kent Smetters of the University of Pennsylvania.

33. Presidential Executive Order, "President's Commission to Strengthen Social Security," May 2, 2001, http://www.whitehouse.gov/news/releases/2001/05/20010502–5.html.

34. Kent Weaver, "The Politics of Pension Reform: Lessons from Abroad," in *Framing the Social Security Debate,* ed. Douglas Arnold, Michael Graetz and Alicia Munnell (Washington, DC: Brookings Institution Press, 1998).

35. Peter Beinart, "Boomerang," *The New Republic, 232* (January 31, 2005): 6.

36. Personal interview with Will Marshall, January 19, 2006.

37. John Aldrich and David Rohde, "The Consequences of Party Organization in the House: The Role of Majority and Minority Parties in Conditional Party Government," in *Polarized Politics: Congress and the President in a Partisan Era,* ed. Jon Bond and Richard Fleischer (Washington, DC: CQ Press, 2000), 31–72.

38. Ryan Lizza, "Hardball 101," *The New Republic, 232* (January 24, 2005): 15–16. It was also the case that, in trying to keep Baucus from working with Bush on Social Security, Reid was pushing on an open door. Robert Draper reports that while Baucus expressed a willingness to work with the administration on Medicare, which he believed faced real solvency problems, Karl Rove insisted that the administration was more interested in Social Security. Draper reports that this "struck Baucus at the time as nonsensical—Social Security was solvent until 2042—until it dawned on him that solvency wasn't what was preoccupying Bush and Rove. This was about privatizing the New Deal." Robert Draper, *Dead Certain: The Presidency of George W. Bush* (New York: Free Press, 2007), 293.

39. Howard Gleckman and Rich Miller, "The Beltway Battle Ahead," *Business Week,* January 24, 2005, 72–5.

40. Jackie Calmes, "How a Victorious Bush Fumbled Plan to Revamp Social Security" *Wall Street Journal,* October 20, 2005, A1.

41. Email communication from David John, January 19, 2006.

42. AFL-CIO, "Wall Street Attacks on Social Security," February 17, 2005.

43. Jim Drinkard, "Seniors Organization Digs in for Fight Over Private Social Security," *USA Today,* December 6, 2004, 1.

44. Robert Pear, "In Ads, AARP Criticizes Plan on Privatizing," *New York Times,* December 30, 2004, 16.

45. Such an argument would draw heavily from Paul Pierson, *Dismantling the Welfare State* (Cambridge: Cambridge University Press, 1994).

46. Described in Altman and Marmor's chapter 5 in this volume, as well as Martha Derthick's *Agency under Stress* (Washington, DC: Brookings Institution Press, 1990).

47. Good examples of this are Joseph Viteritti, *Choosing Equality: School Choice, The Constitution and Civil Society* (Washington, DC: Brookings Institution Press, 1999) and Clint Bolick, *Voucher Wars* (Washington, DC: Cato, 2003).

48. Jeffrey Birnbaum and Alan Murray, *Showdown at Gucci Gulch* (New York: Vintage, 1988).

49. Steven M. Teles, *Whose Welfare? AFDC and Elite Politics* (Lawrence: University of Kansas, 1996); Kent Weaver, *Ending Welfare as We Know It* (Washington, DC: Brookings Institution Press, 2000).

50. Martha Derthick and Paul Quirk, *The Politics of Deregulation* (Washington, DC: Brookings Institution Press, 1985).

51. David Mayhew has famously argued that divided government appears, over time, to be equally conducive to large policy change as unified government. See David Mayhew, *Divided We Govern* (New Haven, CT: Yale University Press, 1991).

52. The lack of business ardor for measures supported by conservative and libertarian think tanks is a fact that has been long bemoaned by the latter. The most spirited defense of the position that business, as currently constituted, is an uncertain—at best—partner for those of conservative principles can be found in Paul Weaver, *The Suicidal Corporation* (New York: Simon and Schuster, 1988), a book sponsored by the Cato Foundation.

# CHAPTER 9

## Education Policy from 1980 to the Present: The Politics of Privatization

*Jeffrey Henig*

As 1980 rolled to a close, Conservative Republicans had every reason to be feeling their oats. Ronald Reagan's victory was an electoral vote landslide. Despite the uphill challenge of running against an incumbent, Reagan earned just fewer than ten times as many Electoral College votes as Jimmy Carter. Republicans also captured a majority of the Senate for the first time since 1954. The ghosts of the 1964 Barry Goldwater shellacking and the Nixon impeachment had been exorcised. Indeed, Reagan seemed ideologically and politically more willing and able to advance a positive conservative agenda; the Nixon administration had disappointed conservative believers in small government by showing that Republicans could control the White House yet fail to reverse or even slow the seemingly inexorable growth of the welfare state.

Education policy had played a role in the conservatives' ascendance, but one that was indirect, low in visibility, and lacking an affirmative vision. As

Patrick McGuinn notes in this volume, resistance to mandatory busing had played a tactical role in Nixon's so-called Southern strategy, and Reagan benefited in Northern white ethnic communities from lingering resentment over what were seen as elitist Democrats' self-righteous insistence that working-class white neighborhoods cede control of their community schools to an aggressive judiciary while hypocritical liberals buffered themselves in suburbs and private schools. While effective as a wedge issue, this political use of education policy was most effective if played out *sotto voce*. Assertions of states' rights and local control in and of themselves provided no road map to guide what should be happening inside schools and classrooms. Education, at the time, was a hole in a doughnut; as a national platform, little wonder, then, that rather than a positive vision of what schools could and should become, Reagan's signature proposal was elimination of the U.S. Department of Education. As one prominent critic summarized Reagan's first two years steering the national education policy, "I have identified a serious problem, and I insist on doing nothing about it."[1]

To the extent that Reagan conservatives offered any kind of a positive agenda for education, it was framed around vouchers. Although the specifics of voucher plans might differ, the core notion is to allow the public dollars raised to support education to travel to whatever school a family selects, even if that school is privately operated, rather than go automatically to the local public school system in the jurisdiction in which the family happens to reside. At the time, vouchers were an extremely divisive issue on three critical dimensions: privatization, church-state relations, and racial and class stratification. By proposing to channel public funding into private schools, vouchers stimulated significant resistance within the public education community, among public employee unions fighting their own battles to protect jobs, and among members of the American public who valued the traditional image of public schools as critical vehicles for imparting community values, socially integrating new Americans, and investing in a skilled workforce and acute citizenry. By opening the possibility of sending public dollars to nonsecular schools, vouchers stirred resistance among many constitutionalists as well as those sensitive to historical manifestations of religious intolerance and efforts by religious majorities—most vividly in other nations, but in the United States as well—to use schools as vehicles of indoctrination. By making it easier for more advantaged families to opt for racially and economically homogenous schools without having to bear the full cost of private school tuition or a move to expensive suburbs, vouchers ignited concerns among liberals and advocates for minorities who feared them as a tool for resegregation. In the political landscape of the times, these factors were sufficient to make an educational platform built around vouchers impossible for even a popular president to bring into fruition. Their function was more symbolic than real, their place in the broader conservative agenda for the 1980s more marginal than central.

The next two decades witnessed sharp and substantial change. Education steadily rose to a much more central role in Republican and conservative strategy. Some of this movement began while Reagan was still in office. Some within the administration concluded that the federal educational initiatives they had inherited were so entrenched that efforts to dismantle them would be futile and self-defeating. "There has been a shift," Secretary of Education William J. Bennett declared early in 1988. "Republicans and conservatives have come to realize that the Federal role in education is here to stay and that you ought not to blow it up. They also realize that it is silly to concede the education issue to the Democrats."[2] In the more contemporary era, both George H. W. Bush and George W. Bush made serious pitches to be considered the "education president." Market-based models for educational reform spread rapidly, hurdling political and constitutional feasibility challenges and building a momentum that has not yet begun to ebb.

The Republican turnabout on education rested in part on the party's need to attend to growing concerns about education among two key constituent groups: corporate America and affluent suburban families. The states' rights concerns that were so prominent in earlier years (see chapters 3 and 6 in this volume) had enough residual strength in 1980 to prompt Reagan-conservatives to wonder aloud whether there was any legitimate role for the national government to play in the traditionally local arena of education policy. With the subsiding of racial issues tied to desegregation, however, these concerns lost much of their animating force. Corporate Republicans were becoming restive about the perceived low quality of American schools even before the famous *Nation at Risk* report dramatized the issue with its powerful evocation of the emerging global economic threat. Having cemented gains in the South, Republicans now had to think more about appealing to the growing population of suburbanites, mostly white, leaning toward the party on grounds of fiscal and tax policy, but socially more liberal and sensitive about appeals based on race. The so-called "soccer moms," an increasingly important potential swing vote, cared a lot about schools—public schools— and wanted an affirmative strategy for making them better. By 2002, with the adoption of No Child Left Behind and the Republican administration's aggressive assertion of its right and responsibility to set standards and hold states and school districts accountable, the notion that conservatives stood foursquare against national involvement in education seemed a bit like a quaint anachronism.

This chapter explores the impact of conservative ideas, interests, and institutions by addressing several puzzles posed by recent education politics and policy. What accounts for the change in the positioning of education on the national agenda of conservatives, from doughnut hole to tactical centerpiece? What accounts for the transformation of school choice from fringe issue to institutionalized reality? How can we understand the Republican Party's seeming reversal from consistent and insistent defenders of a vision of federalism that unequivocally defined education as a state and local responsibility to leadership in passing and carrying out what is arguably the strongest nationalization of education in American history?

I argue that the evolution of conservative education policy is best understood as a combination of intent, happenstance, and opportunism.[3] The Reagan era marked a transition in conservative strategy in at least two ways. First, in an almost classic affirmation of the adage "you stand where you sit," conservative Republicans discovered the merits of authoritative national policy once they found themselves in the position to call the shots. Second, the Reagan era began a slower transition from a substantive core commitment to decentralization to a substantive commitment to choice and privatization within an accountability framework. For the most part, that commitment has remained self-conscious, consistent, controlling, and politically effective. Education initially was carried along for the ride; school vouchers were a logical element to include in a privatization movement, but they were not a featured element because they were politically too hot to handle. A seeming retreat—the embrace of "public school choice"—gave new political life to the market vision of education. The explosive growth of charter schools, initially unanticipated but opportunistically exploited, for the first time gave market advocates a program that was both ideologically aligned with their core agenda (as were vouchers) and an electoral and legislative winner (as vouchers were not). Vouchers—reframed as redistributive programs targeted to liberate low-income minorities from stifling and bureaucratic public systems—remained a part of the package, but, like the antibusing effort, were probably more important for sowing dissension among Democratic constituencies than as a positive vision of where a conservative governance regime would put its emphasis. High-stakes testing, and in particular a strong federal role in a testing-oriented accountability campaign, entered through the back door as way to help George W. Bush capture the White House, but was invited to stay because it proved to be a political winner, not just at the polls but in holding onto an important element of the Republican constituency: corporate interests that were not enthused by an educational agenda defined primarily by vouchers and states' rights. Moreover, somewhat to their own surprise, conservatives discovered that a properly fine-tuned combination of charter schools and standards could win support—or at least neutralize some resistance—from some inner-city minorities and progressive, counterculture-oriented families typically hostile to conservative rhetoric but responsive to initiatives that challenged stultifying local bureaucracies.

## Privatization as a Political Strategy

During the 1970s the idea of privatization as a policy design was nurtured and honed within conservative think tanks and academia both in the United States and, with mutual borrowing, in Great Britain. As a policy strategy, privatization represented a philosophic attachment to individualism and markets linked to a set of policy tools—including deregulation, contracting out, users fees, vouchers, and load-shedding—that could in principle be used to steer key functions from the public to the private sector.[4] During the 1980s, however, privatization took on a different and more aggressive dimension. Rather than a matter of *policy design*—a set of initiatives that conservatives would like to enact if and when they gained sufficient political power—privatization was developed as a *political strategy,* a plan for how they could build on the Reagan Revolution to institutionalize and expand their power base. Education, initially, played a relatively minor role in the formulation and early pursuit of this strategy.

While Reagan generally ran against "big government," his 1980 campaign and first term emphasized traditional themes of federalism, states' rights, and individualism more than market theory per se. Shifting federal support from categorical to block grants as a way to liberate states to innovate and reflect local values were key themes, both generally and in education. Reagan proposed consolidating over 40 grants programs into two block grants that would give states considerable discretion in how they set about helping students with special needs and leveraging improvements in school performance. The 1980 Republican platform portrayed teachers in a positive light, suggesting that federal education policy created the greatest barrier to teachers' freedom in the classroom and thus the greatest barrier to enabling students to meet high standards. Accordingly, the Republican platform argued for deregulation and the elimination of the Department of Education in order to place teaching and learning decisions in the hands of the students, parents, and local education personnel. Other themes included allowing voluntary prayer in schools and providing tuition tax credits to parents, including those sending their children to religious schools. Continuing its subtle exploitation of resentment against the federal courts' aggressive pursuit of racial desegregation, the platform called for elimination of busing, because it "blighted whole communities across the land with its divisive impact," failed to provide achievement results, and the funding used for its high cost could be used for other programs.

Reagan scored some major legislative victories during his first term, most notably in the areas of tax cuts and combining categorical grants into broader (but typically less well-funded) block grants. But his education agenda was pursued tepidly and with little success, in large measure because of the entrenched power of the "education-industrial complex" that McGuinn describes (in chapter 6 of this volume). More significantly, by Reagan's second term, some conservatives were becoming alarmed that even the early victories were being eroded. As seen at the time by Stuart Butler, of the Heritage Foundation: "After some initial success in 1981...Ronald Reagan is now on record as the big spender to end all big spenders—an irony indeed for such a conservative politician."[5]

This chapter puts considerable emphasis on Butler, an influential strategist within the political Right. Butler is credited by Heritage as having helped "to change the course of public policy in America," citing on its web site the fact that "the National Journal, Washington's most influential magazine of politics and policy, named him in the 1980s as 'one of 150 individuals outside government who have the greatest influence on decision-making in Washington.'" For further evidence of Butler's impact, see chapter 8 of this volume. While it probably is correct that Butler has been unusually influential, what warrants attention in this chapter is his clarity, specificity, and unusually explicit presentation of the kinds of strategic thinking that more typically are discussed behind closed doors. It matters less whether Butler originated or simply chronicled the political privatization strategy outlined below.

According to Butler, Reagan's failure to carry through on his promise to shrink government was not due to lack of will but to flawed understanding and strategy. It was not enough to articulate a goal of smaller government—that Reagan did masterfully. What was needed, instead, was a better understanding of the political dynamics that accounted for the growth of government and then a plan to turn those dynamics around. Butler dismissively characterized the Reagan approach as a "supply-side" strategy that sought to shrink government by tightening the flow of money into the federal budget.

> But the administration will never be able to reverse the growth of spending until it learns from its opponents and switches from a supply-side budget strategy to a demand-side approach. It must, in other words, abandon the idea of trying to hold down spending by attempting to apply and sustain spending ceilings. That is a little like trying to stop a pot from boiling over by pressing down on the lid.[6]

Butler argued that the cause of governmental growth was the array of interest groups that benefited from public spending. Because the benefits of government spending were relatively concentrated, those on the receiving end had a powerful motivation to ensure that the spigot stayed open. Because the costs of the programs were spread widely and were not clearly itemized, taxpayers had less motivation to insist on fiscal restraint. Over time, moreover, pro-spending interest groups solidified their standing by linking arms with politicians and bureaucrats who also stood to gain from the growth of the programs they championed and administered. Around this time, some conservatives began referring to this array of interlocking groups as the "Education Blob." Reflecting on the origin of the term, Jeanne Allen, president of the conservative Center for Education Reform, writes:

> The term "Blob" cropped up years ago when reformers began trying to work with the education establishment and ran smack into the more than 200 groups, associations, federations, alliances, departments, offices, administrations, councils, boards, commissions, panels, organizations, herds, flocks and coveys, that make up the education industrial complex. Taken individually they were frustrating enough, with their own agendas, bureaucracies, and power over education. But taken as a whole they were (and are) maddening in their resistance to change. Not really a wall—they always talk about change—but rather more like quicksand, or a tar pit where ideas slowly sink out of sight leaving everything just as it had been.[7]

The "privatization strategy" that Butler laid out "replaces this set of dynamics with another that discourages citizens from demanding public-sector services and encourages them instead to seek similar services from the private sector."[8] Key components of the strategy would include:

- *Emphasize that government can be a guarantor of services without necessarily providing them itself.* Butler argued that conservatives fall into a trap when they argue against any governmental role in the delivery of popular programs. Instead, they should propose ways that government could ensure the provision of the same goods and services via market means. Writing nearly two decades before George W. Bush launched his proposal to privatize elements of Social Security, he observed "no politician in America could expect to be elected after informing a group of senior citizens that the federal government had no role in the provision of Social Security, [but] there would be great political potential in a proposal that tackled Social Security's financial crisis by requiring all citizens to enroll in a pension plan."[9]
- *Use policy tools such as users fees, tax incentives, and vouchers to encourage citizens to rely on the private sector to meet their demands.* Butler labeled this the "heart of privatization," suggesting that it combined "political expediency" with the goal of shrinking government by allowing conservative politicians to "gain points with constituencies by promising more, not less, and by giving people the

freedom to choose the service provider most attractive to them" while simultaneously reducing opposition to budget cuts.[10]

- *Detach elements of the pro-spending coalition: the Education Blob.* Butler cited here what looked at the time to be a compelling example from Great Britain. The Thatcher government had offered discounts to public housing residents to purchase their units, and initial reports suggested that the newly invested property owners were showing weakened allegiance to the opposition Labor Party. Arguing along similar lines, Butler argued that by allowing public employees to bid on contracts with the potential to realize a share in any profits, government unions might be "bought off" to support broad contracting out plans to shift provision to the private sector.

- *Create "mirror image" private sector coalitions that would counterbalance the pro-spending groups.* Privatization would involve the "conscious creation" and nurturing of anti-spending coalitions that would "gel" around targeted tax incentives or regulatory relief. Once in place, these coalitions will battle the pro-spending groups and "take on a momentum of their own."[11]

- *Resist the temptation to directly pursue radical change, in favor of an incrementalist approach that would slowly but more surely lead toward fundamental and sustainable change.* While it is sometimes possible to bring about sharp policy changes, the pro-government forces more typically gained by "creating small, inoffensive programs" that then become the seedbeds for further expansion. Going for big victories means risking big and visible defeats. Learning from their counterparts, "the privatizer should attempt to get a foot in the door" with a small tax or regulatory change and then use that as a platform for expanding the pro-market coalition.[12]

This game plan would later play out very neatly in the education arena. But initially conservatives put their primary efforts elsewhere. Americans' attachments to public education—both the broad ideals it represented and the concrete manifestations within their local communities—made this a politically risky area for conservatives to feature. Even in 1983, when asked shortly after *A Nation at Risk* drew widespread attention for its scathing critique of America's schools, citizens were 50 percent more likely to give public schools a grade of A or B than they were to assign a grade of D or F.[13] Making this latent mass support for the existing system of public education even more significant was the fact that it was topped off by the well-organized and powerful teachers' unions. At the time, too, conservative strategists were primarily focusing on the battle over federal policy; changing education seemed to require fighting many battles in 50 state legislatures and 15,000 school districts. Butler devoted entire sections of his 1985 book on *Privatizing Federal Spending* to the possibilities to privatize the U.S. Postal Service, Amtrak, air traffic control, weapons procurement, and commercial possibilities in space, and even offered a full chapter on Social Security. But the word "schools" does not appear at all in his index; "education" appears only in reference to the unfulfilled Reagan proposal to abolish the Department of Education, and there are only two or three references to school vouchers, in each case submerged in a broader discussion of vouchers in other policy contexts.

## From Vouchers to Public School Choice

Early in 1988 President Ronald Reagan went to Suitland High School in Prince Georges County, a racially changing suburb of Washington, D.C. He stood at a school with a magnet program that had been initiated as part of a judicially monitored settlement to a school desegregation lawsuit filed by the NAACP. Magnets are public schools or programs that are given special themes—such as language immersion, computers, gifted and talented instruction—that differentiate them from other schools in the local jurisdiction and are intended to make them more attractive to some families. Magnets were seen as a way to minimize mandatory busing by using school choice to entice white and black families to send their children to schools outside the residentially segregated attendance zones in which they lived. With the racially mixed but predominantly black student body at Suitland High School as a backdrop, the president drew the link between this very public choice program and the ideas about markets and choice that lay behind his failed voucher initiatives.[14]

For a conservative president who had promoted private school vouchers and criticized federal courts for their aggressiveness on desegregation issues, this certainly seemed like a strategic retreat. It was a case, however, of making one step backward in order to make two steps forward.[15] By adopting a more gradualist version of privatization, the administration reduced anxieties about radical changes that might destabilize the system. This deprived their opponents of the chance to use the voucher threat to rally their own troops and opened the potential to attract new supporters who favored giving families greater options but were wary of market models and school voucher plans.

During his first term, Reagan had succeeded in convincing many that America's schools were in trouble. *A Nation at Risk*, produced by a national commission appointed by Secretary of Education Terrell Bell, announced with great fanfare that the nation's schools were failing to stem a "rising tide of mediocrity" that threatened the nation's economic and moral stature. Rather than building momentum for a radical reform like vouchers, however, the heightened sense of an education crisis ratcheted up pressure on the White House to take an effective leadership role.[16]

Congress, and by most indications the broader public as well, found vouchers to be too speculative and a bit scary. Critics feared that vouchers would wreak administrative and fiscal havoc at the district level, where superintendents and school boards would have to deal with budgetary uncertainty (as public funds would move with students as they shifted among schools, districts, and between the public and private sectors) and principals would not know from year to year how many students to expect or how many teachers to hire. Critics also feared that the market forces unleashed by vouchers would exacerbate racial and economic inequalities as white and middle-class families would use their various advantages to ensure that their children got into "the best" schools, especially if, as many expected, definitions of what was best included preference for student bodies populated by children much like their own. The prospect of breaching the traditional "wall" between government and religious schools was a major concern also, not only to those who expected that vouchers for parochial schools would be found unconstitutional, but also among many who feared the consequences if they were not. And finally, critics questioned whether an untested idea hatched by ivory tower economists had a better chance to raise school performance than relying on the expertise of educators and providing them with the resources they needed to make the current system work better.

By linking the theories and language of markets to magnet schools—an existing and popular public sector reform—conservative strategists helped to breathe life back into the voucher movement by converting it, at least temporarily, into a broader movement for school choice. While vouchers seemed radical and strange, the notion of "choice" was inherently appealing. Conservatives could continue playing into—and stirring up—resentment toward a public sector "monopoly" that used force to extract revenue (through taxes), was often unresponsive to parents seeking input, and assigned children to schools based on attendance zone instead of student interests and needs, but they no longer needed to ask a skittish public to sign on for radical change. Public school choice answered all of the critics' objections: in the form of magnet schools, it had already proven feasible, was linked to integration and equity, did not get government entangled with religion, and was associated with a number of high-performing schools.

During the 1980s and into the early 1990s, though, the tactical pay-off to the school choice platform was less one of making policy inroads than of arming conservative politicians with an answer to the question "so what would *you* do to improve urban schools?" It mattered less whether the answer was politically feasible than that it was intellectually coherent, consistent with the rest of the conservative agenda, and symbolically allowed conservatives to say that they cared just as much as liberals about schools and had a general plan for doing something about them. The target audience was not really the low-income and minority families trapped in the nation's worst schools; these were unlikely converts to a Republican ticket. The group that was of much greater concern was suburban voters. Many of these were attracted by Republican promises to lower taxes, but their commitment was wobbly, especially when education issues were in the fore. While somewhat skeptical of the federal government's capacity to deliver on its promises, these suburban interests were: reluctant to give up on New Deal notions that government can and should solve social problems; broadly loyal to the abstract ideal of the public common schools as a vehicle for social cohesion and economic opportunity; and most immediately protective of the public school systems they had nurtured within their own communities.

Magnet schools were the offshoot of judicial decisions, legislative innovation, political bargaining and compromise. To the extent that they were working and popular, proponents of public-sector reform could have used them effectively to counter the impression that government inevitably generated bureaucracy, bland uniformity, unresponsiveness, ineffectiveness, and waste. But Reagan and conservative thinkers of were quicker to the draw, and as a result won an important early battle establishing the terminological grounds on which the school choice battles would unfold. At the same time that the market metaphor continued to be used by conservatives to promote the idea that government is fundamentally and irredeemably unable to reform itself, by defining magnets schools and public-school choice as indicative of what markets could do, Reagan and the strong market advocates claimed for their own side a series of reforms that were in fact the product of public institutions. While magnet schools were the initial focus, the real payoff came with the rapid emergence of a much broader array of public-school choice policy vehicles, especially charter schools.

## Capturing the Charter School Movement

The Reagan era made it clear that education had evolved into a *national* policy issue; even a staunch believer in reserved powers had to have a strategy for convincing the public that conservative policies would do more than push the issue back down the ladder of federalism and even a staunch believer in the limitations of government had to address the broad desire to reform the public system and not simply replace it. While maneuvering around education would continue to be of growing importance in presidential and congressional partisan politics, however, the traditional battleground for education was at the state and local level and that was not about to change overnight.

National actors, including the political parties and major interest groups on the Right and Left, were actively involved and in many instances calling the shots, but the key battlegrounds where they came head-to-head during the 1990s continued to be in the states. Conservative strategists were aggressive in creating new institutions and tactics to promote market-based reforms in that set of venues.[17] Charter schools, the most dramatic and significant reform initiative, had complex roots and currents, but as with magnet schools managed to distill that brew into a simpler message about the popularity and power of market ideals.[18]

Charter schools are something of a hybrid institution; like the centaur who is half horse and half human, charter schools were designed to combine elements of public and private schools. They are like conventional public schools in the sense that they are funded by government, open to all children,[19] and ultimately responsible to meet standards set by democratically elected authorities. They are like conventional private schools in that they are exempted from many regulations (often including those relating to teacher certification), their basic operating policies are set by a private board (often including at least some parents), and the amount of their revenue depends on the number of "customers" they attract, along with any support they can garner from private donors and the philanthropic community.

In Minnesota, where the first charter school legislation was enacted, the impetus had more to do with locally incubated notions of decentralization, expanding educational options, and energizing school-based communities of parents and teachers than with ideological battles between markets and government.[20] Charter schools in Minnesota were one piece in a package of "choice-oriented" reforms that are better understood as progressive efforts to make the public sector more flexible than as fledgling efforts to institute a market-dominated policy regime. In 1985 the state pioneered a postsecondary enrollment plan that gave 11th and 12th graders a chance to take courses at public or private colleges and universities, with tuition covered by the state and credits earned counting toward their high school graduation requirements. In 1987 the state initiated an open enrollment program that allowed children to attend schools in neighboring districts, with state funding following the child to the receiving school.

The charter school idea proved to be tremendously appealing. Minnesota passed the first charter school law in 1991; just five years later half of the states had charter laws in place. During the 1995–1996 school year there were about 253 charter schools operating nationwide; it took less than four years for this number to increase by over 1,000 and less than six to add another 1,000. By 2005 all but ten states had charter schools laws; there were about 3,400 schools operating; and an estimated one million students were attending charter schools.[21]

Part of the appeal of charter schools was intrinsic and pragmatic, having little to do with broad debates about markets versus government.[22] Indeed, one of the strong selling points of the Minnesota innovation was its potential to take the debate out of the "political and ideological morass" that had plagued prior battles over vouchers and market choice.[23] Just as important, though, was the complicated position that charter schools played in the broader game of ideological and partisan maneuvering.

Conservative groups and moderate Democrats were playing "capture the flag," with the ability to define charter schools being the flag. Some within the conservative movement clearly preferred a more deregulated voucher system, in which existing and new private schools would be the most prominent providers. But the ongoing difficulties of moving that agenda led many to conclude that charter schools could be a viable option for getting a foot in the door. Emphasizing that "charter schools are public schools"[24] made them seem less radical, less akin to vouchers and more akin to magnet schools and other familiar forms of public-school choice. Depending on the particulars of legislative form and bureaucratic implementation, charter schooling could shape up as either a slightly diluted form of vouchers or an incrementally more decentralized form of the traditional public school.[25] Designed to promote a soft version of vouchers, charter school laws could be configured to make approval easy, regulation minimal, and public funding substantial and directly reallocated from the revenues that would otherwise support traditional public school systems. As a incremental adjustment to existing public education, charter school laws could be designed to: give local districts a key role in authorizing and overseeing charters; require charter schools to meet curriculum, teacher preparation, and student testing standards similar to other public schools; limit funding to a portion of operating costs and "hold harmless" funding levels to the traditional districts. In order to muster legislative majorities, conservatives needed to accept provisions that they found objectionable, with the particular point of compromise depending on political factors that differed from state to state. Rather than defend a purist model and go down to defeat, key strategists determined to pursue a long-term plan to get something into place, use that initial wedge to further legitimate the idea of market-oriented policies, and count on the fact that the programs would gradually spawn a new constituency of their own. This new constituency would comprise: parents and educators within charter schools who would favor increased funding and decreased regulation; those on waiting lists who would favor steps to loosen the supply side by eliminating caps and multiplying the number and type of organizations that had authority to issue charters; as well as various support organizations that would emerge to service charter schools, including for-profit companies that would offer curriculum, professional development, and management support.

Liberals and Democrats were not passively standing by. Moderate Democrats, including Bill Clinton, had their own agenda, and charter schools figured in it rather prominently. Competing parties and candidates do not always go head-to-head on a fixed set of issues. Often, each side prefers to concentrate on a small set of issues that they think play to their advantage, battling to convince the public that their priorities are the right ones. In a given election, Candidate A might emphasize security, taxes, and family values, while Candidate B argues that the more important issues are jobs, education, and health care reform. Occasionally, however, a particular issue figures prominently in the strategies of both camps, and that is what occurred with charter schools. Just as conservatives were seeking to define charters as a form of privatization, with the hope that initial versions would "seed" the idea and build momentum for even more marketlike forms, key strategists within the Democratic constituency were drawn to charter schools as a way to introduce some flexibility and reform into the public sector. This was both a defensive strategy—an effort to use charters to derail the perceived momentum toward vouchers—and a proactive one, designed to show disaffected citizens that the Democratic agenda did not stand for bureaucracy and the status quo but for a progressive vision of the public interest and a commitment to use government creatively and pragmatically to improve all citizens' quality of life.

At the national level, the Clinton strategy appeared to pay off. As McGuinn details, Clinton and George H. W. Bush both made education a central theme for their 1992 presidential campaigns.[26] George H. W. Bush ran as an "education president" with a vision that emphasized high standards and accountability, but with the national government supporting but not displacing the states. Pressed by the right wing of the party, many of whom at that point still regarded a purist commitment to privately provided education as litmus test of true conservatism, he became more vocally committed to vouchers as his first administration wound to a close.[27] But this mix did not succeed with voters. Clinton, running as an "education governor," with a position on education that embraced public school choice and charter schools (to the dismay of many in the more liberal wing of the party) was more convincing to voters. As McGuinn reports, "The idea of public school choice—which Clinton championed as an alternative to private school vouchers—was viewed more favorably by citizens than vouchers." And the difference showed itself at the bottom line, when voters went to the polls: "education voters (those who indicated education was the issue mattering most to their vote) supported Clinton over Bush by a more than two-to-one margin (55% to 27% for Whites, and 90% to 7% for Blacks). Clinton did equally well on the education issue among the general electorate, with polls showing that voters thought Clinton better able than Bush to improve public education—by almost a two to one margin, 47% to 24%."[28]

In the 1996 election, the Clinton edge on education was even more pronounced. Like Bush before him, Republican candidate Robert Dole adopted the more market-oriented, anti-government and pro-voucher stance that conservative purists within the party favored. Bush had combined vouchers with calls for state implemented standards and accountability; but Dole was boxed into a position in which vouchers comprised the central element of his education plan. Buoyed by their strong gains in the 1994 Congressional elections, conservative hardliners had resumed the old Reagan education-as-a-state-responsibility position, with the 1996 platform calling again for an end to the Department of Education and an end to all "federal meddling." Education was even more important to voters in 1996 than in 1992, and Clinton's public-school choice position again reaped huge benefits. Clinton soundly defeated Dole and "there was general agreement among the media and campaign staff from both parties that education had been a critical issue...and that Clinton had won the issue decisively. Polls showed that Clinton again massively outpaced his republic opponent on the education question, leading Dole 64% to 31% when the public was asked who would do a better job on the issue."[29]

At the state level, however, the stealthier conservative game plan to use charters as a wedge issue was bearing fruit. Conservative foundations and other donors had begun during the 1970s to found a community of market-oriented think tanks and advocacy groups as part of a plan to create a "mirror image" coalition to reverse the growth of the welfare state.[30] They started at the national level with general purpose and nationally focused groups like Heritage and Cato. But by the late 1980s they had begun to build a network of state-level organizations with the explicit goal of augmenting the abstract ideas of market conservativism with "the 'institutional muscle' essential to grassroots policy success."[31] With funding from conservative foundations like the Olin Foundation, the Richard & Helen DeVos Foundation, the Bradley Foundation and the Castle Rock Foundation, the State Policy Network was formed to build "the institutional capacity of state groups with training programs in the critical areas of organizational and leadership development, marketing, resource development and grassroots mobilization."[32] With funding from some of the same groups,[33] The Center for Education Reform (CER) was created in 1993 as a Washington-based, education-focused organization that could serve as a bridge between the policy ideas being bandied about in Washington and the people in states and communities who were in position to get changes put into place. Headed by a former Heritage Foundation staff member, Jeanne Allen, CER authoritatively positioned itself as a monitor of the charter school movement, combining the collection of descriptive information about state laws with a process of scoring their "strength" as a way to maintain the pressure to push for a more market-oriented, less

regulatory version. Other important beneficiaries of some of the same conservative foundations include: the Institute for Justice,[34] which bills itself as
"the nation's premier libertarian public interest law firm" and has played a key
role in pro-choice and pro-voucher litigation in many jurisdictions, including
Milwaukee, Cleveland, Florida, and the District of Columbia; Chester Finn,
a prominent advocate for choice who received more than one million dollars from the Olin Foundation to support his research and writing between
1988 and 2002; and Harvard University's Program on Education Policy and
Governance, directed by Paul Peterson, which received about $2 million from
Olin and Bradley between 1997 and 2003.[35]

## Reframing Vouchers as a Redistributory and Civil Rights Initiative

Charter schools did not completely eclipse vouchers as a conservative school
reform strategy. But, as with the shift from private-school choice to public-
school choice and charter schools, conservative strategists reframed their proposals to make them less threatening to key constituencies, more likely to
unravel the traditional public school coalition, and more able to support the
goal of creating a new "mirror image" coalition to ratchet down the welfare state. In this instance, the key step was shifting from a conception of
vouchers as a universal policy that would incorporate all school children and
fundamentally reshape the nature of American education to a smaller effort,
targeted at low-income families, those in failing schools, and primarily affecting high-minority and central-city school districts. In doing so, strong market
advocates reduced the threat that their voucher ideas would prove too unsettling to suburban and corporate Republican constituents, claimed for their
own side a set of norms relating to equity that were previously associated
almost exclusively with public schools and progressive political movements
that *laissez-faire* conservatives previously had dismissed as idealistic and misguided, sowed seeds of division within the Democratic coalition, and began
to build an empirical record that they hoped would provide compelling evidence that free markets could outperform government when put into head-
to-head competition.

The Milwaukee Parental Choice Program, initiated in 1990, was the
nation's first serious experiment with a voucher program that provided public
support for families attending private schools. Support for the bill came from
a coalition of strange bedfellows, including Republican governor Tommy
Thompson, State Representative Annette "Polly" Williams, a Democratic,
African American single parent of four children who twice chaired Jesse
Jackson's presidential campaigns in that state, and Howard Fuller, an African

American community activist, who in 1987 had proposed creating a separate school district in the predominantly black portion of the city.[36] Williams and Fuller came around to vouchers out of frustration with the failure of the local system to respond to the black community's demand for high-quality schools in their neighborhoods. They believed that integration, as implemented in the city, had been structured more for the benefit of the city's white population.[37] Their interest in vouchers, then, came less out of a commitment to market ideals than the desire to grab onto a plan—politically feasible because it had Republican support at the state level—that could shake things up and deliver some immediate benefits to their constituency.

The combination of events and actors that spawned the Milwaukee voucher program was not orchestrated by the Right, but conservative forces saw the advantages of capitalizing upon it. Williams and Fuller were adopted as voucher spokespersons and invited to travel and speak widely in favor of vouchers, often as guests of conservative groups. Williams was "lauded by the *Wall Street Journal,* called a 'courageous leader' by President Bush, and introduced to a gathering of Republican notables as 'an American hero' by the director of the conservative Landmark Center for Civil Rights."[38] After his surprise appointment as superintendent in 1991, Fuller combined support for the voucher experiment with promotion of other market-oriented approaches, including charter schools and contracting with private companies to run troubled Milwaukee schools.[39]

During its first five years, the Milwaukee voucher experiment was too small and its longevity too uncertain to have much impact locally, but it served very important functions in the national debate. The initial legislation limited the program to no more than one percent of Milwaukee Public School enrollment, but in the early years voucher participation never reached that mark. Part of the problem was insufficient demand, but perhaps more important was lack of supply. During the program's first year in operation, there were only 22 nonreligious private schools in the city. Ultimately, in order to have educational impact, voucher supporters felt they needed to attract new entrepreneurs and open up the program to include the city's religious schools. While those on the home front knew that the voucher program was a relatively paltry affair, in the national media and public dialogue it loomed large as the concrete evidence that vouchers were politically, legally, and administratively feasible and as symbolic evidence that, rather than being elitist in intent and impact, they could be a tool for addressing the needs of inner-city children and had political champions in the black community who were willing to testify to that.

Because of its symbolic position, it was critical for conservatives to at least keep the Milwaukee experiment alive and well. The Lynde & Harry Bradley Foundation, a locally based foundation established in 1985,[40] played a major role in funding Partners Advancing Values in Education (PAVE), which began offering private scholarships that could be used at religious or secular private schools. Labeled as "scholarships" in order to avoid too direct an association with the controversial notion of vouchers, these private grants were seen by at least some in the conservative community as a strategy for keeping the momentum going while the publicly funded Milwaukee program built its base and was institutionalized. As Hess observed, PAVE "was intended as a stopgap measure, offering educational options to low-income families, stabilizing enrollment at Milwaukee's secular schools, and cultivating a political constituency for the voucher program, while proponents sought to expand the MCPC to include religious schools." Bradley contributed about half a million dollars per year to PAVE during its first three years in operation, and over $2.7 million between 1986 and 1995.[41]

Initially, the redefinition of vouchers as a program for poor and minority students was primarily defensive—to blunt the charge that this was a Republican strategy for avoiding integration (as in the South) or an elitist policy what would benefit wealthy suburbanites while sucking dollars out of the traditional public schools. But advocates of vouchers discovered that framing it as a redistributive issue with a civil rights legacy issue could be a powerful positive weapon in their political battle. Targeting vouchers for the poor kept the costs low and made it less likely that vouchers would have much impact in suburban communities that were protective of their well-regarded public schools.[42] Polly Williams and Howard Fuller realized early on that vouchers had the potential to tap into the deep sense of frustration and betrayal felt in many urban minority communities about the failure of public school systems to deliver on their promises.[43] By 2004, when the 50-year anniversary of *Brown v. Board of Education* had come around, conservatives had developed a series of narratives that redefined vouchers and choice as the intellectual and moral offspring of the civil rights movement.[44] These narratives functioned both as part of a legal strategy orchestrated by the Institute for Justice and as an electoral strategy intended to assuage moderates' concerns that vouchers were a throwback to the racist resistance to desegregation.

While some conservative analysts may have been foresighted enough to recognize this on their own, it seems more likely that they backed into this realization as they witnessed the response that the Milwaukee program sparked. Beginning in 1996, the Joint Center for Political and Economic Studies began releasing polling data showing that support for vouchers was higher among African Americans than the public at large.[45] Because the Joint Center had a strong reputation within the civil rights community and among the progressive Left, these studies could not be as readily dismissed as others that had been produced by scholars or organizations with a known pro-voucher orientation. Subsequent surveys showed even stronger support in the Hispanic community.[46] Voucher proponents like Terry Moe argued that such support—proportionally highest among younger minorities—was a harbinger of a generation gap within the civil rights community and one that Republican and conservative politicians could strategically exploit.[47]

## Building an Empirical Base

In addition to buffering the Conservative agenda from charges that it was elitist and would promote resegregation, the Milwaukee voucher program was also important as a way to build an empirical complement to the theoretical arguments in favor of markets and competition as a spur to educational reform. Many market advocates were convinced that the existing system was so stultified by a self-interested educational bureaucracy that any inroads by more entrepreneurial forces would sparkle by comparison. This had contributed to the intense frustration they had felt when, during the three decades after Milton Friedman began calling for vouchers, no jurisdictions proved willing to even give the notion a try.

Milwaukee opened up a new front in this regard, but to the dismay of conservative market proponents, the initial reports from the field were mixed. John Witte's early yearly reports showed that voucher parents were highly satisfied with their new schools. But here conservatives found themselves backed into a corner of their own making. To justify their arguments about the need for radical change, they had deprecated studies showing that most Americans with children in traditional public schools thought they were doing a good job. Having staked out the position that what mattered was actual performance, they felt constrained to show that the voucher schools were doing more than keeping parents' content. Witte's evaluations suggested that the voucher students were not performing better (or worse) than similar Milwaukee public school students.

Witte was not out to torpedo the voucher idea—he was a sympathetic observer on the general issue of school choice—but on the national ideological battlefield his mixed reports were taken by voucher proponents as a serious threat. Witte became the target of numerous attacks by conservative advocates who considered him hostile to their cause, with the most visible conflicts involving Paul Peterson, a Harvard University political scientist who emerged as possibly the most prominent academic voice in favor of vouchers and choice. Their battle eventually erupted onto the front pages of the *Wall Street Journal,* where a lengthy profile noted "The two men have come to despise each other, with Mr. Witte at the Milwaukee univers_., calling his foe a 'snake' and Mr. Peterson shooting back that Mr. Witte's work is 'lousy.' "[48]

The Peterson and Witte exchanges settled out into something of a stale-mate. Although Peterson's reanalysis of the Milwaukee data claimed much more positive findings about academic achievement, advocates did not get the knockout punch they may have anticipated. Whether in Milwaukee, in a series of subsequent Peterson-directed studies of private scholarships in New York City, Dayton, Ohio, and Washington, D.C., or in a slowly emerging lit-erature evaluating charter school students' performance in various states, the evidence about academic gains associated with school choice proved much more elusive than early proponents had expected. While some researchers seemed to consistently find strong and positive gains associated with vouch-ers and charters,[49] others found negative or mixed effects at best.[50] With both sides charging the other with incompetence or dishonesty, it became difficult for even open-minded observers to figure out what was going on. Many con-cluded that the school choice debate was simply too mired in ideological and partisan conflict to ever be informed by social science research.

Despite the absence of an empirical knockout blow, the effort by conser-vative foundations to fund research on the effectiveness of school choice did serve a number of functions. First, it meant that advocates were no longer limited to making promises based on abstract economic theories; regardless of the controversy over what the evidence really showed, they could claim empirical support. The fact that Peterson's Milwaukee and private scholar-ship studies employed elements of the "gold standard" randomized field trial design enabled them to argue that their studies trumped those studies, more often using presumably weaker cross-sectional or correlational designs, cited by the other side.

Second, the Butler-like strategy of using a limited and highly targeted pro-gram as a wedge and then working to expand it succeeded. Whether vouch-ers had succeeded or not in spurring large achievement gains turned out, at the state and local level, to be less relevant to their political viability than was the fact that they had so far proven to be relatively benign. Through the 1997–1998 school year the conventional Milwaukee public school enroll-ment continued to rise despite the small number of defections to the voucher program, and per pupil expenditures rose as well. Choice proponents, at that point, could and did point out that fears that vouchers would spell the down-fall of traditional public education appeared to be misguided.

In 1995, however, with Republicans controlling the governor's office and both houses of the state legislature, Wisconsin increased the funding and allowable size of the voucher program and, most significantly, approved allow-ing religious schools to participate. The legal status on this remained murky until June 1998, when the Wisconsin Supreme Court finally ruled it consti-tutional. The expansion and institutionalization led to a dramatic increase in enrollments; in Fall 1998 there were 5,740 participating students compared to 1,501 the year before. By the 2005–2006 school year there were 14,517. Per-pupil expenditures continued to rise, but unlike before, the voucher gains were beginning to come at the expense of declining enrollments in the Milwaukee public schools (MPS). After peaking at 101,253 in 1997–1998, enrollment in MPS dropped by nearly 4,100 students by 2005–2006.[51]

Finally, the Milwaukee case was successfully promoted as a model elsewhere. Cleveland's program, begun in 1995, emulated Milwaukee's in many respects, including its targeted nature and initially small size. Enrollment remains relatively small but has increased almost every year, reaching 5,675 by Fall 2004; as in Milwaukee, the program initially did not bite into the enrollments in the conventional Cleveland public school (CPS) system, but after reaching 76,558 in 1998–1999, the number of students in CPS had slipped to about 69,5000 by 2005.[52] Most significantly, in *Zelman v. Simmons-Harris*, the Cleveland program was used as the test case to determine whether the U.S. Constitution permitted public vouchers to be used at religious schools, with the Supreme Court ruling positively in 2002.[53] Florida's Opportunity Scholarship Program and McKay Scholarship Programs for Disabled students were enacted in 1999 and 2000, respectively, and in 2004 Congress enacted a federal voucher program, on an experimental basis, for Washington, D.C.

Despite the slow expansion in the number of voucher programs, and despite the favorable Supreme Court ruling in the 2002 *Zelman* case, vouchers continue to be a harder sell politically than charter schools. But the slow and steady expansion of market-oriented educational options is consonant in a number of ways with the privatization strategy that Stuart Butler laid out over 20 years ago. Between vouchers and charter schools, over a million families have been "weaned" away from the conventional public school system, and these conceivably could become the foundation for a growing political constituency, the "mirror image" coalition to which he aspired. Probably more important from a political standpoint than the family-consumer were two types of organizational entities that provided fully mobilized interests ready to take advantage when windows of political opportunity opened. One, self-consciously planted and nurtured, involved the network of conservative think tanks, foundations, and advocacy organizations that validated and promulgated the voucher and charter school ideas.[54] Perhaps less clearly forecasted, but certainly consistent with the Butler privatization strategy, is the growing size and political muscle of an emerging sector of private sector providers of education and education services.

Before considering this new set of interest groups and the somewhat paradoxical effects they may have on the furtherance of the conservative agenda, it is necessary to attend to one final education policy initiative. The notion that a Republican president and Congress would take the lead in dramatically expanding the federal role in education was unforeseen by even the sharpest prognosticators while Ronald Reagan was continuing to sound themes about the inviolability of states' rights. No Child Left Behind is in many respects anathema to the free-market, anti-government, pro-decentralization ideals that for the most part have defined conservative education policy. But, like charters and vouchers, it is contributing to the emergence of a new set of interest groups that are likely to play a role in defining the policy landscape in the future.

## Backing into Accountability

George W. Bush gave education a much more central role in his campaign strategy than had any previous Republican presidential candidate, and No Child Left Behind (NCLB) was his signature program. On the face of it—and in many ways in fact as well—NCLB also represented a sharp reversal of traditional conservative themes. The 1980 Republican Party platform had proposed eliminating the U.S. Department of Education and dramatically shrinking the federal role. Twenty years later, education for the first time was mentioned in the preamble to the Republican Party platform, which not only acknowledged a federal role but gave that role some substantive content: "to make every school a place of learning and achievement for every child." Somewhat self-consciously walking the line between an assertion of national interest and the traditional conservative commitment to states' rights and localism, the document asserted "We will preserve local control of public schools, while demanding high standards and accountability for results."[55] Once in office, Bush, via NCLB, gave the Department of Education an unprecedented role in defining national educational priorities and holding states and localities accountable for meeting them.

What accounts for this seeming flip-flop, and is the reversal as sharp as it seems? Was Bush rejecting the conservative privatization strategy—which as originally conceived saw states and localities as more likely venues within which to pursue a shrink government agenda? Or is NCLB in some ways a culminating stage of the privatization agenda; does NCLB, as some liberals fear, deliberately set impossible standards precisely so that public school systems, having failed to meet them, will lose their core constituency and be rapidly displaced by a growing for-profit sector?

Both the expanded Republican emphasis on education and the adoption of a national standards and accountability approach are probably best understood as opportunistic adaptations rather than deep philosophical or strategic reversals. Republicans pushed education front and center because they found that a positive education agenda had political advantages; running against a federal role and championing vouchers as an alternative to traditional education were electoral liabilities. Centralized standards and accountability were anathema to many hard-core conservatives, but they appealed to the corporate element within the Republican camp and they were a natural fit for George W. Bush because he had adopted state standards and testing as governor in Texas and had apparent successes there. Moving a state-centered policy regime to Washington, D.C., is *not* an incremental step—at least it would not be one for traditional conservatives weaned on the concept of states' rights. To the extent that Bush was ideological, however, his core commitments related to notions of markets, community, and values much more than to abstract notions of how power should be divided among the levels of government.

While the high-profile testing and accountability aspects of NCLB look more like big government than small, other aspects of the legislation are consistent with the privatization-as-politics strategy outlined by Stuart Butler. Under the Supplemental Education Service (SES) component of the program, parents in Title I schools that have failed to make "adequate yearly progress" for three straight years are eligible for funding to enroll their child in afterschool, weekend, or summer tutoring programs run by for-profit corporations, or by nonprofit community-based or faith-based organizations. The funding comes from the local district's Title I allocation, and while the amount depends on various factors, it runs about $1,500 per student. Siobhan Gorman, of the *National Journal,* calls this "perhaps the federal government's largest free-market experiment in education."[56] In addition, the law establishes conditions under which both schools and entire districts might be slated for corrective action and specifically suggests that turning failing schools over to more market-oriented providers would be one appropriate response. At least potentially, then, NCLB might help to dramatically expand a nongovernmental sector of education providers that has already been growing rapidly. Consistent with Butler's theory, this could be a powerful force in the privatization "ratchet," a new lobbying force for further privatization and deregulation.

## Keeping the Religious Right on Board

Reframing the issue of school choice to put more emphasis on public choice, charter schools, helping minorities, and helping the urban poor enabled conservatives to expand their constituency, but it also presented a challenge: holding on to some of the ardent religious interests that had originally seen vouchers as a vehicle for funding private sectarian schools. While some conservatives would have preferred a much stronger and more public pursuit of this vision, political pragmatists in White House had reasons to keep this element in line.[57] President Bush offered symbolic assurances that he favored faith-based initiatives, combined with strong anti-abortion and anti-cloning rhetoric, to satisfy religious conservatives, but for the most part he avoided the trip wire of linking his education policies directly with volatile issues relating to church and state. In 2000 and 2004, this strategy seemed to be working; certainly, support from fundamentalist groups was seen as playing a major role in the Republicans' electoral success. The prospect that the Bush administration would eventually use its solidified position to bring the choice issue around again to the original voucher vision was enough to keep the religious right on board, although there appeared to be a growing sense of disappointment on this score.

## Constructing Interests: Parents Freed to Choose and The New Corporate and Nonprofit Education Sector

Two emerging developments in the political landscape around education issues appear, at least at first glance, to be particularly potent realizations of Butler's vision of creating a "mirror image" private sector coalition to counterbalance the groups that had propelled the growth of the welfare state. One involves the detachment of parents from a direct stake in the existing public school system. The other involves the substantial growth and consolidation of a corporate sector with a direct stake in the continued privatization of education provision.

The roughly 1.1 million families with children in charter schools and roughly 39,000 in voucher programs in Milwaukee, Cleveland, Florida, and Washington, D.C., may seem like a political drop in the bucket in a nation in which over 121 million voted in the last presidential election.[58] But there are at least five senses in which this may significantly understate the potential electoral impact of programs loosening voters' ties to traditional public education. First, the distribution of parents with children in existing choice venues is highly concentrated. Just six states (AZ, CA, FL, MI, OH, TX) account for two-thirds of the charter school enrollment, and in some local districts like Dayton, Ohio, and Washington, D.C., as many as one in five public school children are now attending charter schools. In select jurisdictions, in other words, the choice contingent is proportionally substantial. Second, based on past trends, the potential for this number to grow is substantial[59] and politicians and parties make tactical calculations not just on the basis of current configurations but on their best guesses of where things may lie in the next electoral cycle and beyond. Third, with the number of programs providing vouchers to private school students growing and with the *Zelman* decision seriously eroding the constitutional barriers to a universal system including religious schools, there is the possibility that parents currently in private schools will begin to see themselves as having a direct stake in the expansion of publicly funded school choice options. Private school enrollment in the U.S. was over 6.2 million in 2001 and is projected to increase by 7 percent between 2001 and 2013 (vs. a projected 4 percent increase in public schools).[60] (National Center for Education Statistics 2003). Fourth, expanding school choices options may weaken the incentive that currently exists for homeowners to support school investment even if they do not have children in the schools.

Wallace E. Oates, in a classic early analysis, found that this increase in value exceeded the added cost of the tax payments the homeowner bore,[61] but this linkage, which makes it rational for homeowners to support local school spending, depends upon the relatively tight geographical nexus between the taxation and the investment. School choice programs attenuate and potentially sever that connection.[62] A final factor supporting the notion that choice programs could substantially alter the electoral landscape is the fact that, as of mid-2008, partisan alignments in the White House and Congress rest on very narrow vote margins; after two presidential elections decided by extremely small margins, potential swing groups have an influence that is disproportionate to the number of votes they represent.

Votes, of course, are not the only currency of the realm when it comes to political power. Interest groups with a strong lobbying presence have the capacity to alter the shape of legislation and regulation in ways that are no less consequential—and possibly are more so—because they happen outside the bright lights of election campaigns. Conservative education policies of the past two decades have opened up new lines of business for the private sector. Educational management organizations (EMOs) are for-profit companies that operate or work with charter schools, contract with districts to manage troubled schools, or provide supplementary education services. Their nonprofit counterparts, typically labeled charter management organizations (CMOs), are different in style and public persona, but also aggressively cultivate an entrepreneurial and management-oriented approach to improving education.

Although the ultimate economic viability of the EMO/CMO industry is still a subject of debate,[63] the existing evidence shows that their inroads are expanding.[64] This expanding private-provider education sector is free to pursue their interests as political actors as well as market competitors. In interviewing politicians and advocacy groups in four states, I and my colleagues have found evidence not only that these organizations are active lobbyists but also that, in at least some cases, conservative proponents of vouchers and less regulated charter school regimes have deliberately cultivated these organizations in order to add muscle and legitimacy to their agenda.[65] NCLB and state accountability programs have also given a huge boost to textbook publishers and testing companies.[66] And the rapid consolidation that is underway makes it likely that publishers, testing companies, and education management organizations will increasingly be vertically integrated and larger in size and market share.

This emerging private education sector may sharpen a previously latent split within the pro-choice movement, as well as highlight the fact that business is not monolithic in its stance toward education reform. As we have seen, some of the key financial support for vouchers and more *laissez-faire* visions of school choice have come from family foundations created by very conservative individuals who made their fortunes in business. More mainstream elements of the corporate sector—as represented, for example, by the Business Roundtable, an association comprising the chief executive officers of some of the country's largest firms—in general have tended to shy away from more radical plans like vouchers, preferring instead to emphasize standards, accountability, and increased achievement, especially in reading and mathematics.[67] Searching on the Business Roundtable's web site[68] using the term "NCLB," for example, returns 50 documents, while searching on term vouchers returns only 9. In culture, size, and interests, the newly emerging education corporate sector is more likely to align with this arm of the business community than with the maverick conservatives that have funded the voucher movement. And rather than a wild and wooly market, they may prefer a more stable and predictable environment in which they negotiate long-term contracts with public officials inclined to be sympathetic because these corporations can make them more effective or because they are a part of the coalition that keeps them in office.

## Concluding Thoughts: A Conservative Strategy Realized or a Thrust Parried?

Much that Stuart Butler laid out in the middle of the Reagan Era has come to pass. The assumption that the public good depends on government growth has been seriously eroded. In education, where loyalties to the vision of the public common school are strong, charter schools—and to a lesser extent vouchers—have taken firm hold, and reliance on traditional school districts as the vehicle for delivering education services is no longer a given. Substantial numbers of families, particularly in some jurisdictions, now look to the private sector for education. Some of the groups that historically have supported public education spending are weaker now (notably the unions), while other occasional allies (local business interests; homeowners) have reasons to be less loyal and committed than in the past. Conservative foundations have spawned a network of think tanks and advocacy organizations in Washington and the states that make it their mission to hone the market ideal and give it a practical political and legal edge. By tactically muting anti-government language, promoting charter schools as "public" institutions, and reframing vouchers as progressive policies, free-market conservatives bypassed some opposition and formed coalitions of convenience that let them enlist as allies groups that would resist signing on to an explicitly libertarian or socially conservative agenda.

In some instances, events seem to have unfolded strictly according to the conservative game plan. The planting and protecting of the Milwaukee voucher program falls into this category, as does the very focused use of foundation resources to meld ideas and action.[69] In other cases, conservatives have proven quick on their feet in adjusting to and exploiting trends that they did not foresee. Examples include their rapid adoption of a charter school movement they did not originate, their reformulation of vouchers as a civil rights initiative, and their use of the accountability movement to enfranchise parent choice and private providers as favored responses when schools and districts fail to meet demanding standards for adequate yearly progress.

It would be a mistake, though, to read this as a story about how canny, united, and foresighted conservatives bested a slow-witted, fractious, and backward-looking Left. Incrementalism, for Butler, was a strategy for surreptitious radicalism, but after more than two decades of small gains, even some patient conservatives are frustrated by the resilience of what they regard as a bloated and reactionary public education sector. That traditional public school districts overwhelmingly dominate K-12 education has made it clearer than ever that the American public retains a powerful allegiance to the idea of publicly funded, publicly delivered education and the goal of a common schooling experience for children of diverse backgrounds.[70] Conservatives, too, had no exclusive franchise on smart politics; although some on the Left interpreted this as capitulation, by refusing to cede charter schools to the free-marketeers, Clinton and a handful of traditionally pro-education interest groups kept alive the notion that charter schools should be considered evidence of the flexibility of public institutions rather than the superiority of markets. That strategy arguably blunted the advance of more radical voucher options. And, by buying time, it allowed empirical evidence to accumulate that choice was not the *panacea* that conservatives had proclaimed it to be.

Ironically, some elements of the conservative privatization campaign may backfire. Butler was alert to fact that some plans to create a mirror image, anti-spending coalition could work the other way. Reflecting on defense contractors[71] and the medical industry, he identified as a major drawback to contracting out the risk that private providers become a part of the pro-spending coalition. Similarly, some interests that conservatives hoped to wean from the public education constituency may yet prove to be part of a new iron triangle that works to keep the basic contours of the publicly funded and regulated system intact. Whether charter school parents will align with private school parents as advocates for further privatization or with traditional public school parents as advocates for greater spending (since charter school funding is usually tied to per-pupil funding in the traditional public sphere) is an empirical question that has not yet been answered. There is some evidence that charter schools are growing at least in part at the expense of private schools, so if these parents do become advocates for more per pupil spending, it is possible that the net effect will be to create more voters in favor of pro-spending candidates. Although charter school advocacy organizations have typically fought to limit governmental oversight and regulatory constraints, high profile closures of dysfunctional charter schools have moderated this, with some advocates calling for stronger and more effective oversight as a way to reduce the risk that embarrassing "bad apples" will tarnish the image of the movement overall.

Finally, it is by no means certain that the emerging corporate sector will be a reliable ally to those who wish to displace government. Corporate providers of curriculum, testing, and school management services may be more comfortable—and more profitable—working with government than individual parent/consumers who can be inattentive, fickle, and hard to reach. Private-sector NCLB supplementary education service providers that can strike deals with local district leadership, for example, get easier access to school buildings as sites of delivery, to teachers as potential part-time employees (as tutors), and to the principal and teachers as endorsers of the notion that their products mesh with the school. Lobbying government, in a range of circumstances, can be a smarter way to do business than selling door to door.

## Acknowledgments

The author would like to thank Jonah Liebert, a doctoral student in politics and education at Teachers College, for his helpful work as research assistant. For editorial suggestions and stimulating notions, he also thanks Brian Glenn, Steve Teles, Patrick McGuinn, David Mayhew, and other contributors to and commentators upon this volume.

### Notes

1. Margaret Caldwell, *The New Republic* (November 7, 1983) 189: 8–12.
2. Edward B. Fiske, "Reagan Agenda: Taking New Tack" *New York Times,* January 27, 1988, B8.

3. Political scientists have paid a great deal of attention in recent years to accounting for sharp policy change in a political system generally regarded as having multiple veto points and a structural and cultural bias toward incrementalism. I draw in part on Kingdon's classic account of the ways in which "windows of opportunity" may allow political entrepreneurs a chance to push onto the agenda policy notions that had been percolating for years. Compared to both Kingdon and Baumgartner and Jones, I place greater reliance here on the ways in which dynamics in *other* policy issue areas may have accounted for the emergence of privatization and vouchers on the education policy agenda (Baumgartner and Jones 1993; Kingdon 1995).

4. E. S. Savas, *Privatization and Public-Private Partnerships* (New York: Chatham House, 2000).

5. Stuart M. Butler, *Privatizing Federal Spending: A Strategy to Eliminate the Deficit* (New York: Universe Books, 1985).

6. Ibid., 3.

7. Jeanne Allen, writing on the Center for Education Reform web site: http://www.edreform.com/info/blob.htm (accessed 10/31/2006).

8. Butler, *Privatizing Federal Spending,* 43.

9. Ibid., 45.

10. Ibid.

11. Ibid., 47.

12. Ibid., 61.

13. Lowell C. Rose and Alec M. Gallup, "The 35th Annual Phi Delta Kappa/Gallup Poll of the Public's Attitudes toward The Public Schools," *Phi Delta Kappan* (2003): 85: 41–52.

14. Leah Y. Latimer, "Reagan Speech Site Fits Bill; Suitland High Showcases Administration Policies," *The Washington Post* (January 20, 1988), B01.

15. Jeffrey R. Henig, *Rethinking School Choice: Limits of the Market Metaphor* (Princeton, NJ: Princeton University Press, 1994).

16. Patrick McGuinn explains the Reagan administration's ambivalence about *A Nation at Risk,* which sharply critiqued the current system—as Reagan would have wanted—but which also seemed to endorse the kind of strong public sector and national responses that Reagan initially campaigned against (McGuinn, *No Child Left Behind and the Transformation of Federal Education Policy 1965–2005* (Lawrence: University Press of Kansas, 2006).

17. See Jeffrey Henig, *Spin Cycle: How Research Is Used in Policy Debates: The Case of Charter Schools* (New York: Russell Sage/Century Foundation, 2008) for an expanded treatment of the political history of charter schools and an analysis of how this affected the polarized presentation of education research in public debate.

18. Ibid., Ch. 3.

19. Most, but not all, states bar charter schools from using admissions criteria to screen out applicants; typically, if oversubscribed they are required to allocate positions by lottery.

20. Tim Mazzoni and Barry Sullivan, "Legislating Educational Choice in Minnesota: Politics and Prospects" in *Choice in Education: Potential and Problems*, ed. W. L. Boyd and H. J. Walberg (Berkeley, CA: McCutchan, 1990); Michael Mintrom, *Policy Entrepreneurs and School Choice* (Washington, DC: Georgetown University Press, 2000); Joe Nathan, *Free to Teach: Achieving Equity and Excellence in Schools* (New York: The Pilgrim Press, 1991); Joe Nathan, *Charter Schools: Creating Hope and Opportunity for American Education* (San Francisco: Jossey-Bass Publishers, 1999).

21. Gregg Vanourek, *State of the Charter School Movement 2005: Trends, Issues, and Indicators,* (Washington, DC: Charter School Leadership Council, 2005).

22. The same kind of communal, anti-bureaucratic, pro-options values that propelled charters in Minnesota gave it appeal to many at the grassroots level in other states. The rapid spread across the states, however, probably had more to do with the pragmatic appeal to legislators (charters initially seemed like a low-cost way for politicians to show voters that they were serious about reform, and, for reasons discussed in the text, one that was acceptable to both Democratic and Republican party elites).

23. Dave Durenberger, "Minnesota's Choice," *Washington Post* (September 10, 1991): A:19.

24. Center for Education Reform, *Just the FAQs—Charter Schools* (2005), http://www.edreform.com/index.cfm?fuseAction=document&documentID=60.

25. Jeffrey R. Henig, Thomas T. Holyoke, Natalie Lacireno-Paquet, and Michele M. Moser, "Privatization, Politics, and Urban Services: The Political Behavior of Charter Schools," *Journal of Urban Affairs* 25, 1 (February 2003): 37–54.

26. McGuinn, *No Child Left Behind.*

27. Ibid.; Henig, *Rethinking School Choice.*

28. McGuinn, *No Child Left Behind*, 81.

29. Ibid., 125.

30. Andrew Rich, *Think Tanks, Public Policy, and the Politics of Expertise* (New York: Cambridge University Press, 2004).

31. State Policy Network, "Why State Policy Network is Needed," (2006), http://www.spn.org/about_spn/purpose.asp (accessed January 28, 2006).

32. Ibid.

33. Early funders included Olin, Scaife, and Bradley.

34. Besides Scaife, Olin, and Bradley, each of which has provided substantial support going back to the organization's earliest year, a major early donor was the Charles R. Lambe Charitable Foundation.

35. All figures on grants are from http://www.mediatransparency.org.

36. Frederick M. Hess, *Revolution at the Margins: The Impact of Competition on Urban School Systems* (Washington, DC: Brookings Institution Press, 2002).

37. Fuller, 2000.

38. Henig, *Rethinking School Choice,* 114.

39. Fuller, after resigning as superintendent in 1995, continued to be a visible and important advocate for vouchers, launching, with support from the conservative Walton Family Fund, the Black Alliance for Education Options [0](BAEO) in the summer of 2000. "Community Voice or Captive of the Right?: A Closer Look at the Black Alliance for Educational Options," *People for American Way*, http://www.pfaw.org/pfaw/general/default.aspx?oid=1404.

40. According to the National Committee for Responsive Philanthropy, a nonprofit organization that has kept a critical eye focused on conservative foundations, Harry Bradley "was a right-wing political activist affiliated with the John Birch Society." The foundation, which received its endowment from the sale of the Allen-Bradley Corporation to Rockwell International, has treated Milwaukee as a "laboratory" for projects furthering its vision that the "good society is a free society." Jeff Krehely, Meaghan House, and Emily Kernan, *Axis of Ideology: Conservative Foundations and Public Policy* (Washington, DC: National Committee for Responsive Philanthropy, 2004).

41. Hess, *Revolution at the Margins,* 88, 105.

42. The Altman and Marmor chapter in this volume notes how conservatives favored model of grants to states targeted at the poor; thus voucher strategy is not *sui generis*. It lowers costs and keeps program constituency limited to groups that are politically weak.

43. Apple and Pederoni suggest that conservative voucher supporters and strange bedfellows like Fuller and Williams may each have been hoping to co-opt the other. Michael W. Apple and Thomas C. Pedroni, "Conservative Alliance Building and African American Support of Vouchers: The End of Brown's Promise or a New Beginning?," *Teachers College Record* (2005) 107: 2068–2105.

44. Lisa M. Stulberg, "School Choice Discourse and the Legacy of Brown," *Journal of School Choice* 1 (2006): 23–45.

45. David A. Bositis, *2002 National Opinion Poll: Education* (Washington, DC: Joint Center for Political and Economic Studies).

46. The 2002 survey by the Joint Center for Political and Economic Studies, for example, found that 60.8 percent of Hispanics supported vouchers, versus 57.4 percent of blacks and 51.4 percent of non-Hispanic whites.

47. Terry M. Moe, *Schools, Vouchers, and the American Public* (Washington, DC: Brookings Institution Press, 2001). I argue elsewhere that conservatives' tactical exploitation of voucher support among minorities has the potential to strengthen the electoral and governance power of Republicans, even if it does not produce any substantial voting support from minorities Jeffrey R. Henig, "Understanding the Political Conflict over School Choice," in *How School Choice Affects Students and Families Who Do Not Choose,* ed. J. R. Betts and T. Loveless (Washington, DC: Brookings Institution Press, 2005).

48. Bob Davis, "Class Warfare: Dueling Professors Have Milwaukee Dazed over School Vouchers—Studies on Private Education Result in a Public

Spat about Varied Conclusions—Candidates Debate the Point," *Wall Street Journal,* October 11, 1996, A1. While there is no doubt that relations between Peterson and Witte were hostile at that time, there is a chance that Davis overstated the intractability of the gulf. After a cooling-off period, the two political scientists came sufficiently to terms that by 2006 they were cooperating on a subsequent study of Milwaukee vouchers.

49. Jay P. Greene, "Choosing Integration," in *School Choice and Diversity: What the Evidence Says,* ed. J. Scott (New York: Teachers College Press, 2005); William G. Howell and Paul E. Peterson, *The Education Gap: Vouchers and Urban schools* (Washington, DC: Brookings Institution Press, 2002); William G. Howell and Paul E. Peterson, "Uses of Theory in Randomized Field Trials: Lessons from School Voucher Research on Disaggregation, Missing Data, and the Generalization of Findings," *The American Behavioral Scientist* 47, 5 (2004): 634; Caroline M. Hoxby, "Does Competition among Public Schools Benefit Students and Taxpayers?" *The American Economic Review* 90, 5 (2002): 1209–39; Caroline M. Hoxby, *Achievement in Charter Schools and Regular Public Schools in the United States: Understanding the Differences* (Cambridge, MA: Harvard University Press, 2004).

50. Alan B. Krueger and Pei Zhu, "Another Look at the New York City School Voucher Experiment," *The American Behavioral Scientist* 4, 5 (2004): 658ff; Helen F. Ladd, "Market-Based Reforms in Urban Education," (Washington, DC: Economic Policy Institute, 2000); Gary Miron and Christopher Nelson, *What's Public about Charter Schools: Lessons Learned about Choice and Accountability* (Thousand Oaks, CA: Corwin Press, 2002); F. Howard Nelson, Bella Rosenberg, and Nancy Van Meter, "Charter School Achievement on the 2003 National Assessment of Educational Progress" (Washington, DC: American Federation of Teachers, 2004).

51. Enrollment data from http://www.schoolchoiceinfo.org.

52. Ibid.

53. 536 U.S. 639 (2002).

54. Henig, *Spin Cycle;* Krehely, House, and Kernan, *Axis of Ideology.* See, for example, Clint Bolick, *Voucher Wars* (Washington DC: Cato Institute, 2003) for an informative, albeit politically slated, insider's account of how conservative-funded legal advocates pursued a judicial strategy culminating in the *Zelman* victory.

55. 2000 Republican Party platform, 1.

56. Siobhan Gorman, "The Invisible Hand of No Child Left Behind" in *Leaving No Child Behind? Options for Kids in Failing Schools.,* ed. Frederic M. Hess and Chester E. Finn, Jr. (New York: Palgrave, 2004).

57. According to one account, Karl Rove and other influential advisors were self-conscious in their efforts to placate fundamentalist leaders whom they ridiculed in private for pushing policies that would be politically damaging. David Kuo, *Tempting Faith: An Inside Story of Political Seduction* (New York: Free Press, 2006).

58. Converting enrollments into potential voters is an inexact process. If we imagined that all choice students represented distinct households comprising two parents, we could double the number and infer that about 2.1 million votes might be at stake. But some households have multiple children within choice venues, and some choice households are headed by single parents. As argued in the text, the precise number of votes directly involved may be less relevant than such matters as the number of households that feel less constrained to the public schools or the extent to which choice families end up as part of the constituency supporting public investment in education or the constituency favoring greater reliance on private investment.

59. Vanourek, *State of the Charter School Movement 2005*.

60. National Center for Education Statistics, *Projections of Education Statistics to 2013*. Washington DC: U.S. Department of Education, 2003.

61. Wallace E. Oates, "The Effects of Property Taxes and Local Public Spending on Property Values: An Empirical Study of Tax Capitalization and the Tiebout Hypothesis," *Journal of Political Economy* 77, 6 (1969): 957–71.

62. Henig, "Understanding the Political Conflict over School Choice"; Randall Reback, "Capitalization under Schools Choice Programs: Are the Winners Really Losers?" (New York: National Center for the Study of Privatization in Education, 2002), occasional paper no. 66.

63. Bill Barket, "Is Edison Schools a Rule Breaker?," *The Motley Fool,* May 4, 2000; http://www.fool.com/portfolios/rulebreaker/2000/rulebreaker000920.htm. Henry Levin, "Potential of For-Profit Schools for Educational Reform" (New York: National Center for the Study of Privatization in Education, 2002), occasional paper no. 47; Chris Whittle, *Crash Course: Imagining a Better Future for Public Education* (New York: Riverhead Books, 2005).

64. 65. Henig et al., "Privatization, Politics, and Urban Services."

66. Bracey, *The War against America's Public Schools;* Andrew Brownstein and Travis Hicks, "Reading First under Fire," in *Title I Monitor, Education Research Funding Council* (Washington, DC: Thompson Publishing Group, 2005); Alex Molnar, *School Commercialism; From Democratic Ideal to Market Commodity* (New York: Routledge, 2005); Kenneth J. Saltman, *The Edison Schools: Corporate Schooling and the Assault on Public Education* (New York: Routledge, 2005).

67. On the role of the mainstream business leaders as a "moderating" force in national education policy, see Christopher T. Cross, *Political Education: National Policy Comes of Age* (New York: Teachers College Press, 2004).

68. http://www.businessroundtable.org/. Search conducted April 13, 2006.

69. National Committee for Responsive Philanthropy, "Axis of Ideology: Conservative Foundations and Public Policy" (Washington, DC: National Committee for Responsive Philanthropy, 2004); Rich, *Think Tanks, Public Policy, and the Politics of Expertise*.

70. Butler, *Privatizing Federal Spending,* 56.

71. Ibid., 93.

# CONCLUSION

## Conservatism and American Political Development

*Brian J. Glenn and Steven M. Teles*

Modern American conservatism is both a cause and consequence of American political development. The preceding chapters showed how conservatives moved from a disparate collection of groups, focused on various domains of public policy, to a remarkably coherent movement capable of collective learning and strategy. The development of modern conservatism was, in large part, a response to the state built by modern liberalism. As liberalism and the state developed, so did conservatism—in terms of its ideals, its coalitional strategies, and its forms of organization. Conservatism was reshaped by the liberal policy regime it sought to dislodge.

Conservatism has also been an important cause of American political development. As liberals began to devote their attention to each of the three issues discussed in this book, the initial response by conservatives was to attack the intervention on fundamental or constitutional grounds: that is, to attempt a reversal of a major liberalism-led developmental shift. While they were typically unsuccessful in halting the state from expanding its responsibilities, the power of conservative interests and ideas in American politics did significantly shape what American state-builders believed was possible. As all our authors made clear, both the character and the extent of American policy development were conditioned by the anticipation of, and in some cases outright confrontation with, conservative interests.

In all three areas, conservatives eventually shifted from constitutional rejection to grudging acceptance of the modern state. Well into the 1970s, this left conservatives in the uncomfortable position of having accepted the fundamental commitments of the modern activist state while lacking the ideas or institutional capacity to offer alternative means by which they could be vindicated. It was not until well into the 1980s that conservatives acquired this capacity, and even then, their ability to reconfigure the modern state significantly has, at least in the areas under study, been limited.

Conservatives have, in short, been far from triumphant. Unable to roll back the liberal state they inherited, contemporary conservatives have instead been forced to offer their own market-based versions of activist government. Despite their inability to enact many of these policies on a broad scale—and their considerable political setbacks in the 2006 election—their strategies still hold the potential for profound long-term policy change.

## Who Were Conservatives? From the Old Right to Modern Conservatism

The ideas and actors that went under the name of "conservatism" at the time of the New Deal were very different creatures from their modern counterparts. Conservatism in the early years of our study was characterized by constitutional opposition to the growth of the state and a philosophical aversion to liberal norms of equality and a role for government in correcting market failures. As liberalism became more entrenched, this antistatist form of conservatism gradually gave way to a statist, or modern, conservatism that accepted liberalism's goals while claiming that its means had become ossified and ineffective in achieving the goals to which they aspired.

Consider first Social Security. As Berkowitz and DeWitt argue, the "conservative" argument at the time of Social Security's passage (enunciated by, among others, the Republican Party's 1936 nominee for the presidency, Alf Landon) was that the provision of universal pensions on a national scale violated the enumerated powers of the federal government. When this argument lost traction, many conservatives claimed that Social Security was not what its supporters claimed it was—insurance—but rather an unsustainable welfare program doomed to collapse under its own weight. Conservatives mocked the program's actuarial unsoundness and looked forward to the day when they would pick up the pieces when the program fell apart. In the meantime, conservatives believed that the best they could do was keep a lid on the program's growth and ensure that taxes kept up with benefits, in order to prevent a politics of "something for nothing."

Altman and Marmor show that, as time went on and Social Security failed to collapse, conservatives in Congress settled for directing the program's development from positions of institutional strength rather than shouting in the wilderness. This position frustrated libertarian-leaning politicians and intellectuals such as Barry Goldwater and Milton Friedman, who believed that Alf Landon's uncompromising position represented the true faith. Neither the conservatism of the congressmen who accepted their role as the right wing of the program's establishment nor that of the root-and-branch critics succeeded in halting the growth of the program, and, by the late 1970s, critics of the program had become convinced that Social Security was politically "uncontrollable."[1]

By the early 1980s, conservatives had carved out the foundations of a new approach to Social Security. Even conservative and libertarian true-believers no longer questioned a role for the federal government in guaranteeing a standard of living for the elderly, nor did they simply promise a slightly smaller, more fiscally sound version of the liberal vision. Instead, conservatives began to advocate their own, market-driven mechanisms for achieving liberalism's goal of widespread retirement security, and sought to change the political conversation through judging Social Security by its "rate of return." This approach accepted the existence of coercive taxes for the purpose of retirement insurance, but argued that those taxes could produce greater wealth if invested in private accounts rather than Social Security. Markets could beat Social Security at its own game.

A similar shift can be seen in the environment. When modern environmentalism burst on the stage in the mid-1960s, conservatives held firm to the previous bipartisan orthodoxy: production was good, nature was resilient, the effect of pollution on human health and the ecosystem was vastly overstated, private property was inviolate, and states and localities should decide on the use of their own resources. Conservatives also questioned the constitutional propriety of modern environmentalism, especially its transformation of federalism and the role of courts in agency decision making.

Starting in the late 1970s, the position of conservatives toward environmental policy shifted. As Richard Harris describes, the first critics out of the box were environmental economists, most of whom were not self-described conservatives. They accepted the goals of environmental protection but questioned the efficiency and effectiveness of the modern environmental regime.

Following these economists were "free-market environmentalists" who, as Judy Layzer shows, also accepted the reality of environmental dangers but argued that private property rights were superior to command and control for delivering on ecological goals. Finally, conservatives argued that in contrast to the purportedly sensible, empirical approach of modern conservatives, environmentalism had transformed itself into a new secular religion that was a threat to American institutions and traditions.

In no other area of our study is the difference between anti-statist and modern conservatism as stark as in education. Here, as Gareth Davies argues, conservatives once combined a claim to defending the tradition of a constitutionally limited federal role with a suspicion of the efficacy or desirability of education to promote the social or political equality of the poor and racial minorities. Patrick McGuinn shows that, in the wake of the 1960s explosion of federal government activism in education, conservatives began to shift their ground, accepting the goals of equality of educational opportunity, especially for urban blacks, but claiming that increased spending through federal categorical programs showed little effect on the achievement of disadvantaged groups. By the 1980s, as Jeffrey Henig demonstrates, conservatives had moved from critique to construction, arguing that liberal-controlled institutions were part of the cause of the poor educational performance of disadvantaged groups, especially African Americans. In order to attain the goal of educational equality, competition and accountability needed to be injected into schooling through vouchers and charter schools, but targeted precisely at the groups that earlier conservatives hoped to let whites flee: poor, inner-city black children.

In all three of these cases, conservatives adapted to the standards—retirement security, environmental protection, and educational opportunity—of the regime they previously sought to displace. How did this happen? How did conservatism move from a challenge to the legitimacy of a strong federal state, a defense of untrammeled private property, and an enemy of egalitarianism to a faith that claimed that it could use national power to achieve the goals of equality and efficiency more effectively than could liberalism?

## The Quandary of Antistatist Conservatism

Conservatism as we now know it did not exist prior to the New Deal, or indeed, for quite some time afterward. American politics was not organized by the ideas of liberalism and conservatism primarily because the issues that give those concepts meaning in contemporary politics—such as social insurance, environmental regulation, and education policy—were almost wholly nonexistent at the national level. The federal government did not even have an income tax until the Sixteenth Amendment to the Constitution made it possible, and as a result, most Americans did not feel the weight of taxes on their shoulders as they later would. Indeed, the few existing *progressive* social safety programs were so meager that they were later adopted as the *conservative* alternative to the New Deal.

This is not to say that there was nothing conservative about American public policy. In fact, almost everything about American public policy at the federal level up through the 1930s would now be considered extremely conservative. Redistribution was extremely limited, unions were weak, governmental involvement with the national economy did not reach far beyond tariffs, antitrust, and delivering the mail, and the mighty president of the United States had a staff of fewer than a dozen. Progressives found themselves repeatedly stymied by the U.S. Supreme Court, and *laissez-faire*, with a few important exceptions, ruled the day.[2]

Franklin Delano Roosevelt's election during the Great Depression helped produce the conditions that facilitated the growth of modern conservatism. Coming into office with a mandate from the people to "do something," FDR introduced a broad range of policies designed to stabilize the economy, regulate the workplace, and put in place a social safety net. His administration also brought with it a vision of liberalism in which administrative power would be used to protect the social and economic rights of an increasingly wide range of Americans.

The lasting importance of New Deal liberalism lies in the fact that, more than just a series of policies, liberalism was also an ideology, and one whose sweeping ambition struck fear in the hearts of those unconvinced by FDR's belief in a benevolent state. From fear came mobilization, and the antistatist conservatism that emerged in the wake of the New Deal was fundamentally about being *against* liberalism, far more than being *for* something. The first generation of conservatives were united by opposition to government intervention in social and economic spheres that had previously either been left to the states and localities, or had not been considered part of the public realm at all.

## Coalition Building against a Rising Establishment

> *You need not be taken in by the solemn whisper that the Establishment has a president, an executive committee, a constitution, bylaws, and formal membership requirements, to believe that there do exist people of varying prestige and power within American Liberaldom; that we speak here of the intellectual plutocrats of the*

*nation, who have at their disposal vast cultural and
financial resources; and that it is possible at any given
moment to plot with fair accuracy the vectors of the
Establishment's position on everything.*
                                    —William F. Buckley

The "establishment" of which Buckley spoke was made up of liberals found in all corners of the federal government, elite universities, the *New York Times,* and institutions like the Council on Foreign Relations and the Ford Foundation. Combined with the political power of the Democratic Party and the rising force of the union movement, the liberal establishment was an impressive ideational and policy-making force—impressive, that is, where it directed its attention. As Davies and Eisner both reveal in their respective chapters, through the 1950s liberals did not devote significant attention to education or the environment, and, as a result, there was little conservative mobilization either. Of the policies examined in this book, the one that produced the earliest conservative countermobilization was the Social Security Act of 1935.

While today we think of Social Security as a public policy primarily targeting the elderly, as Berkowitz and DeWitt show, it was initiated as a broad antipoverty program. Its primary opponents were the businesses that would have to start paying taxes on their employee's wages, and aside from a handful of large, progressive manufacturers, industry large and small was unified against the Social Security Act. These businessmen were the original conservatives, desperately clinging to a *laissez-faire* doctrine they believed had served their interests—and the nation as a whole—quite well since the founding.

This generation of antistatist conservatives were typically in favor of an unregulated market, but were primarily motivated by suspicion of and resistance to centralized, bureaucratic national government that they saw as threatening to social traditions and local government. Their earliest objections to the expansion of government into new areas, therefore, typically centered on the claim that a given intervention was unconstitutional rather than simply unwise or poorly designed. This idea had important implications for conservative political strategy and coalition formation, and helps explain the relative inefficacy of conservatism in responding to the growth of the state.

## Elite Actors in the Face of the New Deal Tidal Wave

The conservatism that emerged from the New Deal was composed of the disparate opponents of the growing American state, who were lacking in strong organizations or networks to coordinate a coherent response to modern liberalism. Many conservatives put their faith in the courts, which they hoped would save them—as they had in the Progressive Era—by ruling the new programs unconstitutional. Consequently, when they developed at all, grassroots battles were fought on a policy-by-policy basis rather than being coordinated with one another.

While interested parties were (for the most part unsuccessfully) battling in the courts and Congress to prevent liberal policies from being enacted, there was another group of conservative actors competing for the hearts and minds of Americans at the level of high theory. Public intellectuals such as Russell Kirk, Albert Jay Nock, Richard Weaver, William Henry Chamberlin, and Friedrich Hayek sought to convince Americans of New Deal liberalism's dangers and the advantages of returning to life prior to its ascension. While some of these authors reached a mass audience—Hayek would sell a million copies of *The Road to Serfdom* and become a household name—conservatives still lacked an intelligentsia as broad or as institutionally well-positioned as that of their liberal opponents. Through the 1940s and 1950s, conservatives slowly built new kinds of organizations, like the Mont Pelerin Society, to marshal their intellectual forces, but at the time, little of this activity resonated with practical policy making.

Thus, up through World War II, conservatives had yet to coalesce into anything resembling a movement. They fought new federal policies on a piecemeal basis, and had few ideas of their own to offer up as viable alternatives. Their program was a call for returning to the pre–New Deal *laissez-faire* politics. Unfortunately for them, the memory of the Great Depression stood fresh in Americans' minds, and thus "the good old days" did not look all that good.

## Old Ideas in a New Era

Clinging to the past, antistatist conservatives in all three areas initially challenged the constitutionality of the new federal programs. They had done so successfully in education since the founding, and as Davies notes in his chapter, up through the 1950s there was still a bipartisan consensus that education was a state and local issue. While anticommunism, antistatism, a fear of bureaucracy, and the idea of parental control all informed conservative arguments against federal intervention, even FDR's own administration believed education was a local affair, despite powerful arguments in favor of a well-educated polity. The same held true for environmental regulation. Roosevelt, Truman, and Eisenhower largely ignored environmental issues, in part because their attention was elsewhere, but also in part because, with a few exceptions, they believed the federal government's proper role was to allow the economy to flourish through utilizing the nation's vast natural resources. Until the 1960s, constitutional constraints on the federal government helped divert attention away from these two fields.

Social welfare was different. By the time of the Social Security Act of 1935, 30 states or territories had old-age pension laws on their books, and the common law doctrine preventing states from granting pensions to anyone who had not given hazardous duty had been toppled. Despite these changes, Berkowitz and DeWitt point out that Social Security's passage was anything but guaranteed. Conservatives both inside and outside Congress challenged the Act's increased taxes, questioned the wisdom of maintaining an enormous financial reserve, and called upon the constitutional grounds of federalism and freedom to contract. Despite these arguments, old-age pensions were popular with the public, as we know from the success of state campaigns where both Democratic- and Republican-controlled legislatures passed them after witnessing strong grassroots support. Despite substantial mobilization of resources and ideas in opposition to the Social Security Act, opponents utterly failed to generate grassroots opposition.

In summary, there was no real "conservative coalition" before the 1960s, at least not one visible in the world of Washington policy making.[3] Opponents of federal expansion in the three policy areas did not see themselves as having a common set of interests, and although they were unified by a belief that the constitution limited the powers and reach of the federal government, that idea carried little weight once the liberal coalition directed its attention to a new area of public policy.

## *The Lack of a Conservative Infrastructure*

In addition to lacking ideas and coalitions, conservatives had few coordinating organizations either within or between issue areas. Where conservative organizational capacity is the story of the final chapters, it might fairly be said that the consequences of a lack of such capacity is the story of the early ones. By the 1940s, the executive branch, including the White House, had developed large, well-funded staffs of experts capable of generating policy proposals connected to social science research, and from this point on, government itself became a powerful impetus for change. At the same time, Washington think tanks and national research universities expanded as a source of policy ideas, generally with an expansionary (if not always particularly ideological) bias. Conservatives were woefully unprepared to compete with the analytical and agenda-shaping prowess of these governmental and nongovernmental actors, and consequently engaged with politics almost exclusively at the electoral and intellectual level.

In most policies, both foreign and domestic, conservatives lacked the organizational capacity to confront "the establishment" on its own terms until well into the 1980s. Their lack of organizational capacity limited their ability to generate alternatives to the policies proposed by the modern state, or to reach out to like-minded legislators and the general public. As Berkowitz and DeWitt note, once the Social Security Act passed Congress and was challenged in the courts, both sides had to prepare briefs for the several cases that followed, most significantly *Helvering v. Davis* (1936). The Committee on Economic Security, which after the bill's passage morphed into the Social Security Board, brought in the best minds on social insurance in America. It drew from academe, the American Association of Labor Legislation, and its own staff of highly trained economists, actuaries, and attorneys. These specialists generated a 221-page study, "Economic Insecurity in Old Age: Social and Economic Factors Contributing to Old-Age Dependency," which argued that the Great Depression had fundamentally altered the nature of poverty in America. As our authors note, this research formed two-thirds of the government's brief in front of the U.S. Supreme Court. The plaintiffs, on the other hand, relied on the Old Right notion that the entire scheme was predicated on unconstitutional powers, and their 61-page brief was entirely doctrinal. The Court forthrightly declared that the Great Depression had consigned older ideas of federalism to the jurisprudential graveyard, arguing that "the purge of nationwide calamity that began in 1929 has taught us many lessons. Not the least is the solidarity of interests that may once have seemed to be divided."[4] Out-organized at the elite level, conservatives could not compete in the new intellectual context produced by the New Deal.

The period immediately following the passage of the Social Security Act presented the best opportunity to besmirch it in the minds of the general public, as workers were paying taxes in the middle of the Great Depression without seeing any benefit from them for a significant number of years into the future. When they handed out paychecks, employers opposed to the new legislation included slips of paper pointing out the loss of income from taxes, and combined them with arguments against the various programs—all to no avail. While no one wanted to pay more in taxes, Americans then and now were willing to pay for benefits they thought worthwhile, and old age protection was one of them. What opponents of Social Security lacked was a viable alternative, as the private pension programs they had put their faith in failed in the face of the economic downturn. Conservatives turned to welfare capitalism—the program of a previous generation of progressives. Meanwhile, as Martha Derthick has argued, the Social Security Administration rolled on with sophisticated public relations defending the program and offering endless justifications for expanding it.[5]

In summary, where activism in the policy realm was concerned, conservatism as a movement and an ideology had to be constructed *de novo*. The idea of conservatism had developed largely as a response to the liberalism of the New Dealers and lacked an institutional base in think tanks or universities where public intellectuals and policy specialists could develop and diffuse ideas. On the grassroots level, conservative policy responses developed in a piecemeal fashion, reacting to proposals of liberals with little to offer as alternatives, other than the largely discredited doctrine of *laissez-faire*. Many of the groups that would later join the conservative coalition (such as religious conservatives, Southerners, and many working-class whites) had yet to be mobilized in the early years for the simple reason that the Roosevelt and Truman administrations did not seek to interject the federal government in areas that would cause them to rethink their political allegiances. While there were intimations of tensions in the Great Society coalition in the 1950s, it would take the remarkable extensions of Democratic liberalism under Lyndon Baines Johnson and the Great Society to provide the opportunity for conservatism to bring in new groups, ideas, and strategies.

## Why Conservatism Changed

The transition from antistatist to statist conservatism was driven by three large social and political shifts. First, the changes produced by the growth of the state and the transformation of liberalism dislodged the attachments of many parts of the New Deal coalition. Second, as a result of the entry of new actors into the conservative movement, an increasing recognition of the failure of antistatist conservatism, and the identification of opportunities that came from the actions of liberals themselves, the way was opened for a new conservative approach to the state. Third, conservatives added organizational and policy entrepreneurs based in Washington, D.C., to their previous collection of high-level intellectuals, grassroots activists, and elected officials. These new actors argued for challenging liberalism on the basis of conservative alternatives that might serve the ends of equity, opportunity, security, or environmental protection better than liberalism had.

### *Changed Coalitional Dynamics*

Modern conservatism could not have existed before the expansion of state activism and dramatic social changes produced by the wave of policy making beginning with the Johnson administration and extending into the Nixon era. Refugees from Great Society liberalism provided conservatism with connections to new social groups, policy expertise, and political savvy that the movement had previously lacked.

We can see the effects of the Great Society on the conservative coalition most dramatically in the area of education. On the one hand, education was the most prominent site of contention in desegregation, beginning with the Supreme Court's decision in *Brown,* but also, as McGuinn shows, in the use of federal educational funds to spur compliance with the Court's decisions and the recently passed civil rights laws. The reaction to the federal government's increasingly assertive role in education helped push Southern partisans of racial segregation into the Republican Party and led to the near-elimination of Southern progressive officeholders,[6] while the extension of desegregation to the North (through busing) had a similar impact on white ethnics.[7] The federal government's attempt to strip Southern "academies" (largely, although not exclusively, designed to skirt the desegregation of public schools) of their tax exemptions also helped mobilize Southern evangelicals and fundamentalists, adding yet another cog to the modern conservative coalition.

While it is less frequently commented upon, the environmental regulation of the 1970s had a similar coalitional effect. Up through the mid-1960s, much of the mountainous West was still characterized by vigorous partisan competition. The transformation of federal environmental regulation had a significant impact on the politics of Western states, dependent as they were on federal land for ranching, farming, and mining. The "sagebrush rebellion" and subsequent conflicts driven by the Endangered Species Act (for example, over the spotted owl and the snail darter) allowed conservatism to appeal to Western voters with modest means who had previously been sympathetic to the Democrats.

The changes and dislocations associated with the growth of the modern state, in short, helped to transform previously liberal or noncommitted social groups into conservatives. As a result of attracting these newly disaffected groups, conservatism itself changed. What was once the ideology of the mine and forest owner became increasingly attractive to the miner and logger. A movement associated with mainline Eastern Protestantism became increasingly populated by ethnic Catholics and Southern evangelicals. While many would question whose goals it served in government, there is little doubt that, as an electoral matter, American conservatism had gained a powerful popular base driven by backlash against the growing American state.

## New Ideas and Elite Actors

The changed agenda of the modern state and modern liberalism helped add cadres of talented elite actors to the ranks of conservatism, to go along with its new mass base. Liberal professors and public intellectuals like Nathan Glazer, Irving Kristol, and Seymour Martin Lipset reacted against what they saw as the flawed policies of the Great Society and the tenderhearted approach of university leaders to campus disruption. Lawyers like Peter Schuck and David Schoenbrod, who were once important figures in the public interest law movement, became influential critics of the movement in academe. These defectors from liberalism, who came to be known as neoconservatives, had no armies of voters behind them but provided something equally valuable: the ability to challenge liberalism on its own terms, on the basis of professional expertise and elite credentials. The magazines they led, such as *The Public Interest* and *Commentary,* provided a venue for the publication of some of the earliest critiques of the policies studied in this book, including Martin Feldstein on Social Security,[8] Daniel Patrick Moynihan and others on education,[9] and multiple articles on the environment.[10] These critiques, grounded in social science rather than political philosophy, provided analytical foundations for conservative policies that they had previously lacked.

The entry of these new actors into the conservative ranks also led to a shift in the movement's approach to policy change. Statist conservatives now challenged liberalism on the basis of its results rather its constitutional legitimacy. This outcome-based critique of liberalism was harder for defenders of the modern state to ignore, opening the way for conservatives to claim that liberalism had failed by its own standards. This provided an opportunity for conservatives to introduce their own strategies for ensuring old-age security, environmental protection, and educational equity. The failure of antistatist conservatives in the early Reagan administration to curb the growth of Social Security and environmental policy or to eliminate the Department of Education further suggested that their approach was a political nonstarter.[11] This process gained steam in the wake of the "Republican Revolution" of the mid-1990s, giving credibility to advocates of transforming (but not eliminating) the modern state through providing services via the market or civil society. Whether it was the introduction of private accounts in Social Security, free market environmentalism, faith-based initiatives, or educational vouchers, modern conservatism increasingly argued that state action could serve conservative goals of efficiency and individual choice, allowing them as well to reach out to voters who had previously supported liberalism.[12] This approach, which was controversial in the 1980s when it went under the heading of "big government conservatism," became the movement's conventional wisdom when reintroduced by George W. Bush under the rubric of "compassionate conservatism" and the "opportunity society."

Accompanying this new intellectual approach was an alternative vision for how conservative ideas could be made politically viable. As both Teles and Derthick and Henig show, statist conservatives increasingly began to adopt a strategy of "radical incrementalism," looking for policies that could create stresses in existing liberal coalitions, attract new groups to conservatism (such as young workers in Social Security, and the inner-city poor in education), and lay the foundations for more comprehensive changes in public policy (as with expanded IRAs as a strategy for making the public sympathetic to Social Security privatization). The appeal of this new form of conservatism to more traditional conservatives was its promise that, by detaching government spending from centralized state provision, the political foundations of liberalism would weaken, making it possible to whittle down the state in the long term.

## New Infrastructure

Well-developed ideas alone are inadequate, of course, as they need mechanisms in order to be transmitted to either policy elites or the mass public. Accompanying new conservative actors and ideas was a vastly expanded infrastructure of think tanks and conservative public interest law firms, directed by policy entrepreneurs informed by modern conservatism's normative and strategic insights. Where conservatism in earlier periods had been an outsider movement, these new tools gave conservatives access to information, analytical capacity, and the ability to coordinate action strategically—tools that had hitherto been the exclusive property of advocates of state expansion.

As we saw above, in the growth stages of Social Security, environmental regulation, and federal aid to education, conservatives had been comprehensively out-strategized. They lacked the resources to challenge (or in some cases even understand) liberal proposals, or to generate and push for alternatives of their own. Starting in the 1970s, and accelerating thereafter, this began to change. Think tanks like the Heritage Foundation, American Enterprise Institute, and the Cato Institute generated critiques of liberal policies, and operated as sites for coordinating strategic approaches to undermining them. For example, neither the conservative strategy for privatizing Social Security nor its mission of voucherizing education would have been nearly as carefully constructed without the strategic leadership of Heritage's Stuart Butler, and he would not have been in a position to exercise that leadership without the think tank's close relationship with conservative members of Congress and their staff. Conservative foundations like Olin (which began in earnest in the late 1970s) and Bradley (started in the mid-1980s) provided funding for an even more ambitious set of institutions, including public-interest law firms, academic research, parallel professional societies, and interest groups.[13] These foundations helped encourage learning across different parts of the new conservative infrastructure, by funding ideas that built on past successes and pulling the plug on failures.

The power of this new conservative infrastructure came not just from its various parts, but from the increasingly dense networks that connected them. As Judith Layzer shows, in environmental policy, public-interest law groups like the Pacific Legal Foundation were connected to think tanks such as the Competitive Enterprise Institute, foundation-funded academic researchers, local activists, and a Republican Congress increasingly hostile to environmental regulation. When combined with the changed character of business representation in Washington, a consequence of the Republican's "K Street Project,"[14] conservative activists were increasingly in a position to coordinate and direct business's response to the environment, reversing the co-optation that had, as Harris shows, neutralized its power in the 1960s and 1970s. Jeffrey Henig, in chapter 9, describes a similar network pattern in the area of education, where advocates of vouchers have put together networks that span professors (such as Harvard's Paul Peterson and Carolyn Hoxby), activists (like Howard Fuller at the Black Alliance for Educational Options), lawyers (Clint Bolick at the Institute for Justice), and activists like Chester Finn, who combine the roles of public intellectuals and movement strategists. While it lacks the substantial political muscle still possessed by the public school lobby and teachers' unions, this network is much denser than that which conservatives possessed when the idea of school choice was still in its infancy. These networks also facilitate rapid transmission of information, ideas, and political strategies, allowing for a coordinated approach that would have been difficult or impossible two decades before.

In short, a movement that had once been long on high-level philosophy and grassroots activists has now become firmly ensconced in Washington and, increasingly, in elite positions in the professions and academe, where conservatives are now able to generate viable policy alternatives and transmit them effectively to elite policy makers and the mass public. While conservatives continue to hold a self-image as insurgents, they are increasingly well-institutionalized insiders. What this transition has produced in terms of tangible change in public policy is the subject to which we now turn.

## How Conservatism Shaped the Modern State

Activist government in the United States has been decisively shaped by the presence of conservative interests and ideas. Of course, political scientists have explained many of America's policy outcomes by looking at the constraints that business[15] and defenders of racial hierarchy[16] have put in the way of state development. Looking over the sweep of the past 75 years, however, conservatives have done much more than stand in the way of state expansion. They have also supported an expanded state role, been co-opted into accepting its growth, or inadvertently assisted the expansion of government through the unintended consequence of their efforts to keep it in check. Conservatives, in short, have been both contributors to, as well as constraints on, the development of the modern American state.

The traditional story of conservatives as constraints on the growth of the American state certainly does appear very strongly in our cases. Davies and McGuinn show that Southern segregationists vigorously resisted a directive federal role in education out of fear that it would be used to chip away at racial hierarchy and the supply of cheap agricultural labor. Catholics supported the tradition of a limited federal role in education out of concern that they would be cut out of the newly created governmental largesse. Finally, mainstream conservatives and many local officials used "constitutional tradition" to tar national aid to education as an alien intrusion on the American culture of localism. These combined forces were sufficient to prevent the extension of the New and Fair Deals into education policy, protecting education from progressive change until the triple shocks of Sputnik, the Great Society, and the 1964 election.

As Berkowitz and DeWitt show, conservatives were also surprisingly effective in slowing the growth of Social Security in its early days. Drawing on still-strong traditions of federalism, their generally silent influence limited the extension of social insurance to Old Age Insurance, leaving the rest of the Social Security Act a mish-mash of joint federal-state programs. Important parts of the Act were written with the traditionally conservative Supreme Court in mind. The anticipation of conservative opposition also led defenders of Social Security to market their creation as based on the model of contributory insurance, and to keep initial benefits relatively low. In the area of Social Security, in short, the influence of conservatives was largely invisible and anticipatory, with architects of the modern welfare state building conservative assumptions into the program in order to forestall attacks.

Conservative ideas and actors also helped to influence the character and timing of American environmental policy. Eisner shows how business interests and the power of the states, along with the underdeveloped idea of ecology, prevented large-scale environmental policy from getting on the agenda through the early 1960s. While conservatives, especially business, were soundly routed in the environmental area in the 1960s and early 1970s, the fear of business power decisively shaped the character of modern environmental politics. Concerned with the disproportionate influence of "concentrated" (primarily business) interests on environmental policy, especially in Congress, the founders of the modern environmental state created a political system designed to go around business power, composed of administrative policy makers, courts, and congressional subcommittees and coordinated by new public interest environmental groups. As Layzer argues, this new political system would later be seized by conservatives, who were able to eat away at previous environmental policy development at the margins using the same low-profile mechanisms that liberals had used to build up environmental protection. Layzer also sees conservatives as an important constraint on the trajectory of environmental policy in the 1990s, where they were able to use their recently created organizational apparatus and power in Congress to prevent environmental policy from being updated to take account of new risks and gaps in previous legislation.

Our story, however, is not simply one of conservatives as a drag on state development. There are abundant examples of where, either intentionally or inadvertently, through their action or failure to act, conservatives played a role in expanding the modern state.

Perhaps most interesting and unexpected are the cases in which conservatives inadvertently contributed to the growth of the state through strategies designed to constrain it. For example, McGuinn shows that while the Johnson administration favored relatively simple redistribution of educational funds to poor states, conservatives calculated that limiting federal aid to narrowly targeted categorical assistance would keep the growth of educational spending in check. Their strategy backfired: categorical aid facilitated the growth of educational interest groups, because the narrow categories made the job of organizational entrepreneurs easier. These narrow categories also facilitated the use of federal aid to education for congressional credit-claiming, cementing its popularity among the holders of its purse strings. The groups that formed around these categories became mobilized to protect federal spending, forming the core of what conservatives would later refer to simply as the "blob."

A similar story is told by Altman and Marmor. By the early 1960s, conservatives concluded that the greatest danger posed by Social Security was that program benefits would outstrip taxes, giving liberals the ability to promise "something for nothing." To avoid this, conservatives held firm to the idea that all increases in benefits should be accompanied by corresponding increases in payroll taxes. This strategy put conservatives in the ironic position of maintaining the tax spigot that allowed for continually increased benefits during periods of economic expansion. In addition, sensing the increasing pressure to enact Medicare, conservatives pushed for a substantial increase in Old Age Insurance cash benefits, in the hopes that this would dry up funds for federal health insurance. While this gambit succeeded in producing congressional deadlock in 1964, it also pushed the issue past that fall's elections, allowing Medicare to be taken up by the most liberal Congress in the twentieth century.

Conservatives' role in expanding the state was not simply a matter of inadvertence. A number of our authors point to the role that conservatives—or at the least, actors whom we would expect to be conservative—played in the growth of activist government. Berkowitz and DeWitt show that, once its sputtering early years had passed, many large businesses actively supported the growth of Social Security cash benefits, either because of its linkage to their own company pensions, or because, as in the case of the life insurance industry, they were able to piggyback on the program's popularization of the insurance idea. Harris provides evidence that, once environmental laws were on the books, large corporations saw them as a way to push costs onto their smaller competitors. Both McGuinn and Henig argue that corporations have increasingly seen aid to education as a contributor to their competitiveness in a global economy, and have lobbied to protect the federal role and, in many cases, to expand it. Finally, McGuinn shows that federal aid effectively made the states, which had previously been eager to preserve their autonomy, a powerful part of the lobby for preserving national education spending.

Conservatives also played a role as much for what they did not do as for what they did. A number of our authors trace out the ways that conservative actors were effectively co-opted by either the strategies of liberals or the unfolding logic of the programs they created. Davies points to how the rhetoric of national security and anticommunism helped to weaken conservative opposition to federal education aid. McGuinn shows that Catholic opposition to federal education spending withered in the light of the 1965 Elementary and Secondary Education Act's tactical decision to fund individual students rather than public schools. Altman and Marmor document how congressional conservatives abandoned opposition to Social Security's expansion as long as they preserved a role in shaping its development. Teles and Derthick show that the financial industry, which conservatives hoped would strongly support Social Security privatization, sat out the debate over the Bush plan because of their fear of retaliation from unions, and because tax-subsidized IRAs and 401 ks already gave them access to the most lucrative market for retirement savings.

The role of conservatives in the growth of the modern state has taken a final step in the last decade, as many of them concluded that outright opposition to government had ceased to be a plausible strategy and that they should seek instead to use government to serve their own ends. In Medicare, conservative opposition to the addition of prescription drug coverage was muted by the creation of a market for providers. In education, conservatives dropped their opposition to a strong federal role, and in fact consented to a substantial increase in national education spending, as long as it was accompanied by standards of state performance. We may have reached a turning point in the development of activist government, therefore, when the growth of the state will be driven just as much by the goals of conservatives as those of progressives.

## The Limits of Counter-Mobilization

Until recently at least, the standard narrative of most stories of modern conservatism—oddly enough, especially when it is given by liberals—ends with conservative victory. A movement once in the wilderness has become the dominant source of policy ideas in American politics, carried forth by an infrastructure in Washington and across the country that dwarfs the capacities of liberals. Accompanying these changes, of course, is the growing electoral power of an increasingly conservative and disciplined Republican Party. Using these electoral and organizational resources, conservatives have dramatically altered American domestic and foreign policy: cutting taxes, weakening unions, increasing military spending, and dramatically reshaping foreign policy. The story of the conservative movement, as many see it, is a triumphal one.

Seen through the prism of our three cases, the conservative triumph is more ambiguous. While conservatives succeeded in injecting market forces into Medicare Part D, for example, this was a success embedded within the most expensive entitlement passed since the creation of Medicare. Social Security privatization, which was to be the centerpiece of George W. Bush's second term, was a stunning failure that never managed to build any political momentum. While conservatives have succeeded in nipping at the edges of the nation's major environmental laws through litigation and bureaucratic guerrilla warfare, none has been repealed or even dramatically altered. The most that conservatives can claim is that, at least, no major new environmental laws have been passed, and even here there are signs that significant action on global warming may be just around the corner. In education, every year sees the introduction of additional small school choice plans, alternative certification programs, and a growing charter school movement. That being said, these are still changes at the margins. Only a small percentage of all public school students attend charter schools (that are still substantially underfunded compared to public schools), and the number of students using private school vouchers is miniscule. The power of teachers' unions is still imposing, and few teachers enter the profession without going through the schools of education so hated by conservatives.

Is this a story of success or failure? Obviously, the yardstick one uses matters a great deal. Thirty years ago, few conservatives would have allowed themselves to believe that ideas like school vouchers, market strategies for controlling pollution, or Social Security privatization would be part of mainstream discourse. Almost none would have predicted that they would become the official positions of the Republican Party. On the other hand, in the wake of their electoral breakthrough in 1994, most conservatives—and a large number of liberals—thought that changes like these were right around the corner and that the modern activist state was about to be brought to its knees. In short, conservatives have been wildly successful in changing the character of mainstream policy debate, but far less successful in moving from agenda setting to policy passage. Why?

The first and most obvious explanation is that, while conservatives have grown stronger, many of their old adversaries are still around, bloodied but not bowed. One of the most important obstacles to George W. Bush's Social Security privatization gambit was the strong opposition of the AARP, a group whose financial muscle and membership still dwarfs anything Republicans can manage. In the area of the environment, groups like Environmental Defense, the Natural Resources Defense Council, and the Sierra Club continue to have millions of members, led by lawyers and lobbyists who pay close attention to any effort to change existing laws. As Lazyer demonstrates in her chapter, whenever conservatives directly attack existing environmental policies, these groups only increase in membership and funding. Finally, the educational establishment—teacher's unions, schools of education, and the Washington-based education lobby—continue to have substantial resources and a huge organizational presence in every school district in the country. These organizations came into being as a result of the growth of the modern state, and despite conservatives' best efforts, they remain. The modern conservative policy infrastructure, in short, is very impressive where old Republican chestnuts like taxes, unionization, and foreign policy are concerned, but it is still no match for what liberals can bring to bear in the policies examined in this book.

Second, most of the programs under study in this volume continue to be widely popular with the American public. Conservatives have succeeded in raising doubts about the future of Social Security, but those doubts have not substantially shaken the fact that most of the public likes the program as it is. While conservatives have made suspicion of the environmental movement an increasingly powerful cultural trope, few Americans trust conservatives with the issue, and most support strong measures to reduce pollution and other environmental dangers. Conservatives have been most successful in shaking the public's faith in public schools, especially those in the inner city, but most Americans continue to feel that while everyone else's public school may be bad, their own are fine, and vouchers present more risk than reward.[17]

Third, despite the best efforts of conservatives, all of the policies under examination in this book continue to be strongly identified in the public's mind with liberals. While the public has become increasingly convinced that there may be significant costs and inefficiencies associated with modern environmental policy, they do not trust conservatives to fix these problems while preserving environmental protection. The public is worried about Social Security's long-term health and interested in private alternatives to social insurance, but the elderly in particular continue to harbor suspicions of the Republicans' desire to preserve the program. In education, conservatives have begun to break the identity between the interests of teachers and students, but the public continue to see Democrats as the natural party of education.

Fourth—and connected to the continuing popularity of these programmatic areas—is the continuing attractiveness of the activist state for office seekers. The environment, for example, has become a valence issue for many middle-class swing voters, and few politicians in contested races are willing to risk being branded as opposed to clean air or water or in favor of global warming. Even conservatives now accept that guaranteeing educational opportunity, especially for the poor, is a national obligation, and they have found it difficult to attack core parts of the education lobby's power without being successfully branded as being "anti-education." Finally, Social Security's blame avoidance dynamics continue to be as powerful as ever, and conservatives have not yet discovered a way to make the cuts in benefits necessary for any successful privatization program palatable for election-minded politicians.

Fifth, the programmatic structure of the modern activist state, combined with the complicated character of American political institutions, still poses significant challenges to efforts at major reform. As Teles and Derthick note in chapter 8, transition costs continue to be a major stumbling block for Social Security privatization.[18] The continued decentralization of schooling in the United States means that conservatives must fight thousands of battles in order to introduce educational choice. In the environment and other areas of domestic policy, conservatives have found it difficult, and in most cases impossible, to overcome the multiple veto points associated with separation of powers. Consequently, conservative successes have been incremental (the slow growth of charters and vouchers), indirect (the increasing public comfort with defined contribution *private* pensions), or obstructionist (the prevention of new environmental laws).

Sixth and finally, despite the efforts of many in the Washington-based conservative policy community, issues like the environment, education, and Social Security are still not the priority of most grassroots activists or Republican politicians. Opposition to gun control is still a more potent force for riling up the Republican base than reform of environmental laws. When faced with a choice, conservative politicians prefer tax cuts to Social Security privatization. A hard-line foreign policy continues to be a stronger glue for the Republican Party than using choice to bring educational opportunity to the inner city. Until conservatives can convince their own base and politicians to take risks in these issues equal to those that they have taken for tax cuts and the war in Iraq, change will continue to be measured in inches.

## Parting Thoughts

Conservatives have been most successful in these traditionally liberal policy areas when they created a coalition for change reaching beyond their own ranks. Consider first three areas outside the scope of this book. Conservatives complained for years about the inefficiency created by a complicated tax code, but they were only able to enact tax simplification in 1986, when the issue was taken up by liberals like Bill Bradley and Dick Gephardt.[19] While conservatives were able to use welfare very successfully for electoral purposes, reform only came when the idea was embraced by Bill Clinton.[20] Finally, conservative economists were the first to criticize the costs of regulation, but major deregulation only passed when liberals like Ted Kennedy signed on.[21]

There are important lessons from these instances of conservative success, and the near misses in this book. At least some Democrats have historically been willing to consider reforms originally pushed by conservatives when they had sufficient political power to ensure that their interests were protected. As Teles and Derthick show, this explains why Democrats, including Bill Clinton, were willing to consider Social Security privatization in the 1990s when they controlled at least one branch of government, and why they have been almost wholly opposed since. Many Democrats have supported market-based policies when they have been associated with the expansion of government (such as Medicare Part D, control of sulfur dioxide in the 1990 Clean Air Act, and today with global warming), but have resisted them when they were not part of a bipartisan policy trade. Educational vouchers and charter schools have gotten more support in states and cities when they have been pushed by liberal Democrats, especially African Americans, than when they were supported by exclusively conservative policy coalitions.

This points to a significant developmental point. We believe that the three areas under examination in this volume have attained quasi-constitutional status. These functions of government are not seen by the public, and thus by politicians, as "normal" acts of government, but as foundational public commitments. As a result, conservatives have been reduced to chipping away at the margins of these policies, and others like them, through indirect, legal, or bureaucratic means, except when they have been able to garner a broader than normal scope of political consent.

This points to a final irony. The American system of government is not hard-wired for rapid, comprehensive change, but its weak parties and multiple veto points have been effective in facilitating the broader coalitions that are required for policy change of the kind that many modern conservatives want. While the increasing partisan polarization of American politics has helped conservatives achieve some of their goals, such as tax reduction, it may have made it more difficult to push through changes that require a broader mobilization of consent. If this is right, it suggests that conservatives—especially in an era when their power in Congress has been diminished—may find that their future successes will come less through raw party power, and more through a modern strategy of "Whig Men and Tory Measures."

## Notes

1. Martha Derthick, *Policymaking for Social Security* (Washington, DC: Brookings Institution Press, 1979).
2. While the federal government was certainly highly limited before the 1930s, government activism at the state and local level was widespread. As William Novak argued in *The People's Welfare: Law and Regulation in 19ᵗʰ Century America* (Chapel Hill: University of North Carolina Press, 1996), America had a very interventionist "police power" state in the 19ᵗʰ century. The activities of this localized state never produced a clean liberal-conservative divide, however, because its provision of public goods and regulation of behavior were supported by business and socially traditional interests.
3. Of course, there was a conservative coalition in Congress, composed of conservative Southern Democrats and Republicans, who held considerable institutional power and used it aggressively to frustrate liberal policy goals. But this institutional coalition was not connected to a real extra-institutional interest coalition of the sort that began to develop in the 1960s and 1970s.
4. 301 U.S. 641.
5. Martha Derthick, *Policymaking for Social Security* (Washington, DC: Brookings Institution Press, 1979).
6. Michael Klarman, *From Jim Crow to Civil Rights* (Oxford: Oxford University Press, 2004), chap. 7.
7. See, for example, Ronald Formisano, *Boston against Busing: Race, Class and Ethnicity in the 1960s and 1970s* (Chapel Hill: University of North Carolina Press, 2004).
8. Martin Feldstein, "Toward a Reform of Social Security," *The Public Interest* 40 (1975), 75–95.
9. Daniel Patrick Moynihan, "Equalizing Education: In Whose Benefit?" *The Public Interest* 29 (1972), 69–89; Milton Friedman, "A Free Market in Education," *The Public Interest* 3 (1966), 107.
10. Myrick Freeman and Robert Haveman, "Clean Rhetoric and Dirty Water," *The Public Interest* 28 (1972), 51–65; R. Shep Melnick, "Pollution Deadlines and the Coalition for Failure," *Public Interest* 23, 123–134 (Spring 1984); Michael Greve, "Environmentalism and Bounty Hunting," *The Public Interest* 97 (1989), 15–29.
11. The reader may have noticed by this late stage how small a role Ronald Reagan has played in our analysis of policy-relevant conservatism. President Reagan's failure to restructure either Social Security or education policy and to do little more than halt the advancement of environmental regulation is

truly remarkable, not only given the apparent mandate he claimed to enjoy, but also factoring in the stagflation the nation was experiencing when he was first elected, and also the decline in unions—which for the better part of the century up to his election had formed the very backbone of the Democratic Party and to a great extent of liberalism itself. The failure of the Reagan administration to displace any of these policies speaks not only to the inability of the antistatists to offer what at the time were considered viable alternatives, but also to the deep acceptance on the part of the American polity of the goals that liberalism had articulated for these policies. This acceptance goes far beyond mere institutionalization of the policies in interest groups and government policy. They have, we argue, reached the stage where they are literally part of America's unwritten constitution—a point we develop further in the very last section of this chapter. If this claim is correct, then arguments for abandoning their commitments will fail, and what will be needed instead are alternative means for achieving the same goals through methods that are deemed more acceptable to conservatives.

12. A good example of this "harm reduction" approach to the welfare state can be seen in *The New Consensus on Family and Welfare,* ed. Richard John Neuhaus and Michael Novak (Washington, DC: American Enterprise Institute, 1987).

13. Steven M. Teles, *The Rise of the Conservative Legal Movement: The Battle for Control of the Law* (Princeton, NJ: Princeton University Press, 2008).

14. The K Street Project was the largely successful effort by Congressional Republicans, starting in 1995, to put strong partisans in the leadership of Washington-based business organizations. Nicholas Confessore, "Welcome to the Machine," *Washington Monthly,* July/August 2003, 30–37. The K Street Project grew out of the long-standing frustration of conservatives with business support for the growth of the state, or at least their limited ardor for shrinking it. A wonderful case of this attitude is Paul Weaver, *The Suicidal Corporation: How Big Business Fails America* (Washington, DC: Cato, 1988).

15. Colin Gordon, *New Deals: Business, Labor, and Politics in America, 1920–1935* (New York: Cambridge University Press, 1994); Ellis W. Hawley, *The New Deal and the Problem of Monopoly: A Study in Economic Ambivalence* (Princeton, NJ: Princeton University Press, 1966); Charles Lindblom, *Politics and Markets: The World's Political Economic Systems* (New York: Basic Books, 1977); Martin J. Sklar, *The Corporate Reconstruction of American Capitalism, 1890–1916* (New York: Cambridge University Press, 1988); Stephen Skowronek, *Building a New American State: The Expansion of National Administrative Capacities, 1877–1920* (New York: Cambridge University Press, 1982), chap. 5 and 8; Peter A. Swenson, *Capitalists against Markets: The Making of Labor Markets and Welfare States in the United States and Sweden* (New York: Oxford University Press, 2002).

16. Robert Lieberman, *Shifting the Color Line* (Cambridge, MA: Harvard University Press, 1998); Ira Katznelson, Kim Geiger, and Dan Kryder, "Limiting

Liberalism: The Southern Veto in Congress," *Political Science Quarterly* 108 (Summer 1993): 283–306.

17. Terry Moe, *Schools, Vouchers and the American Public* (Washington, DC: Brookings Institution Press, 2001).

18. See also Paul Pierson, *Dismantling the Welfare State: Reagan, Thatcher, and the Politics of Retrenchment* (New York: Cambridge University Press, 1994).

19. Jeffrey Birnbaum and Alan Murray, *Showdown at Gucci Gulch* (New York: Vintage, 1988).

20. Steven M. Teles, *Whose Welfare: AFDC and Elite Politics* (Lawrence: University Press of Kansas, 1996).

21. Martha Derthick and Paul Quirk, *The Politics of Deregulation* (Washington, DC: Brookings Institution Press, 1985).

# AFTERWORD

## An Attenuated Reconstruction: The Conservative Turn in American Political Development

*Stephen Skowronek*

It has been more than a quarter century since the "Reagan Revolution" gripped American government; nearly a half century since Barry Goldwater unveiled *The Conscience of a Conservative*. In practical political terms, the change is unmistakable. A conservative insurgency pushed its way to power, transformed national discourse, realigned political conflict, and brought new priorities to the fore. No longer consigned to bit parts in political developments driven by their opponents, conservatives have written a new script and claimed a leading role for themselves in determining the shape of things to come.

And yet, as the chapters of this volume document, the redirection of American government has been anything but straightforward. Close examination of policy initiatives that have attended the conservative turn expose an attenuated reconstruction, one far more equivocal than the insurgents' rhetorical repudiation of the liberal regime might lead us to expect. These findings raise important questions, both about the dynamics of American political development generally and the significance of this new phase in particular. In this concluding essay, I would like to reflect what is being said in these pages back on American political development (APD) at large. I want to consider how insights drawn from past transformations might illuminate the conservative turn, as well as how studies of the conservatives' policy impact might advance APD as a scholarly enterprise.

Potential gains are not difficult to discern. APD scholarship has long been interested in the fate of ideologically charged insurgencies. It has taken aim at the consensus theory of American politics, disaggregated our allegedly all-encompassing liberal tradition, and rediscovered the high stakes and substantive weight of conflict in American political history. For the most part, however, scholarly attention has focused on alternative visions generated by the dissenting Left. Moreover, in examining these alternatives and establishing their integrity as distinct political pathways for the nation, this work has, in the main, retrieved ideals that fell by the wayside in contests for national power and that illustrated the limits of the Left.[1] Against this backdrop, the progress of the conservative insurgency to date stands out as a gold mine of untapped insights. In reversing the field of vision, this volume opens up to historical reflection a relatively unattended wellspring of popular mobilization and formative political action, and in pointing to problems of follow-through on the Right, it casts a very different light on what was achieved by the other side.

Whatever the angle of vision, the underlying question is the same. These pages challenge us once again to come to terms with political change in America. The ingenious structure of the volume forms a mosaic, its different pieces combining to illuminate the same developmental event, and as an overall image emerges in composite, it prompts us to rethink what is at stake in such events generally. A different mix of policies—welfare policy, tax policy, and foreign policy, for example—might yield somewhat different conclusions about the course and impact of the conservative insurgency, as might more sustained attention to action on the judicial side of the conservative reconstruction, but the three policy areas taken up by these authors are of sufficient weight and variety to ensure that the developmental sequence of which they are a part is not construed too narrowly or rigidly. The issue that keeps bubbling up in each of the policy domains under review concerns the scope, depth, and potential durability of the political transformation under way, and that issue lies at the very heart of the APD enterprise.

The chapters reveal several different dimensions of this issue, and though they show them to be tightly entwined, it might be useful in an overview assessment like this to sort through them. One dimension is intellectual and takes as its point of departure the developmental status of political alternatives to "liberalism" in America's past as well as today. What is "conservatism" in contemporary America? What is it an alternative to? How extensive, aggressive, and coherent is its critique? A second dimension concerns processes of change. What are the common elements of prior reconstructions of American government, and how are they manifested in this one? How have political alternatives in the past negotiated the transition from opposition to power, and how does the progress of the alternative before us stack up against prior experience? A third concern follows directly: can systemic effects be calibrated? Some political changes construct a new platform for all future action; others prove to be more fragile and susceptible to the back-and-forth swing of democratic politics; most developmental episodes contain elements of both. What, then, are the general indicators of a more a durable effect? Are they evident today? Where do the policy changes in view seem to fall on this continuum? The following pages do not pretend to answer any of these questions conclusively or to exhaust what the existing APD literature has to say about them. They are meant to highlight these different dimensions of the material at hand and to point to a few avenues of exploration that might prove analytically productive.

## Conservatism as a Political Alternative

Ideological conflict at the elite level tends to be tightly contextualized in America and highly susceptible to tactical political maneuvering; the conceptual exchanges and programmatic inversions we observe over time seem to defy generalization. Historically speaking, conservatism has been particularly hard to pin down as an ideological standard. Ever since the Constitutional Convention met to consider ways to restrain the state legislatures, stabilize the polity, and secure the nation, conservatism has been an integral part of high politics in America. Conservatives in America have often advocated reform, and more often than not, these reforming conservatives have proclaimed themselves true champions of liberal principles. Leaders labeled "conservative" are to be found on different sides of hotly contested issues, and that makes it even harder to say what conservatism entails in the American political tradition or who the real conservatives are. Alexander Hamilton's programmatic efforts on behalf of an active and expansive federal government were considered harbingers of a conservative reaction in their day, but by all accounts, John C. Calhoun was also an ardent conservative, and he sought to limit national power and defend states' rights. Conflicts between Hamilton and James Madison in the 1790s, between John Quincy Adams and Andrew Jackson in the 1820s, and between Stephen Douglas and Abraham Lincoln in the 1850s all harbored political alternatives of real consequence for the nation in their time, but they do not map neatly or consistently onto a coherent discursive divide between conservatism and liberalism—likewise the early twentieth-century positions staked out by William Jennings Bryan, Theodore Roosevelt, Woodrow Wilson, and Herbert Hoover.

This volume begins to track a "conservative" response to "liberalism" with the advent of the New Deal, and indeed, the current sense of an ideological standoff between liberalism and conservatism in American national politics gets more pronounced as we move forward from the 1930s. This period specificity alerts us to the construct's historically contingent and politically reflexive character. Contemporary conservatism has gained definition against the institutional articulation and programmatic expansion of the social welfare state. The emergent frame has equated liberalism with policies designed to concentrate power at the center, redress imbalances in social and economic relationships, and standardize applications through national bureaucratic instruments; conversely, it arrays conservatism on the side of limiting governmental interference in social and economic relationships, loosening bureaucratic standards and restraints, and protecting the autonomy and diversity of civil society. As the apparent inversion of these positions in the abortion debate would seem to suggest, political alternatives fashioned in this way—that is, reactively and in the moment—harbor deep ambiguities. In fact, today's liberals will not defend bureaucratic regimentation or oppose economic freedom any more than today's conservatives will defend inequality and oppose the liberation of the oppressed. To the extent that these alternatives trade off politically against values that Americans widely share, they continue to leave substantial play for the exchange and manipulation of elements.

Thus, though the failure of consensus theory to predict the current ideological standoff may seem obvious, it does not seem impertinent to ask just how far current conditions have departed from the premises of that theory. It is certainly no coincidence that consensus theory grew to prominence just as the welfare state and its surrounding debates were beginning to take shape, and it is well worth remembering that consensus theorists never denied the pervasiveness or intensity of political conflict in America. The question that these theorists posed was whether political conflicts in America cut deep enough to actually displace one alternative with another. Louis Hartz found political conflict in America relatively unproductive because he saw that the combatants continually stopped short of direct engagement with their competitor's core principles: so long as American liberals refused to renounce capitalism and American conservatives refused to renounce equality, the alternatives they articulated would, he concluded, continually collapse into one another in practice.[2] This, it seems to me, is still the baseline proposition against which we need to evaluate the current state of affairs. Let me consider three responses.

One is that the value conflicts in American politics today are not nearly as insular or provincial as Hartz observed them to be in America's past, that American conservatives are more secure in their philosophical bearings and self-conscious in their political commitments than they were before. America's social-democratic turn followed the general pattern of political development in the West closely enough to lend the conservative critique of the welfare state a cosmopolitan outlook and to deepen its sense of a worldwide drift of the principles of liberal government into incoherence. The title of Richard Weaver's 1948 manifesto, *Ideas Have Consequences,* not only captured the faith of later generations of conservative theorists, it also sharpened their understanding of the connection between theory and practice and of their key role in the larger project of recovering standards. Few other reconstructive movements in American politics have drawn inspiration so directly from disciplined thinkers and holistic systems of thought.

This is an important distinction, and one to which we will have occasion to return. But it is notable that even at the level of high theory, the conservative critique has not been all of a piece. Different voices—Adam Smith and Edmund Burke, Frederick Hayek and Russell Kirk, Milton Friedman and Leo Strauss—can still be heard, and those voices are often in tension with one another programmatically. Not the least of the attractions of Weaver's manifesto was that it mixed the traditionalist and libertarian values of modern conservatism so freely. Combinations like that may harbor potent strategies for political mobilization, but they also make it harder to say what the critics are aligned for than what they are arrayed against. Proposals for school vouchers and the privatization of social security are suggestive of the growing prominence of libertarian themes in conservative policy circles, but there is reason to suspect that conservatism still cannot stray too far from its traditionalist roots, much less renounce them altogether in favor of a more principled libertarian stand, without losing much of its popular appeal.

Let me follow up with a second, very different response to Hartz, one that reconsiders the core values that have contended historically within American popular culture. Rogers Smith has argued that Hartz found political conflict in America unproductive because he was too fixated on the European ideological antinomies between capitalism and socialism. Smith posits a culturally engrained conflict in America that arrays the contending civic ideals somewhat differently, and he examines the ideas and policies put forward in the nineteenth century according to their practical effects in advancing institutionally one or the other of these underlying ambitions. He finds one tradition of thought and action that seeks to greater equality among citizens by broadening individual rights and opportunities, another that seeks greater cohesion through the perpetuation and defense of established social hierarchies.[3] The programmatic thrusts of Hamilton and Calhoun, though starkly different in their economic outlook and institutional prescriptions, were both "conservative" by this standard as their prospective political effect would have been to insulate and promote established social and economic hierarchies against political threats mobilizing against them.

This schematic is useful in directing attention to the political foundations of post–New Deal conservatism. As several of the papers in this volume indicate, conservative opposition to liberalism gained political strength in the 1930s and 1940s though an alliance of Republicans and Dixiecrats. This was no more natural an alliance than a coalition of Hamilton and Calhoun would have been. Nor was it easily arranged, as the New Deal served and protected Southern interests in many crucial respects. What drove these strange bedfellows closer together over time was not opposition to government intrusion or bureaucratic governance per se but the New Deal's displacement of a repressive system of control over the industrial labor force and its protection for the rights of workers to organize and act collectively in their own interests.[4] In a Smithian sense, modern American conservatism was forged out of the common threat to corporate governance and Southern apartheid posed by labor's newfound prerogatives and political clout, and by extension, out of the enhanced prospects for further social leveling implicit in the labor model of mass mobilization in pursuit of governmental redress.

By these criteria, American political development since the New Deal has decidedly not driven to a stand off on matters of fundamental value, nor have the alternatives tended to collapse into one another. What we observe instead is a historic rout of conservatism's traditional defenses by waves of social groups that successfully mobilized for greater freedom and equality. The unprecedented intellectual energy that has gone into a reformulation and reinvigoration of conservatism in our day is, in this sense, an acknowledgment that its traditional props are collapsing fast and that there is no turning back. Part of the appeal of regrouping around libertarian themes is that those are the ones best able to acknowledge and accept these permanent changes in the American political universe. Note, however, that concern with social cohesion—an engrained cultural value that may actually be gaining in political potential in light of liberalism's advances—is not a libertarian priority. To the extent that conservative intellectuals today are driven to libertarian themes, their ability to respond to something Americans really care about may turn out to be quite limited.

This leads me to a final response to Hartz. The ideological standoff between liberalism and conservatism may be sharper and more firmly grounded theoretically than prior conflicts, but it may *also* be less productive. Put another way, Hartz may have been wrong about the productivity of political conflict in America's past, but his charge of inherent limits does seem to capture something unfolding before our eyes in the current standoff over the fate of the welfare state. Opposition insurgencies in the past have repeatedly demonstrated their authority to forthrightly repudiate and successfully dislodge governmental commitments vital to the operations of the received order. Bank wars, civil wars, and court battles have arrayed stark alternatives against one another, and breakthrough political victories have generated governmental transformations. But by this very American standard of the authority to repudiate and dislodge, today's conservative insurgency has proven to be a markedly contained event.

Ronald Reagan recalled the reconstructive ambitions of prior insurgencies with his forthright repudiation of big government. In clear libertarian terms, he denied that bureaucratic government offered solutions to current challenges and identified it instead as the centerpiece of the nation's problems. But since then, American government has grown larger and more bureaucratic. Save perhaps for Reagan's rhetorical targeting of "welfare queens," an assault that bore fruit some years later when Bill Clinton consented to a dismantling of parts of the old welfare system, conservatism has advanced most effectively not through the repudiation and displacement of modern liberalism's superstructure but through accommodation, manipulation, and studied neglect.[5] As the papers in this volume trace the transition within the conservative insurgency from opposition critique to positive policy provision, the coherence of their alternative gets murkier, and the substantive commitments associated with modern American liberalism remain very much intact. On the evidence collected here, Hartz's thesis that insurgent alternatives in America cannot resist their opponents' values and are destined to collapse into some accommodation with them seems quite correct.

This pattern is clearly marked in the changing conservative stance on education where forthright opposition—first to any federal role and then to a cabinet-level department—was eviscerated, and where "now conservatives as well as liberals embrace tough federal mandates and penalties in the name of educational opportunity."[6] The resilience of liberalism is most powerfully demonstrated in these pages in the domain of social security, long the cornerstone of the American welfare state. Here, in fact, conservatives would seem to have had more success affecting the shape of policy early on, during the New Deal and its immediate aftermath, than in later years when, presumably, they have more fully come into their own as a political force to be reckoned with. Ronald Reagan and George W. Bush both flubbed their confrontation with this centerpiece of New Deal liberalism, the former electing for a compromise on social security after a stillborn assault and the latter accomplishing even less with his plan to "save" Social Security by conservative means. Even in the environmental case, where the liberals' advance came relatively late and the conservative rollback has proceeded furthest, direct confrontation and forthright repudiation have been rare. As Judy Layzar tells it, public opinion remains a powerful constraint. As conservatives have been careful to endorse environmental protection in principle, they have been left to insinuate their commitments into policies that acknowledge the problem as one to which government must respond. Rollback on these terms proceeds indirectly and behind the scenes: success comes in the form of "obstructing new legal mandates and capitalizing on the low visibility of bureaucratic decision making to make administrative changes that reduce the stringency of environmental protections."[7]

The three-stage sequence of development in each of our policy areas carries with it the implication that we are well beyond the era of Eisenhower (and Hartz), and indeed the Eisenhower strategy of accepting liberal policy commitments while promising a different way of meeting them has been renounced repeatedly by conservative insurgents from the early years of William Buckley and Barry Goldwater to the heyday of Ronald Reagan and Newt Gingrich. But, if these papers are any guide to the actual practice of conservative governance, something very much like Eisenhower-style obfuscation would still seem to be the only effective game in town. From the New Deal forward, forthright repudiation has marginalized conservatism as a policy alternative; its policy advances have elaborated instead upon the Eisenhower playbook. Compare the policy content behind FDR's rhetorical repudiation of economic royalists or Lyndon Johnson's rhetorical repudiation of Southern apartheid with the policy content behind Ronald Reagan's rhetorical repudiation of big government. Railing against bureaucratic regimentation is a popular move that may serve to stigmatize liberalism and advance alternative interests, but attacking a hierarchy so conspicuously abstracted from clear societal referents leaves modern liberalism insulated at its base and narrows the practical range of the alternative proposed.

As these chapters tell it, from the time of the New Deal to the time of the Great Society, there was a real debate between liberals and conservatives about what American government should do, and since that time these "essential boundary questions between public and private responsibility" have become less central to political disputes.[8] Conservatives today are more likely to offer policies that promise to do the same thing better than to propose reconstructing governmental commitments altogether. Ironically, and quite unlike reconstructive moments in the past, the scope of the substantive discussion has diminished, while the political competition between the alternatives has grown more intense.

Accordingly, this volume depicts a polity riveted by issues of policy design. There are, to be sure, high stakes in a politics of policy design; the conservative's great investment on the intellectual side is testimony to that. But the design possibilities are nearly limitless and the devil is stuck in the details. As I will suggest below, the intensity of this politics in our day is the fruit of prior developments as these are reflected in the less contained and more diverse universe of stakeholders able to speak to design issues. Those developments have made a decisive turn in a new direction, any direction, more difficult to negotiate. Rather than portending a transformation, the politics of policy design suggests a polity still reeling from the transformations of the recent past and just trying to figure out how to proceed.

## Transformative Processes

I do not want to overstate the importance of ideological coherence and consistency in catalyzing durable political change. Reflecting back on past political transitions and governmental redirections calls attention to other components of these processes that operate in conjunction with ideological conflict to mark a departure and determine its extent.

One, detailed by David Plotke in his analysis of the New Deal transformation, is the emergence of a "reform block" or alternative governing cadre.[9] This is an elite group of actors with a new outlook on politics and a different strategy for gaining and wielding governmental power. Finding its mission in response to problems and opportunities arising within the old order, the reform block emerges while the old order still appears very much intact. Its members work across a broad front, if not in deliberate concert, to undermine the received common sense with new assumptions and to promote institutions that will govern on different premises. Carving out strategic positions for themselves in the public and private spheres, they stand ready to take charge of governmental affairs when the opportunity arises. A second component found in significant departures in the past is an exogenous shock that disrupts established political patterns and exposes received political assumptions and governing premises to popular scrutiny. Shocks do not necessarily play to the advantages of a gestating reform block, but when accompanied by an electoral break that cuts their way, the reform block is there to speak to the popular demand for new solutions. Using the opportunity afforded to demonstrate their alternative assumptions, they secure their institutional foothold on governmental power. The third element in this process, institutional consolidation, is very much dependent on sustaining the electoral advantage. A new regime emerges when new forms of institutional support are provided to potent social and economic interests in the electorate. By extending the hold of a new class of politicians and locking new priorities into governmental action, the regime establishes itself in a new commonsense understanding of what American politics is all about.

Were we to examine in detail prior redirections of American government—those achieved by the Federalists in the 1780s, the Jeffersonians of the 1800s, the Jacksonians in the 1830s, the Republicans in the 1860s, the progressives in the 1900s, and the liberals in the 1930s and 1960s—we would find these elements in varying degrees and combinations. While no two episodes are exactly alike, careful attention to the different combinations has something to tell us about depth and durability of each.

In two of the three periods addressed by the papers in this volume, it is the liberal reform block that holds sway. The story of liberalism's expansion and consolidation plays out in the background of this volume as we watch its conservative opponents struggle to find their voice, but the methodical linking together of societal interests and administrative services under liberal premises is very much at issue. It is not just the extended time frame and scale of this consolidation that stands out as novel but also the characteristic form assumed by institutional relationships in this regime. What we now call "interest group liberalism" is a regime composed of multiple networks of bureaucratic and social power, and the density of these networks complicate the problem of reconstruction for anyone, liberal or conservative, who might be contemplating it. There is nothing of comparable resilience in the Jeffersonians or Jacksonians regimes, which were consolidated largely through party organizations, or even among the Civil War Republicans who added a series of constitutional proclamations.

There is some evidence in the three papers on the formative period of the liberal regime—the period between the New Deal and the Great Society— that conservatives were complicit in the rise of these relatively impenetrable new structures of power. In their determination to resist stronger federal controls, conservatives seem to have promoted policy compromises and program modifications that opened the door to what Gareth Davies calls "expansion by stealth." As he tells it, conservatives first came to the support of "impact aid" as an alternative to a more explicit federal role in local education and as a remedy for the alleged damage already done by federal intrusion upon the localities on other fronts. Trying to keep impact aid limited and remedial, they helped set in motion a policy so attractive at the local level that it soon began to expanded of its own accord. The initial design debates over Social Security, in which opponents and proponents alike seemed bent on demonstrating a conservative bias against central direction and control, produced a similar result.

The second period under study, looking forward from the 1960s, unfolds in a more bifurcated frame. Liberalism was still ascendant in this period; indeed, it took a great leap forward. But new institutional strongholds for conservatism began to emerge in private foundations, think tanks, economics departments, and law and policy schools. With new venues opening up to offer sustained support, conservative intellectuals began to act and think like an alternative governing cadre; more savvy and self-conscious, this reform block began to seek out and exploit new linkages between politics and policy alternatives. As Altman and Marmor note, there were more than just facts on the ground to stoke public concern with liberal commitments in the 1970s; there was a new class of "intellectual entrepreneurs" taking advantage of emerging problems to assault the assumptions of the liberal regime and alter the terms of political debate.[10]

These institutional resources for an enhanced conservative presence have not only deepened analytic capacities and contributed to a higher policy profile, they have also deepened political capacities and contributed to a more sharply competitive national politics. It is the political achievements of this reform block that stand out for attention, for there was nothing preordained about the transformation of the shaky cross-party coalition of the 1930s and 1940s into a robust conservative party with organizational clout in every section of the country. That was a political transformation negotiated with great intellectual insight and tactical subtlety.[11] The steady pool of talent now being provided on the political side to seize control of the state, and on the policy side to manage it, is the strongest indicator we have to date that something of profound developmental significance has occurred. Conservatism seems durable at least to the extent that election for election, and proposal for proposal, conservatives now have the capacity to pace and contest liberals long into the future.

On comparative examination, however, there are some distinctive aspects of this development that deserve to be flagged. It is notable, for example, that the Jacksonians outmaneuvered the old guard of their day by drawing elite talent from a different class of men altogether. More willing to engage in popular mobilization than the gentleman class of the early national period, the Jacksonians built institutions that required entirely new skill sets to manage. So too the progressives: they drew their talent from institutions like the emerging graduate schools and professional associations in which the old guard of their day was relatively weak and in which new skills of increasing value to the government could be developed. In contrast, the conservative reform block has developed strongholds that parallel liberal counterparts in the same domain; they come from the same social background and the same sorts of institutions, and they develop the same sorts of skills.[12] Whereas the Jacksonians and the progressives were organized to bypass their opponents, conservative insurgents of today have organized to go head-to-head with theirs. The capacities they have developed to counter liberals, election for election and policy for policy, also make them less likely to displace liberalism in any politically decisive sense. They have leveled the playing field and challenged the common sense of mid-twentieth-century politics, but rather than establish a new one, they have settled in for a great debate.

Well they might, for the electoral side of the conservative reconstruction has turned out to be a series of non-events. The contemporary period is chock full of exogenous shocks and electoral swings, but none of these has decisively indicted the old order or severed the liberals' grip on power. The third period reviewed in these policy studies is punctuated by several jolts forward for the conservative advance—the elections of 1980, 1994, 2002—but none has come close to the elections of 1864, 1934, or 1964 in clearing the field. Meanwhile, events like Hurricane Katrina in 2005 and elections like the 2006 midterm have tugged strongly the other way.

On this count, the experience of the early progressive reformers at the turn of the twentieth century may deserve a second look. Events and elections never decisively broke their way either; like today's conservatives, they always had more talent than political clout. The early progressives advanced on power slowly, haltingly, and uncertainly, working their way over time with whatever opportunities were provided by the twists and turns of electoral politics. At the national level, progressive reform became a matter of slogging away, persistently and unevenly, at established political and institutional relationships. In the end, they insinuated a variety of new ideas into government policy without decisively eradicating those previously in place or consolidating their gains. To this day, it is hard to characterize the achievement of the early progressives or to calibrate their break with the past. We can follow a near-constant renegotiation of governing arrangements between the time of McKinley and the time of Harding, but at the end of that run the progressive cadre found itself frustrated, the continuities of governance in the 1890s and the 1920s far more impressive than the redirection. It is not just that older commitments remained intact through these years; for when the electoral uncertainty of the intervening years shook itself out in the 1920s, these older commitments proved capable of a powerful resurgence, one that marginalized and nearly overwhelmed the changes that the reformers had so painstakingly negotiated. By contrast, the changes punctuated by the elections of 1864, 1934, and 1964 were abrupt and decisive; there was no going back on the new governing commitments made in their wake. Even when the losers regrouped and regained the initiative, they were compelled to deal with an entirely new state of affairs.

There are several different ways to read these similarities with the early experience of progressives. One is that short of a decisive shock and electoral rout, redirection will remain uncertain and attenuated. Another is that the greater success of today's conservatives in taking over one of the major parties and enhancing its electoral competitiveness portends greater success for redirection over the long haul, that the advances here and there on multiple fronts might be sustained more effectively and eventually add up to something more categorical. Nor should one forget that, notwithstanding the reversals of the

1920s, the progressive departure turned out to be but a prelude to two far more decisive transformations, both of which were inspired by the national bureaucratic thrust of their vision. The electoral breakthroughs that brought the New Deal and the Great Society followed upon and deepened the progressive state-building program.

Though the emergence of a robust reform block or alternative governing cadre may not be sufficient in and of itself to complete a transformation, those resources, once developed and secured, can have great staying power. The proper historical perspective on the conservative turn may, then, be very long indeed. Taking a cue from progressivism's long reach, we may mistake the significance of this insurgency and overstate its limits if we compare it exclusively to the New Deal and Great Society departures, for these were themselves second- and third-round offensives, all pushing the reconstruction of American government in the same general direction. But let's not go too far too fast with that speculation. Historical processes admit certain common components, but as we have already noted, the redirection of American politics has had a substantive side that cautions against any purely mechanical calibration of the possibilities.

## Calibrating Change

In a purely mechanical sense, the progressive and conservative reform movements frame twentieth-century governance in America with intriguing symmetry. With the emergence in the 1870s of new institutions promoting an alternative governing cadre, progressive reformers began to challenge the sufficiency of market mechanisms and to push for national bureaucratic and regulatory remedies. Then, with the emergence in the 1970s of new institutions of their own, conservative reformers have begun to challenge the efficacy of bureaucratic and regulatory solutions and to push for a return to market mechanisms. One is tempted to go even further: the progressive's bureaucratic vision advanced itself against the then-dominant party state and its extensive patronage supports; the conservative's assault on the bureaucratic state and its clientelistic supports relies today on a revitalization and redeployment of the tools of party government.

If these portents of an architectural inversion of the constituent parts of modern American government—of a meta-historical trade-off between bureaucratic power and party power in American political development—hint at the outer boundaries of creative redesign, they point even more directly to the vulnerabilities of a liberalism that left the instruments of mass democracy to atrophy and to the paradox of a conservatism that pins a vision of limited government on expanding its capacities for popular mobilization.

These curious juxtapositions remind us of the peculiar sequence of political development in America, where mass democracy long preceded demands for an extensive national bureaucracy. Progressivism came by its antiparty stance reflexively, just as conservatism has come by its antibureaucratic stance. But by the same token, this peculiar sequence of development makes it easy to misunderstand the historical relationship between democracy and bureaucracy in the emergence of modern America. To the extent that these are not antithetical developments—to the extent that today's national bureaucratic controls are themselves an expression of the expanded scope of American democracy—the current drive to harness mass democracy in an assault on modern bureaucracy is likely to prove self-limiting.

While it is true that a robust party democracy flourished in nineteenth-century America in the absence of extensive national administrative controls, it is most decidedly not the case that this was a system of limited government or control by market mechanisms. Party democracy was one of several different governing systems in operation at the time; extensive legal controls over labor, blacks, and women excluded their collective interests from the public sphere and kept them subordinate. The most durable work of political insurgency in America, and the most reliable metric of changes that have raised American politics onto a new platform and reset the terms of all future development, is to be found in the dismantling of these separate systems of legal authority and the political incorporation of previously excluded populations. So it was that the American Revolution dismantled the authority of monarchy and aristocracy; the Jacksonian Revolution dismantled the legal privileges of the guild and the patrician classes, the Civil War dismantled the master/slave relationship, the New Deal dismantled the master/servant relationship, and the Great Society dismantled legal foundations of apartheid. Even the progressive insurgents, whose liberation work was less decisive than these others, moved against the social foundations of patriarchy by extending to women the right to vote.

Each of these reform movements was prompted to create new institutions to cope with a radical alteration in the mix of authoritative controls and to effectively govern a more liberated society. In that sense, each has had a conservative aspect. The progress of social liberation and political incorporation has in fact been strongly correlated with, and facilitated by, the displacement of controls that were judicially mandated and locally enforced by controls that are congressionally mandated and bureaucratically enforced.[13] In the nineteenth century, this relationship was most poignantly expressed in the negative: during Reconstruction, the weakness of national administrative capacities clearly and severely limited the potential gains from emancipation. A more extensive system of bureaucratic governance has followed the intrusion of labor, women, and blacks more forcibly into the public sphere. This ureaucratic turn has been characterized by conservatives as an abandonment of freedoms provided by the self-regulating market and as the opening of a new road to serfdom, but the formal political subordination of these new forms of control to elected officials who represent the individuals subject to their rules marks them as far more democratic than the older forms they replaced.

These democratic foundations of the modern bureaucratic state present a profound dilemma for today's conservative insurgency, for the evil it rails against expresses the progress of the very people it needs to mobilize. Much of what has been said about the studied intellectualism of the libertarian critique and about the halting progress of the conservative's institutional reconstruction boils down to this core difficulty. The promise of political liberation, a hallmark of all of America's greatest and most successful insurgencies, has cut deepest when it has been accompanied by an equally clear promise of societal reincorporation. Where political interest in liberation from bureaucratic control is widest, it tends to be shallow and abstract; where it runs deepest, it tends to be narrow and particular. All told, the cultural resonance of the promise of limited government is quickly dissipated by the broad-ranging and concrete attractions of bureaucratic recognition, protection, and service. In this regard, the most significant finding in these pages may be that the administration of George W. Bush squandered a historical opportunity to revamp the old Social Security system by prioritizing tax cuts. Martha Derthick and Steven Teles tell us that this decision dealt the prospects for conservative reconstruction a major setback, but if the administration was in fact making the more savvy calculation of political advantage, one has to wonder about whether conservative reconstruction is really a prospect at all.

In reflecting the findings of these chapters back on American political development more broadly and trying to come to terms with the events they encompass as parts of a single developmental event, I have dwelled on the apparent limits of the departure. But lest this be construed as a brief for the safety and security of the old regime, I should hasten to add in conclusion that the resilience of liberalism's handiwork under what has become a sustained and multifaceted assault is hardly proof of its vitality. Liberalism perseveres, but it remains on the defensive. The infusion of fresh policy ideas and the newfound intensity in the politics of policy design that has accompanied them have come from its critics, and to the extent that neither party to this standoff carries the day, government is left to drift, or worse, to atrophy. One thing that a developmental perspective makes clear is American government has remained vital only because it has periodically undergone thoroughgoing reconstructions. Whatever the limits of the conservative reconstruction in terms of political power or transformative vision, it stands as an appropriate reminder that we are long overdue.

## Notes

1. Karen Orren and Stephen Skowronek, *The Search for American Political Development* (New York: Cambridge University Press, 2004), 66–8. A few of the many examples of the theme of alternatives lost are Eric Foner, *Reconstruction: America's Unfinished Revolution* (New York: Harper, 1988); Eldon Eisenach, *The Lost Promise of Progressivism* (Lawrence: University Press of Kansas, 1994); Alan Brinkley, *The End of Reform: New Deal Liberalism in Recession and War* (New York: Vintage, 1995). For a partial exception to the rule see Anne Norton, *Alternative Americas: A Reading of Antebellum Political Culture* (Chicago: University of Chicago, 1986).

2. Louis Hartz, *The Liberal Tradition in America* (New York: Harcourt Brace, 1955); Orren and Skowronek, *The Search for American Political Development,* 56–8.

3. Rogers Smith, "Beyond Toqueville, Myrdal, and Hartz: The Multiple Traditions in America," *American Political Science Review* 87 (September 1993): 549–66; see also Rogers Smith, *Civic Ideals: Conflicting Visions of Citizenship in U.S. History* (New Haven, CT: Yale University Press, 1997).

4. Ira Katznelson, Kim Geiger, and Daniel Kryder, "Limiting Liberalism: The Southern Veto in Congress, 1933–1950," *Political Science Quarterly* 108, 2 (1993): 283–306.

5. Ange Marie Hancock, *The Politics of Disgust: The Political Identity of the Welfare Queen* (New York: New York University Press, 2004); Jacob Hacker, "Privatizing Risk without Privatizing the Welfare State: The Hidden Politics of Social Policy Retrenchment in the United States," *American Political Science Review* 98 (2004): 243–60.

6. Davies, this volume, chap. 3.

7. Layzer, this volume, chap. 7.

8. Berkowitz and Dewitt, this volume, chap. 2.

9. David Plotke, *Building a Democratic Political Order: Reshaping American Liberalism in the 1930s and 1940s* (New York: Cambridge University Press, 1996).

10. Altman and Marmor, this volume, chap. 5.

11. Joseph Lowndes, *From New Deal to New Right: Race and The Southern Origins of Modern Conservatism* (New Haven, CT: Yale, 2008).

12. See for example, Steven M. Teles, *The Rise of the Conservative Legal Movement: The Battle for Control of the Law* (Princeton, NJ: Princeton University Press, 2008).

13. Karen Orren, *Belated Feudalism: Labor, the Law, and Liberal Development in the United States* (New York: Cambridge University Press, 1991); Orren and Skowronek, *The Search for American Political Development,* 180–1.

# Index